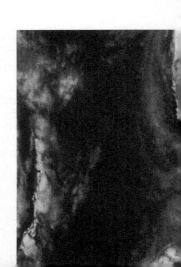

# THE WORLD OF

# CHARLES AND RAY EAMES

Edited by Catherine Ince with Lotte Johnson

Thames & Hudson    barbican

Foreword and Acknowledgments                                    10

Something about the World of Charles and Ray Eames              12
*Catherine Ince*


**LIFE IN WORK**   17        A Contemporary Practice: The Eameses in the 1940s    20
                             *Eames Demetrios*

                             An Affection for Objects                             41
                             *Esther McCoy*


                             Slideshow: *G.E.M.*                                  53


**AT HOME WITH THE EAMESES**   61        Eames House                              85
                                         *John Winter*

                                         Charles and Ray Eames, the Proto-Brutalists    98
                                         *Steve Parnell*

                                         'At Home' with the Eameses: Performance,
                                         Hosting and Hospitality                  112
                                         *Pat Kirkham*


                                         Slideshow: *Movie Sets*                  129


**ART OF LIVING**   137        The Dress of Charles and Ray Eames                 148
                               *Alison Moloney*

                               Context as Destiny: The Eameses from Californian
                               Dreams to the Californiafication of Everywhere     164
                               *Sam Jacob*


                               Slideshow: *Circus*                                169

# CELEBRATION AS A HUMAN NEED 177

Poetry of Ideas: The Films of Charles Eames 193
*Paul Schrader*

The Travelling Eameses 210
*Pat Kirkham and Elizabeth St George*

Celebrating Connections: From Aby Warburg's
'Iconology of the Interval' to the 'New Kinds of Models'
of Charles and Ray Eames 214
*Lotte Johnson*

Slideshow: *India* 217

# SAMPLE LESSONS 225

Art X: The Georgia Experiment 233
*George Nelson*

Towards a Communication-Oriented Society:
The Eameses' *India Report* 242
*Anthony Acciavatti*

Slideshow: *Tanks* 257

# INFORMATION MACHINES 265

Communicating America: Moscow, 1959 268
*Luke Naessens*

Squaring the Hypothetical Circle: Getting
Around *Mathematica* 276
*Kristen Gallerneaux*

Think 286
*Amy Gallick*

Peaks of Perpetual Excitement: Exhibition-Making
at the Eames Office 290
*Barbara Fahs Charles*

The Artefacts of Innovation 302
*Eric Schuldenfrei*

Selected Chronology 306
Notes 308
Contributors 315
Index 316
Image Captions and Credits 318

# Foreword and Acknowledgments

Charles and Ray Eames are among the most important designers of the twentieth century. They are widely celebrated for their extraordinary work at the Eames Office, a 'laboratory' where, together with their collaborators and staff, they produced an array of pioneering and influential projects.

The output of the Eames Office is characterized for most people by designs for furniture and products, yet the Eameses' avid interest in addressing the needs of any given problem led them to design and communicate using a wide variety of tools and media. The range of their projects would astonish even the most interdisciplinary of practitioners today – from architecture, furniture, graphics and product design to painting, drawing, film, sculpture, photography, multimedia installations and exhibitions, as well as new models for education. Charles and Ray Eames moved fluidly between the mass production of objects for everyday use and the transmission of ideas through exhibition, film or installation, in anticipation of the global 'information age'. They were driven by philosophical ideals that favoured knowledge, discovery and discipline; embraced the potential of technology and science for the common good; and saw no separation between life and work. The Eames Office itself was a site of experimentation – a testing ground – where the Eameses and their staff continually challenged themselves to tackle new subjects, materials and approaches.

The exhibition and accompanying publication *The World of Charles and Ray Eames* present a complex portrait of the formidable couple and their collaborators. It is the first major exhibition in the UK in fifteen years to showcase the work of Charles and Ray Eames, offering an opportunity to re-examine their work and legacy, and the legacy of post-war modernism.

It is apposite that this exhibition should take place at Barbican Art Gallery. In the past decade, the gallery's exhibitions have illuminated the work of leading figures and movements in the fields of architecture and design, including Alvar Aalto, Le Corbusier, Rem Koolhaas (*OMA/Progress*), the Bauhaus, Pop art and design and, most recently, *Constructing Worlds*, which explored photography's relationship to architecture. Within the context of the multidisciplinary venue of the Barbican Centre, where the visual arts, dance, film, music and theatre happily coexist, the gallery has a history of mounting exhibitions that probe interdisciplinary practice and explore the cross-pollination of ideas across mediums. *The World of Charles and Ray Eames* extends this trajectory; for the Eameses themselves, design was not a contained practice but rather a way of life.

*The World of Charles and Ray Eames* has been curated and edited by Barbican Curator Catherine Ince, who has realized a stimulating and thought-provoking exhibition and publication. She worked closely with Assistant Curator Lotte Johnson, Exhibition Assistant Luke Naessens and Curatorial Trainee Mairia Evripidou.

A project of this scale and complexity would not have been possible without the support of numerous individuals and institutions. First and foremost, we would like to thank the Eames family and the Eames Office LLC for collaborating with us on the production of both the exhibition and the publication. They have provided invaluable insight into the world of Charles and Ray Eames, supported our ambitions from the outset and shared their expertise and time with us most generously. From the Eames family, we remain grateful to Eames Demetrios, Llisa Demetrios, Carla Hartman, Lucia Atwood and Byron Atwood; at the Eames Office, we sincerely thank Genevieve Fong and David Hertsgaard; and at the Eames Foundation, we thank Catherine Davis.

The exhibition has been enriched by the incredible generosity of public and private collections in the US and Europe. Our sincere thanks are due to Eames Collections LLC, Los Angeles;

Mateo Kries, Serge Maudit, Susanne Graner, Andreas Nutz and Boguslaw Ubik-Perski at the Vitra Design Museum, Weil am Rhein; Martin Roth, Christopher Wilk and Jana Scholze at the Victoria and Albert Museum, London; Jock Reynolds and John Stuart Gordon at Yale University Art Gallery, Connecticut; James H. Billington, Roberta Shaffer, William Jacobs, Rachel Waldron, Ford C. Peatross, Helena Zinkham, Greg Marcangelo, Margaret McAleer, Tracey Barton, Mike Mashon and Amy Gallick at the Library of Congress, Washington DC, and Culpeper, Virginia; Marc Greuther and Kristen Gallerneaux at the Henry Ford Museum, Dearborn, Michigan; Glenn Lowry, Juliet Kinchin and Paul Galloway at The Museum of Modern Art, New York; Robert Staples and Barbara Fahs Charles; Kevin Roche; Dr Steve Parnell; Professor Pat Kirkham; and other individuals who wish to remain anonymous.

Both the exhibition and the catalogue benefited from the expert knowledge and guidance of scholarly advisers Pat Kirkham and Eric Schuldenfrei. We are extremely grateful to the authors who provided illuminating contributions to this publication: Eames Demetrios, Dr Steve Parnell, Professor Pat Kirkham, Alison Moloney, Sam Jacob, Elizabeth St George, Anthony Acciavatti, Kristen Gallerneaux, Amy Gallick, Barbara Fahs Charles and Dr Eric Schuldenfrei.

This publication has been produced in collaboration with Thames & Hudson. We appreciate the contributions of Commissioning Editor Lucas Dietrich and Editorial Assistant Bethany Wright. Mark Ralph expertly edited the texts and Louise Ramsay ably handled production. The book, exhibition graphics and marketing campaign have been beautifully designed by John Morgan, Teresa Lima, Adrien Vasquez and Øystein Arbo at John Morgan Studio. The exhibition has been thoughtfully designed by 6a architects, which responded to the exhibition's contents with sensitivity; we would like to thank directors Tom Emerson and Stephanie Macdonald and associate Owen Watson, assisted by Sebastian Oswald and Timothée Gauvin.

Many other individuals have provided invaluable expertise and research assistance to the curatorial team: Jack Masey; Jehane Kuhn; Alex Matter; Kevin Roche; Stephen and Hilary Benn; Valentin Bontjes van Beek; Thomas Weaver and Edward Bottoms at the Architectural Association; Gregory M. Wittkopp, Leslie S. Edwards and Shelley M. Selim at the Cranbrook Art Museum and Cranbrook Center for Collections and Research; Sam Grawe, Ben Watson, Mark Schurman, Gloria Jacobs and Linda Baron at Herman Miller; Ray Smith at the Corita Art Center; Rolf Fehlbaum and Stine Liv Buur at Vitra; Ivan Harbour, Vicki Macgregor, Mike Fairbrass, Dan Rogers and Kelly Darlington of Rogers Stirk Harbour and Partners; the Smithson family; Christian Spencer-Davies of A Models; John Berry; Linda Scinto at KRJDA; Daniel Ostroff; Zoe Ryan at the Art Institute of Chicago; Jennifer Dunlop Fletcher at the San Francisco Museum of Modern Art; Anna Mason at the William Morris Gallery; Catherine Whalen; Beatriz Colomina; Neil Jackson; Elizabeth Smith; David Yeomans; Jane Pavitt; David Senior; and Salvatore Licitra from the Gio Ponti Archive. We are grateful to Elizabeth St George and Athena Angelos, both of whom carried out research on our behalf at the Library of Congress, Washington DC.

The curator would like to extend special thanks to Abraham Thomas; Ellis Woodman; Corinna Gardner; Louise Jones; Richard Wentworth; Matt Connors; Tom Hall; David Reinfurt; Wayne Daly; Clare Cumberlidge; Paul Elliman; Pedro Gadanho; Milena Høgsberg; Benjamin Reichen; Prem Krishnamurthy; Mathias Schwarz-Clauss; Alexander von Vegesack; Catharine Rossi; Lydia Yee; Carol Swords; Susan Morgan; Pete Collard; Nina Due; Sara de Bondt; Anne Massey; Noam Toran; Onkar Kular; Mark Cousins; and her colleagues at the Barbican Art Gallery.

An undertaking as ambitious as this requires a huge collective effort from the Barbican team. We thank Katrina Crookall, Zoe Jackman and Priya Saujani in the Art Gallery; Peter Sutton, Margaret Liley and Bruce Stracy in the Production team; Ann Berni and Ariane Oiticica in Media Relations; Kate Davis, Siobhan Ion and Aine McGuinness in Marketing; Lynette Brooks and Caroline Harris in Development; Emma Ridgway, Orlagh Woods and Lauren Monaghan-Pisano in Creative Learning; and Gali Gold in Cinema. Exhibition logistics were expertly handled by Alice Lobb, Exhibitions Manager, and Ulrika Danielsson, Exhibition Organizer. Former curatorial interns Audrey Chan, Stephanie Hirst and Jazia Hamoudi supported the project in its research and planning phases, and Temporary Exhibitions Assistant Lotte Allan assisted in the later stages of the project.

Key supporters have helped make this exhibition possible. We are enormously grateful to the Terra Foundation for American Art for their generous support. Government indemnity for part of the exhibition has been provided by the Department for Culture, Media and Sport, and administrated by the Arts Council England. Thanks are due to the Design History Society for their 2014 research grant. Ivan Harbour and Rogers Stirk Harbour and Partners have kindly supported the production of the model of Case Study House No. 8. We have been fortunate to have *Elle Decoration* as our media sponsor.

Finally, we acknowledge Charles and Ray Eames, for their extraordinary work and ongoing legacy, which continues to inspire designers, architects, artists, film-makers, photographers and a myriad other practitioners today.

Jane Alison    Head of Visual Arts, Barbican Centre

# Something about the World of Charles and Ray Eames

## Catherine Ince

The titles that Charles and Ray Eames gave to their projects are satisfying formulations in their own right, and reveal as much about the designers' approach to work as the projects themselves. A class billed as *A Rough Sketch for a Sample Lesson for a Hypothetical Course*, for example, could not fail to entice even the most reluctant student, while the enigmatic-sounding film *Banana Leaf: Something about Transformations and Rediscovery* conjures for the viewer an expansive idea that promises to be poetic and informative, even a little surreal. The Eameses borrowed from Hollywood's tradition of using working titles for a film production prior to theatrical release, because the working version, unlike a final title, need not be 'acceptable'.[1] Instead, the working title usefully admits to ideas in progress or the necessary contraction of a complex subject.

The rich and complex history of Charles and Ray Eames, their lives, their Office and its prolific output is almost impossible to summarize. This publication, like the exhibition it accompanies, does not attempt to provide a definitive account of the Eameses' history, but foregrounds work and ideas that continue to resonate today. What follows here and throughout tells you *something about* their world; it is consciously 'a rough sketch'.

The film world was the source of several useful lessons for Charles and Ray. Visual communication was integral to their practice from the outset, and it was not long before their interest in forms of visual presentation expanded from still photography to include experimentation with moving images. By the early 1950s the Eameses had developed their multi-image lecture technique and completed the first of their many short films.[2] The couple greatly admired the craftsmanship involved in film-making, and, for them, life on set represented the values inherent in discipline, finely honed technique and hard work. Charles had first-hand experience of this world, and on arrival in Los Angeles he found work in the art department of MGM Studios; a few years later, after forming a friendship with the émigré film director Billy Wilder, he accompanied Wilder on many of his shoots, documenting the action behind and in front of the camera. The resulting body of photographs was assembled into *Movie Sets* (pages 129–36), a three-screen slideshow (a format that became the Eameses' preferred method of presenting still images) that conveys their regard not only for the technical intricacies of film-making but also for the seductive intimacy of the film set itself.

In his first lecture as Harvard University's prestigious Charles Eliot Norton Professor of Poetry (1970–71),[3] Charles borrowed again from the world of Hollywood film production to elucidate his ideas on the process of solving problems in a disciplined way: 'there's a saying that's often used if the company is out and the going is really tough, and you're having to pack motion picture equipment up a mountain of rough terrain, nothing ... happens as it should, why somebody'll always turn to the other guy, and he'll say, "the blood will never show".' Making a film, he continued, was a 'terrible, enjoyable bloody sort of operation'.[4] The analogy was apt, and the character of the Eames Office was undeniably shaped by the atmosphere of the movie industry and the optimistic culture of invention that defined California at the time. The Eameses delighted in detail and worked through difficult problems from every angle with their staff, collaborators, consultants and – on occasion – friends; they studied form and structure, adapted components and processes, and tested the details again and again. Their approach was dedicated, hands-on and, like the best film director or circus ringmaster, carefully orchestrated to 'never let the blood show'. For them, this rewarding experience was all part of 'getting on with the business of life'.[5]

### The Business of Life

Charles and Ray Eames established their studio in the 1940s against the backdrop of the Second World War.[6] On arriving in Los Angeles from the Cranbrook Academy of Art in Michigan in the summer of 1941, the Eameses' first experiments in design were conducted in the couple's spare time at their small apartment in West Hollywood. Their goal was to devise a way to mass-produce the moulded-plywood furniture Charles and his friend and collaborator the Finnish architect Eero Saarinen had designed for the competition 'Organic Design in Home Furnishings' held by The Museum of Modern Art (MoMA) the previous year.[7] The work was a practical process of trial and error and immediately all-consuming. An opportunity to apply their rudimentary experiments to the war effort quickly emerged, leading them to develop their first mass-produced product: an emergency transport splint in moulded plywood and shaped to the human form (see pages 26–7). The design of the splint was a pivotal project for the Eameses. Not only did it enable a new level of research into manufacturing techniques, but also it marked the formation of a business, one that would eventually evolve into the Eames Office, located at 901 Washington Boulevard, Venice, Los Angeles, California, where the office would remain throughout its history.

Charles and Ray surrounded themselves with a resourceful and committed team who were as keen as the Eameses to model ideas through a form of rough-and-ready, ad hoc experimentation. The cast of talented staff grew and changed over the decades, but several key figures – Don Albinson, Robert Staples, Deborah Sussman and John Neuhart among them – stayed for many years before establishing their own offices and were critical to the realization of some of the Eameses' best-known products and projects. Like a film set, the Office possessed an informal and almost magical quality quite different from the quietly restrained design offices of the period. Jehane Burns joined the Eames Office in 1969, and although the Office was a sizeable operation by this point, its essential character seemed set from the beginning. She remembers that

> every surface seemed to be levels deep in eloquent things and images; residues of projects, things left by friends, things kept because they worked well or because they didn't; models, mock-ups, doodles, diagrams and charts of every kind and scale; drafting boards, cameras, a wood-shop; an understated but cherished kitchen. Off-white Celotext panels, C-clamped to two-by fours, half-enclosing and half-displaying the current state of some topic. Pools of light and shadowy corners; buff, faded pink and raw umber. Informal, accumulative, but full of breathing-space; controlled so as to work well: for work, for hospitality, for collaboration.[8]

A photograph taken at 901 in the early 1950s (right, top) attests to the condition of the Office as both 'shop' (in the American sense of the word) and studio set. Stacked wire chairs await their upholstered seat pads, which are being stitched together on the sewing machine in the foreground. At the right of the frame a wood sculpture of a whale rests on an Eames Storage Unit (ESU), as if waiting for the prop master to place it on set (the whale did in fact make several appearances in photographs, and was also deployed in the Eames-designed Herman Miller showroom in Los Angeles when not in residence at the Eames House and studio). In front of the ESU is a standard wire basket of the type interrogated by Office staff to determine how to apply the basket's same inexpensive tooling and welding technique to a three-dimensional form. In the background, spotlights and a white backdrop have been arranged to photograph, one assumes, the new furniture range. Charles and Ray are centre-frame and engaged in conversation across bolts of upholstery cloth, while waiting to direct the shoot.

A vast body of this type of photography documents 901 in action. Some images capture moments of activity (like the making of the making of a photograph shown here), while others are evidently posed: photographs constructed to communicate Charles and Ray Eames and their world as much as the designs they produced. See, for example, the highly staged photograph of the Eames Office team at 901 on page 4. It is interesting to note the way in which such representations are interpreted over time. Looking back on her career in an interview with Ralph Caplan, Ray discussed the circumstances that led to one of the most famous portraits of the Eameses, in which she and Charles are captured lying underneath their chair bases, like model figures pinned to the floor. Her reflection is revealing. She describes being tired at the end of the day after photographing products for a Herman Miller advert with Don Albinson, who, after seeing the couple lie down on the photoshoot floor, suggested they try out an idea with their final film. For some, it is a spontaneous, enjoyable gesture; for others, a studiously constructed proposition. The tension is powerful and speaks to the centrality of the image in aiding mythology.[9]

Nevertheless, both forms of photography are fascinating, because they provide the viewer with a rich visual biography of

Charles Eames, Ray Eames and Eames Office staff working at 901, December 1951

Fibreglass armchair shells with drawings by Saul Steinberg at 901

Tableau of The Toy and plywood children's furniture set up at 901

the studio as experienced *and* as intended to be seen. But photography was not used only to record the life of the Office. Photographs of all descriptions were taken and applied in numerous and inventive ways – for advertising and other forms of publicity; for use in film or public lectures; sometimes for a one-off slideshow designed to share new projects with visitors to the Office; or simply for pure pleasure. Photography was not only a cherished medium but also an indispensable tool, particularly for Charles, who taught himself wet-plate photographic processing as a child and is rarely captured in a photograph without a camera. 'I'll do anything to give an excuse to take photographs', Charles once said.[10] At the Office, taking pictures was actively encouraged, and staff members were behind the camera as often as Charles, or indeed Ray. The Eames Office generated most of its own images, but when a project called for a greater number or variety of photographs – the Eameses' seven-screen film *Glimpses of the U.S.A.* (1959), for example – they were typically sourced from relevant libraries and photo agencies; on occasion, friends and associates were called on to 'get the pictures'.[11]

Image-making as both document and idea was integral to the Eameses' world, and it is logical that the designers extended their use of visual media from two dimensions into the realm of space and environment.

*Visual Thinking*

By the late 1940s the Eameses' capacity as visual thinkers was already evident in their plywood experiments, photography and graphic work for such clients as *Arts & Architecture* magazine or the Herman Miller Furniture Company. Their skill in composition reached new heights at the end of the decade with a series of startlingly original architectural projects. The most iconic of these is the Eameses' own house: Case Study House No. 8 (1945–9), the foremost example of Charles and Ray's work with light, space, form and colour, and one of the most expressive of their simple yet layered ideas of 'arrangement' and 'functioning decoration'.[12]

The same year the Eames House was completed, Charles and Ray were asked to devise a full-size room for the exhibition *For Modern Living*, which was being organized at the Detroit Institute of Arts by their friend and colleague Alexander Girard (see page 143). Their new furniture designs, including the ESU, folding dining table and DCM chairs, were showcased alongside an eclectic selection of objects and a photo-mural of High Sierra bark created by Charles. The room also presented an opportunity to debut the

'striking, good-looking and inventive' sculptural prototype chaise longue (La Chaise), first realized for MoMA's 'International Competition for Low-Cost Furniture Design'.[13] The Eameses' design represented an elegant and modern approach to domestic space; it is most illuminating, however, when viewed as a *concept*, one that expresses an attitude towards the 'business of life' through the lively visual interplay of colour, form, object (new and old, precious and everyday), image and space.

Material and spatial elements conceived for the model room in Detroit were reprised in 1950 when the Eameses designed the installation for *Good Design*, an exhibition co-organized by MoMA and the Merchandise Mart in Chicago, where it was staged. In the entrance area of the building's vast exhibition hall, the Eameses juxtaposed artworks (a Kandinsky painting, a thirteenth-century Madonna sculpture) with pieces of modern furniture and a graphically sparse mural composed of enlargements or details of historic examples of 'good design' (a fork, scissors, a Thonet café chair, Greek pottery).[14] The main space was divided into pavilions by such industrial materials as rope, rods, chains and string. In a similar fashion to the design of *For Modern Living*, spotlights were suspended from standard conduit pipework and an array of everyday objects hung from golf tees plugged into a wall clad with perforated acoustic panels. Both spaces were visually playful and captivating compositions, and were well received in the American design press.[15] Like the Eameses' House of Cards (1952), a simple construction toy in the form of a deck of illustrated cards, their environments muted the didacticism of conventional display methods and, instead, emphasized their interest in drawing out new and surprising relationships intended to enrich one's experience of life.

By the early 1950s the impact of the Eameses' distinctive visual language had spread to Europe. The Eames House was published widely (see pages 61–128), but it should also be noted that the holistic vision of their exhibition designs found an enthusiastic audience too. In 1953 the Swiss designer and artist Richard Lohse published *Neue Ausstellungsgestaltung* (New Design in Exhibitions), his impressive anthology of contemporary display design in which Eames Office exhibitions featured alongside installations by such progressive European figures as Ernesto N. Rogers, Pier Giacomo and Achille Castiglioni, and Max Bill. In 1961 Richard Hamilton, the British artist and Independent Group member, was invited by *Design*, the journal of the Council of Industrial Design, to reflect on the 1951 Festival of Britain. He lamented the general quality of design on show at the festival, and called attention to its poor display techniques by citing international examples that he felt particularly 'successful [in their] manipulation of space', notably the Eameses' work from the previous decade and many of those displays in Lohse's overview.[16]

*Design as a Method of Action*[17]

Although the ambition of such programmes as MoMA's 'Good Design' series was to stimulate among consumers an appreciation of modern, well-designed products, for some the project was – and remains – an exercise in the construction of good *taste*. The Eameses were undeniably optimistic about the benefits of design, and in particular the application of design thinking, to society. With regard to objects and material culture, however, their philosophy derived not from the judgment implied by distinctions between 'good and bad' or 'old and new', but from a perspective of design that was centred on satisfying the needs – spiritual or physical, to use Charles's words[18] – of the user. They aimed to produce designs that were better to use, to enjoy and to live with, and expressly acknowledged the inherent value and integrity of things possessing such qualities. In a television interview with

Charles made in around 1951, the host asks him about his view on taste in relation to architecture. Charles begins by defining architecture as encompassing 'planning, objects, and extensions of man, as well as buildings' before stating that 'those things that we recognize as taste are often the most negative aspects of an architect's work. It's the area in which he isn't quite sure of himself and falls back on this highly personalized thing to fill the gap. And I don't mean to confuse taste with an intuitive sense of what is good.'[19]

The Eameses were often quoted as saying that they designed for themselves. This did not mean their approach to design was a mode of self-expression; in fact, on a number occasions they spoke frankly against self-expression in design.[20] For them, design was the expression of an objective and a process of action – a problem to be solved by applying a curious intellect and engaging with surrounding technological and social conditions. In a talk given at the 1951 International Design Conference in Aspen, Colorado, titled 'Design, Designer and Industry', Charles underlined his and Ray's position against originality for its own sake. He discussed ideas from such 'original thinkers' as their friend Buckminster Fuller that chimed with their own attitude towards design: 'if our objectives are clear, and if we proceed to work towards them, then the need for originality is gone – and the work stands a chance of being as big as the objective.'[21] The Eameses' ambition to 'provide the best for the most for the least' is their most oft-quoted maxim.[22] Their belief in the power of design to address the needs of society was a goal common to many in the immediate post-war period, particularly in the context of a buoyant American economy in which ambitious industry leaders valued excellence and were open to new ideas about design, manufacturing and doing business.[23] For Eames Office staffer Deborah Sussman, corporations were discovering the roots of art, design and architecture at this time, and were led by 'visionaries like Thomas J. Watson [IBM] or D. J. De Pree [Herman Miller], who wanted quality, who wanted to discover, who could take risks ... they needed new corporate-identity programs, they needed buildings, and they needed ways of describing what they were doing on a very high level.'[24]

Charles and Ray Eames were astute about these relationships, and such opportunities enabled their ideas to flourish, resulting in a body of work that has given shape to the twentieth century. Yet the Eameses' practice went further than that of any of their contemporaries in mirroring the trajectory of society and culture at that time, from the heyday of the consumer era of mass production to the post-industrial age of knowledge and information transmission. Charles and Ray's expansive approach to design was ultimately one that saw the communication of ideas as central to everything, a viewpoint that ensured theirs was a natural and logical transition from object to idea. The process – life itself – was a journey of perpetual discovery, and it is fitting that the corporate slogan of their most supportive client, International Business Machines (IBM), was THINK.

*Opposite*
Installation view of *Good Design*, Merchandise Mart, Chicago, 1950

*Above*
Eames Office staff member working on model of the Ovoid Theater for the IBM Pavilion, New York World's Fair, 1964

### The Language of Vision

The first seeds of the Eameses' interest in communication and information theory were also sown in the early 1950s. With George Nelson and Alexander Girard, the Eameses devised *A Rough Sketch for a Sample Lesson for a Hypothetical Course*, a multimedia lecture about fundamental concepts of communication and visual thinking carefully crafted to impart a significant quantity of information in a short period of time. The ambition was to help students 'form a coherent picture of human activity ... to form independent judgements, and above all, to learn to relate isolated bits of information in terms of a large context.'[25]

ANTHONY WEDGWOOD BENN
12, HOLLAND PARK AVENUE,
LONDON,
W. 11.
PARK 5503

A dazzling designer called Eames
So excelled at a myriad schemes
That his rocketting mind
left the world far behind
Now in orbit his genius gleams

A.W.B.
London
15·VIII·61

The idea of the 'larger context' – the connectedness of concepts and things to one another as well as their overlapping areas of interest – was integral to the Eameses' working methods and philosophy. They placed significant emphasis on one's ability to model ideas with these constellations of relationships in mind:

In practice, we think of ourselves as tradesmen – it's a kind of custom trade; people come to us for things. The products, for the most part, are models, in one sense or another. There are 'models before the fact' – like an architect's proposal model for a building that's not yet built – and there are 'models after the fact' – like a scientist's model of a giant molecule or a galaxy. In both cases, the model is something you build in order to communicate about a structure that interests you. If there was a particular training that prepared us for this trade, it was the training and the concerns of architecture.[26]

The idea of the conceptual and physical model as a tool of enquiry and communication is one of the most vital aspects of Charles and Ray Eames's legacy. All projects were the result of this rigorously applied methodology and a vehicle for the transmission of their ideas. If the *Sample Lesson* was a radically ambitious educational model of the potential of the 'language of vision', then *Glimpses of the U.S.A.*, the Eames Office's multi-screen film for the American National Exhibition in Moscow in 1959, pushed their enquiry into communicating complex ideas even further.[27] Here, the challenge was to convey a nuanced picture of an entire nation, one that would ring true for audiences in Moscow who were eager for *images* of the country familiar to them from the rhetoric of politics. The Eameses created a powerful experience in the form of a seven-screen, 10-minute film montage of more than two thousand images that they felt presented a '*fair*' picture of a diverse country by 'establishing credibility and avoiding superlatives'.[28] The resulting installation was epic on many levels, but with their next attempt at

communication as environment the Eames Office reached new heights in the mastery of technology and concept. The now legendary IBM Pavilion at the 1964–5 New York World's Fair was a 'total environment', in which visitors were exposed to the history and theory central to the advances of computer technology. The latest IBM products and services were on show in a carnivalesque display of interactive exhibit and demonstration booth. At the centre of the pavilion stood the Ovoid Theater, home to the 'Information Machine', an immersive and stimulating multimedia experience designed to explain computer processing and data modelling to fair visitors in a tightly controlled theatrical 'performance'. Although each project had a different but unified visual expression, the fundamental idea remained the same: to find the best means of communicating complex ideas in an accessible way.

Over the years, Eames Office clients included government departments, cultural and academic institutions, centres of scientific research, public broadcasters and large-scale corporations. In the late 1960s and 1970s, the Eameses were especially preoccupied with disseminating their long-held values around knowledge, learning and the connections between people and ideas through continued work in film, exhibition and consultancy for such bodies as the Massachusetts Institute of Technology, IBM, the Smithsonian Institution and the Metropolitan Museum of Art, to name but a few. They felt strongly that these organizations shared a collective responsibility to provide access to their educative resources for the benefit of society as a whole, and that they should exploit new technologies and modes of communication to achieve this. Exploring new ways of thinking about the world served as the foundation from which all Eames Office projects materialized.

In January 1949 Charles Eames drafted some notes of advice to students, which remain a relevant description of the way the Eames Office worked for more than four decades.[29] Like all of the Eameses' projects, Charles's insights are simple yet deeply layered, and sound as fresh today as they must have first seemed more than half a century ago:

Make a list of books
Develop a curiosity
Look at things as though for the first time
Think of things in relation to each other
Always think of the next larger thing
Avoid the 'pat' answer – the formula
Avoid the preconceived idea
Study well objects made past recent and ancient but
   never without the technological and social conditions
   responsible
Prepare yourself to search out the true need – physical,
   psychological
Prepare yourself to intelligently fill that need

The art is not something you apply to your work
The art is the way you do your work, a result of your
   attitude towards it

Letter from the Eameses' long-time friend
Anthony Wedgwood Benn to Charles Eames,
15 August 1961
Ink on paper, 22.9 × 17.8 cm (9 × 7 in.)

The Papers of Charles and Ray Eames, Manuscript
Division, Library of Congress, Washington DC

# LIFE IN WORK

Ray Kaiser trained as a painter, studying in New York under the avant-garde artist Hans Hofmann, with whom she undoubtedly honed her talent in the use of form, structure and colour. During her time on the East Coast, Ray moved in progressive artistic circles; she had a keen interest in modern dance, attending classes led by Martha Graham, and was a founding member of American Abstract Artists – a radical group that campaigned for the exhibition of non-representational art.[1] Charles Eames demonstrated an interest in photography from an early age, and while studying architecture developed his practical skills in lithography and etching, as well as in building and design. Supposedly thrown out of architecture school for a precocious appreciation of Frank Lloyd Wright,[2] Charles went on to open his own practice in St Louis after travelling on his honeymoon in 1929 to Europe, where he and his first wife, Catherine Dewey Woermann, visited sites of modernist architecture by Ludwig Mies van der Rohe, Le Corbusier and Walter Gropius. A residential project in Missouri led to a meeting with Eliel Saarinen, who in 1938 offered Charles a fellowship to resume his architecture and design studies at the Cranbrook Academy of Art in Bloomfield Hills, Michigan, where the Finnish architect was director. In the autumn of 1940, at the urging of a friend, Ray began a course at Cranbrook, stating on her application form a desire to 'concentrate on crafts' and noting her inexperience in handling tools or machinery.[3] By then, Charles was head of the academy's Department of Industrial Design and worked part-time in Saarinen's architectural office.

Cranbrook's curriculum fused the values of arts and crafts with the visionary thinking represented in Europe by such schools as the Bauhaus. As an American crucible of modernism, the academy played a vital role in the development of Charles and Ray's conception of modern design. In 1940 Charles collaborated with his friend and fellow instructor Eero Saarinen, Eliel's son, on designs for The Museum of Modern Art's 'Organic Design in Home Furnishings' competition. They were assisted in the preparation of submission drawings and models by Ray and fellow student Don Albinson (who would later become an important member of the Eames Office), along with instructor Harry Bertoia. This was to be the first of many fruitful experiments in moulding wood in three dimensions for application to furniture design.

Charles's friendship with Ray blossomed. In May 1941 he divorced Catherine Woermann, and in June of that year he and Ray were married, relocating to Los Angeles almost immediately. Ray was a native Californian, and the couple chose the West Coast as their base in order to dedicate themselves to their work, away from the tensions of life in Michigan or the distractions of New York. In California they found a new creative and cultural environment suited to their interests and working life: modernist aesthetics and social ideals flourished, and the local film and technology industries provided a hotbed of productivity and innovation crucial to their continued experiments in design and architecture.

*Previous page*
Ray Eames working on the first iteration of the plywood stretcher, 1942

Charles Eames, early 1940s

*Left*
Charles and Ray Eames, early 1940s

Darling

Among people I might see in Cal - is the guy interested in paramount "shorts" DO you think that between the two of us we could write the scrip for and direct subjects like

"modern arch - in U.S."
" ⌐ Skulpter - - "
" - Painting . . . "
"Beauty in useful objects" ?
etc -

It seems like if its given the right slant it would have punch for producer public & US —

well it was just an idea -

If I could only talk them into letting us try one

Maximum says rug stays here for exhibit —

XX

Letter from Charles Eames to Ray Kaiser,
27 February 1941
Ink and coloured pencil on paper,
32.2 × 19.1 cm (12 ⅝ × 7 ½ in.)
Eames Collections LLC

Ray Eames
Design for cover of Arts & Architecture,
April 1942, with photograph by Charles Eames
Paint and photo collage on card,
15.9 × 12.7 cm (6 ¼ × 5 in.)
Eames Collections LLC

Charles and Ray Eames are probably more famous today than they were in their lifetimes. And as those lifetimes recede into the past, their work and ideas remain of, and often ahead of, our time. Consider Charles's comment from 1971: 'Beyond the age of information is the age of choices.'[1] While at its heart this is a structural statement, a design statement, it resonates with many people – designers or otherwise – as an expression of the world today. Similarly, his observation that 'If we are going to feel secure, we must feel secure in change'[2] seems ever more prescient, complementing tenderly a credo of Ray's: 'What works good is better than what looks good ... [what] looks good can change, but what works, works.'[3] It was design ideas such as this that guided and linked their endeavours from the 1940s to the end of their lives.

The Eameses' achievements seem almost inevitable: the furniture is part of countless lives, the Eames House a cultural treasure, *Powers of Ten* a film as well as a term of art in Hollywood,[4] the House of Cards toy still given as a present around the globe, their graphic designs still delighting, and such exhibitions as *Mathematica: A World of Numbers ... and Beyond* still on display decades after they first opened. As few designers ever have, the Eameses worked at the highest level in many different media.

But their personal measure of themselves was not uniqueness at all. The Eameses believed that if something was well designed, then the idea of it having been designed at all would never come up. 'Way-it-should-be-ness', they called it.[5] Yet ironically, it took a great deal of effort. And as we begin to consider *how* it was achieved, the Eameses' early years of struggle and creation become quite intriguing, because they show us a recognizable and familiar experience, even a contemporary one – not simply for designers, but for all of us. (Even setting a table is an act of design, as Charles once observed.)[6]

Charles and Ray's passion was not a monomania for furniture, but rather a polymania for design itself and the problems it could address. This meant that even at the start of their career together, when their resources and their bandwidth might have seemed narrowest, the spectrum of their work was a constellation of inspirations. And this breadth unfolded in the same decade the Eameses first saw each other on the campus of the Cranbrook Academy of Art – a time that no one *ever* thought would become known as the 'Eames Era'. That is what makes this part of their story important. If the finished canvas of their lives teaches us something every day, what might a glimpse of the first tentative brushstrokes tell us?

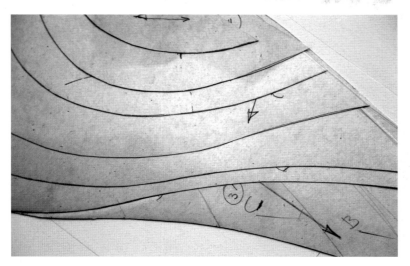

In 1940 The Museum of Modern Art (MoMA) in New York announced the now legendary competition 'Organic Design in Home Furnishings'. For young designers, first prize would be the best possible start to their careers: a guaranteed manufacturer for the winning designs. Charles Eames and Eero Saarinen submitted chairs to be made of exposed moulded plywood formed into compound curves with the seat and back united; in the case of their side chair, the seat and back were to be a single piece.[7] In common with most every other entrant, they presented their designs in the form of images of full-scale plaster models (naturally, MoMA could not handle 585 full-size chairs).[8]

When the Eames–Saarinen team won in early 1941, the work of production began and Charles and Eero soon realized that the initial technique for moulding plywood they had in mind was not practical. They tried another standard technique, but in the end there was no technology available to shape plywood as they required. The chair shells that the manufacturer was able to make – laboriously and expensively – were so splintery, crude and difficult to remove from the mould that they needed to be upholstered. In the summer of 1941, as the low quality of the shells became clear, Charles wrote from his and Ray's new home in Los Angeles to Eliot Noyes, director of the Department of Industrial Design at MoMA, saying, 'I suppose Eero has told you of our finally getting around to some cast iron dies – It makes me sick that we didn't insist on giving it a trial months ago.'[9]

As Ray later recalled, the whole idea was that she and Charles wanted to design chairs where the act of mass production made the chair *better*, not worse.[10] The Eameses did not blame the manufacturer; rather, they realized that, if you want the design to flow from the manufacturing process, then *you*, the designer, must figure out how to make it. With the 'Organic' chairs, Charles and Eero had made a mistake familiar to any designer today who has created a three-dimensional form on a computer only to find that it works less well in real life. Each of Charles and Eero's winning photographs depicted a plaster model that was merely a design of the *form*, not its materiality – not the complete, real thing. Charles and Ray would never make that mistake again.

After a few months in Los Angeles, Charles was forced to take a job at MGM Studios.[11] Significantly, Charles and Ray did not go to the opening of the *Organic Design in Home Furnishings* exhibition in New York in the autumn of 1941; instead, they traded the prestige of such an occasion (and saved the money it would have cost to attend) for more time to spend on the task of figuring out how to mass-produce moulded plywood with compound curves – in particular, a chair whose seat and back were one. Carried out in their apartment near the University of California, Los Angeles, this work involved very little theory. Rather, it was trial-and-error experimentation. It was also a form of very serious play.

Charles's artisanal skills and Ray's painting expertise link them directly to the pragmatic, hands-on, can-do, blue-collar skill set of Industrial Revolution America. The Eameses are often described as artists, their works shown in museums as well as showrooms. But they described themselves as 'tradesmen' who happened to use 'tools connected with the arts'.[12] This account of their practice was consistent with their push against the modern tendency to regard the rewards of creativity as the sole province of the arts, rather than a reasonable expectation of everyday life.

In later years, during Charles's delivery of the Norton Lectures at Harvard University in 1970, for example, the Eameses would cite Chen Ning Yang and Tsung-Dao Lee – Nobel laureates from 1957, recognized for their convention-challenging work in particle physics – as belonging to that richer definition of creativity.[13] They also felt passionately about Henry Ford's original mission for his museum in Dearborn, Michigan, of collecting one of each type of a huge swathe of industrial and pre-industrial objects (shoes to tractors), rather than choosing the 'best' or the most popular.[14] Ford felt that, often, the so-called failures had more to teach us. Similarly, the time spent by the Eameses experimenting and understanding is strikingly akin to the year away from Kitty Hawk in North Carolina that Orville and Wilbur Wright spent in Dayton, Ohio, determining experimentally the co-efficient of lift through a series of wind-tunnel tests (the equations that describe lift would not be developed for decades). What all these kindred spirits had

*Opposite and right*

*Organic Design in Home Furnishings*, The Museum of Modern Art, New York, 1941; installation view and catalogue (right) with prototype chairs by Charles Eames and Eero Saarinen

*Above*

Paper template for ply layers to form plywood sculpture, 1943

*Overleaf*

Experimental prototype for the moulded fibreglass chair shell, manufactured by John A. Wills, *c*. 1949
Fibreglass and metal trash-can base, 81.3 × 71.1 × 58.4 cm (32 × 28 × 23 in.)
From the Collections of The Henry Ford, Dearborn, Michigan

Detail from the competition drawing. Three-dimensional study of the form of these chairs was made in small models of copper. The small model for this relaxing chair and the method of constructing the full size plaster study are shown in the photograph at the right.

14

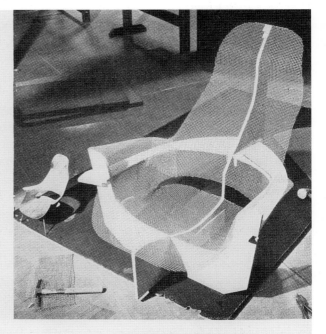

DESIGNS BY SAARINEN AND EAMES

in common was a willingness to rebuild from scratch (or, in Ford's case, create opportunities to do so) the foundation on which their future efforts would be based. No relying on hearsay.

In a sense, this is what the Eameses were trying to do with their furniture: rebuild from first principles their understanding of plywood itself. They even made cardboard models of their lyrically curved moulded-plywood sculptures (see page 36), detailed in such a way that each individual layer of veneer that made up the plywood was represented by a thin, correctly scaled piece of cardboard. Although the Eameses' goal remained furniture, there was still much to learn when events at Pearl Harbor in December 1941 focused all industrial activity in the United States towards the Second World War.[15] Hearing that metal splints were exacerbating battlefield wounds, the Eameses decided that their technique for moulding plywood, even at that early stage, could make a moulded-plywood splint that would save lives. In June 1942 Charles settled his debts with Cranbrook and wrote a note on a piece of veneer: 'I have had to take a leave of absence from MGM so Ray and I can devote all our time (and I mean all) to experiments for the Navy.'[16] Note 'Ray and I'.

The Eameses' splints were certified by the military in August 1942. It was time for Charles to quit MGM for good. While the Eameses were working on the splints, they were also becoming involved in John Entenza's *Arts & Architecture* magazine. Often using Charles's photographs and drawings as material for collages, Ray created some of the most compelling magazine covers of the era. They still dazzle. These graphic works were just the first of many creative seeds that the Eameses would plant during this first decade together, and which would flourish throughout their lives.

In addition to creating covers and experimenting with plywood, Charles and Ray were beginning to figure out their own working rhythms. One pattern emerged clearly. With just about every new medium and even material that the Eameses explored, there was almost always a period during which they investigated possibilities on their own. Even when they were working with a larger staff, it was Charles and Ray who travelled together to India first, or made such early films as *Blacktop* (1952), or conducted their first experiments in plastic. As Ray said, they could make more mistakes that way, without feeling they were wasting other people's time.[17]

This 'exploration time' was extremely important to the Eameses, allowing them to operate, for example, in the manner of the Skunk Works at Lockheed Corporation.[18] But it also reflected a notion that Charles once shared with a group of students. In a lecture delivered at the University of Manitoba, Winnipeg, on 7 March 1977, Charles observed that just about everyone, no matter how busy or how short of money they might be, has a 'margin' in their lives, a bit of extra time or some additional resources to draw on. The trick, he said, was to not waste that margin and to use it 'selfishly' and effectively. And seizing those margins was something that the Eameses were good at, even when Charles was paying the bills with his salary from MGM.

This seeming luxury of having time to discover and explore came not from wealth but from wisdom. In fact, economically, the 1940s were a pretty tough decade for the Eameses. Ray was twenty-nine when they married in 1941, Charles thirty-four. Of their parents, three were gone, and Charles was also supporting his daughter from his first marriage.[19] With their splint approved, a group of backers was found by John Entenza to invest in the Eameses' creation. Although small and insufficient, this funding did allow production issues to be resolved, to the point where the Eameses finally received a major order from the US Navy: 150,000 splints, way beyond the fiscal resources of the investors. Contract in hand, Charles secured the support of Evans Products to reward (and buy out) the backers, while letting the Eameses retain their intellectual property and gather a team to scale up

production. Such creative figures as Herbert Matter and Harry Bertoia sought to participate, joining Margaret 'Percy' Harris and others from MGM. From late 1943 to 1946, Charles received a salary for overseeing production – his only regular income at that time. There were other experiments and explorations: the epic glider nose cone, the vertical aircraft stabilizer and, of course, the exquisite stretcher (see pages 27 and 32–5). Then, at last, the war was over and the world faced the challenge of transition.

Tragically, the final year of the war also saw the death of Colonel Edward S. Evans, the head of Evans Products. With the consumer-oriented furniture business now less of a fit, Evans Products agreed to fund one last trade show at the Barclay Hotel in New York in December that year.[20] Ultimately, this led to the happy connection of the Eameses with the Herman Miller Furniture Company.[21] It was also at this show that the Lounge Chair Wood (LCW), an item of furniture that *Time* magazine would later call the design of the century, was first seen.[22] Importantly, even though this chair celebrates complex curves, its seat and back are separate; in the end, Charles and Ray felt this was the most honest use of the plywood. A unified seat and back would be achieved one day, but it would require a completely new material.

It was also in 1945 that Charles first delivered *Lecture 1*, a slide presentation that allowed him to weave images in and out of his stories and explanations of the Eameses' design philosophy. Lectures featuring slides would become a major aspect of the Eameses' practice. It was a way to express their ideas and thinking, and also a perfect use of Charles's vivid photography. Eventually, the single screen of *Lecture 1* would become three screens, then seven, and sometimes more. At the same time, Charles and Ray pushed their margin even further, creating their first toys: the moulded-plywood elephant and other animals. In a sense, this was a natural extension of the plywood work, but it was also less forgiving. After all, a toy has to capture the intangible

essence of something – and any child is a qualified judge of whether a toy elephant fails or not. It is an excellent test of mastery, of way-it-should-be-ness. Even today, children and adults are delighted by the Eames Elephant, proof indeed that it was a successful test of the Eameses' facility with moulded plywood. Alas, each part of the two-piece elephant was more expensive to make than the LCW, so it was shelved for sixty years.

Amid all the financial pressure, the Eameses still explored. Even though their plywood chairs were well received, it would be some time before they were deemed a success. There were also cash-flow issues that any start-up of today would recognize. In 1946 the Eames Office and Evans Products were selling the chairs direct, with Herman Miller distributing for a few years, but already Evans was consolidating, moving the tooling to one of its factories in Michigan. At that point Charles and Ray's income from sales of the chairs was on a royalty-only basis, which meant that, while things were being moved, set up and the sales pipeline filled, they received no income for the best part of a year. Everyone was laid off. Don Albinson, an Eames Office staffer, remembered going to the studio in Venice, California, to see whether there was any paid work yet.[23] The space was so utterly empty that when Charles and Ray wanted to take a break, they indulged in some archery practice – shooting arrows down the length of the vast former bus garage they were fighting to keep. (If it all sounds like a storyline from Silicon Valley, that gives a flavour of their challenge.)[24]

In 1948 MoMA organized the 'International Competition for Low-Cost Furniture Design' and invited the Eameses to take part. Charles and Ray were still fine-tuning the plywood chairs, deep into production, because, as George Nelson said years later, for Charles, 'every [design] is a loved infant' to be worried over.[25] Nevertheless, the Eameses saw the competition as an ideal opportunity to pursue the shell chair, and in the autumn of 1948 they were awarded second prize for a single-piece shell stamped in metal. However, they soon switched to plastic reinforced with fibreglass,[26] and were finally satisfied with their choice of material after Charles commissioned the famous 'trash can' chair.[27] Things were moving fast – but new chairs in a new material were no fit for Evans. In 1949 a new deal was signed, Evans left the picture, and Herman Miller took over the licence and the tooling and started making the plywood chairs directly with the Eameses. Meanwhile, designs for the plastic shell chair were advancing well. On 19 November 1949 Charles wrote to Eero Saarinen to say that 'the die is cast'.[28] The first metal mould for an Eames plastic chair – in fact, any plastic chair ever – was ready for work.

Around that time, another extraordinary project in yet another medium – architecture – was coming to fruition: Case Study House No. 8, the Eames House. First designed in 1945 then redesigned in 1948 and built in 1949, the house pushed the Eameses' margin to the limit. Charles recalled that they had to 'hock everything' in order to raise the money to build it.[29] Indeed, they were able to achieve their goal only because the house was being erected on then inexpensive land with prefabricated parts.

During the building of the house, the Eameses set down yet another marker in a medium to which they would contribute greatly, making their first filmed images together by documenting the house's construction. Never completed, the footage is now believed lost. Yet this was not their first brush with moving images. Working in film had been part of their original plan in moving to Los Angeles, and for the 1939 faculty exhibition at Cranbrook, Charles had made and screened a short film on Maija Grotell.[30]

The Eames Office also designed its first exhibitions in the 1940s. If film had been part of the Eameses' ambitions from their first months together, it was in exhibition design that Charles and Ray probably had the most shared experience. Ray's participation in numerous artists' communities in the 1930s was critical, as was

Charles's work on the faculty show at Cranbrook. But it is also fair to say that they produced richer work together, and the Eames room for the exhibition For Modern Living (1949) is magical even in collage form (see pages 144–5).

Charles and Ray moved into the Eames House on Christmas Eve, 1949. This first stay was brief. Their New Year would really get under way in Chicago, where they planned to install their expression of the Good Design show at the Merchandise Mart.[31] It would still be a year or two – ten years on in their life together – before they achieved something close to financial security with the success of the plastic chairs. To them, however, it felt as though they had achieved something greater already: the real possibility of a life driven by their holistic vision of design.

In another context, the Eameses would quote the early Sanskrit poem Bhagavad Gita, part of the Hindu epic Mahabharata: 'You have the right to your labour, but not the fruits of your labour.' At this moment, and throughout their lives, they treasured that labour more than its compensations. Maybe that is why the Eameses never regarded their chairs as finished, continually improving that plastic chair whose die was cast. One of the most successful chairs of all time, and they were always trying to make it better – materials, bases, forms, sustainability, colour.

Perhaps a particular genius of the Eameses' was to learn from Charles's eight months in rural Mexico in the early 1930s. He observed that, although the people he encountered there were often exceedingly poor, they had rich cultural, emotional and spiritual lives. This showed not only that one really could live on just about nothing, but also, for Charles, that he had to stop using the need to make a living as an excuse for doing things he did not believe in; that way, he noted, 'you can bring your whole self to it'.[32] This realization changed his practice. Later, he and Ray would always come from a pure place in their work, forever expanding their margin by exploring new ideas, new media, and by facing new and worthy problems.

So the Eameses continued to follow their hearts and their play, and yet did so in a way that was not about fetishizing their uniqueness, but about connecting 'to the universal part' of themselves. Interestingly, such seemingly secondary projects as the film A Communications Primer (1953) turned out to be very good decisions financially. The Eameses recognized that you will always be happy if you do your best work, and that no work should be undertaken purely in the hope of it resulting in a particular job. As Charles observed, 'that leads to all sorts of bad habits'.[33]

Under the Eames Office roof were full-colour and black-and-white photo labs, a film-editing area, movie cameras (eventually, even special-effects facilities), furniture production, research areas, and the means to fashion all sorts of prototypes for exhibitions, create graphics and perform myriad other tasks. In the digital era we take such tools for granted, although ironically we often find ourselves using them to go faster, not slower and more thoughtfully. One would think that, with all the time we are able to save, we would spend more of it on reflection.

People often speculate about what Charles and Ray, if working today, would have done with all those new tools. Who knows what they would have come up with? What we can feel confident about is the first thing they would have done with the Internet, with 3D printing, the personal computer, mobile phones and everything else they never experienced (but in some cases foresaw): they would have played. And they would have invited others to play.

And then, Charles and Ray would have played some more – because play is a form of love for the world and a perfect way to unlock possibilities. After all, as they themselves acknowledged, 'whatever the way, at all times love and discipline have led to a beautiful environment and a good life.'[34] And in that sense, leading by example, they still lead the way.

Charles and Ray Eames in their
apartment, Strathmore Avenue,
Los Angeles, California, early 1940s

On their arrival in Los Angeles
in 1941, Charles and Ray Eames
moved into the Strathmore
apartment building designed
by the architect Richard Neutra
in 1937, living there until they
completed their own house in
1949. Their new setting epitomized
modern Californian architecture
and was ideally suited to the
Eameses' aesthetic. The couple
turned their second bedroom into
a laboratory – equipped with tools
purchased from a nearby outlet of
Sears, Roebuck & Co. – in order to
continue their experiments with
compound-curved plywood
furniture. Charles's home-made
device for heat-bonding plywood
sheets was christened the 'Kazam
Machine' – a 'magic box' from which
moulded seat shells emerged, and
which enabled the Eameses to hone
their basic moulding technique.

'Kazam Machine' in the Eameses'
apartment, Los Angeles, 1941

Experimental moulded-plywood
chair shell, *c*.1943

Note from Charles Eames to
Ray Eames, 7 February 1942
Pencil on paper, 20.3 × 12.7 cm
(8 × 5 in.)
Eames Collections LLC

KEEP OUT
OF THE
KAZAM
Please

Following a visit from Wendell G. Scott, a medical doctor involved with the military and an acquaintance of Charles's from St Louis, the Eameses adapted their technical experiments with furniture to develop a moulded-plywood leg splint for use by the US Navy. The prototype was accepted in the summer of 1942, and in November of that year the US Navy placed its first order for 5,000 splints from the newly established Plyformed Wood Company.[1] A plywood stretcher to support lower spine injuries was also developed, but the design did not progress beyond the prototype stage.

*Opposite*

Leg splint production, 1943

*This page*

Charles and Ray Eames for the
Molded Plywood Division, Evans
Products Company
Leg splints, *c.*1943
Moulded plywood with a birch
(left) and mahogany (right) veneer,
birch: 106.7 × 20.3 × 11.4 cm
(42 × 8 × 4 ½ in.), mahogany:
106.7 × 20.3 × 10.8 cm
(42 × 8 × 4 ¼ in.)

Charles and Ray Eames for the
Molded Plywood Division, Evans
Products Company
Stretcher, 1943
Moulded plywood,
213.4 × 76.2 × 30.3 cm
(84 × 30 × 11 ⅞ in.)

Both Eames Collections LLC

Man lying in the second stretcher
prototype, 1943

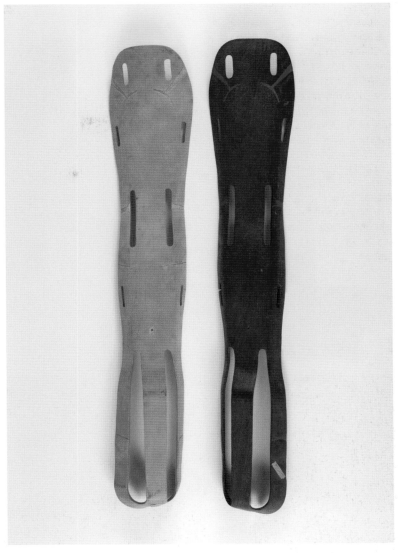

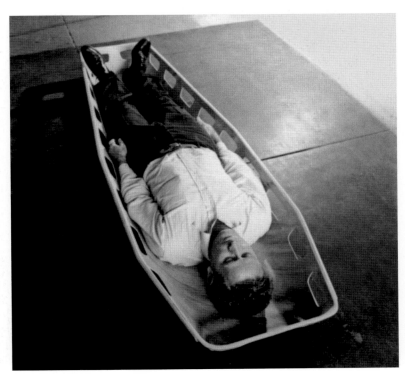

*This page*
Molded Plywood Division's splint-production staff posing at the Rose Avenue shop to celebrate achieving the goal of manufacturing 200 splints per day, 1943

Ray Eames
Study for business card for Molded Plywood Division, Evans Products Company, 1943
Collage and ink on card, 9 × 11.8 cm (3 ½ × 4 ⅝ in.)
Eames Collections LLC

Ray Eames
Business card for Plyformed Wood Company, 1942
Photomechanical print and pencil on card, 4.8 × 8.7 cm (1 ⅞ × 3 ⅜ in.)
Eames Collections LLC

*Opposite*
Packaged leg splints, 1943

Ray Eames
Packing label for leg splint, 1943
Photomechanical print on paper, 8.7 × 11.3 cm (3 ⅜ × 4 ½ in.)
Eames Collections LLC

In 1943 the Plyformed Wood Company moved to larger premises and took on additional staff, but company operations were compromised by cash-flow problems. As a result, Charles entered into talks with Colonel Edward S. Evans, head of Evans Products Company, a Detroit-based manufacturer and lumber supplier. In October 1943 Evans bought the rights to produce and distribute the Eameses' splints, and thus the Plyformed Wood Company became the Molded Plywood Division, a West Coast subsidiary of Evans Products Company. Charles was named 'Director of Research and Development', and Ray designed a new logo for the subsidiary; the packing label for the splint featured the new logo and the existing circular trademark of Evans Products.

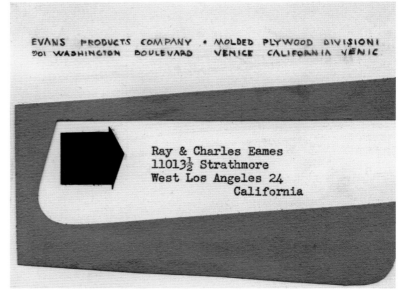

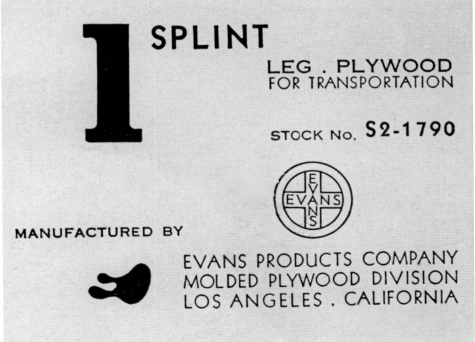

# NAV
# MARINE

# A NEW-TYPE SPLINT

with a famous war record

is now ready to give outstanding civilian service too

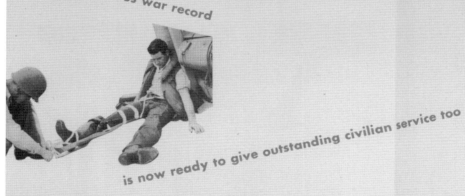

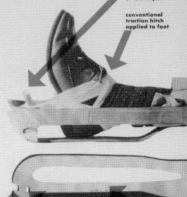

traction by means of tourniquet

conventional traction hitch applied to foot

traction hitch secured by passing through notch

hole provided to receive cord when dead-weight traction is used

affo... nee... heel...

light weight and easy to carry—will nest compactly for storage and transportation

THE EVANS PRODUCTS COMPANY'S TRANSPORTATION LEG SPLINT WAS DEVELOPED FOR THE UNITED STATES NAVY TO FILL A NEED CLOSELY PARALLELING THE ONE THAT EXISTS UNDER CIVILIAN EMERGENCY CONDITIONS—THIS IS DEMONSTRATED BY THE FOLLOWING EXCERPT FROM THE UNITED STATES NAVAL MEDICAL BULLETIN, VOL. XLI, NO. 5:

"In the 'front line' zones the medical efforts are principally emergency measures for saving a man's life, alleviating pain, and preserving an injured part until the casualty can be evacuated to a base. In such combat zones the hospital corpsmen render a large part of the initial emergency treatments, which should always be reduced to the simplest, safest, and quickest methods. It was in the hope of simplifying the initial treatment and evacuation of men with lower extremity wounds under combat conditions that the 'emergency transport' splint was produced."

SINCE ITS OFFICIAL ACCEPTANCE BY THE U. S. NAVY BUREAU OF MEDICINE AND SURGERY IN 1943, DOCTORS AND CORPSMEN USING THE SPLINT UNDER THE MOST TRYING CONDITIONS HAVE GIVEN IT THEIR UNQUALIFIED APPROVAL. THOUSANDS OF SAILORS AND MARINES ON HARD WON BEACH HEADS HAVE BENEFITED FROM THIS MODERN ORTHOPEDIC DEVICE —THEY HAVE BEEN SPARED MUCH SUFFERING AND IN MANY CASES PERMANENT DISABILITY.

THE EVANS MOLDED PLYWOOD SPLINT CAN NOW PERFORM THIS SAME SERVICE FOR EMERGENCY HOSPITALS; FIRST AID STATIONS; FOR CITY, COUNTY, STATE, AND FEDERAL DEPARTMENT OF HEALTH; FOR INDUSTRIAL ACCIDENT COMMISSION; FOR MEDICAL ASSOCIATIONS; FOR LOGGING CAMPS, MINES, AND OTHER HEAVY INDUSTRIES WHERE LEG FRACTURES OCCUR FREQUENTLY—

## ITS NATURE

The splint is a simple molded plywood shell free from "mechanical gadgets" or features to break loose or get out of order—has no appendages, hooks, or appliances, yet the contour and form are so engineered that it can be applied to either left or right leg quickly by untrained personnel, without risk of further injury due to application.

The splint needs no preparation, lacing with bandages, or padding before application. It forms a protection from any extraneous movement and harm often incurred during rapid transfer and transportation. The rigid molded shell accomplishes this with a minimum of weight and restrictive binding.

In addition to giving immobilization at all points during the transportation of the victim, complete provisions have been made for traction and countertraction which can be used when necessary.

## ITS PHYSICAL PROPERTIES

The contoured plywood shell that forms this splint is accurately molded under heat and pressure, the component laminations being bonded with a high grade thermosetting resin—maximum rigidity for minimum weight is made possible by introducing additional laminations where the stress is greatest— the splint is a truly integral structure.

The splint is surfaced with a hard wood, and has a synthetic resin finish—it is completely waterproof—a three hour boil test has no effect on its form or the strength of its glue bond.

| | |
|---|---|
| WEIGHT | 1.5 pounds |
| LENGTH | 42 inches |
| WIDTH | 7½ inches |
| DEPTH | 3½ inches |
| MATERIAL | Face plys hardwood inner plys gum |
| RESIN GLUE | Melamine-Urea Formaldehyde (waterproof) |

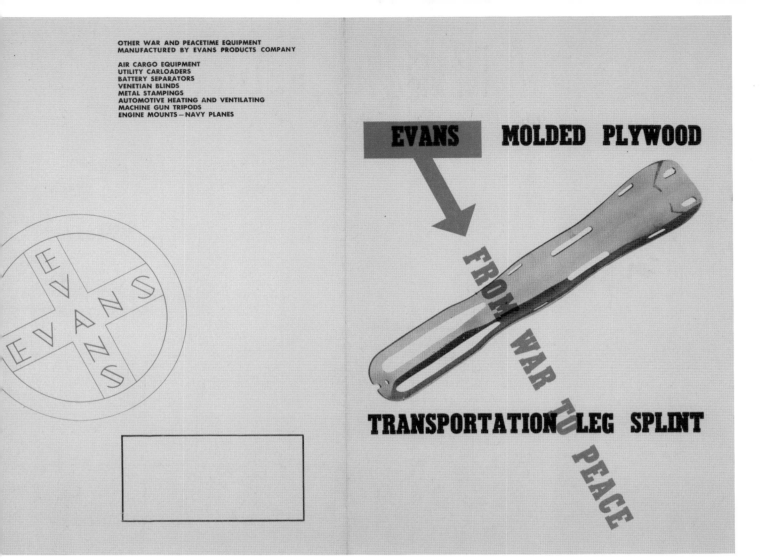

OTHER WAR AND PEACETIME EQUIPMENT
MANUFACTURED BY EVANS PRODUCTS COMPANY

AIR CARGO EQUIPMENT
UTILITY CARLOADERS
BATTERY SEPARATORS
VENETIAN BLINDS
METAL STAMPINGS
AUTOMOTIVE HEATING AND VENTILATING
MACHINE GUN TRIPODS
ENGINE MOUNTS — NAVY PLANES

EVANS    MOLDED PLYWOOD

FROM WAR TO PEACE

TRANSPORTATION LEG SPLINT

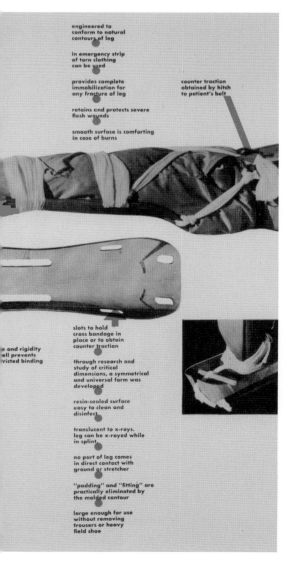

engineered to
conform to natural
contours of leg

in emergency strip
of torn clothing
can be used

provides complete
immobilization for
any fracture of leg

counter traction
obtained by hitch
to patient's belt

retains and protects severe
flesh wounds

smooth surface is comforting
in case of burns

e and rigidity
ell prevents
tricted binding

slots to hold
cross bandage in
place or to obtain
counter traction

through research and
study of critical
dimensions, a symmetrical
and universal form was
developed

resin-sealed surface
easy to clean and
disinfect

translucent to x-rays,
leg can be x-rayed while
in splint

no part of leg comes
in direct contact with
ground or stretcher

"padding" and "fitting" are
practically eliminated by
the molded contour

large enough for use
without removing
trousers or heavy
field shoe

Charles and Ray Eames for the
Molded Plywood Division, Evans
Products Company
'From War to Peace', brochure for
transportation leg splint, c.1945
Photomechanical print on paper,
22 × 48 cm (8 ⅝ × 18 ¾ in.)

The Work of Charles and Ray Eames,
Prints & Photographs Division,
Library of Congress, Washington DC

*Opposite*
Moulded-plywood aeroplane
stabilizer, *c*.1943

*This page*
901 Washington Boulevard, Venice,
Los Angeles

Moulded-plywood pilot seat, *c*.1943

The Molded Plywood Division developed parts for Vultee Aircraft and other aircraft manufacturers. In addition to horizontal and vertical stabilizers for the Vultee BT15 Trainer, the Evans Products subsidiary developed plywood gas tanks, wheel doors, hinges and structural angles, although not all were put into production. An experimental moulded-plywood pilot seat, in which a folded parachute served as a seat cushion, was presented to the Lockheed Corporation but not taken further. More workshop space was required as operations expanded, and by the end of 1943 the company (with the exception of splint production) had moved to 901 Washington Boulevard in Venice, Los Angeles, which was to become the home of the Eames Office for the next forty-five years.

In 1943 the Molded Plywood Division was contracted to produce the nose section of the CG-16 'Flying Flatcar', an experimental military glider designed by Hawley Bowlus of Airborne Transport, Inc. The glider was intended to transport personnel and equipment between home and battleground. To produce a set of two curved blisters, the team went through a long period of trial and error, devising new machinery and tooling, and rented additional production space to deliver the commission within the two-month deadline. The glider was flown but soon discontinued, following a fatal test-flight accident. Moulded plywood was quickly replaced by aluminium as the major structural material for aircraft.

*Opposite*

Christmas card from Hawley Bowlus
to Molded Plywood Division staff,
1943

Glider production with the blisters
in place, 1943

*Above*

Molded Plywood Division staff
members with a blister for a glider
nose section, 1943. From left:
Norman Bruns, William Francis,
Marion Overby, Harry Bertoia,
Charles Eames, Ray Eames and
Gregory Ain

Between 1941 and 1943, while the Eameses experimented with the properties of moulded plywood for both military and domestic products, they began a series of sculptural experiments, testing to what extremes the compound curves they were developing could be pushed. The results were powerful undulating forms that explored the expressive possibilities of the medium. These twisting sculptural volumes not only showcased the strength and vitality of moulded plywood, as Ray acknowledged, but also positioned them as works of art in their own right. Ray featured one (now lost) sculpture on the cover of *Arts & Architecture* magazine in September 1942 (see page 40). She continued these sculptural experiments alongside the Molded Plywood Division's production of plywood splints, teasing out the templates into organic forms.

*This page*
Untitled, 1943
Moulded plywood, 94 × 66 × 30.5 cm
(37 × 26 × 12 in.)

Ray Eames
Study for plywood sculpture, early 1940s
Pencil on paper, 23.8 × 13.5 cm (9 ⅜ × 5 ¼ in.)

Both Eames Collections LLC

*Opposite*
Ray Eames
Untitled (splint sculpture), 1943
Moulded plywood, 107.6 × 20.3 × 7.6 cm
(42 ⅜ × 8 × 3 in.)
Eames Collections LLC

Charles and Ray Eames posing for their 1944
Christmas card with a splint sculpture

Ray Eames
Study for plywood splint sculpture, early 1940s
Ink and pencil on paper, 12.7 × 11 cm (5 × 4 ⅜ in.)
Eames Collections LLC

Life in Work

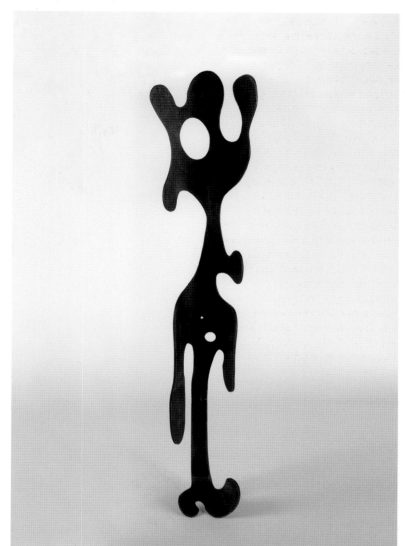

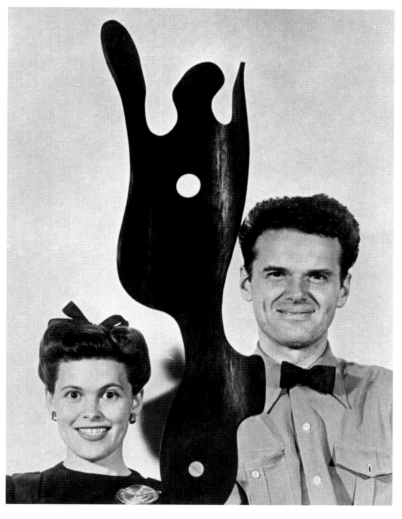

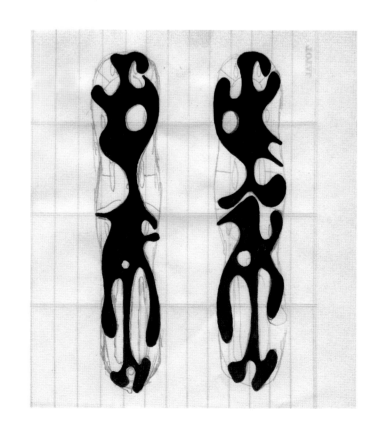

37

LINE AND
COLOR DEFINE
VOLUME
THAT VOLUME
CAN BE TANGIBLE
OR NOT BUT THE
SPACE BETWEEN
TWO TANGIBLE
VOLUMES IS
NEVERTHELESS
        A VOLUME

*ray eames*

it is impossible to talk about painting without bringing up the whole weary subject of aesthetics philosophy and metaphysics.

the fact is that without any talk we are influenced by the world in which we live and by the synthesis of the experiences of the world by all creators ● the engineer mathematician sculptor physicist chemist architect doctor musician writer dancer teacher baker actor editor the man on the job the woman in the home home and painters

for the past many years the western world has been working back through the maze of surface decoration and meaningless gloss to the fundamentals of form ● sometimes this has been an economic necessity as in the present war years other times it comes from an aesthetic demand ● where the people through the sensibilities of the creators find it necessary to rediscover values and to cast aside the non-essentials ● hindrances of the past

why is it that today we are more concerned with the materials and design of a chair than with its covering or ornament? why are we more concerned with the quality of the music than with the personal idiosyncrasies of the conductor? why are the uniforms the word itself becomes strange so varied and differ so radically from those of former wars? why are our houses being designed from the inside out rather than fitting the living to a predetermined style on the outside? why indeed do we not only accept but also admire and feel intensely proud of the jeep? a superb example of a healthy direction of thinking and feeling

in spite of prejudice and confusion we are becoming aware slowly of true and good and vital and therefore beautiful form.

my interest in painting is the rediscovery of form through movement and balance and depth and light ● using this medium to recreate in a satisfying order my experiences of this world with a desire to increase our pleasure expand our perceptions enrich our lives

*Arts & Architecture*,
September 1943
Letterpress on paper,
32.5 × 24.7 cm (12 ¾ × 9 ¾ in.)

Collection Vitra Design Museum

Ray Eames
Untitled, early 1940s
Paint on paper, 22.9 × 30.5 cm
(9 × 12 in.)

Eames Collections LLC

Ray Eames
*for c in limited palette*, 1943
Casein on Masonite panel,
21.6 × 27.9 cm (8 ½ × 11 in.)

Eames Collections LLC

Ray Eames
Untitled, early 1940s
Crayon on paper, 27.6 × 21.3 cm
(10 ⅞ × 8 ⅜ in.)

Eames Collections LLC

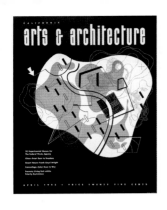

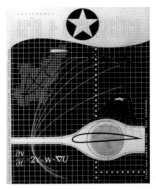

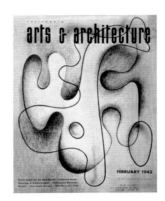

# An affection for objects

**Whether applied to ideas or objects, communications or chairs, Charles and Ray Eames have been exploiting technology as a prime element of design for 25 years**

Follow the back streets of Venice, L.A.'s rundown beach community, past wooden Gothic houses, Spanish Colonial stuccos with tile roofs, Greene-and-Greene type bungalows squeezed in between a lumber yard, factories and little shops, and you come to a clean industrial structure enclosing 20,000

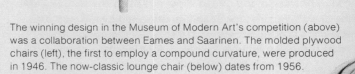

The winning design in the Museum of Modern Art's competition (above) was a collaboration between Eames and Saarinen. The molded plywood chairs (left), the first to employ a compound curvature, were produced in 1946. The now-classic lounge chair (below) dates from 1956.

sq ft of space, for over a quarter of a century the office of Charles and Ray Eames.

Inside is the same kind of mixed use as the surrounding neighborhood: furniture design, film-making, preparation of exhibitions. Each project leaves an alluvium. A 1967 film on a proposed National Aquarium (a joint project with Roche & Dinkeloo) left behind a dozen glass tanks swimming with small life of the sea. Ray Eames appears and slides back a shield on one tank to expose an unborn shark moving softly in its transparent egg case. Then Eames comes in and follows the movement of the octopus with his finger on the glass tank. They stand transfixed as if entering into the structures of the organisms.

Left over from films on toys are tables of building blocks, magic lantern slides, an armada of wood and tin vessels sailing on a mylar sea, awaiting a day, as Eames puts it, "when I will have a little time to do a few things I've saved up." Posters abound, some from three decades ago when he first fell in love with the circus. One of his Charles Eliot Norton lectures at Harvard last year was on the circus, its discipline, and that of all nomadic peoples. Now the American Philosophical Society has invited him to deliver its 1974 Penrose lecture on the same subject.

There is a scale model of the IBM Exhibit Center with the recent installation of the Copernicus exhibition. Around work tables are clusters of Xeroxed material being collected for three other shows: a small one on calendar reform which by now has been joined to the Copernicus show, one on Isaac Newton to replace the Copernicus at the end of 1973, another on Jefferson and Franklin to open at the Grand Palais in Paris and return to the U.S. for the bicentennial celebration.

In the furniture workshop, new bases for existing chairs are being studied. On high racks are examples from the past—several versions of the 1946 molded plywood chair, prototypes that never went into production, a chaise on which Saul Steinberg drew a reclining woman.

Eames's design of furniture began in St. Louis as an extension of architecture—for buildings designed by his own short-lived office and a partnership cut short by the depression. Eames designed not only furniture but lighting fixtures, rugs, mosaics, vestments and vessels for a church. He came out of the tail end of the crafts movement, Cranbrook and the Bauhaus and, as Craig Hodgetts says, "he then invented the notion of improvised environment and recognized that if you designed correctly the environment would become like a good auto repair shop."

Eames's first recognition in furniture design came after he left practice and went to Cranbrook on a scholarship, with some teaching duties. By that time he was interested in photography (his father was an amateur photographer) and ceramics (he had built a kiln for himself in St. Louis); he had traveled to Europe and Mexico, had seen folk art, Mies and Corbu. It was 1939, he was 29. Cranbrook was then dominated by the spirit and architecture of Eliel Saarinen, and at the school were Eero Saarinen, Ralph Rapson, Harry Weese, Edmund Bacon, Florence Knoll, Harry Bertoia and Ray Kaiser, the painter-sculptor Eames married in 1941.

When the Museum of Modern Art's newly formed Department of Industrial Design, directed by Eliot Noyes, announced the Organic Furniture Competition in 1940, Eames and Eero, assisted by Ray, collaborated on molded plywood chairs and cabinets. Marcel Breuer, a juror, recalls that he

Solar toy, 1956

The Eames' own house characterizes their loyalty to the framework of a structure of an idea and the variation of objects or images within it. The house has remained almost unchanged since 1948.

## An affection for objects

was "very positive" about the choice of the Eames-Saarinen entries in two categories for first place.

The program called for furniture which reflected the aesthetic tendencies and technological possibilities of the day—a brave program for a time when quality and handcrafting were synonymous. The machine technology on which the Eames-Saarinen pieces were based was more envisioned than actual, and Eames soon discovered the gap between designing for mass production and finding someone who could produce. The best offer for manufacturing the molded plywood chairs was $75. This put them back in the luxury class that the competition had been set up to bypass. (Less than 10 percent of the population had an income over $5000 a year in 1940.)

Eames's wartime activities developed the technology to produce chairs. With John Entenza, he set up a company in Los Angeles to produce an Eames-designed molded plywood leg splint. Most of the staff were architects and artists—Griswald Raetze, Herbert Matter, Harry Bertoia, Gregory Ain. Ain, known for his fine social housing, had the title Chief Engineer and worked with equipment, he says, which could have come from Renaissance woodcuts of machinery. From splints, production branched out into components for plywood planes.

At the end of the war, the plant went into production of molded plywood furniture, and in 1946 the Museum of Modern Art showed both the famous molded plywood chair and the production process, finally justifying its hopes for the 1941 competition. The crisp doubly curved back and seat, attached to the steel-rod frame by large rubber shock mounts, began immediately to show up in photographs of post-war houses—often three-quarter profile with the back overcut with a lone broad leaf of a philodendron. It was one of the few chairs readily available that was in scale with the new interiors, and often a single one was moved from room to room with the camera, then loaded on the photographer's van to go on duty again.

The chair is still made by Herman Miller, Inc., which has produced the Eames group since 1946, but its sale is limited compared with such high-production pieces as the 1949 fiberglass chairs—singly, stacking or in tandem. Originally the Eames group was used mainly in homes, but today 90 percent go into offices, board rooms, restaurants, airports, etc. What has now grown into a multimillion dollar enterprise gained momentum when the 1950s boom in civic and office buildings created a need for well-designed lightweight seating that would take tough wear. The Eames group met the criteria. Moreover, it reflected the growing weariness with monumentality; and the stackable chairs coincided with the new mobility and impermanence.

## Images on film

Films were begun in 1950 with one on toys. Here the magical hand of Ray Eames is strong. She is modest about her participation in furniture design although it is there. Deborah Sussman, long with the Eames office, saw her often come along and "refine a shape." Gregory Ain remembers that in the war production plant Ray could "bring things into relation with one another and could find the inner order in whatever she touched." Alison Smithson wrote in *Architectural Design* (Sept. 1966) "I can see the part played by Ray Eames in all

The Eames staff photographed in front of a mock-up and facing a simulated audience used in determining scale (above) and the office force (below) on the set of a 1960 film "Introduction to Feedback."

that they do: the attention to the last detail of the collected material, the perserverance in finding what exactly is wanted; although the seeker may not know the exact object until it is finally seen."

The films are audacious both technically and in the selection of objects. The Eameses have an affection for objects and a love of facts—a toy, an equation, a computer or an altar. A film on tops says everything there is to know on tops; the films sharpen a fact to the point where it pierces as painlessly as acupuncture. They don't teach, they inform.

In 1944 they were using a technique of fast cutting for slide shows; "A Sample Lesson," with George Nelson and Alexander Girard, 1952, was the first multimedia production. The 1958 "The Information Machine," for the IBM pavilion at the Brussels Fair was multi-image. At the 1959 American Exhibition at the Moscow Fair, "Glimpses of the USA" was a 12-minute presentation of 2200 images on seven screens. Film, slides, animation, graphs, diagrams—all work together to support a central theme.

Of the 50 or so films made in the last 23 years, many were

commissioned by institutions, governments or corporations, including a film for the Smithsonian on its 200th anniversary and the aquarium film for the Department of the Interior. Among the many commissioned by IBM was the 1972 "Computer Perspective." "Powers of Ten," made in 1968 for the Commission of College Physics, is a science-fiction reality of time/space between the nucleus of a carbon atom and the farthest known point in space. The eight-minute zoom from a man lying on a Miami beach into outer space and back ends with an examination of the structure of the nucleus, with chronometers on the split screen registering distances traveled. Craig Hodgetts calls it "a clear exposition and a poem, too. Eames communicates an ethical view of the world."

### Images on walls

Work on exhibitions started also in 1950, but it was with the 1961 Mathematica exhibit for IBM that all the Eameses' talents in this field suddenly meshed into what Donlyn Lyndon calls "a vision of complexity." In their exhibitions, he says, "a wall is a manifesto of what architects should try to do. It carries information in all directions, backward or forward, and you make your own connections."

"Nehru: His Times and His India," a 1965 show commissioned by the Indian Government, was unusual for its lyricism in the presentation of visual biography. There was a three-dimensional representation of Nehru's prison cell, through which one could walk, and on whose walls were fastened excerpts from Nehru's prison writings. Like the other shows, it demonstrated the same meticulous care with detail, the love of the object for itself, the imagination in the selection of object or fact, the harmony unexpected juxtapositions, ellipses that give the viewer time to make his own connections.

The exhibitions are usually developed along a time line. The one currently at the IBM Center which celebrates the 500th anniversary of the birth of Copernicus follows the advances of astronomy and relates them to the social landscape of each period. In exhibitions more than in films, the strictness of the framework leaves room for a play of imagination and opportunities to establish human scale. In "A Computer Perspective," of which fortunately there is a permanent record in a book of the same name (Harvard University Press, 1973) there is a handwritten letter starting "Dear Mother," sent by Alan Turing, author of "On Computable Numbers," which, juxtaposed to illustrations of SSEC and UNIVAC, makes the computer very friendly indeed.

But the Eameses have always been experts at using change of scale to surprise the mind and the eye. A case is their own living room. It was one of the early houses to adapt industrial materials to residential use, an *Arts & Architecture* magazine Case Study house; the two-story living room wall of factory sash, sliding glass and solid wall painted in primary colors, the exposed steel beams and decking establish a large scale; countering this is a small quiet sitting corner under one of the balcony bedrooms, and around the space is a shelf holding a changing collection of objects, small and beautiful, fine and folk. At eye level, they invite close examination and handling. "This is," says Charles Moore, "the miniature world the Eameses care so much about." They were the first to fill in the spartan framework so acceptable to modern architecture with a varied and rich content. Robert Venturi claims that the Eameses "reinvented good Victorian clutter. Modern architects wanted everything neat and clean and they came along and spread eclectic assemblages over an interior."

Eames would call the rich content "goods." And, he says, "When goods become one of the new covetables, quality will stop degenerating."

Young designers may call Eames "too harmonious," his chairs "commitments" rather than just useful objects like the Thonet chairs, but all would agree that he was created a new set of covetables. [Esther McCoy]

The IBM Computer Perspective show (left) and the Mathematica exhibit (above) are both organized on a time line which depicts a rich social landscape as related to that particular subject and its context.

*Page 40 and below*

Ray Eames
Covers for *Arts & Architecture*,
1942–7
Letterpress on paper, dimensions
variable

Various lenders, including Eames
Collections LLC; Collection Vitra
Design Museum; Collection of
Dr Steve Parnell

In 1942 Ray Eames began designing
covers for *Arts & Architecture*
magazine, with some assistance
from members of the Eames Office.
In 1943 alone she designed ten
covers; by the end of 1947 she had
designed a total of twenty-six.

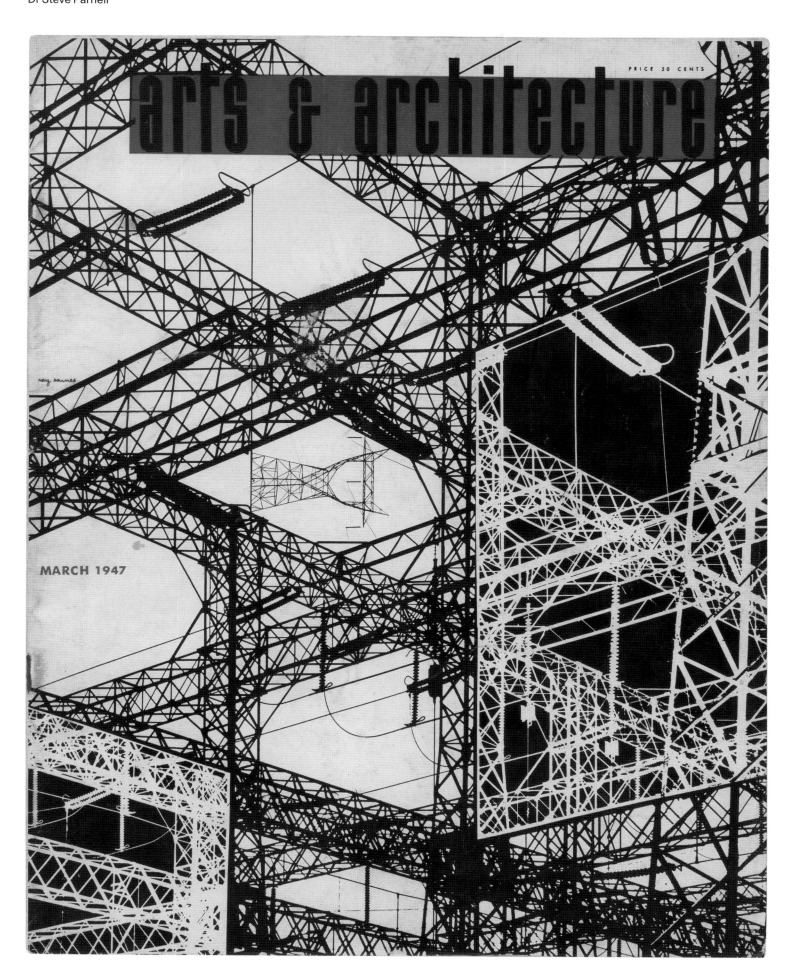

arts & architecture

PRICE 50 CENTS

MARCH 1947

*Arts & Architecture*, September
1946, cover (right) and interior
spread (below) designed by
Herbert Matter
Letterpress on paper,
32.3 × 25 cm (12 ¾ × 9 ⅞ in.) closed,
32.3 × 50 cm (12 ¾ × 19 ⅝ in.) open
Collection Vitra Design Museum

As demand for military products
dwindled, experimentation with
furniture continued with renewed
intensity. The ambition was to mass-
produce simple, low-cost, high-
quality designs. Knowledge
gained from military projects and
technologies was applied to a vast
series of tests and prototypes
modelled at full scale. The challenge
of refining plywood contours and
thicknesses, and connecting
materials with precision, yielded
a series of chairs of varying
configurations – from split-back
one-piece shells to a two-piece
seat and back with tilt-back, three-
or four-legged bases in wood
and metal. Ray's sketches express
the variety of forms explored. In
the September 1946 issue of *Arts
& Architecture*, devoted to Charles
Eames with cover and interior
collages by Herbert Matter,
the critic Eliot Noyes noted the
'aesthetic brilliance and technical
inventiveness' of the furniture
designs.[1]

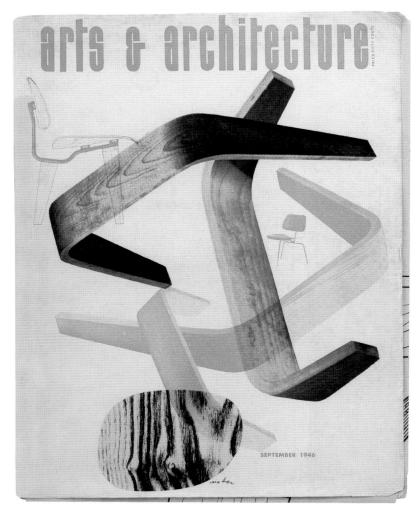

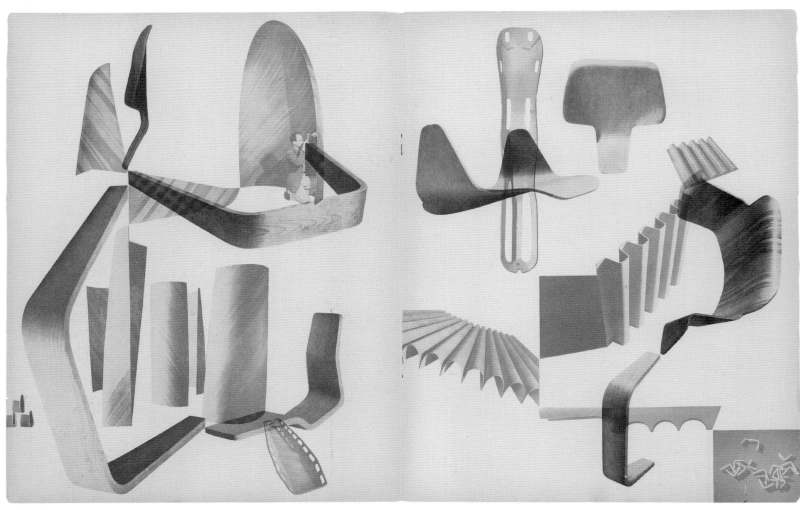

*Clockwise from above*

Ray Eames
Early concept sketch for lounge chair, with
sketches of various chairs and tables, *c.*1948
Graphite on paper, 27 × 13.5 cm (10 ⅝ × 5 ¼ in.)

The Work of Charles and Ray Eames, Prints
& Photographs Division, Library of Congress,
Washington DC

Experimental moulded-plywood chair, 1941–2

Charles and Ray Eames for Molded Plywood
Division, Evans Products Company
Tilt-back chair, *c.*1944
Moulded walnut plywood, lacquered steel bars
and rods, rubber shock mounts and rubber glides,
66 × 54.6 × 72.4 cm (26 × 21½ × 28½ in.)

The Museum of Modern Art, New York.
Gift of the manufacturer, 1946

*Top, left and right*

Charles Eames posing on an LCM (Lounge Chair Metal; left) and a DCM (Dining Chair Metal; right), 1954

*Above*

Ray Eames sitting on an experimental lounge chair, 1946

This example is one of a series of studies for a plywood lounge chair. Its form prefigures the upholstered Lounge Chair and Ottoman produced in 1956.

*Right*

Doris Nolan sitting on a tilt-back side chair, *c.*1946

Life in Work

Don Albinson and Charles Eames
outside 901, with two-piece
plywood chairs

Charles and Ray Eames
Pre-production DCM (Dining Chair
Metal), 1946
Plywood with rosewood veneer,
zinc-coated metal and rubber,
72.4 × 50.8 × 53.3 cm
(28½ × 20 × 21 in.)

Yale University Art Gallery, Gift of
Randall Garrett, BA 1972, MA 1975

Describing the evolution of the
moulded-plywood chairs, Charles
Eames said: 'Solid steel seems the
best way to get the most strength
with the thinnest line ... Four legs
again seemed best; the frames
began to take their final forms.
The contours of the seat and
back were refined in terms of the
complicated functions of the edges
and the relation to each other.
We became more conscious of the
surface texture, of heat transfer,
finishes, the balance, the ease
of handling, the colours, the
woods, and the heads of the bolts.
A chair should look equally good,
approached from above or from
below. If it's going to be a chair,
it should be a whole chair.'[1]

Alex Matter sitting on a moulded-
plywood elephant, 1945
Photograph by Herbert Matter

Plywood children's chairs, 1945

Stacked plywood children's
chairs, 1945
Photograph by Herbert Matter

Experimental three-legged
chairs, 1945

Photo collage of plywood
chairs, 1951

In 1945 the Eameses produced
a small collection of children's
chairs, tables and stools in a trial
run of 5,000; the plywood furniture
was available in a natural finish as
well as in aniline-dyed colours.
The range proved difficult to market
and was discontinued. At the same
time, a prototype plywood elephant
was developed as an offshoot of
the plywood furniture series, but
was not put into production.

Having refined the moulding
process, Evans Products prepared
tooling to manufacture the plywood
chairs in bulk. The seats and backs
were connected to wood or metal
frames by a rubber shock mount.
Initially, the Dining Chair Wood,
Lounge Chair Wood and a three-
legged Dining Chair Metal were
deemed most suitable for
production. Following their
presentation at the Barclay Hotel,
New York, in December 1945,
the prototype three-legged chair
was eliminated from the range
and replaced by two four-legged
versions; the range was first mass-
produced in the summer of 1946.
Work continued on a series of
tables, case goods and a flexible
partition screen.

*Above*

Publicity photograph for moulded-plywood furniture group, with double exposure of Ray Eames

An exhibition titled *New Furniture Designed by Charles Eames* was presented at The Museum of Modern Art, New York, in March 1946.[1] George Nelson had seen the furniture at the Barclay Hotel display and urged D. J. De Pree, president of the Herman Miller Furniture Company, to view it.[2] De Pree visited MoMA with James (Jim) Eppinger, sales manager at Herman Miller, and by October that year Evans Products had granted Herman Miller exclusive rights to market and distribute the plywood furniture. Three years later Herman Miller acquired the manufacturing rights.

*Opposite*

Frames from *G.E.M.* 3-screen slideshow consisting of a wide range of images addressing the meaning of 'quality' and prompting the viewer to look anew at familiar details, many of which were pulled from previous slideshows. Originally titled *Excellence*, *G.E.M.* (*Government, Education, and Management*) was first shown at an IBM event in March 1967

ONE·PENNY·IN·THE·SLOT

TICKETS

3 8

No 11

68

TAUTZ & C.°

11

G. THOMAS.
Court Hair Cutter.

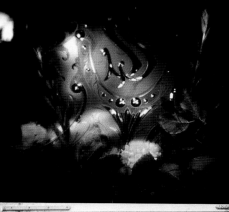

A. WEBSTER & C.°

FRIA

# AT HOME WITH THE EAMESES

In the years following the end of the Second World War, *Arts & Architecture* magazine was refashioned by its editor, John Entenza, into the principal mouthpiece for West Coast modernism. Entenza and his circle were particularly interested in the ramifications of new lifestyles and technologies for residential architecture. In 1945 the magazine launched the seminal Case Study House programme, initially commissioning eight California-based architects to design and build modern homes. Unlike pre-war modernist housing projects, the programme did not aspire to establish universal prototypes for standardized housing, but rather invited responses to the needs of specific clients and locations.

Charles and Ray Eames designed Case Study House No. 8 for themselves. The completed building was published in *Arts & Architecture* in December 1949, the month the Eameses moved in. For the couple, the house was to be the centre of productive activities and a 'background for life in work'.[1] It is the most potent and iconic expression of their attitude towards living, and marked a new take on the modernist principles of the preceding decades; although faithful to the edict of 'truth to materials', the Eames House is pragmatic, unselfconscious and informal.

The finished building is remarkable for its simplicity and lightness. A pair of two-storey pavilions are arranged facing each other across a small courtyard. The larger block contains the domestic spaces, the smaller the Eameses' studio and guest facilities. The alternating use of coloured panels and glass on the façade creates kaleidoscopic effects of light and shade on the interior, effects elaborated by shadows and reflections of foliage on either side of the windows, which were captured beautifully in *House: After Five Years of Living* (1955), a film montage of photographs taken by the Eameses after the house's completion.

The house was not conceived as a static architectural object, but as a structure that could be effortlessly adapted to the Eameses' particular ways of living and working. This shifting backdrop functioned as both exhibition space and theatre set and, over time, generated a dynamic constellation of relationships between inhabitants, objects and space. The Eames House is, in the words of British architects Alison and Peter Smithson, 'architecture as a direct result of a way of life'.[2]

In a filmed interview about their work, Charles and Ray reflected on the process of designing the house and described their use of off-the-shelf standardized materials, the importance of the adjacent meadow to the building and site, and the challenge of combining these elements to achieve a structure suited to their needs. 'It's like a game,' Charles said, 'building something out of found objects, which is the nicest kind of exercise you can do.'[3] In the preceding years this game had already begun with their work in furniture, and continued long after the construction of the Eames House with their further experiments in design, and with toys, images and film-making. This hands-on, improvisatory and inventive approach to architecture and design has come to define the Eameses' legacy and wide appeal.

Working at first with Eero Saarinen, Charles Eames was invited to design Case Study Houses Nos. 8 and 9. The former was to be the Eameses' house and studio, while the latter was designed as the home of John Entenza. Reflecting the close relationship between the Eameses and Entenza, the houses shared the same Pacific Palisades site. The houses had significant media exposure at every stage of the design and construction process. Throughout 1949 and 1950, readers of *Arts & Architecture* witnessed the development of the projects in regular instalments featuring drawings, models, construction shots and, finally, photographs of the finished buildings.

When it was first presented in 1945, Case Study House No. 8 was a cantilevered Miesian box suspended over an open meadow. Looking towards industrial architecture, Charles and Ray Eames chose to construct a frame from prefabricated steel components with glass infills. Owing to a steel shortage in the post-war years, however, construction could not begin until 1949. By that point the design had changed considerably. While the idea of a simple steel-framed box remained, the structure was brought down to the ground, significantly reducing the amount of steel required. The house was rotated 90 degrees and set into the hillside, sheltered behind a row of eucalyptus trees. The architecture became a discrete and minimal addition to the landscape, leaving the large meadow entirely intact.

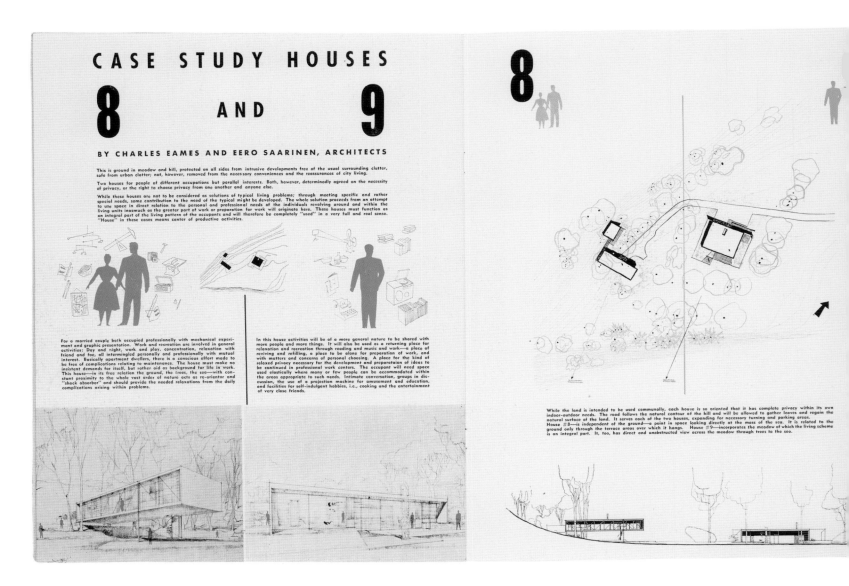

*Opposite*

First presentation of designs for Case Study
Houses Nos. 8 and 9 in *Arts & Architecture*,
December 1945
Letterpress on paper, 32.3 × 50.5 cm
(12 ¾ × 19 ⅞ in.)

Collection Vitra Design Museum

*This page*

'Life in a Chinese Kite', *Architectural Forum*,
September 1950
Photomechanical print on paper, 32 × 24 cm
(12 ⅝ × 9 ½ in.)

Collection Vitra Design Museum

Presentation of Case Study House No. 9
in *Arts & Architecture*, July 1950
Letterpress on paper, 32.3 × 49.2 cm
(12 ¾ × 19 ⅜ in.)

Collection of Dr Steve Parnell

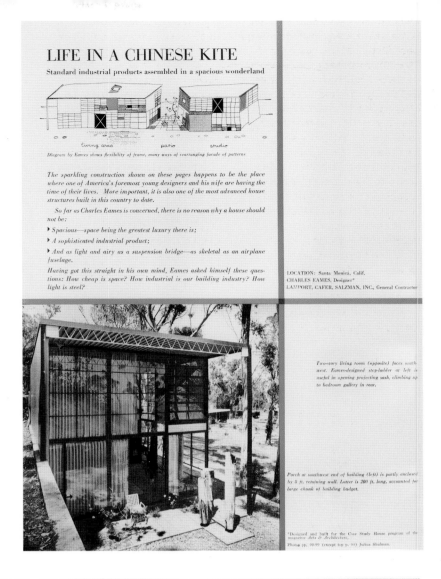

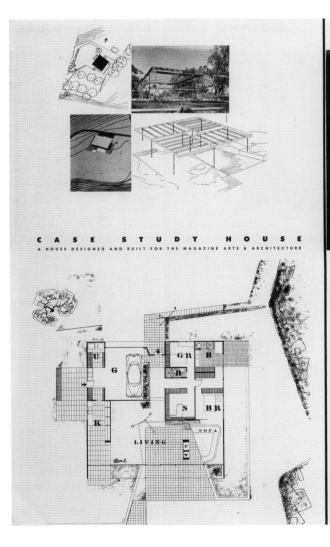

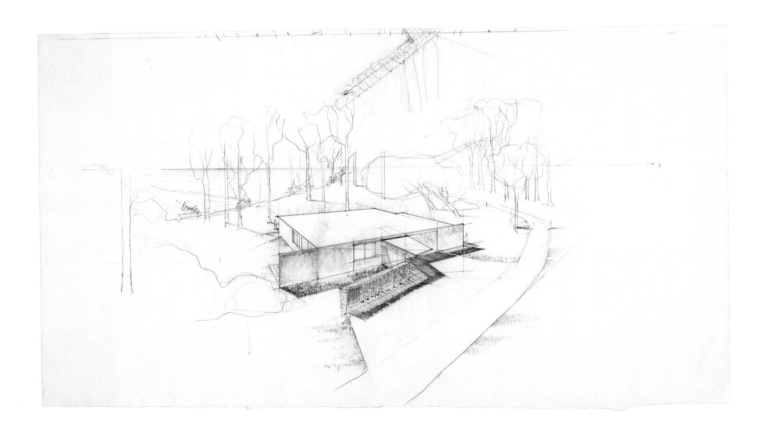

*Clockwise from opposite, top*

Charles Eames

Perspective rendering of Case Study House No. 8
(Bridge House version) for Charles and Ray Eames,
Pacific Palisades, Los Angeles, California, 1945
Graphite, with coloured pencil note at bottom,
on tracing paper, 27.9 × 45.7 cm (11 × 18 in.)

Elevations of Case Study House No. 9 for
John Entenza, 1948
Diazo print, coloured paper and coloured pencil,
58 × 70 cm (22 ⅞ × 27 ½ in.)

Façade study for Case Study House No. 8
for Charles and Ray Eames, 14 October 1948
Graphite, coloured pencil and watercolour
on diazo photoprint with coloured paper collage,
50.6 × 90 cm (19 ⅞ × 35 ⅜ in.)

Perspective rendering of Case Study House
No. 9 for John Entenza, 1948
Graphite on tracing paper, 38 × 68 cm
(15 × 26 ¾ in.)

All from The Work of Charles and Ray Eames,
Prints & Photographs Division, Library of
Congress, Washington DC

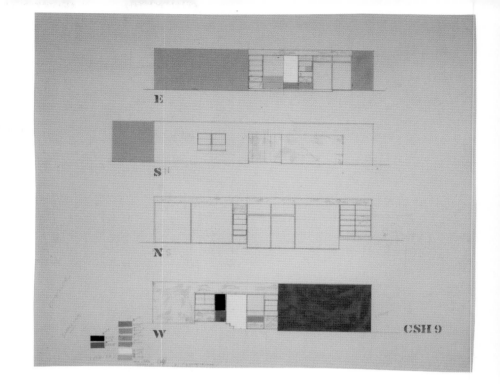

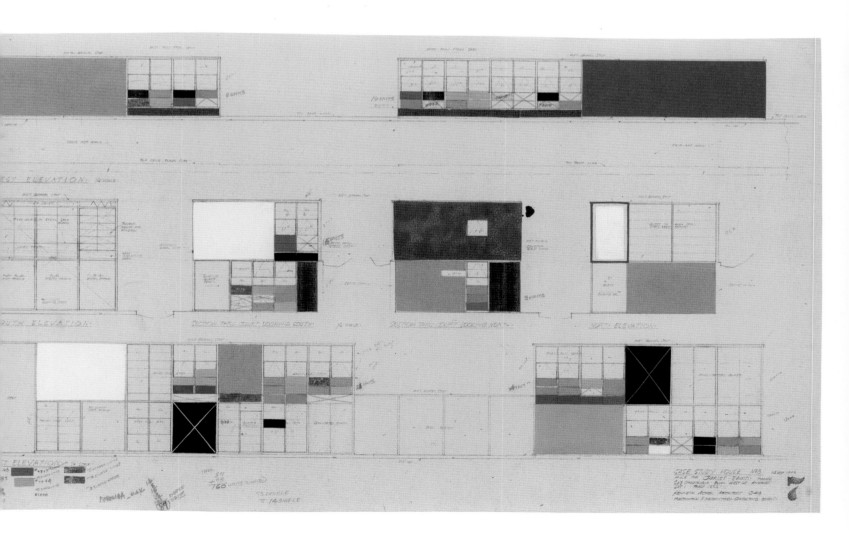

*This page and opposite, top*
Charles and Ray Eames posing with steel frame during construction of Case Study House No. 8, 1949

*Opposite, bottom*
Envelope with sketch for photo collage of Charles and Ray in the frame of Case Study House No. 8, n.d.
Ink and pencil on paper,
9.2 × 21.7 cm (3 ⅝ × 8 ½ in.)
Eames Collections LLC

The use of prefabricated components meant that Case Study House No. 8 could be assembled at great speed. Once the materials had arrived on site, the frame was apparently assembled in a mere 16 hours. The Eameses quickly took a series of photographs in which they posed together, both standing underneath and clambering over the structure, holding a model bird. The images prefigure the way the house would become a site of continual experimentation and play for the designers.

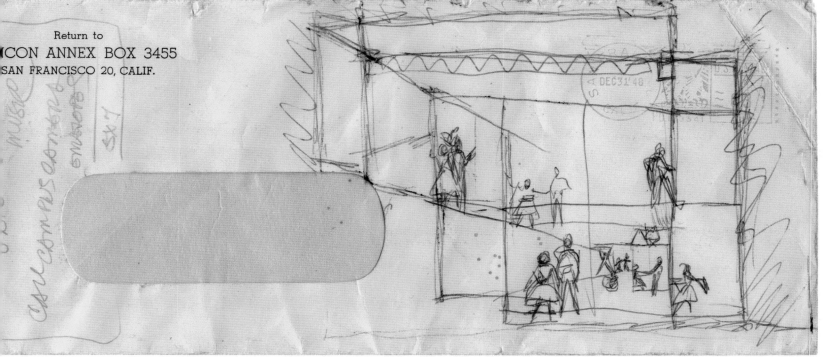

*This page, clockwise from top left*

Construction of Case Study House
No. 8, 1949
Photograph by Lucia Eames

Installation of curtains in Case Study
House No. 8, 1949

Worker painting exterior panels
of Case Study House No. 8, 1949

Case Study House No. 8 during
construction, 1949

*Opposite*

John Entenza during construction
of Case Study House No. 9, 1949
Photograph by Lucia Eames

Charles and Ray Eames with
John Entenza during construction
of Case Study House No. 9, 1949
Photograph by Lucia Eames

The Eameses' fondness for exposed steel frames was not dogmatic. John Entenza was a more reclusive client than the Eameses themselves, even harbouring a dislike of strong sunlight; the radical transparency and openness of Case Study House No. 8 would not have been appropriate for him. The architects accordingly chose to clad the structural skeleton of Case Study House No. 9 in wood panelling and plaster, creating a more enclosed and private space. This modified approach demonstrated the flexibility of prefabricated materials when applied to different briefs.

Eames House, Pacific Palisades,
Los Angeles, California

*Clockwise from above*
1950, 1958, 1949, 1950

Photographs by Julius Shulman

At Home with the Eameses

Once the construction process had been completed, images of the photogenic Case Study House No. 8 were disseminated internationally in architectural journals. Today, the most celebrated images remain those taken by Julius Shulman in 1949, 1950 and 1958. The Los Angeles-based photographer first came to prominence with the photographs of Case Study Houses he shot for *Arts & Architecture* in the 1950s. Shulman's technically meticulous photographs of the houses presented them as vehicles for a glamorous, idealized Californian lifestyle. He portrayed Case Study Houses Nos. 8 and 9 not as empty, formal structures but as domestic, comfortable and *inhabited* spaces.

Eames House, Pacific Palisades,
Los Angeles, California

*Clockwise from above*
1950, 1958, *c*.1950, 1950

Photographs by Julius Shulman

At Home with the Eameses

Case Study House No. 9 is a low-lying, single-storey block housing small private spaces clustered around an open-plan central space. The brief emphasized the house as a site of relaxation and retreat. Although a sunken living area opens out on to a patio through a large glass wall, the division between inside and outside is more conventionally defined than in Case Study House No. 8. With its low ceiling and solid partitions, Entenza's house retains more of a sense of interiority. The open plan could be partitioned off into smaller enclosed spaces, and Eames and Saarinen even included a windowless study in the centre of the house.

Case Study House No. 9, Pacific Palisades, Los Angeles, California, 1950
Photographs by Julius Shulman

In 1950 the Eameses were invited
to design a house for their close
friends Billy and Audrey Wilder.
They proposed a long, freestanding
building not dissimilar to their
own house. The design was
characterized by its open plan,
creating a series of flexible spaces
that would form the backdrop for
the Wilders' expanding art
collection. A prefabricated steel
structure featured once again,
although the treatment was to be
more formal than at the Eames
House. The Eameses produced a
model and a series of drawings that
emphasized the design's clarity
and simplicity. Ultimately, however,
the project was never realized.

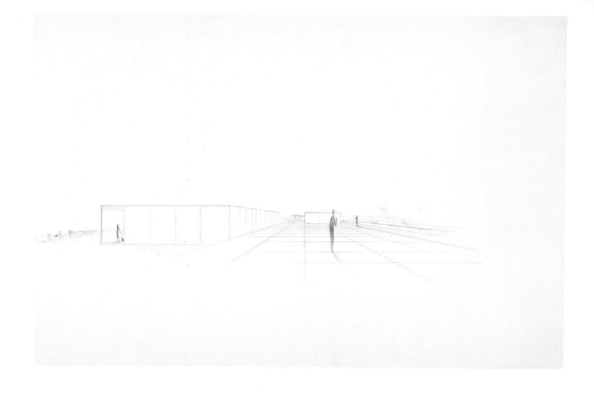

House for Billy and Audrey Wilder, 1950

*Opposite and this page, centre*
Perspective rendering
Graphite on tracing paper, 54 × 79 cm
(21¼ × 31⅛ in.)

Bird's-eye perspective rendering
Graphite on tracing paper, 22 × 28 cm (8⅝ × 11 in.)

Bird's-eye plan rendering
Graphite on tracing paper, 54 × 93 cm
(21¼ × 36⅝ in.)

All from The Work of Charles and Ray Eames,
Prints & Photographs Division, Library of
Congress, Washington DC

*Right and bottom*
Ray Eames working on model; detail of model, 1950

*Overleaf*
Charles and Ray Eames with Wilder House model
Photograph by Peter Stackpole for *Life*

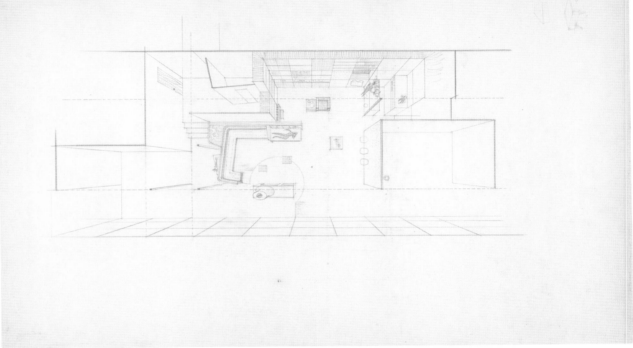

*Opposite*
Charles and Ray Eames at home, 1950

*Above and right*
Charles and Ray Eames in the Eames House
studio, 1950

Photographs by Peter Stackpole for *Life*

The Eameses and their house quickly gained recognition in the mainstream media. In its September 1950 issue, *Life* magazine ran a profile of Charles Eames, with a particular focus on the house. To accompany the article, the magazine commissioned staff photographer Peter Stackpole to take a series of portraits of the Eameses. The couple were photographed over two sessions in January and August 1950, at work and play in their house, in Entenza's house and at the Eames Office.

Kathie Stackpole on the staircase of the Eames House, 1950

Ray Eames, 1950

Ray Eames with model of Case Study House No. 8 (Bridge House version), 1950

Photographs by Peter Stackpole for *Life*

At Home with the Eameses

# CHAPTER 7

# EAMES HOUSE

Chatauqua Way, Santa Monica, California

Charles and Ray Eames, a husband-and-wife team, were among the most influential designers of the 1950s. They have not only produced a series of beautifully designed objects, but are responsible for a whole new way of looking at things. Though the Eameses are international figures, they are based in Los Angeles and they have used native Californian techniques, largely by-passing the European high-art, serious-culture tradition. They combine the technical confidence of Californians with a keenness for picking up images and objects from widely different cultures. They collect peasant objects and mass-produced objects (never art objects in the conventional sense) and put them together with wit and charm to make a colourful display of unsophisticated things, selected with sophistication and made into films, cards and simply placed in their house.

In 1940, the Eameses, together with the architect Eero Saarinen, won a competition for the design of a chair sponsored by the New York Museum of Modern Art. At that time their design was too sophisticated from a technical point of view, and no manufacturer could be found to produce their chair, which demanded the bonding together of different materials. During the war, however, glueing techniques developed enormously, as did methods of forming plywood, the latter partly as a result of the Eameses' own research. In 1946 the moulded plywood chair went into production and during the next twenty years new models in various materials have been added to the range. Since 1950, parallel with their continuing work on chairs, the Eameses produced films, toys, exhibitions and displays of great quality, which, together with the chairs, produced the Eames approach—a new and happy way of looking at objects. They also altered the attitude of architects, for pre-Eames modern

*The terrace at the southern end of the Eames house. The precision of the house is contrasted with exuberant natural shapes—wild vegetation and rotted old tree trunks standing up like sculpture.*

Left, bric-à-brac in the Eames house. Film, natural objects and peasant objects from ancient and modern cultures placed together summarise the revolution the Eameses have brought into our way of looking at things.

Right, a photograph of the house under construction showing how it is squeezed between the hillside and the eucalyptus trees, making necessary the long concrete retaining wall to allow the building to be cut into the slope.

Below, a plan of the building as built, showing the house and studio, separated by a court, set in a straight line between the hillside and a row of eucalyptus trees.

architecture was rather serious, with objects carefully placed and well related; the Eames influence led to informal interiors with light furniture, which could be moved at will, and to the replacement of serious art like painting and sculpture with the cult of collecting amusing bric-à-brac. This could either be the work of peasant cultures, such as Mexican figures, or Chinese toys or the non-high-art images of a period, as produced by the advertising industry. It is too early to assess how permanent this last change is, but it was very understandable at a time when painting had not the importance for architects it had in the 1920s, and when the advertising industry was producing images which made more impact and seemed more relevant to architects, both for the technical quality of their production and for their implications of a better life through the use of more machine-made products.

Southern California is the home of the movie industry, the air-craft industry and later the aerospace industry, and the Eameses are at home in this environment. Early modern architecture in Europe had a passionate commitment to the machine; the buildings tried to look machine-made even when they were hand-made, but their architects, for all their emotions about machines, were often ama-teurs when it came to actually using them. The Eameses, on the other hand, are not very emotional about machines; they just use them with immense competence. From the movie industry, they have taken the technique of film making and adopted it to suit their own ends. From the aircraft industry, they have studied the way alumi-nium and plastics, wood and steel are joined together and they have used this knowledge to make furniture.

The Eameses are not architects by profession, and apart from a small showroom their own house is their only built work. Yet because their minds were fresh and unencumbered with precon-ceived ideas, they were able to produce one of the most significant houses ever built and at the same time one of the most pleasant to live in. The story of the house began in 1947, when the Eameses were asked by the West Coast magazine *Arts and Architecture* to design and build a house as a 'case-study house'—one of a series of such houses commissioned by the magazine to examine the typical middle-class suburban house and to try to raise the standard by example. The Eames case-study house was to be for their own occupation and stands on a plot in Santa Monica, in the north-west part of the Los Angeles conurbation. The site was not an easy one on which to design a house, for it sloped steeply away from the sea,

*Opposite, top, a general view across the meadow-like garden showing the house on the left and the studio on the right. The steel frame, the windows and all other elements of the building are stand-ard items from catalogues. The result is not architecture in the conventional sense, consistent to the smallest detail, but an attractive collection of ready-mades, like a collage.*

*Opposite, bottom, the house seen from the studio, looking across the brick-paved court. The retaining wall and hillside are on the right.*

and was well wooded with eucalyptus trees. The first published design shows a large living area, raised above the ground to accommodate the slope and to take advantage of the views over the Pacific. The structure consisted of four steel posts and, since the distance between them was considerable, the steel structure is predominant and is expressed like a bridge; it is in fact a development of an idea for a steel house sketched by Mies van der Rohe twenty years earlier. At right angles to this house in the air, a studio was to have been built, cut into the hillside so as to be two-storeys high on the entrance side, and one-storey high at the back.

This design was abandoned, however, before the house was built. In the final scheme, the studio remained where it was, and the house was swung round to become a continuation of it, separated by a patio, so the house too is cut into the hillside—a fundamental change from a bridge-like structure held up in the air to an earth-hugging house cut deep into the hillside. The house has now become a two-storey building with the living area on the ground floor. This sacrifices the fine distant views, but in compensation, the living room is taken up through two floors opening out on to a covered terrace. So there are now generous internal views to make up for the distant ones that have been lost. All these changes are in sympathy with the fundamental alteration into a more introverted house. The new siting of the house in the bank behind the line of 90-foot eucalyptus trees enabled the trees to be preserved and to shelter the house from the sun, and the flat part of the site could revert to meadow—a process encouraged by cultivating only plants that were native to the site.

In 1949 the house was built. First a strong reinforced concrete retaining wall, 200 feet long, to hold back the hill and give a flat base for the house, the studio, the patio and the terrace. Then a light structure was built for the house itself, made of standard elements out of catalogues, which resulted in a house that was cheaper than average, with that non-arty quality possessed by assemblies of ready-mades, collections of other peoples' work stuck together like a collage. And because local industry offered a generous array of products, the Eameses were able to select what they needed, so that the finished building on its site is a unique and magical place. It represents a novel way of building houses: not the one-off handicraft way, for in a technically advanced society such houses can only be for the rich. (In any case, such a method seems irrelevant at a time when the best products are machine-made.) Nor is it a

*A view of the timber walkway linking the house and studio.*

*Another view of the timber walkway alongside the house. The diagonal braces take the wind load and enable the construction of the house to be very light. It is this lightness that gives the house its charm and slightly unreal quality.*

standardised dwelling produced by the promoters of industrialised building systems, for they leave us no freedom of choice and our needs and tastes are not all identical. The Eames house shows that out of an array of mass-produced, machine-made components we can select those we need and build an individual building. Thus we reap the benefits of mass-production and of technologically sophisticated components yet are free to assemble them in our own way. It is like a giant Meccano set.

The Eames house and studio have a skeleton of steel, with 4 inch by 4 inch steel columns regularly spaced at intervals of 7 feet 4 inches along the long sides. Spanning between these two rows of columns, 20 feet apart, are 12-inch deep open truss joists. Wherever the external skin is placed across the building between two columns the 12-inch joist is omitted and the roof is supported on the mullions. As a result of this simple device, the glass on all sides can be taken right up to the roof, not up to the underside of the beam. So the roof shows an edge only a few inches thick all round and this makes the whole house look paper thin. The building and its steel frame not only are light and elegant, but also appear so. This aspect of the design is further emphasised by hiding the heavy edge beam to the upper floor and by making the steel columns too thin to take any but vertical loads and by taking wind loads on clearly expressed diagonal braces.

The steel columns and the open joists spanning them are all clearly

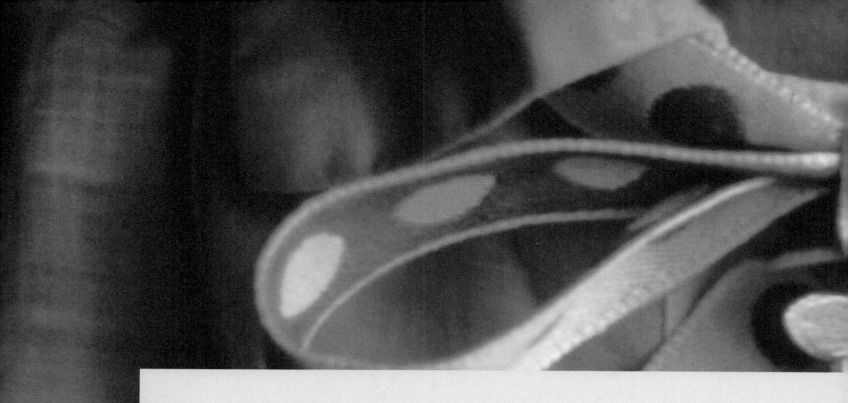

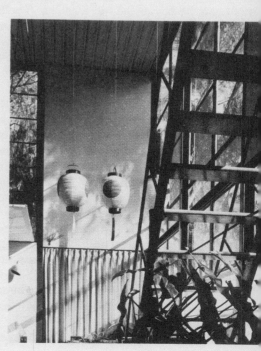

*Left, a view looking into the front door of the Eames house showing the plywood and steel spiral staircase.*

*The landscape is reflected in the glass as we look into the living room, right, along the passage to the entrance door. The living room is the full height of the house and the front of the gallery makes a thick white band above head height.*

*Below, the inside of the studio, which, like the living room, is a two-storey-high space with a gallery. All the elements—staircase, ceiling, windows—show the same light touch with off-the-peg, machine-made items.*

exposed, as is the industrial steel decking that spans between the joists to form the upper floor and the roof. The skin stretched between the columns is glazed or solid as necessary; the design can accommodate either in any position and indeed allows for them to change at a later date. The solid panels are steel industrial sheeting, plastered to give a smooth finish; the glazing is standard industrial sash, the window units selected are subdivided into small panes so that the window does not disappear but is seen as part of the membrane enclosing the space. This is further reinforced in places by glazing with wired glass, so that the glass itself becomes a visible part of the enclosure. The nature of the house is further emphasised by colour: the steel, both structural frames and window frames, are painted dark grey, and some of the infill panels in light primary colours.

When handed over, many modern buildings are completely finished; little alteration is expected and the owners have only to maintain them in their original condition. But the Eameses were building for themselves, and they knew that they would continually change the house as they designed new chairs, collected new objects or threw out old ones. Therefore the house was never designed as a finished article but as a place capable of change. The design as a

*Above, a view of the spiral staircase just inside the front door; beyond the cupboard is the high living room with the terrace beyond.*

whole is not symmetrical or formal in any sense; the number of columns along the sides is not of crucial design importance as it is in, say, a Greek temple. In fact, the building could have been built longer or shorter without detracting from the design. Moreover the windows are placed wherever convenient without relation to any preconceived idea of architectural order. This represents a fundamentally different view of architecture from the Renaissance belief that a design was perfect only when nothing could be added or taken away without spoiling it. The Eames approach is sometimes called 'additive architecture', because it is an assembly of pieces added together, not an unalterable harmonious whole. Inside the house there is the same lack of permanence. Photographs taken in 1949 show the living room as elegant, sparsely furnished, with bare white walls; ten years later the room had become a museum of collected items, overflowing everywhere. The pristine look had gone, replaced by one that was cosy and highly decorated. The house can accept the changes. It was designed to.

The arrangement of the various rooms within the house is sensible, and much has been sacrificed to make the living room and the studio a generous size and the full height of the building. The result is the same wonderful sense of spaciousness as the similar arrangement of its contemporary, Le Corbusier's Unité d'Habitation at Marseille (described in Chapter 1). In the house the upper floor covers about half the area and is reached by an elegant spiral staircase without a handrail—this is an adults only house! The two bedrooms are on

*Opposite, the living room photographed twelve years after completion. Originally the room was white and rather severe, but it has acquired a new character as it has become filled with objects and furniture over the years.*

this upper floor, and as well as normal windows opening on the out-side, they have sliding panels so that they can be opened to become balconies looking down into the big living room; underneath these bedrooms is a low annex to the living room forming a cosy corner for more intimate occasions. The living room, 24 feet by 20 feet by 17 feet high, seems even larger than it is because the ceiling continues into the bedrooms and out over the terrace. The house must be one of the finest ever built in which to enjoy a sunny climate, with its easy relationship of high inside room to paved terrace with sheltering retaining wall and trees, a roof extending 7 feet 6 inches beyond the glass line to cut out the high summer sun and windows on three sides to catch the breezes. The terrace is paved with brick divided into square panels as an extension of the same geometry of the house's structure; and here there are often new designs of Eames chairs, which they are trying out themselves and a cluster of tree trunks set up like sculpture.

After completing the house, the Eameses started making films and built no more. And although the influence of the Eames way of looking at objects has been taken up by designers all over the world, the house as a building has had little direct influence, and the many possibilities it opens up for domestic architecture are still largely unexplored. Many of the later case-study houses commissioned by *Arts and Architecture* are also framed in steel, but they have reverted to a heavier, more formal architecture, as opposed to the delicate, sophisticated informality of the Eames house. The Eameses themselves reinforced their message with a design for a house for the film director Billy Wilder, prepared shortly after they moved into their own house, but it was never constructed. The Billy Wilder house emphasises, even more than their own house, the lightness of steel construction and an informal, almost rambling disposition of rooms and terraces. Other architects, under the influence of Mies van der Rohe, admired steel structure for the simplicity of their members and the regular layout it seemed to imply. But the Eameses made the layout wander to suit their requirements and made their beams not of simple I-sections but of built-up trusses so that individual steel members are very small and the whole effect is so light that it appears almost unbuildable.

Architects tend to be rather serious about their work. Perhaps the greatest lesson of the Eames house is that it showed that it was possible to design a serious building that is relaxing to use and to decorate it in a way that amuses as well as pleases.

*A house designed for the film director Billy Wilder by Charles and Ray Eames after completing their own house. This design takes the ideas of the Eames house a stage further; not only is the steel frame more light and elegant than ever, but the plan is allowed to wander informally.*

Charles Eames outside Case Study
House No. 9, 1950

Charles Eames, 1950

Charles and Ray Eames in the Eames
House living room alcove, 1950

Photographs by Peter Stackpole for *Life*

On 16 June 1958 the up-and-coming British architect Peter Smithson wrote to Charles Eames:

Dear Charles Eames,
When we met for 60 seconds in London, I said I was coming your way (D.V.) this year. I arrive N.Y. on 6th Sept & depart 4th Oct. I want to go to Chicago mainly & am trying to find someone who will give me a lecture there. (I've written P. Johnson & D. Haskell) You said you might be able to fix something at U.C.L.A. or Berkeley. Can you? I need money to get around, you see, & would v. much like to visit you in your native habitat. [HOMO SAPIENS CALIFORNII VULGARIS [?]]
Fraternally,
Peter Smithson[1]

Charles agreed to help, and a lecture and visit were duly organized. Smithson followed up in September from the Illinois Institute of Technology in Chicago with advance information about his lecture, and some brief biographical notes:

Born 1923.
Practiced [sic] architecture since 1950 with wife ALISON.
Inventor of 'New Brutalism'
Member of C.I.A.M. & destroyer of ditto.
Founder of 'TEAM X'
Designer of Hunstanton School & 'House of Future' etc. etc.
Writer on Town-Building theory
Since 1957, 5th year Tutor at ARCHITECTURE [sic]
ASSOCIATION SCHOOL LONDON.[2]

Neither Peter nor Alison Smithson attempted to hide their admiration for the Eameses, and on discovering in the mid-1960s

*Opposite*
Installation view of *Parallel of Life and Art*,
Institute of Contemporary Arts, London, 1953
Photograph by Nigel Henderson

*Above and below*
Alison and Peter Smithson
Secondary Modern School, Hunstanton, 1949–54
Photographs by John Maltby

that their students at the Architectural Association were ignorant of the work of their Californian counterparts, the British husband-and-wife architects guest-edited an issue of *Architectural Design* magazine. Published in September 1966, the issue was called 'An Eames Celebration'.

Only five years later, the architectural historian Reyner Banham wrote that 'the Eames House has had a profound effect on many of the architects of my generation in Britain and Europe. It became the most frequently mentioned point of pilgrimage for intending visitors to Los Angeles among my friends, some of whom were later to edit a special issue of the English magazine *Architectural Design* devoted to Eames's work, and to his house.'[3] The house received much international press coverage after it was completed in December 1949,[4] and it is impossible to imagine that the Smithsons did not see any of it early on, especially given the fact that they would meet at Banham's house on Sundays to leaf through the latest architectural magazines,[5] and that magazines, particularly those from America, were soon to form a focus of the Independent Group, of which the Smithsons were key members.[6] Although it is impossible to say exactly when the Smithsons first came across the Eames House,[7] I wish to use this radically

influential building and well-established influence of the Eameses on the Smithsons to argue the bigger, perhaps more surprising point that the American couple should in fact be considered proto-Brutalists.[8] Accepting this, I believe, will help us understand what Brutalism – as a movement rather than a style, or as an ethic rather than an aesthetic – was then and has since become.

As an aesthetic, Brutalism continues to attract considerable debate. Not only is it, as a style, unpopular among the general public (being of a certain age, its buildings are commonly nominated for demolition), but also it represents a certain politics of resistance. It helps that it photographs extremely well, too, especially in black and white. However, the movement that Peter Smithson claimed to have invented in his note to Charles Eames was quite different, and was founded on an architectural 'ethic' that Smithson recognized in the Eameses' designs in general and the Eames House in particular.

The provenance of the 'New Brutalism', as it was originally known, has been well rehearsed: the Independent Group and its exhibitions, from *Parallel of Life and Art* (Institute of Contemporary Arts, London, 1953) to *This is Tomorrow* (Whitechapel Art Gallery, London, 1956); the term's first usage by the Smithsons in the December 1953 issue of *Architectural Design*, in reference to their project for a house in Soho, London; the *béton brut* (raw concrete) of Le Corbusier's Unité d'Habitation in Marseille, finished in 1952; the reception of the Smithsons' Hunstanton School on its completion two years later; their New Brutalism manifesto in the January 1955 issue of *Architectural Design*; Banham's article in that year's December issue of the *Architectural Review*; and so on. For a comprehensive history of the New Brutalism as aesthetic, I refer the reader to Anthony Vidler's extensive Banham-centric commentaries.[9] It was Banham himself, however, who published the movement's canonical history, *The New Brutalism: Ethic or Aesthetic?* (1966), in which he concluded that, 'For all its brave talk of "an ethic, not an aesthetic", Brutalism never quite broke out of the aesthetic frame of reference.'[10] This summary is not surprising given that Banham, as an art historian and critic, was only ever really interested in what could be represented on the page – that is, in the aesthetics – as his book, replete with crisp, seductive photographs of raw concrete and exposed brick, amply demonstrates. Its enigmatic subtitle, *Ethic or Aesthetic?*, essentially asks whether Brutalism should be considered on the Smithsons' terms or Banham's. Indeed, the book could just as easily have been called *The New Brutalism: Secundum Smithsons or Banham?*[11] Importantly, as Robin Middleton noted in his largely overlooked review of the book in *Architectural Design*, the Smithsons were not consulted in its writing. In his review, Middleton perceptively identifies the Smithsons' debt to the Eameses: 'The combination of the Mies aesthetic with the Eames concept of arrangement proved electrifying when interpreted by the Smithsons.'[12] I shall return to this 'concept of arrangement' below.

Banham's much-cited 1955 *Architectural Review* article on the New Brutalism starts by acknowledging that architectural historians had identified two main types of 'ism': 'one, like *Cubism*, is a label, a recognition tag, applied by critics and historians to a body of work which appears to have certain consistent principles running through it ... the other, like *Futurism*, is a banner, a slogan, a policy consciously adopted by a group of artists.'[13] There were always at least two flavours of Brutalism: Banham's aesthetic flavour was the critic's label, whereas the Smithsons' ethical flavour was the architect's banner. The aesthetic flavour was derived from Le Corbusier's *béton brut*, but the ethical flavour was exemplified by the Eames House. Neither of these influences, of course, would subscribe to any 'movement' – they were, after all, the leaders, the originators, the source. The ethical aspect of Brutalism, which was

*Opposite*

Installation views of exhibit by Group 6 (Alison and Peter Smithson, Nigel Henderson and Eduardo Paolozzi), *This is Tomorrow*, Whitechapel Art Gallery, London, 1956
Photographs by John Maltby

*Top*

Alison and Peter Smithson Upper Lawn Pavilion, Fonthill Estate, Wiltshire, 1959–62

*Left and above*

Eames House, 1958 (left) and November 1978 (above)
Photographs by Peter Smithson

35

36

## Santa Monica House

**35-40** Eames' house brings to the variability and change of its contents—its pattern of growth—the fixture of an imposed order. There is a double reality. One is the continuous dark grey web, inside and outside, of the steel frame, its panels, and its roof. This is the primary form. The other is the sense of secondary form, accepting activity for practical ends—storage systems, or the experience of visual spectacle. To the primary form is added a courtyard, a paved platform or a floating, horizontal decorated plane—conceived spatially but dependent on the more powerful primary form. Elimination of ritual is not necessary; activity does not conflict with form.

In the past, temples and cathedrals have pos this organization, where a strong stone or system has supported the roof, and within this, s ary structures for shrines or tombs combin furniture and equipment to create another syst

▷466

always described by the Smithsons as the idea of 'the simple life, well done',[14] or 'architecture as the direct result of a way of life',[15] has been almost entirely neglected or misunderstood in architectural historiography in favour of the aesthetic. This is not to say that the Eames House influenced the design of the Smithsons' Hunstanton School, the first building in Banham's Brutalist canon.[16] The chronology is impossible, and in any case that accolade goes to the Mies aesthetic manifested in his campus for the Illinois Institute of Technology (1938–58). However, on discovering the Eames House, the Smithsons immediately identified it as representing their Brutalist sensibility, or 'ethic'.

The history of the Eames House is well documented,[17] and I shall not repeat it here other than to reiterate that it was conceived for, and published in, John Entenza's *Arts & Architecture* magazine, appearing in its final, constructed form as Case Study House No. 8 in an article for the December 1949 issue.[18] In that article, Entenza himself notes that 'it is as an attitude toward living that we wish to present [the house]'.[19] This sentiment makes a striking reappearance in the Smithsons' 'architecture as the direct result of a way of life' ethic of the ordinary, the 'as found', the everyday, and was reiterated by Charles Eames in an interview years later: 'the rewarding experiences and aesthetic pleasures of our lives should not be dependent solely upon the classic fine arts, but should be, rather, a natural product of the business of life itself.'[20] For her part, Ray took a similar view, the house no longer being as important as the life it enabled: 'The structure long ago ceased to exist. I am not aware of it.'[21]

Besides this attitude to everyday life, there are several other characteristics of the Brutalist ethic evident in the work of the Eameses that the Smithsons discuss throughout their careers. One concerns the appropriate handling of materials, whatever they might be. The Dutch architectural historian Dirk van den Heuvel points out that 'the idea of "doing", finding form in the handling of materials and in the making process, is the second measurement of the Brutalist ethic, next to and closely linked to the first one ... the correspondence between appearance and actual material construction.'[22] This statement echoes that of Michael Brawne, writing in 'An Eames Celebration': 'This awareness and emphasis on the need to make objects on the basis of what is right in use rather than what is best in terms of production is already evident in the house.'[23]

Another characteristic concerns associations: collections, fragments or 'contrapuntal games'.[24] This 'conglomerate ordering',[25] as the Smithsons later referred to it, is most obviously apparent early (probably unconsciously) and coincidentally in their exhibition *Parallel of Life and Art* and the interior of the Eames House. The exhibition aimed to submerse the visitor in images, by hanging them from every available surface. Watching the Eameses' *House: After Five Years of Living* (1955), an 11-minute film consisting solely of hundreds of images of the inhabited house, we can see the interior in a similar way – as an exhibition or arrangement of objects and images, including some suspended from the ceiling, completely surrounding the occupants. According to van den Heuvel, 'To the Smithsons then, domestic order is not just about architecture as the built structure and its principles of ordering, it also concerns the order of things, in and around the house, and how this corresponds to a way of life. The house is a dynamic constellation made up by the very collection of things in and around the house and the house itself. As such it provides a framework for the routines and events of everyday life.'[26] This quote could easily be applied to the Eames House, and resonates with the articles in 'An Eames Celebration' by Brawne and Peter Smithson himself.[27] Crucially, this 'dynamic constellation' of the Eames House, which the Smithsons found

so resonant with their own everyday sensibilities, is a constructed 'system of images',[28] as opposed to Banham's single 'memorability as an image', which he identified as the first of his three fundamental characteristics of Brutalism in his 1955 piece in the *Architectural Review*.[29]

There are other characteristics, such as Japanese-ness, that could be referenced as evidence of the hypothesis that the Eameses are the quintessential proto-Brutalists. But how is the Brutalist ethic of the Eames House evident in the work of the Smithsons? It is everywhere in their writing, most explicitly in the book *Changing the Art of Inhabitation* (1994),[30] which describes a genealogy of modern architects that starts with Mies and leads to the Smithsons via the Eameses. In particular, the commonalities between the houses of each architect – Mies's Farnsworth House (1945–51), the Eames House (1945–9) and the Smithsons' own Solar Pavilion at Upper Lawn, Wiltshire (1959–62) – are discussed several times.[31] Each house is described as an idyllic pavilion, 'as a place wherein to be restored to oneself; as a source of one's energies. The pavilion is thus seen as a place made idyll; a dream of a stress-free way of life, a domain – often a greater garden – often in the pretend wild; that is, in nature.'[32]

Returning to Peter Smithson's request to visit the Eames House (designed for their own use) at the beginning of this essay, it is probably no coincidence that only a few months after Smithson's return to England in October 1958, he and his wife finally bought the land on which they would construct their own weekend house, the Solar Pavilion. And it is here that Brutalism-as-ethic – the overlooked side of Brutalism's duality – is most perfectly exemplified.

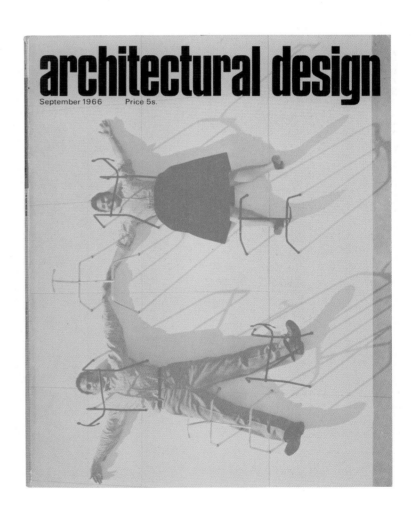

Cover (above) and interior (opposite)
of *Architectural Design*, September 1966
Letterpress on paper,
30.4 × 23.8 cm (12 × 9 ⅜ in.)
Collection of Dr Steve Parnell

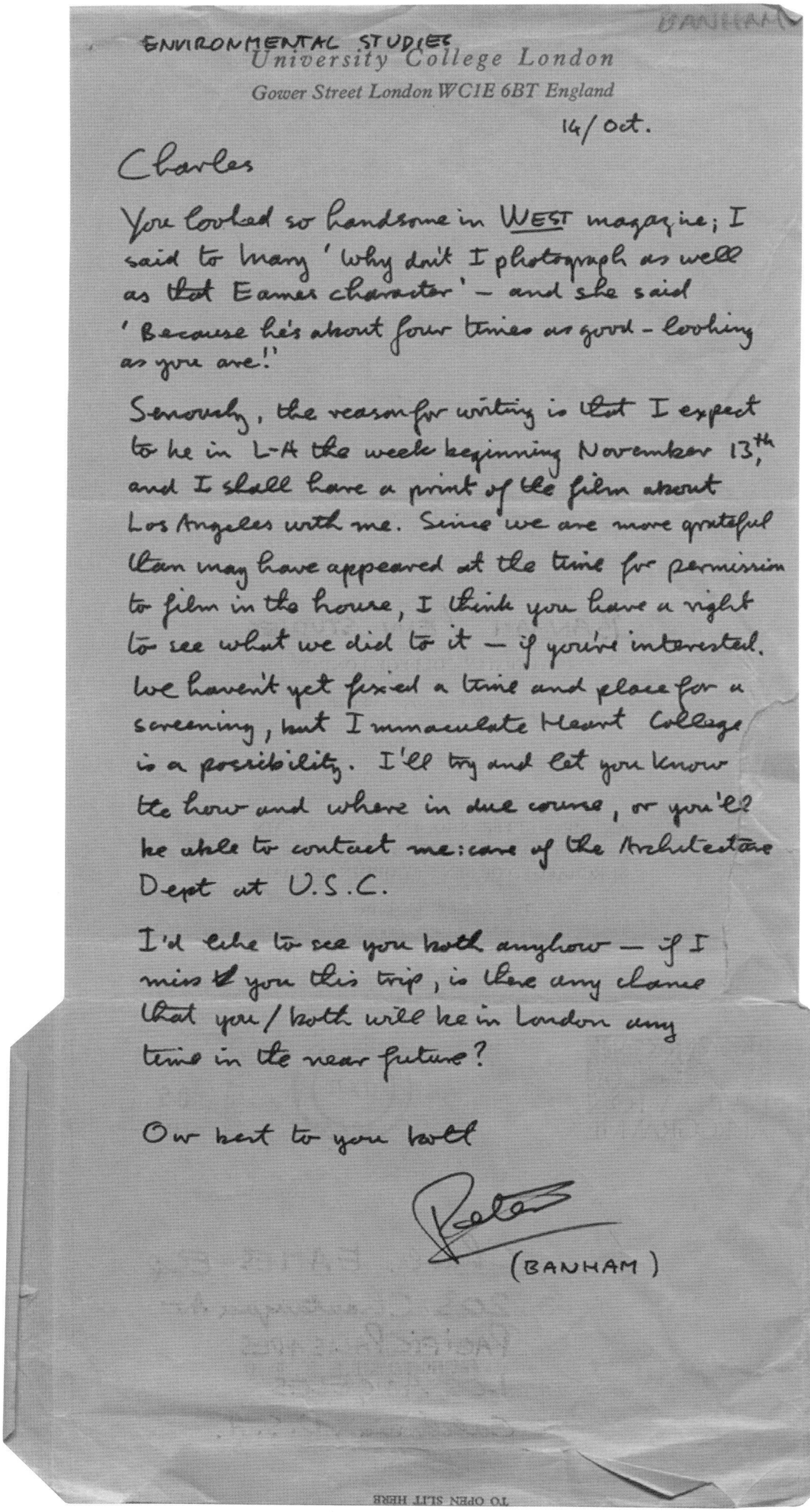

BANHAM

ENVIRONMENTAL STUDIES
University College London
Gower Street London WC1E 6BT England

14/Oct.

Charles

You looked so handsome in WEST magazine; I said to Mary 'Why don't I photograph as well as that Eames character' – and she said 'Because he's about four times as good-looking as you are!'

Seriously, the reason for writing is that I expect to be in L-A the week beginning November 13th, and I shall have a print of the film about Los Angeles with me. Since we are more grateful than may have appeared at the time for permission to film in the house, I think you have a right to see what we did to it – if you're interested. We haven't yet fixed a time and place for a screening, but Immaculate Heart College is a possibility. I'll try and let you know the how and where in due course, or you'll be able to contact me: care of the Architecture Dept at U.S.C.

I'd like to see you both anyhow – if I miss you this trip, is there any chance that you / both will be in London any time in the near future?

Our best to you both

Peter
(BANHAM)

TO OPEN SLIT HERE

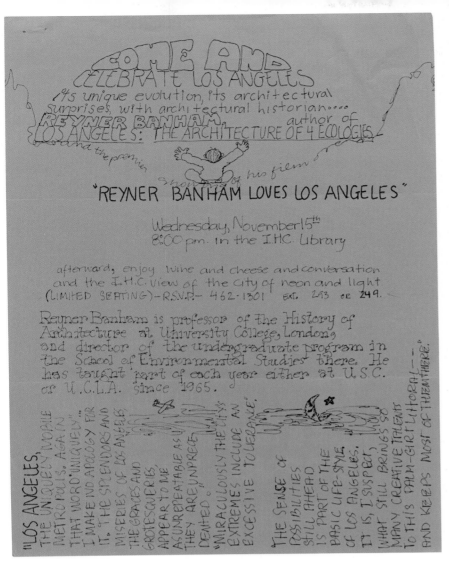

Reyner Banham was a great proponent of Charles and Ray Eames; he admired their technical ingenuity and common-sense approach to design, and regularly wrote about their work in such publications as *The Architectural Review*. A year after publishing *Los Angeles: The Architecture of Four Ecologies* (1971), his persuasive portrait of the Eameses' home city, Banham made a BBC documentary on the subject. In *Reyner Banham Loves Los Angeles* (1972), the striking 'Englishman abroad' takes the viewer on a driving tour of the city's 'four ecologies': Surfurbia (beach), Foothills, the Plains of Id (flatlands) and Autopia (freeway). Banham had hoped to film at the Eames Office, but this was not possible and only the Eames House is featured. The documentary was made for the BBC series *One Pair of Eyes* (1967–84), which explored subjects from the perspective of the guest presenter.

*Opposite*
Letter from Reyner Banham to Charles Eames, 14 October 1972
Ink on paper, 31.7 × 18 cm (12 ½ × 7 ⅛ in.)

*This page*
Artist Unknown
Leaflet for screening of *Reyner Banham Loves Los Angeles* at Immaculate Heart College, Los Angeles, California, 15 November 1972
Photomechanical print on paper, 28 × 21.6 cm (11 × 8 ½ in.)

Artist unknown
Poster for screening of *Reyner Banham Loves Los Angeles* at University of California, Los Angeles, 14 January 1974
Photomechanical print on paper, 28 × 21.6 cm (11 × 8 ½ in.)

All from The Papers of Charles and Ray Eames, Manuscript Division, Library of Congress, Washington DC

The Eames House was a flexible venue for a wide spectrum of activities, both professional and personal, formal and informal. During the 1950s Ray Eames kept a visitors log, and her records indicate the varied ways the house was used (see pages 108–9). The log records both the mundane activities of everyday life, including cleaning and gardening, as well as more unusual occurrences. The house also functioned as a showcase for the Eameses' designs, and they often agreed to show the space to students and business associates. On 23 April 1957, for example, the British architect Sir Hugh Casson visited for lunch.

*Clockwise from above*

Charles and Ray Eames at home, 1950

Charles Eames in a kimono, *c.*early 1950s

Charles and Ray Eames at home, *c.*early 1970s

Lisa Ponti with Charles Eames

*This page*

Students and teachers from the
Immaculate Heart College visiting
the Eames House, 1957

Charles photographing objects

*Overleaf*

Ray Eames
House log, vol. 2, April 1957
Pencil and ink on paper,
27.9 × 21.6 cm (11 × 8 ½ in.)

Ray Eames
House log, vol. 1, July 1956
Pencil and ink on paper,
28.2 × 21.5 cm (11 ⅛ × 8 ½ in.)

All from The Papers of Charles
and Ray Eames, Manuscript
Division, Library of Congress,
Washington DC

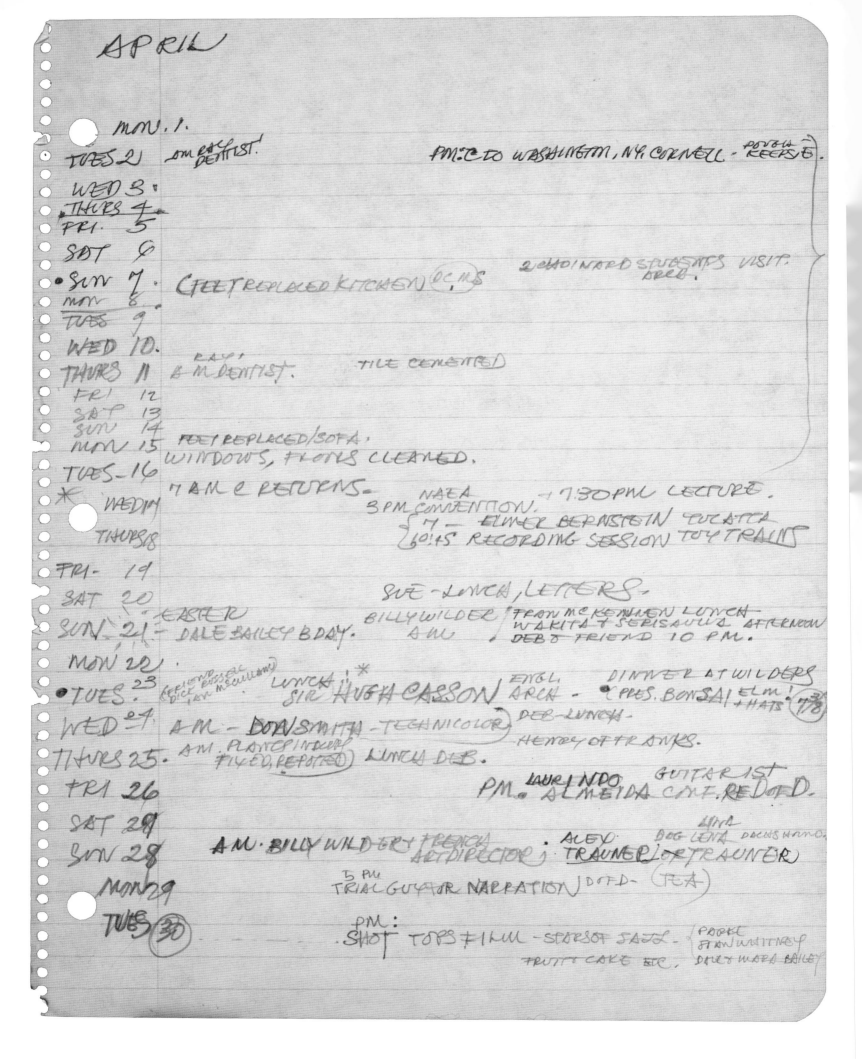

# APRIL

MON. 1.

TUES 2  DR. ... DENTIST.                    PM: C TO WASHINGTON, NY, CORNELL - POUGH-KEEPSIE.

WED 3.

THURS 4

FRI. 5

SAT 6

SUN 7.  C FEET REPLACED KITCHEN (DC, MS)          2 CHOINARD STUDENTS VISIT. DRB.

MON 8.

TUES 9

WED 10.

THURS 11  RAY: A.M. DENTIST.          TILE CEMENTED

FRI 12

SAT 13

SUN 14

MON 15  FEET REPLACED/SOFA.
         WINDOWS, FLOORS CLEANED.

TUES 16

* WED 17  7 A.M. C RETURNS.       NAEA  + 7:30 PM LECTURE.
                                3 PM CONVENTION.
                                 7 — ELMER BERNSTEIN EUCATTA
                                10:45 RECORDING SESSION TOY TRAINS

THURS 18

FRI. 19

SAT 20                  SUE - LUNCH, LETTERS.

SUN 21  EASTER          BILLY WILDER   FRAN McKENNEN LUNCH.
        DALE BAILEY BDAY.    AM    WAKITA + SERISAWUS AFTERNOON
                                 DEB & FRIEND 10 PM.

MON 22

TUES 23  (FRIENDS OF DICK RUSSEL IAN McCULLAM)  LUNCH : *
         SIR HUGH CASSON  ENGL. ARCH -  DINNER AT WILDERS
                                        C PRES. BONSAI ELM! + HATS 178

WED 24  A.M. - DON SMITH - TECHNICOLOR  DEB - LUNCH.
                                        HENRY OF FRANKS.

THURS 25  A.M. PLANE INDOOR  FIXED, REPOTED   LUNCH DEB.

FRI 26                  PM. LAURINDO  GUITARIST
                           ALMEIDA CMF. REDOTED.

SAT 27

SUN 28  A.M. BILLY WILDER: FRENCH  ALEX  DOG LENA DACHSHUND.
             ART DIRECTOR ; TRAUNER / TRAUNER

MON 29       5 PM
         TRIAL GUITAR NARRATION  DOTED - (TEA)

TUES 30       PM:
         SHOT TOPS FILM - STORS OF SALE -  PROPS STAN WHITNEY
                        FRUTT CAKE ETC.  DALE MARA BAILEY

JULY

SUN JULY 1
MON 2 — WORKED ON L/N THE AFT.
   TUES 3 — PICNIC        " ...        TO WARNERS (KINEY!)        NEVADA!
   WED 4 — LUNCH & DAY SISTERS  GORITA MAY MARY  2 ASST. PHOTO.
                    PM - VISITORS -  MAY  FRISCH! + 2 .   SWISS ARCH. CASPEN

THURS 5
FRI   6
SAT.  7                   1.Q. JONES, EMMONS + 2 ARCH.     STEEL HOUSING.
SUN   8
MON 9 AM REECE (5) BARNES / MAREN & KATHIE
                    HOWARD / JENNIFER  MEREDITH TRENT'S DAVENPT
TUES 10  TO STUDIO (20TH C.FOX) DINNER, TUES BFAST - & 6 OF FAM.
WED  11 (AM  KATHERINE            DINNER,
              PICS FREI STANS) PM. SAUL BASS,  MR & MRS  ENGLAND
                                        MICHA BLACK        (DRINKS)
THURS 12   OFF TO SANTA BARB - AFTER, BFAST -
FRI. 13  C RETURNS!  (THURS BABE  BFAST, LUNCH DINNER)
                                                    TEDS;
SAT 14
SUN 15  AM BABE RETURNS / LOOK PHOTO. TOS.        BABE DINNER
                    2 ARIZ ARCH.  12 RALEIGH N CAROLINA; ERNST WIEMANN
MON   AM BABE TEDS  AT F.R.  BFAST .  PM. ALLON SCHOENER  & CINCINNATI
TUES    BFAST (3) ALLONS.              DINNER / DRINKS     GUEST TL
WED 18  BFAST & ALLON OFF - EARLY!
THURS 19
FRI 20  C MEETING SAM BORNSTEIN + PROX.    8:EVE  BERNARD MRS
                                                  BENSON  ( DRINKS
SAT. 21  STUBBES BDAY. (3 WIND UP BOATS)     ACIELINS (BERNARD  OE (STEVENS)
                                                        ROSS)      BIZ.
SUN 22 .                        (JAPANESE FESTIVAL)


MON 23 .
TUES 24 .
WED 25 .      2:PM (50) SISTERS  IMMAC Q  LEAVE 5:30 MRS.  4 FRIEND;
                                          C TALK; ARRIVE; LISA AABEL / JENSEN'S
THURS 26                                                          WHOLESALE
                                          MRS MRS    ST. LOUIS  OSKAR  MERCHANDISING
FRI 27                    PM. FELIX BONTON. 4 MET MRS  DANE (EX56823)
                                                        DRINKS.
SAT 28  ⚭

SUN 29 BFAST      4 JIM CLARK +GA!    8 PM TO 12:30   DAVID SCHULLN DRINKS.
       PAUL ROSELAND (KANSAS CITY) /  NIGHT DAVID & HENR & CITLIN + H'S SISTER/
                                           COMMON DRINK.
                                           PARADE / TRAIN.
MON 30
TUES 31 . S                       EVE GIRARDS ARRIVE / DINNER /


109

The Eames House living room,
*c.*1950s

Charles and Ray Eames treated
their home as a three-dimensional
canvas: paintings and sculptures
were suspended from the ceiling,
rugs and ornaments arranged
precisely on the floor, and toys and
other artefacts filled every shelf.
They were particularly interested in
the role played by objects in rituals
and festivities, and the Christmas
season offered an opportunity
to practise their original approach
to decoration. They explored
the ways objects could be used
to activate the architecture of the
house, transforming it from a space
of the everyday into one of
celebration.

# 'At Home' with the Eameses: Performance, Hosting and Hospitality     Pat Kirkham

To visit 'at home' with Charles and Ray Eames was to enjoy both their many excellent qualities as hosts and the beautiful Eames House itself. Located in Pacific Palisades, California, the house was one of their most important joint ventures and one of their abiding joys. This essay focuses on the Eameses' performance(s) of hospitality, their approach to hosting, and the Eames House as the backdrop to 'at home' entertaining.

The Eameses received a wide variety of visitors at the house but did not keep a formal guest book there. Ray, however, kept informal lists, and a handwritten log of house visitors (from 1952 to 1959/60, when it tails away) has recently become available to scholars.[1] Writing in pencil in a spiral-bound notebook, she recorded the date of the visit, the visitors' names and, if she did not know them already, sometimes their occupations and where they came from.[2] She noted whether they visited in the morning, the afternoon or the evening, and whether they also went to the Eames Office. And, if they brought spouses or guests with them, she tried to jot down their names too, as if to ensure that such information would be at hand if they visited again. Similarly, she would occasionally make a note of the food that was served.

### Range of visitors
Some of the visitors to the house were business associates from such firms as Zenith Plastics, the Herman Miller Furniture Company, IBM and Tigrett Enterprises, organizations for which the Eameses created products, exhibitions, films and multi-screen presentations. These business associates usually visited the Office as well as the house, whereas the film composer Elmer Bernstein, who collaborated with the Eameses on many of their films, recalled doing all his work with them at the house.[3] Among the more famous meetings of collaborators at the Eames House were those held in order to plan the American National Exhibition – part of the USA–USSR cultural exchange held in Moscow in 1959 – for which the Eameses produced the multi-screen presentation *Glimpses of the U.S.A*. George Nelson, the exhibition's organizer, and Jack Masey, coordinator of design at the United States Information Agency, spent a weekend at the house in November 1958, and Nelson later recalled that all the basic decisions about the exhibition were made at that time.[4] Photographs taken then, as well as correspondence between Nelson and the Eameses, confirm that the film director Billy

Wilder, a close friend of Charles and Ray's, was also actively involved at the beginning of the project.[5]

Other visitors to the house included Eames Office staff members. Occasionally, the whole office was invited for a party or a picnic in the meadow, while some came on their own, to work on particular tasks. Among those staffers invited as friends was Don Albinson, an Office employee from 1946 until 1959 and, together with his wife, Nancy, a former student of Charles's at the Cranbrook Academy of Art in Bloomfield Hills, Michigan (Albinson also knew Ray from the academy). Another such staffer was Deborah Sussman, who, a few months after beginning an internship at the Eames Office in 1954, found herself house-sitting for the Eameses while they took a trip to Europe that autumn. 'Could life be more beautiful?' she asked when writing to her parents from the house.[6] A great favourite of the Eameses, Sussman was a regular visitor.

Other local visitors ranged from Wilder and his wife Audrey to Tony Rosenthal, a sculptor whom the Eameses had known at Cranbrook, and his wife Halina, a designer. In March 1952, for example, the Rosenthals were invited to the house at a time when Enrichetta Ritter, the then editor of the Italian design magazine *Domus*, was visiting. According to Ray's log, they all dined out, returning to the house for candy and liqueurs.[7] Regular visitors from out of town included Charles's daughter, Lucia, and her family, and the architect/designer Alexander Girard and his wife, Susan, both of whom shared the Eameses' interest in collecting and displaying objects.

Besides socializing with friends and business associates, the Eameses also hosted a large number of architects, designers, artists and others from around the world who wanted to see the house and meet the Eameses themselves. Group sizes varied, but between twenty and fifty was not uncommon. In May 1954, for instance, the house was visited by fifty nuns and graduates of the Immaculate Heart College, a centre of art-education outreach in Los Angeles supported by Charles and Ray; in July 1956, another party of fifty from the same college made the same trip.[8] Forty art teachers from the Los Angeles public-school system and sixty-five art teachers attending a conference in Los Angeles toured the house in March and April 1952 respectively, and such group visits lasted until Ray's death in 1988. Indeed, only a few months before she died, she accepted a request to host 100 members of the American Institute of Architects at the house, with a picnic on the lawn.[9]

*Opposite*
Eames House, 1958
Photograph by Julius Shulman

*Right*
Masked tree outside the Eames
House, 1950

### The home as a personal statement

The Eameses believed that, within the home, personal statements should be made by the occupant, rather than a professional designer, using 'the accessories of his or her own life' as props; their own home, meanwhile, reflected the British designer William Morris's philosophy: 'Have nothing in your home that you do not know to be useful, or believe to be beautiful.'[10] The inside of the Eames House owed much to Ray's painterly eye and her talents in collage and interior decoration (a term she and Charles studiously avoided), and reflected their joint enthusiasm for collecting and displaying objects.[11]

Visitors were afforded a glimpse of Ray and Charles's personal 'accessorizing' as they approached the house and saw the boldly coloured Mondrian-like panels on the façade that marked the building as an artistic space. Just as the panels disrupted the concept of a modernist 'glass box', so too the geraniums, impatiens (also known as busy Lizzies) and other commonplace plants in traditional clay pots along the front of the house, together with the folk-art doorbell, rattled people's preconceptions of what a modern house should look like. By their very ordinariness and *lack* of modernity, the plants indicated to visitors that they were

## 'Functioning decoration' and 'extra-cultural surprise'

The interior of the Eames House was an ever-changing backdrop for Charles and Ray's performance of hospitality, and the horse heads and masks mentioned above were among the many items that served as props not only for the eclectic assemblages of objects within the house but also for the couple's many projects, including the films and the showrooms. The Eameses sometimes used the term 'functioning decoration' to refer to the startlingly juxtaposed yet carefully arranged groupings of objects that differed in scale, size, colour, texture, type, cultural origin, age, materials and monetary value.[17] It was an aesthetic of addition, accretion, juxtaposition, wit, whimsy, and the de- and re-contextualization of objects and images.

Deborah Sussman recalled that one of the many pleasures 'chez Eames' was these assemblages of objects.[18] She delighted, she said, in the 'shifting shadows from, and reflections of, the trees' that added additional patterns to the groupings of objects arranged on almost every surface: floors, tables, sofas, walls, ceilings and even the kitchen worktops.[19] The Eameses' tastes were catholic, and each object in their huge collection was treated with equal reverence, from pebbles, sea shells, combs, starfish, feathers and driftwood to candles, candelabra, toys, souvenirs, Mexican piñata, Native American baskets and kachina figures, Indian cushions, Japanese lanterns and pottery, Christmas decorations, potted plants, and cut flowers. Many objects were handcrafted and/or 'found', natural, commonplace, and from cultures and countries 'other' to the United States. When placed in unusual groupings, these objects created what the British architects Peter and Alison Smithson called 'extra-cultural surprise'.[20] The choice of objects and the ways in which they were displayed both reflected and were informed by the multiculturalism of the post-war period, and made visits to the house akin to 'being inside a veritable treasure trove'.[21] The objects and their arrangement also served to personalize and humanize what might otherwise have seemed an impersonal, 'machine age' space.[22]

entering a space in which they would find some familiar markers – one in which the everyday and the 'old-fashioned' were valued as much as the extraordinary and the new.

For a while in the 1950s, visitors to the house were greeted by a masked tree. The Eameses had personalized one of the tall eucalyptus trees at the front of the house by attaching a large paper mask to it, thus transforming it into a totem pole. This tree-masking took place around the time when Charles, Ray and Office staff were engaged in mask-making, and when the American actor, art historian and collector Vincent Price, with whom the Eameses were on friendly terms, erected in his garden a genuine Native American totem pole from the Pacific Northwest.[12]

Sometimes, Charles and Ray would be wearing masks when they greeted visitors, and impromptu performances with masks were occasionally part of the 'chez Eames' experience.[13] A birthday card drawn by Charles for John Entenza, editor of *Arts & Architecture* magazine from 1938 to 1962 and a friend and neighbour of the Eameses, suggests that all manner of performances took place in the adjacent houses.[14] Ray in particular loved performance: her family had close connections to vaudeville, and she herself had studied both classical ballet and modern dance.[15] At home, Ray participated in performances with various friends. On one occasion, she, Charles, Entenza and the architect Konrad Wachsmann wore papier mâché horse heads; on another, she and Wachsmann sported Chinese masks.[16] Furthermore, once the Eameses had started making slideshows, films and other audiovisual presentations, they began rounding off the 'at home' visits with short programmes of their work displayed on a pull-down projection screen installed in the living room.

*Opposite*
Charles and Ray Eames wearing animal masks for an impromptu performance, 1945

Ray Eames and Konrad Wachsmann wearing Chinese masks, August 1951

*This page*
Ray Eames posing with cat photograph, December 1970

Charles Eames posing with Picasso photograph, December 1970

### Host–guest relationship

The Eameses considered design and lifestyle in terms of a good host–guest relationship. Among the many couples whom Charles admired for their qualities as hosts were the architect Eliel Saarinen, first president of the Cranbrook Academy of Art, and his weaver/designer wife Loja, first head of the academy's weaving department. During Charles's time at Cranbrook (1938–41), he became 'best friends' with the Saarinens' son, Eero, a fellow architect and designer, and it was the two young men who came up with the comparison between good design and good hosting.[23] In 1972 Charles recalled how, some thirty years earlier, he and Eero had decided that 'the role of the architect, or the designer, is that of a very good, thoughtful host, all of whose energy goes into trying to anticipate the needs of his guests – those who enter the building and use the objects in it. We decided that this was an essential ingredient in the design of a building or a useful object.'[24]

Key to Eliel and Loja Saarinen's success as hosts was Loja's artistic presentation of their home; she was especially admired for her table settings.[25] When Ray married Charles, she, like Loja and most married women in the United States at the time, took on certain gender-normative domestic responsibilities, including the housekeeping and entertaining. If there was food to be prepared or served, Ray would do it (although in later years the Eameses employed a cook at the Office, which became like a second home; see below). Ray enjoyed nurturing through hospitality, and her 'at home' performances blurred the boundaries between her roles as wife, friend, and artist, designer and film-maker with Charles.

### Staging the performance

Before the arrival of friends for an 'informal' evening at home, Ray, like a stage manager, art director or production designer, would oversee a small Eames Office team assigned to preparing the house for the coming performance of hospitality. Candles had to be burned down to specified lengths, pillows fully plumped up, and every object placed exactly where Ray wanted it. Don Albinson likened these behind-the-scenes preparations to those preceding a play or film shoot: 'It was all theatre. Every visit was totally staged. Ray storyboarded it all in her head … Everything had to be "just so".'[26] Staff were under strict instructions to be out of the house well before guests arrived, because seeing the 'stagehands' would lessen the magic of the performance. 'Ray liked our cars to be well clear … before guests arrived', recalled Albinson. On one occasion, however, he and his fellow workers were running late:

> We were mid-way across the patio as Charlie drove up to the house with Billy and Audrey Wilder. Ray was clearly very upset but it was comical in a way. What could we do? There is only a narrow drive and you couldn't fail to see our cars parked there. Even if we had hidden in the bushes they would have seen the cars. And now they couldn't miss us running to them. 'Hey, Don,' Charlie called, 'good to see you. What are you doing up here?' He seemed genuinely surprised to see us. I wondered if he had any idea just how much work went into those 'informal' evenings but realized Charlie knew everything that went on.[27]

### Big picture, minute detail

The Eameses' ability to keep sight of what Ray called 'the larger picture' while paying attention to the smallest of details, and what critic Esther McCoy referred to as their 'affection for objects', are everywhere apparent in their choreography of hospitality through food and its presentation.[28] Ray specified the food for guests with the same precision with which she specified items for the 'dressing' of Eames exhibitions and films, thus helping transform the rituals of eating and daily life into memorable experiences.

Many visitors to the house recall the 'super simple yet scrumptious' food that the Eameses offered their guests.[29] By focusing on simple, good-quality food that, for the most part, did not require cooking or preparation, the Eameses greatly reduced the time needed to prepare for 'at home' entertaining. They served large platters of fresh fruits, along with cheeses, ice-creams, cookies, 'home-baked' breads, crackers, candies and cakes (chocolate and coffee were favourites), and regularly ordered in steaks (chateaubriand from Ted's Grill was another popular choice). Fruit juices, good strong coffee, beer, liqueurs, champagne and 'hard liquor' were among the drinks served, depending on the occasion and time of day.

The time that Ray saved by serving such food, and by using Office staff to help prepare the house, was spent by her on creating the 'tablescapes', or 'trayscapes', that were part of the Eames 'at home' experience. If, as claimed by William Lethaby, the grand old man of the Arts and Crafts Movement after Morris's death in 1896, a beautifully laid table was a work of art, then Ray was a gifted artist indeed.[30] Featuring a variety of items arranged in artistic and unusual ways, her tabletop designs recreated in microcosm the wider 'functioning decoration' of which they were part. Each element of a tablescape, from the tablecloth, napkins and napkin rings to the serving dishes, cutlery, flowers and vases, was carefully selected not only for its own form, colour and decorative qualities, but also for how it related to the other items in the same arrangement, including the food. Composition, colour and colour coordination were central to Ray's table-laying, and she drew on her large collection of crockery, from finely made Japanese pottery in plain bright colours to Royal Copenhagen's prettily patterned tableware in blue and white. A range of woven baskets (some in her favoured heart shape) held breads, with several varieties often offered at once. Besides the food, dishes, tablecloths and napkins, the main features of her tabletop designs were the more conventional ones of floral arrangements and candles in holders.

*Opposite*

Photograph of birthday card for John Entenza (with nine head shots), 1947 Photograph of collage, 10.2 × 12.7 cm (4 × 5 in.)

Eames Collections LLC

*Below*

A table setting at the Eames House. From left: I. Bernard Cohen, Patricia Arfman, Charles Eames, Frances Cohen, Michael Sullivan and Owen Gingerich Photograph by Ray Eames

Charles's well-known dislike of parties, especially cocktail parties, and other large social gatherings (he begged off a coveted invitation to President John F. Kennedy's inauguration citing fear of crowds) extended to eating in restaurants unless he could hear everyone who spoke.[31] He preferred instead the three-sided multipurpose alcove at the Eames House designed by him and Ray to serve as a conversation area, and, for the most part, the Eameses entertained in small groups. Often, but by no means exclusively, it was just them and another couple. Because they had a large number of friends, they entertained on a regular basis, particularly throughout the 1940s and 1950s; indeed, even thereafter, when they cut back on their socializing and transferred much of it to the Office, they still continued to host considerable numbers of friends and business contacts at the house.

From about the late 1950s onwards, the Office became a second home to the Eameses. They hired a professional chef to cook for them and their guests, and, weather permitting, ate outdoors. Charles and Ray lunched mostly in private, reviewing work and family matters or just soaking up the sunshine and relaxing; sometimes, individual staff members were invited to join them to discuss work-related issues. 'I remember feeling quite jealous if someone else was called in; it was a *big deal* to be asked', recalled Deborah Sussman. 'I remember that once, as Glen Fleck [a fellow staff member] was on his way to join them for lunch in the office, I felt so jealous that I had to pinch myself and remember that I had been to the house so many times that other people were probably jealous of my relationship with them.'[32] Ray loved celebrating holidays and birthdays, even though Charles became less keen on the latter the older he got. For Charles's fiftieth birthday in 1957, staff members decorated one of the walls in the Office to serve as a backdrop for his birthday cake. The decorations remained in place thereafter, marking the site for Office birthday celebrations and the place where indoor meals were served to guests visiting the Office.

Billy and Audrey Wilder were frequent guests at the Eames House, especially from the late 1940s to the early 1960s. The Wilders credited much of the 'magic' of the 'at home' evenings to the Eameses' 'warmth', to Ray's 'flawless taste' and 'brilliant eye', and to her ability to find 'joy in food'.[33] Audrey, a noted hostess in her own right, appreciated just how much effort and talent went into creating those 'visually delightful arrangements of objects', as well as a 'wonderfully relaxed atmosphere'.[34] She also recalled Billy enjoying the lengths to which Ray had gone to acquire some of the foods he liked, including German breads and cakes.

The photographs of the Wilders and the Eameses at the Eames House in 1961 were taken by a professional photographer working for *Look* magazine. The photographs are clearly posed, but the Wilders were such regular visitors to the house that they probably felt quite relaxed and 'at home'. In one photograph, they and the Eameses are pictured sitting in the conversation alcove amid a host of objects. All four are making personal statements with their attire. Billy, who was renowned for being a snazzy dresser, sports a blazer-style jacket and a smart shirt and tie, while Audrey, a former model, 'Glamourette' and singer with the Tommy Dorsey band, wears a show-stopping strapless dress in a bold print. The Eameses' clothes, by contrast, are more studiously artistic and more casual, although Ray wears court shoes with a mid-height heel, as opposed to the espadrilles and ballet shoe-style footwear she wore on an everyday basis.

The Wilders spoke of their friendship with the Eameses as an 'extremely close and easy' one, pointing out that, by the time of the photo shoot for *Look*, it had been that way for more than a decade. Billy, a great raconteur who was constantly delivering witty one-liners, recalled having fun on every visit to the house. He, Audrey and Ray enjoyed telling 'amusing stories' about people they knew and things that had happened to them, whereas Charles, according to Billy, 'was quieter ... more of a sort of dreamer' who loved to share his ideas. 'Our job', quipped Billy, 'was to keep him on the ground.'[35] Audrey recalled that Ray and Charles sometimes encouraged her to sing – 'They loved music, and singing', she observed – but, for the most part, they just talked, with the conversation flowing easily from one thing to another, from work and trips they might all take together to the latest items they had bought for their collections.[36]

500 COLUMBIA STREET, SOUTH PASADENA, CALIFORNIA

*Doris + Henry at an Eames Candy Ceremony.*

*thank you very very much D + H.*

*Opposite*

An Eames Office group photo on Charles's fifty-third birthday, 1960. From left, front row: Robert Staples, Nancy Kane, Charles Eames, Glen Fleck and Ray Eames; back row: Gordon Ashby, Bill Reithard, Mariea Poole, Richard Donges, Robert Hostick, Peter Pearce, Lucia Capacchione, Dale Bauer, Michael Raugh, John Neuhart and Richard Bungay

*This page*

Charles and Ray Eames with Billy and Audrey Wilder in the Eames House living-room alcove, 1961 Photograph by Paul Fusco for *Look*

Letter from Henry Dreyfuss to Charles Eames, n.d. Ink on paper, 26 × 18.4 cm (10 ¼ × 7 ¼ in.)

The Papers of Charles and Ray Eames, Manuscript Division, Library of Congress, Washington DC

*This page*

Tea ceremony at the Eames House, 1951. From
left: Isamu Noguchi, Ray Eames, Yoshiko (Shirley)
Yamaguchi, Sosei Matsumoto, Charlie Chaplin,
Henrietta Lederbom, Iris Tree, Betty Harford,
Christian Lederbom and Ford Rainey
Photograph by Charles Eames

Yoshiko (Shirley) Yamaguchi in the Eames
House, 1951

*Opposite*

Tea ceremony at the Eames House, 1951

### Hosting: a tea ceremony

One instance of hosting for which the Eameses pulled out all the stops was a Japanese-style tea ceremony held in 1951 in honour of two house guests from Japan: the Japanese-American sculptor and fellow Herman Miller designer, Isamu Noguchi, and his wife-to-be, Yoshiko (Shirley) Yamaguchi, a popular Japanese film star and singer who had come to Hollywood to make *Japanese War Bride* (1952).[37] Also attending the tea ceremony was Charlie Chaplin, who greatly admired Japanese culture and had already visited Japan on three occasions.[38] These visits had taken place in the 1930s, when Yamaguchi was living in Manchuria, and it seems unlikely, therefore, that she knew Chaplin from before the Eames event; later photographs indicate that they met up again at least once.[39]

Another participant in this particular Eames 'at home' was Sosei Matsumoto, a Japanese-American woman who opened a tea-ceremony school in Los Angeles in the same year that the Eameses engaged her to perform their ceremony.[40] Two other guests were, like Chaplin, British-born cosmopolitan types: Iris Tree, a bohemian poet and actor whose thespian father, Herbert Beerbohm Tree, had introduced her to Chaplin more than thirty years earlier, and her son, the screenwriter Ivan Moffat. Also in attendance was the American actor Ford Rainey, with whom Tree had been acting in California, and who was then in the process of building a career in film.

Assisted by Noguchi, the Eameses transformed the double-height space in their living area into a more fitting location for the performance of the tea ceremony, albeit an Eamesian version. Astutely, the Eameses did not aim at authenticity, openly using several of their own low metal-rod tables and refraining from 'dressing up' in kimonos, even though they owned some. Indeed, only Matsumoto and Yamaguchi wore traditional Japanese dress. The latter, however, who had been born in China and had spent much of her life there, still felt more comfortable in Chinese garments; when she had first visited the United States in 1950, for example, she had brought with her only 'two or three kimonos for the stage'.[41] The fact that Yamaguchi chose to wear a kimono for the Eameses' tea ceremony supports a reading of the event as theatre, as does the presence of Chaplin, at that time the most famous performer in the Western world, who, during the informal socializing after the ceremony, posed and gestured with a Japanese fan.[42]

### Hosting: a candy ceremony

Around the time of the Eameses' tea ceremony, and possibly when the living area was still set up for that event, Charles and Ray hosted a Japanese-style ceremony with a difference. In attendance were the industrial designer Henry Dreyfuss and his wife, Doris Marks Dreyfuss, and their undated 'thank you' note to the Eameses refers to a 'candy ceremony'.[43] The drawing shown here (see page 119) suggests that kimonos were worn, and that Charles and Ray substituted the passing round of confectionery, a regular feature of many Eames 'at homes', for the serving of tea. The Dreyfusses shared the Eameses' interest in all things Japanese, and shortly after the tea ceremony at the Eames House, the two couples attended the dedication of a Buddhist temple in Pasadena, where the 'Way of Tea' was performed.[44]

### Conclusion

The various kinds of 'at home' entertaining conducted by the Eameses, from intimate evenings with a couple of friends to tours of the house for groups of architects, students, teachers (including nuns) and members of professional associations, show just how inventive and adaptable they were as hosts, and just how much work they put into their entertaining. Even though Charles and Ray's evening 'at home' with the Wilders in 1961 was recorded by a photographer, thus blurring the lines between a private gathering of old friends and a photo shoot – some of the results of which would be widely circulated in a popular magazine – it demonstrates their preference for intimate evenings with only one, two or three other people present. Moreover, it was a reiteration of many similar evenings spent with close friends over a period of more than a decade; the 'candy ceremony', by contrast, involved a couple whom Charles and Ray knew far less well.

A one-off in terms of the type of event and the mix of attendees, the tea ceremony of 1951 was an example of the Eameses hosting up to ten guests, with Matsumoto serving as a quasi-host for part of the time. Although the Eameses, and Ray in particular, always spent a great deal of time and effort on ensuring that each visit was as perfect as possible, when they invited Noguchi and Yamaguchi to stay as their house guests in 1951, they upped the ante considerably, putting an enormous amount of work into staging the tea ceremony. As producers and directors, Charles and Ray spent more time on the preparation and choreography of this particular event than they did on most of their other 'at homes'. In typical Eamesian fashion, however, it was both extremely simple and richly layered. Taken as a whole, the various aspects of the Eameses' performances of hosting discussed here illustrate how Charles and Eero Saarinen's point about good design being like a good host flowed both ways, and that good hosting was akin to good design. The tea ceremony, together with all the other examples of 'at homes' cited above, shows that the Eameses approached hosting with the same attention to the 'big picture' and simultaneous focus on the details as they did all their projects.

In a letter to Eero and Lily Saarinen dated 29 August 1950, Charles Eames mentions ongoing work on a toy intended to be 'large, colourful and cheap enough to be expendable'. Several ideas were developed, including a series of 'huge masks'. The second concept – or 'structural phase' – was to be made up of triangular and diamond-shaped units, 'which go together to form columns, blocks, huts, solids, all Bucky Fuller-like stuff'.[1] The masks, and the cardboard toy seen on the opposite page, did not develop beyond prototype stage. The design for a structural toy did evolve, however, and the following year Tigrett Enterprises manufactured The Toy, a kit consisting of large square and triangular panels of bold-coloured, plastic-coated paper, wooden dowels, and wire connectors. The Eameses photographed different playful scenarios to advertise the toy, from theatrical sets to tents and houses.

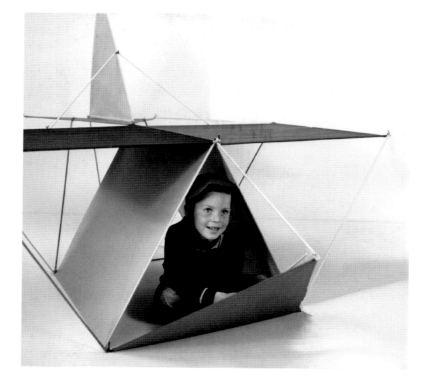

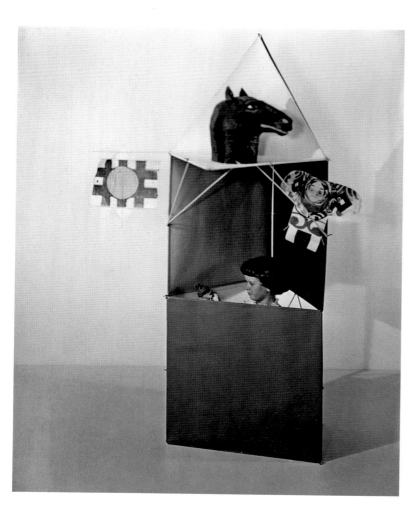

*This page*
The Toy, 1951

*Opposite*
Children playing with prototype for
The Toy outside the Eames House, 1950
Photograph by Peter Stackpole for *Life*

*Pages 124–5*
Lawrence Alloway, 'Eames' World',
*Architectural Association Journal*,
vol. LXXII, no. 804, July–August 1956
Photomechanical print on paper,
24.1 × 35 cm (9 ½ × 13 ¾ in.)
Architectural Association

At Home with the Eameses

# EAMES' WORLD

by Lawrence Alloway

SIR HERBERT READ, laying down the law for art,[1] explains the unity of effect of Gothic cathedrals as usually 'due to a single controlling mind, that of the master-builder, a man who was capable of conceiving the monument, not as a shell to be adorned (or as a Christmas tree to be 'decorated') but as an organism, every particular cell of which is morphologically and functionally related to the whole'. This kind of talk belongs to philosophers who can by means of it strip artistic phenomena down to a few perfect cases, or possibly none at all, leaving the world full of flawed objects that don't reach up to the philosopher's fictions. Probably, Charles Eames would be more interested in the Christmas tree, because its decorations can be organised in ways that approximate to the facts of life – seasonal, untidy, changeable, non-ideal. Eames' is a designer who shows how this can be done.

The key to Eames' world is his toys. The *House of Cards* (picture deck) is described on the instruction sheet as 'Pictures gathered from sources all over the world. Familiar and nostalgic objects'; the *Giant House of Cards* as 'graphic design(s) taken from the arts, the sciences, the world around us'. Collecting visual images in this way is typical of Eames. In Venice, California, where he lives, he often carries a camera with which he snaps anything he notices – stones on the beach, people exercising, his companions, objects in windows. He has a relaxed and yet constantly manipulative way of using the objects of the day as they come up. To make the film *Black Top*, for example, Eames borrowed a camera after chancing to see a school playground washed down.

The first of Eames' toys to go on the market six years ago was a multi-purpose assembly kit of coloured stiff paper panels (four squares, four triangles), dowels, and pipe-cleaners for linking. To quote from the instruction sheet:

THE TOY is designed for many colorful hours of fun for the whole family, and each member can share and enjoy THE TOY in his own way –

THE BABY as a bright world to grow [in] –

THE SMALL CHILD as houses and tunnels and tents to play in –

THE BOYS AND GIRLS as towers, puppet theaters, large and exciting structures –

THE HIGH SCHOOL AGE as brilliant party decora-

tions, plays and pageant sets –

IN COLLEGE as campus and house decorations, tastic and brilliant hanging objects to hover ( a junior prom –

YOUNG MEN AND WOMEN, clubs, civic organisatie floats and festivals.

Common to all Eames' toys is a large margin permissiveness regarding usage and interpreta by the spectator. Such control as Eames wants exercises by means of a module, as used in his house at Venice, his storage units, and in the I man Miller Furniture Company showrooms. In showrooms a floor and ceiling grid-system, holding vertical struts, contains, along with mov screens, various objects: Japanese kites, seed pack wicker basket with coloured cubes, photogra enlargement of a feather, and so on, were recom by a visitor in 1953.[2] In the recent toys (unlike early ones which were pure colour and patt there is a similar range of visual symbols sup menting the constructional possibilities. Eames m tains a sort of remote control by the given struc of his six-slotted cards and by his initial choic images.[3] But the toys are meaningful only w assembled and in doing that the user has been c mitted to a chain of decisions. Eames cannot for exact combinations of the cards: it is the choic the user that organises each house built by the c Eames has found, especially in the picture (marketed by Summit Games in England), a de system that permits the creation of other syst The user's system validates that of the designer.

Eames has managed to re-think the problem w continually exasperates architects – the existenc people, whose circulation patterns and change or obstinate usages often constitute a system inir to the architect's design. By leaving the use o designs to the spectator Eames opposes the kir thinking revealed by Sir Herbert and by archi interested in ideal situations. Eames has found a to integrate human moves in a design system. toys, and in particular the picture cards (see co are a symbol and example of an approach to d defined by the conditions of use and by peo basic, involuntary symbol-making capacity.

Eames' film on his own house is a series of sti household objects and architectural details. (

54

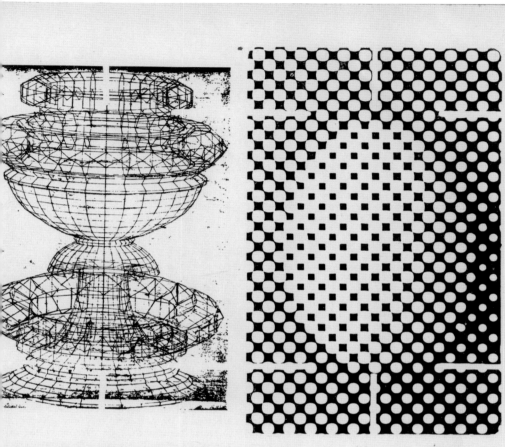

*...systems of transmitting information. Left, perspective drawing of a chalice by Paulo Uccello. Right, greatly ...ified half-tone print of an egg*

...l with a pre-war film consisting of rapid shots ...jects, Léger's *Ballet Mécanique*, there is more ...ence than the use of colour film. For Léger ...ts were geometry; for Eames they are semantics ...urface as well as form. The sharp good taste of ...ay with objects touches, in mood, on a Gene ... musical.

...1954 Eames, with George Nelson and Alex ...d, created ART X, an application of industrial ...iques to education at the University of Georgia. ...s an audacious play with the possibilities of ...channelled communication, rich in the codes ...symbols which fascinate Eames: audio-visual ...rces (films, slides, three screens, recorded ...d) were, at one point, supplemented by odours ...e ventilating plant. This study of the possibilities ...mmunication is a central interest of Eames, as ...*Communications Primer*, made for ART X. Now ...n see some ambiguities in the film, for example, ...t the meaning of information in cybernetics,

but it is still an impressive as well as a glittering film. By dramatising aspects of transmitter-message-receiver systems Eames stresses design as a process of transmission rather than design as approximation to a canon. He thinks in terms of relationships rather than aesthetic standards of form.

[1]Sir Herbert Read: *The Architect as Universal Man* (*Arts and Architecture*, May, 1956).
[2]The author is indebted to Geoffrey Holroyd for information and ideas about Eames and to Frank Newby and Laurence Backmann who spoke at a discussion on Eames' toys and films at the Institute of Contemporary Arts in April, 1956.
[3]For similar problems of remote control in sculpture, see article on John McHale by the author: *L'intervention du spectateur* (*Aujourd'hui*, November, 1955).

**Cover illustration**
Gold thimble, embroidering scissors. Old American toy railroad station. Chinese dominoes. Chinese patchwork quilt.
*Block given by Summit Games Ltd.*

**55**

*This page*
House of Cards, pattern deck, 1952

Giant House of Cards, 1953

*Opposite*
House of Cards, picture deck, 1952
Printed card, each 8.9 × 5.7 cm
(3 ½ × 2 ¼ in.)

The 54-deck House of Cards picture and pattern sets include images of 'familiar and nostalgic objects from the animal, vegetable and mineral kingdoms', or graphic patterns and solid colours. The decks of slotted cards came with an instruction leaflet, which listed the printed images as well as 'sample building procedures' and photographs of potential constructions, including the United Nations Headquarters in New York, an aircraft hangar, a dome and a fun house. The Giant House of Cards followed in 1953, and each of its twenty cards features a 'graphic design taken from the Arts, the Sciences and the world around us', with brightly coloured squares on the reverse.

The cards encouraged play and experimentation with structure, as well as reflection on everyday artefacts that the Eameses felt should be appreciated as both useful *and* beautiful.

At Home with the Eameses

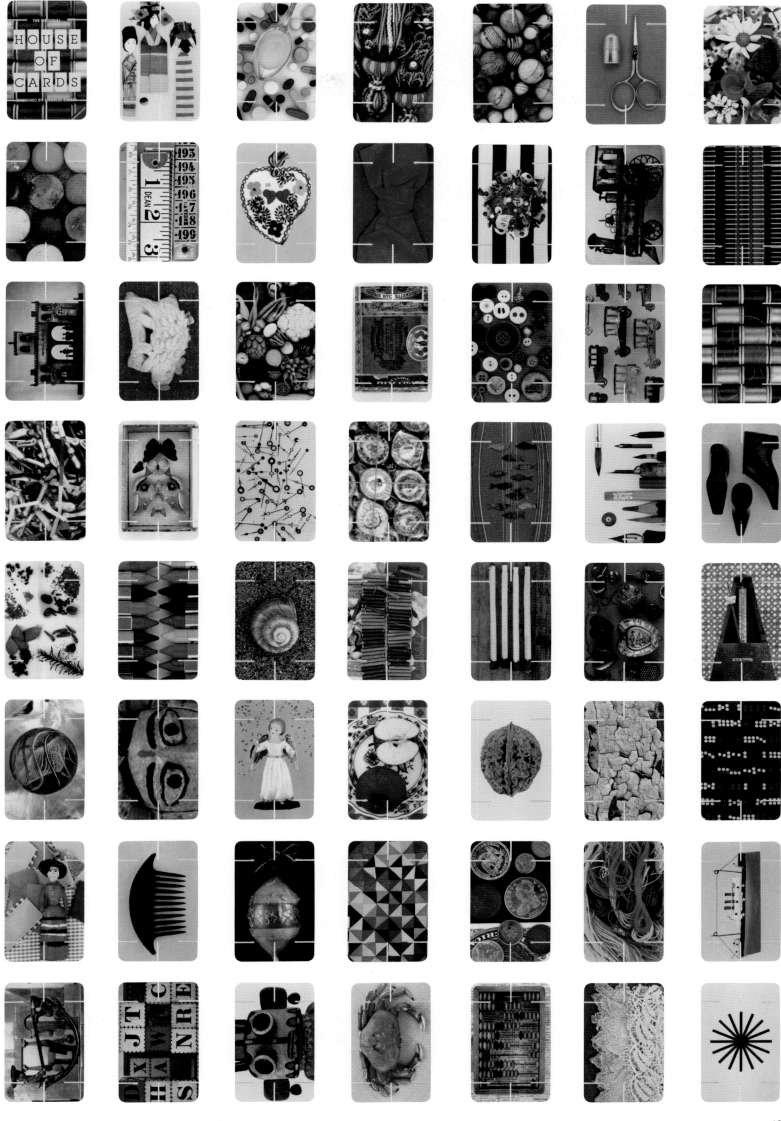

In the late 1960s the Eames Office developed a new card game, Pairs, which reprised the 'images of good things' presented in the House of Cards picture deck. Objects considered for depiction in the game were grouped by colour and category (animal, vegetable and mineral), and included such familiar Eames items as tops, bells, buttons, hearts, paper clips, tools and food.

Pairs did not go into production, and all that survives is a series of contact sheets featuring images of potential source material along with corresponding lists of subject groups, sample cards showing images of objects and studies for a title card.

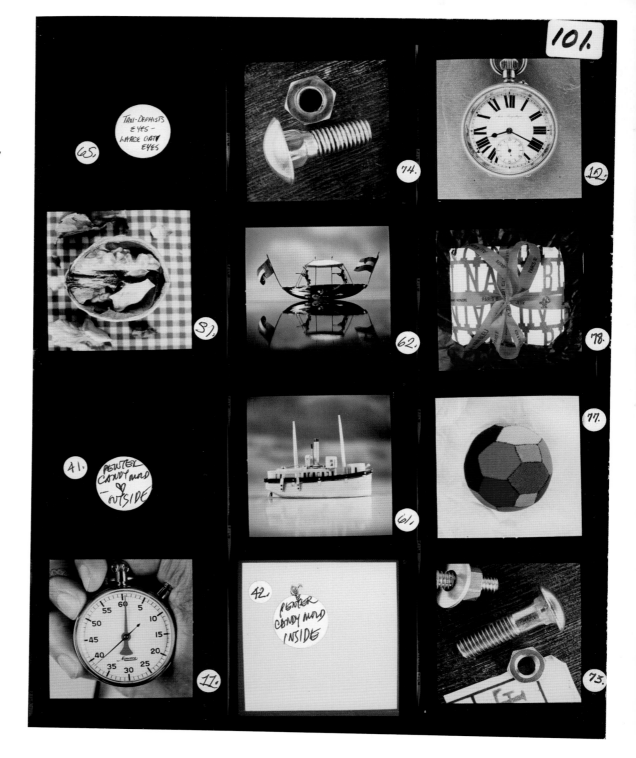

*This page*

Contact sheet #101 for Pairs card game
Colour photograph, 25.4 × 22.6 cm (10 × 8 ⅞ in.)

Studies for title card for Pairs card game
Graphite on card, 6.6 × 6.6 cm (2 ⅝ × 2 ⅝ in.)

The Papers of Charles and Ray Eames, Manuscript Division, Library of Congress, Washington DC

*Opposite*

Frames from *Movie Sets* 3-screen slideshow consisting of images of the sets from Billy Wilder film productions, including *Ace in the Hole* (1951), *Sabrina Fair* (1954), *The Spirit of St Louis* (1957) and *Irma La Douce* (1963)

At Home with the Eameses

# ART OF LIVING

view from A

'Eames is pleased, but still not entirely satisfied, with his new chair. It will sell for $28 and he wishes he could design just as good a chair for less. "The objective," he says solemnly, "is the simple thing of getting the best to the greatest number of people for the least."'[1]

Charles and Ray Eames saw design not as the pursuit of originality for its own sake, but as a process of thinking about problems and their connection to surrounding historical, social and technological conditions. They advocated for students of design to be curious and inquisitive, and discouraged formulaic solutions or preconceived ideas. This original and rigorous approach yielded some of the most innovative and iconic designs of the twentieth century.

In the late 1940s the challenge was to produce inexpensive high-quality furniture using existing methods of mass production. By 1950, having exploited technical and material advances in plastics made during the war years, the Eames Office, collaborating with Herman Miller and Zenith Plastics, brought to market their most successful chair design. In contrast to the avowedly architectural seating by such modern masters as Mies van der Rohe and Le Corbusier, the lightweight and durable moulded-plastic shell chairs sat comfortably in any setting, making them a popular choice for residential, public and office spaces. In 1956 the Eameses changed tack, creating the now iconic Lounge Chair and Ottoman using luxurious woods and leather upholstery. Endlessly fascinated by the potential of materials, the Eameses next experimented with aluminium – a malleable and lightweight metal with high tensile strength – and developed the Aluminium Group, a sculpturally elegant collection of chairs and tables. Their structural and material elements formed the basis of the Tandem Seating range, a highly robust system first designed for public areas in airports. These Eames designs have come to define the look not only of our homes, but also of corporate and public spaces worldwide.

The Eameses' conception of design, however, was not limited to fundamental questions surrounding the production of specific objects, but represented an *attitude* towards living in the modern world. Although later resistant to the notion of 'good design' promoted by The Museum of Modern Art in New York throughout the 1940s and 1950s, Charles and Ray Eames were integral to the mission, and took part in several influential projects organized by MoMA and participating department stores during that period.[2] In these exhibitions the Eameses' aesthetic echoed that of their own house and juxtaposed modern industrial designs with handcrafted objects, works of art, photographs or material drawn from the natural world. The same visual language was adopted for Eames Office displays conceived for Herman Miller showrooms from 1949 until the late 1960s. Eclectic and playful props and images were assembled to inspire the consumer to be individual and, above all, human in their day-to-day living. Both Charles and Ray possessed a sharp eye for scenography, but it was Ray who truly excelled in art direction. A highly organized and visual person, Ray kept detailed lists of objects to be used in displays and arrangements in showrooms, exhibitions and photoshoots. In her handwritten list of 'Helpful Hints' for the Revell Toy House (see pages 160–61), she writes: 'what finally matters is that your house works the way you want it to. And that it is a pleasant place to be in.'

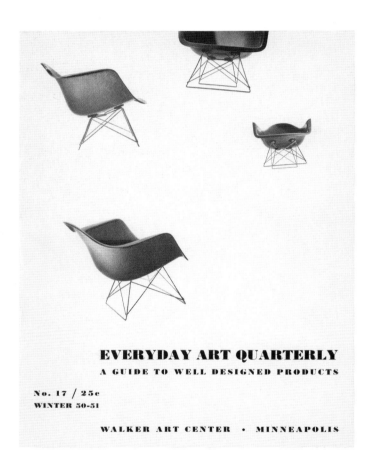

Art of Living

*Opposite*
Cover of *Everyday Art Quarterly*, no. 17,
Winter 1950–51
Photomechanical print on paper, 27.7 × 21.5 cm
(10 ⅞ × 8 ½ in.)
Private collection

*This page*
Photoshoot of Eames furniture, including
a LAR (Lounge Armchair Rod base) with
drawing by Saul Steinberg, at 901, January 1951

Photoshoot of Eames furniture at 901,
November 1955

## LOW COST FURNITURE, QUALITY CONTROLLED, MASS PRODUCEABLE

The form of these chairs is not new nor is the philosophy of seating embodied in them new— but they have been designed to be produced by existing mass production methods at prices that make mass production feasible and in a manner that makes a consistent high quality possible.

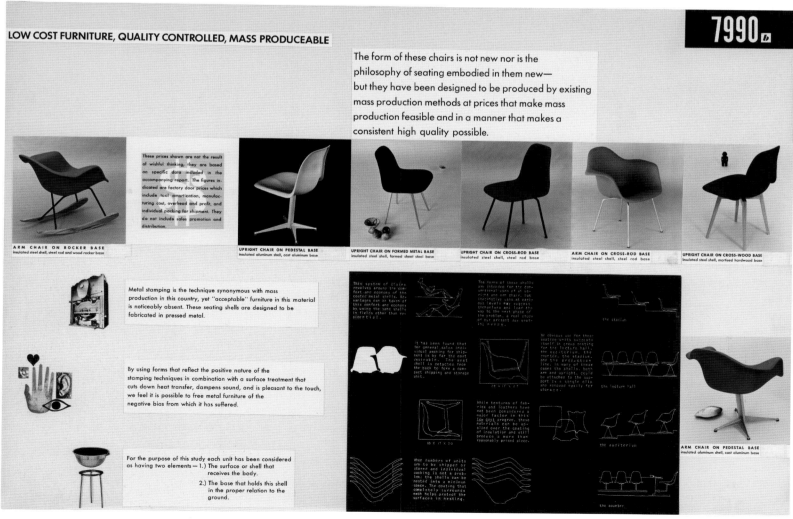

These prices shown are not the result of wishful thinking, they are based on specific data included in the accompanying report. The figures indicated are factory door prices which include tool amortization, manufacturing cost, overhead and profit, and individual packing for shipment. They do not include sales promotion and distribution.

**ARM CHAIR ON ROCKER BASE**
insulated steel shell, steel rod and wood rocker base

**UPRIGHT CHAIR ON PEDESTAL BASE**
insulated aluminum shell, cast aluminum base

**UPRIGHT CHAIR ON FORMED METAL BASE**
insulated steel shell, formed sheet steel base

**UPRIGHT CHAIR ON CROSS-ROD BASE**
insulated steel shell, steel rod base

**ARM CHAIR ON CROSS-ROD BASE**
insulated steel shell, steel rod base

**UPRIGHT CHAIR ON CROSS-WOOD BASE**
insulated steel shell, mortised hardwood base

Metal stamping is the technique synonymous with mass production in this country, yet "acceptable" furniture in this material is noticeably absent. These seating shells are designed to be fabricated in pressed metal.

By using forms that reflect the positive nature of the stamping techniques in combination with a surface treatment that cuts down heat transfer, dampens sound, and is pleasant to the touch, we feel it is possible to free metal furniture of the negative bias from which it has suffered.

For the purpose of this study each unit has been considered as having two elements — 1.) The surface or shell that receives the body.

2.) The base that holds this shell in the proper relation to the ground.

**ARM CHAIR ON PEDESTAL BASE**
insulated aluminum shell, cast aluminum base

Art of Living

The 'International Competition for Low-Cost Furniture Design' was announced by MoMA in 1948 and sought new designs for seating and storage units. Jurors included Catherine Bauer, a housing expert; architect Ludwig Mies van der Rohe; and Gordon Russell, the then director of Britain's Council of Industrial Design.[1] Working with the engineering department at the University of California, Los Angeles, the Eames Office submitted a series of competition boards (three of which are shown opposite and overleaf) and produced full-scale model chairs, which were a step closer towards realizing a mass-produced single-piece chair shell.

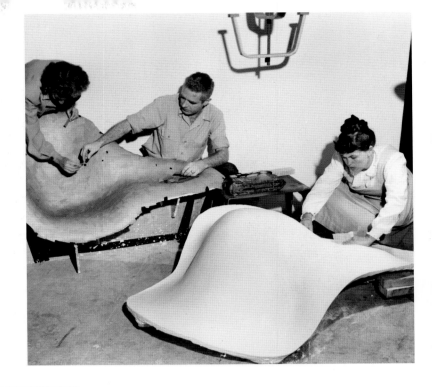

*Opposite*
Entry panels for MoMA 'International Competition for Low-Cost Furniture Design', *c*.1950
Gelatin silver print (top) and photo collage (bottom) mounted on paper board, each 50.8 × 76.2 cm (20 × 30 in.)
The Museum of Modern Art, New York. Gift of the designers, 2008

*This page*
Frances Bishop, Robert Jacobsen and Ray Eames working on the mould for 'La Chaise', 1948

Eames Office staff, 1948. From left: Robert Jacobsen, Don Albinson, Jay Connor, Charles Eames, Ray Eames, Charles Kratka (reclining), Fred Usher and Frances Bishop

Robert Jacobsen joining the three-piece stamped aluminium chair, 1948

# conversation, rest & play

Gondola,Confortable,Duchesse,Psyche,Kangaroo; are some names of the past for a type of seating that fills a difficult-to-define need of the time.

THE FORM OF THIS CHAIR DOES NOT PRETEND TO CLEARLY ANTICIPATE THE VARIETY OF NEEDS IT IS TO FILL. THESE NEEDS ARE AS YET INDEFINITE AND THE SOLUTION OF THE FORM IS TO A LARGE DEGREE INTUITIVE. THE FORM CAN ONLY SUGGEST A FREER ADAPTION OF MATERIAL TO NEED AND STIMULATE INQUIRY INTO WHAT THESE NEEDS MAY BE.

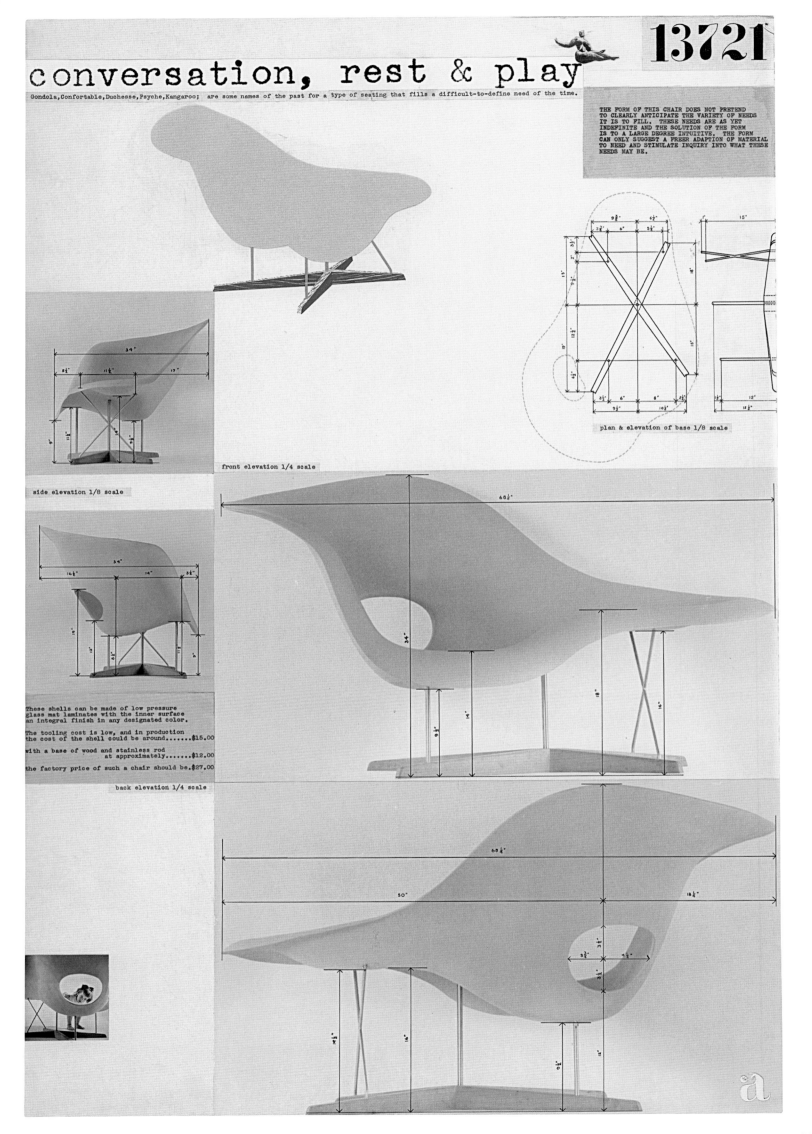

plan & elevation of base 1/8 scale

front elevation 1/4 scale

side elevation 1/8 scale

These shells can be made of low pressure glass mat laminates with the inner surface an integral finish in any designated color.

The tooling cost is low, and in production the cost of the shell could be around.......$15.00

with a base of wood and stainless rod at approximately.......$12.00

the factory price of such a chair should be.$27.00

back elevation 1/4 scale

The exhibition *For Modern Living* was designed and directed by Alexander Girard. Staged at the Detroit Institute of Arts in 1949, it presented objects, materials and room sets to 'suggest new and interesting solutions to the many and varied problems of modern living'.[1] Seven contemporary rooms were devised by such figures as Alvar Aalto, Florence Knoll, Bruno Mathsson and Eero Saarinen, along with Charles and Ray Eames. Ray's preparatory collage (overleaf) gives a sense of the vibrant colour palette of their room set, noted in the exhibition catalogue for its *attitude* towards space and the everyday objects with which one lives.

*Above*

Cover of catalogue for the exhibition *For Modern Living*, with drawing by Saul Steinberg, 1949
Photomechanical print on paper with plastic comb binding, 28 × 25.3 cm (11 × 10 in.)
Private collection

*Left and below*

Installation views of the Eames Office room display for the exhibition *For Modern Living*, Detroit Institute of Arts, 1949

*Opposite*

Entry panel for MoMA 'International Competition for Low-Cost Furniture Design', *c*.1950
Photo collage mounted on paper board with pencil, 76.2 × 50.8 cm (30 × 20 in.)
The Museum of Modern Art, New York. Gift of the designers, 2008

*Overleaf*

Ray Eames
Study for a room display for the exhibition *For Modern Living*, 1949
Graphite, paper and photo collage on paper, 21 × 30 cm (8 ¼ × 11 ¾ in.)
The Work of Charles and Ray Eames, Prints & Photographs Division, Library of Congress, Washington DC

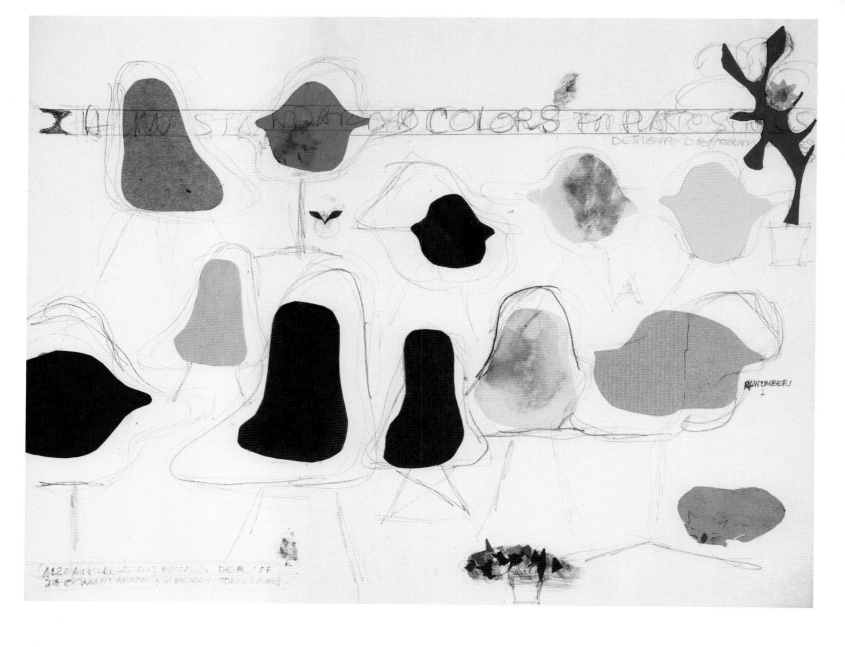

Study for chair shell colours, n.d.
Pencil and collage on paper,
21.6 × 27.9 cm (8 ½ × 11 in.)

The Papers of Charles and
Ray Eames, Manuscript
Division, Library of Congress,
Washington DC

Moulded fibreglass armchairs with
Herman Miller packaging, 1950

Using technologies developed during the Second World War, the Eameses were able to adapt stamped-metal chair designs from the MoMA competition to be produced in fibreglass-reinforced plastic. An initial rough model was made at Charles's request by the boat-builder and fabricator John Wills (see page 22). In 1950 the first plastic armchairs – available in three colours – were manufactured by Zenith Plastics for Herman Miller. A side chair was added to the range, and a greater variety of colours, upholstery options and a choice of bases soon became available. The lightweight Wire Chair quickly followed, with a similar choice of bases and upholstered seat pads. For architects Alison and Peter Smithson, in contrast to the heavy wood designs available in Britain at the time, the Eames plastic and wire chairs were like a 'message of hope from another planet'.[1]

Art of Living

*Clockwise from left*
Stacking fibreglass chairs, 1957

Charles Eames, 1954

Peter Smithson, Eduardo Paolozzi, Alison Smithson and Nigel Henderson on Limerston Street, Chelsea, photographed for the catalogue for the exhibition *This is Tomorrow*, Whitechapel Art Gallery, London, 1956 (Eames Wire Chair far left and Dining Armchair Rod Base far right)
Photograph by Nigel Henderson

At first glance the dress of Charles and Ray Eames may appear incidental in the wider context of their prolific and influential body of work. Yet by taking a closer look at their garments, it becomes clear that their relaxed, workwear aesthetic was an integral part of a carefully considered image, one that complemented the practice of the Eames Office, its philosophy and the Eameses' own resolute work ethic. Everyday objects can often be highly revealing, and the everyday clothes of Charles and Ray Eames offer not only an alternative biographical source but also insights into the American couple as designers, collaborators and life partners.

The Eameses played with the conventional dress codes of the era – Charles in a pair of casual trousers and a shirt accessorized with a bow tie or cravat (a style of dress not dissimilar to that of his contemporaries), Ray in flat shoes and a wide skirt, or, most often, a pinafore dress with a white short-sleeved blouse and a waist-length jacket. They honed their individual styles and, most distinctively, wore these uniforms for more than forty years.

Ray's look was more striking than Charles's, and her choice of outfits, especially the pinafore dress (named after a form of apron worn by domestic staff, the bib of which was pinned to the front of a dress), reflects both a bohemian sensibility and her artistic roots. It is difficult, however, to place Ray's style within a particular category of dress. On a basic level, her look resembled that of other working women of the 1930s and 1940s, when American fashion designers were producing clothes that presented subdued versions of popular feminine styles. As the fashion historian Rebecca Arnold has noted, 'Such restrained styles were symptomatic of women's needs to construct an image of authority and discretion within both office and city street, in order to conform to social and cultural expectations of femininity.'[1]

Some critics have focused on the feminine qualities of Ray's clothes, examining her appearance in the context of the role she played in her working partnership with Charles: 'Ray's self-consciously feminine guise underscored the role she adopted within their relationship of Charles' younger, adoring protégé and underplay[ed] her contribution to their work, which contrasts with the picture painted by Charles himself of a gifted, energetic woman.'[2]

Ray is frequently positioned as Charles's understudy, and it is difficult to know whether or not she consciously adopted this role. Perhaps, in part, it was her 'feminine guise' that gave this impression, although to suggest as much is to equate femininity with subservience. Ray's aesthetic *was* feminine – unsurprisingly so, given the era in which she was working – but it is the habitual wearing of the same style that is most telling, and which, instead, reveals her to be uncompromising and non-conformist. She was swayed neither by the fashions of the time nor by the dress of the Hollywood elite. Some believe that Ray maintained the same style as she was too busy with work to be distracted by changing fashions;[3] others think she simply found a style that suited her figure.[4] The Eames historian Pat Kirkham has noted the potential influence on Ray of the nineteenth-century dress reform movement, a group of mostly middle-class women reformers who promoted the adoption of less restrictive and more comfortable clothing. The Pre-Raphaelite circle adopted the ideas of Victorian dress reform, and 'advocated an end to the distortions and restrictions of fashion, especially women's fashions, and searched for a permanently beautiful form of clothing that would put an end to the fashion cycle'.[5]

The ideas of the dress reform movement still held sway in artistic circles during Ray's time at art school,[6] and it is evident that throughout her life Ray sought perfection in her clothing. She put together an image and wardrobe – possibly with the help of her friend Dorothy Jeakins, an Oscar-winning Hollywood costume designer – that both enabled her hands-on role within the Office

*Opposite*
Charles and Ray Eames posing with metal chair bases, 1947
Photograph by Don Albinson

*Above*
Ray Eames
Illustrated clothes list, n.d.
Ink and coloured pencil on paper,
15.2 × 10.2 cm (6 × 4 in.)
Eames Collections LLC

*Overleaf*
Letter from Ray Eames to Charles Eames (pages 3 and 4),
25 August 1955
Ink and collage on paper,
27.9 × 21.7 cm (11 × 8 ½ in.)
The Papers of Charles and Ray Eames, Manuscript Division, Library of Congress, Washington DC

*Page 151*
Production photograph during the filming of *S-73 (Sofa Compact)*, 1954

Still from *S-73 (Sofa Compact)*, 1954
Film, 10:40 min.

Charles and Ray Eames, 1974
Photograph by Ian Cook for *The Observer*

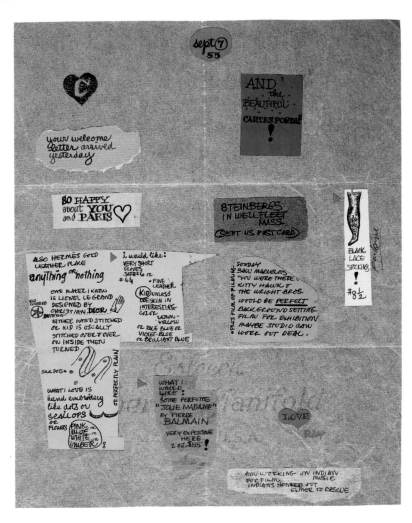

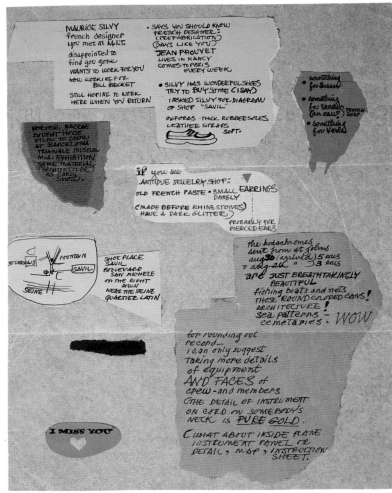

and reflected her artistic roots, while not alienating the American public or the Eameses' professional clients. The papers of Charles and Ray Eames, held at the Library of Congress in Washington DC, include numerous fashion sketches and illustrations by Ray that demonstrate the exacting attention to detail she paid to her clothes, from the quality of the fabric to the complex seam construction. She would even cover the buttons on her dresses with the same fabric she had used for the dresses themselves.

Yet Ray's restrained and functional aesthetic was often juxtaposed with, and contradicted by, carefully selected accessories: bows, brooches, necklaces, bracelets and earrings. The bows, in particular, spoke more to Victorian and Edwardian dress than to the modern look of American fashions of the time. They also held specific memories for Ray. In an interview conducted in 1980, Ray is asked about receiving, with Charles, the first Kaufmann International Design Award twenty years earlier. Ray, referring to the velvet ribbon she is wearing, replies: 'You know what, I put this on because I was reminded. I wore that for the receiving of the award. That goes back – when was it, 1960?'[7]

Ray was an obsessive collector and hoarder, and designed her clothes to accommodate this quirk. She incorporated into her dresses vastly oversized pockets, which increased in size over the years as new clothes were made. According to Barbara Fahs Charles, who worked in the Eames Office in the late 1960s, among the items in her pockets were her cigarettes. 'Ray was a smoker. She liked Benson & Hedges, which had silver paper inside, and she would write notes on the white side. Other people have notebooks, Ray had piles and piles of little notes on these cigarette papers.'[8] Designs for new outfits were often sketched on these papers, as well as on the backs of envelopes that Ray had found in the Office. The sketches, including those for evening dresses, which would be made in more luxurious fabrics, always followed the same silhouette.

Ray's unchanging look belied her interest in fashion. From an early age through to her teenage years, she would make countless paper dolls accompanied by skilfully crafted and intricate outfits. Her fashion illustrations, accessorized with handbags and shoes, also included fabric swatches. One sketch, which may have been made during her time at May Friend Bennett School in Millbrook, New York, in the 1930s, depicts the fashionable evening attire and swimwear of the period.[9] Ray's interest in fashion can also be seen in the Eameses' magazine subscriptions, which, although dominated by such architectural and scientific publications as *Domus* and *Analog Science Fact and Fiction*, included *Vogue* and *Harper's Bazaar*. Ray's luggage was from Louis Vuitton, while her diary, complete with a removable leather cover that she would re-use each year, was from Hermès.[10] In a letter to Charles from 1955, written when he was on business in Paris and composed of individual notes and drawings, Ray updates him on news from the Office and provides detailed descriptions of possible gifts he could bring back. The list is meticulous, with illustrations of gloves from Dior, a sketch of lace stockings and a request for Balmain perfume – noted for being less expensive in Paris.[11]

These luxury accessories were used discreetly, and Ray was aware that her restrained yet distinctive look perhaps contradicted her playful personality. Her garments featured details hidden from view; there might be a bow on the inside of a pinafore dress at the nape of the neck, for example, or a brightly coloured patterned lining on the inside of a jacket. Tina Beebe, an artist who worked in the Eames Office from 1977 to 1980, recalls: 'She would give a little giggle and take you aside to show you she had [a] purple polka-dotted lining inside her jacket.'[12]

While Ray concealed the more flamboyant side of her personality in the linings of her clothes, Charles was happier to put his personality on display. His confident and charismatic character found expression in his relaxed clothing style and numerous bow ties, cravats and shirts. The bow ties in particular were colourful and patterned, some checked, others in gentle shades of blue and pink. One was eccentrically decorated with vividly coloured numbers.

Despite Charles's more relaxed look, his clothes were deeply considered. He was frequently photographed wearing a suit, the jacket of which was usually single-breasted with four buttons. Shirts were bespoke and made at Larry's of Beverly Hills in checked, striped or polka-dot fabrics in soft pastel shades. Sometimes they were customized with shiny Navajo buttons.[13] Occasionally, Charles is seen wearing a casual pullover-style shirt, a design noted for being less functional and more time-consuming to put on than one that unbuttons in the manner of a coat.[14] His shirts were well worn, as evidenced by numerous repairs, and reflected the Eameses' make-do-and-mend mentality, which extended to all aspects of their lives, from their routinely darned pillowcases to their wedding-gift toaster, which was said to be constantly repaired.[15] This slightly dishevelled aesthetic, or, as Library of Congress archivist Margaret McAleer describes it, 'disciplined rumpledness',[16] is carried through to photographs of Charles in which his bow tie hangs loose around his neck or the top button of his shirt is undone. According to Barbara Fahs Charles, 'He liked being a Midwesterner and not some New Yorker. His look was not Savile Row or Madison Avenue at all. It was slightly casual, with rougher materials but always with a bow tie. It was a designer statement and an individualistic statement. "I'm a designer but I'm not wearing Italian clothes".'[17]

Charles's practical, Midwestern attitude was most apparent in his choice of shoes, which tended to be casual, soft-leather lace-ups from Sears, a department store and mail-order business that catered for the average American and, at the time, was America's largest retail chain. An article about the Eameses from 1975, written to coincide with the couple's visit to London to oversee the installation of *The World of Franklin and Jefferson*, begins with a discussion of Charles's shoes. On that occasion he and Ray were wearing Earth Shoes by the Swedish manufacturer Kalsø. Noted for their comfort, the shoes are described by Ray as 'life-saving'.[18] A letter to Ray, written in 1975 from an advertising agency, suggests that the Eameses turned down an invitation to make a 'how-it-works' film about the Kalsø footwear.[19]

Although Ray designed robes for the Herman Miller choir in 1952,[20] and contributed to the design of the uniform worn by the stewards at the Eameses' IBM Pavilion at the New York World's Fair of 1964–5,[21] the Eameses never designed clothes on a commercial basis. Garments were, however, integral to the couple's film-making, in which costume was used to convey a character's personality, social status or profession. In the film *S-73* (1954), two couples demonstrate the assembly of the Sofa Compact, with varying degrees of success. It is the 'average couple', dressed in sensible workwear, who are manually capable and who put the sofa together swiftly and with ease. The 'less experienced couple', with the female character depicted in the glamorous daywear of the era, take considerably longer to complete the task.[22]

The Eameses themselves were filmed and photographed extensively throughout their careers. They are seen both at home and at work, either on their own or with the wider Eames Office team. The Eameses played a central role in the art direction and styling of these images, and their dress was key to the images' effectiveness. In one photograph, which perhaps captures most pointedly their acute awareness of the messages clothes can convey, the pair are seemingly pinned to the floor by their chair bases. In this staged photograph the Eameses place themselves as objects within the frame. Ray is wearing her familiar full skirt and flat shoes, while Charles is in casual trousers; yet what is most striking about their appearance is their matching gingham shirts.[23] They are unified through their clothing, and together their casual attire speaks more to the language of modest workwear than to a glamourized image of two high-profile designers, with Ray presented as an equal collaborator rather than a woman in the shadow of her partner.

*This page*

Letter from Ray Eames to Charles Eames (page 1), 25 August 1955
Ink on paper, 27.9 × 21.6 cm (11 × 8 ½ in.)

The Papers of Charles and Ray Eames, Manuscript Division, Library of Congress, Washington DC

Stills from *Eames Lounge Chair*, 1956
Film, 2 min.

*Opposite*

Charles Eames posing in the Lounge Chair and Ottoman. Photograph for an advertisement, 1956

Philippa and Miranda Dunne in the Lounge Chair. Photograph for an advertisement, November 1955

Lounge Chair and Ottoman photographed in the Eames House

In 1956 the Eames Lounge Chair was debuted during a television interview on NBC's *Home*. To accompany their brief interview, the Eameses made a short film in which Herman Miller employee Dick Hoffman assembled, disassembled and packaged the chair. By concentrating on the chair's constituent parts, the film conveyed the object's roots in the Eameses' earlier experiments with mass production and standardization. Many other presentations of the Lounge Chair emphasized the more traditional qualities of comfort and luxury, depicting it as a modern version of the Victorian club chair.

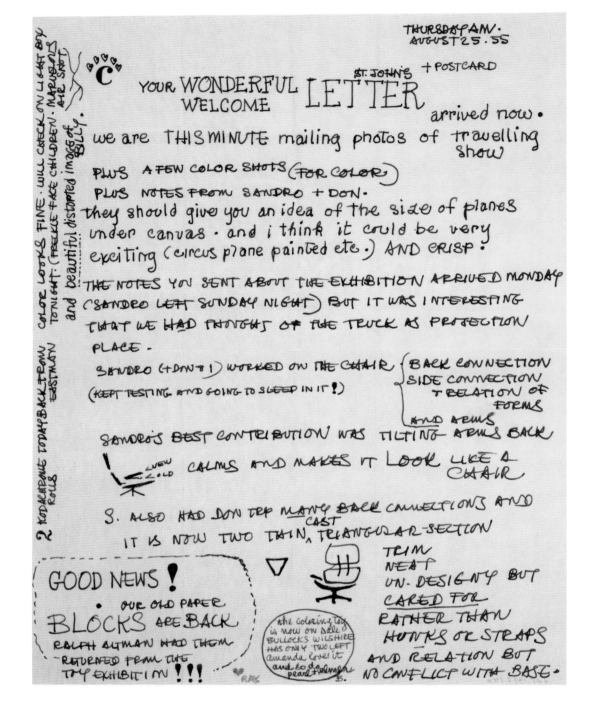

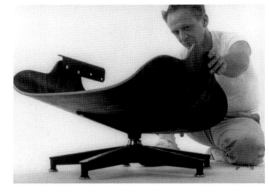

In 1958 Eero Saarinen asked Charles and Ray Eames to design a set of outdoor furniture for the industrialist J. Irwin Miller, whose home he was designing in Indiana. Following a series of tests and experiments at the Office, they developed the Aluminium Group furniture. Moving away from the concept of the solid shell, the chairs and accompanying ottomans were comprised of cast-aluminium profiles supporting saran mesh seats stretched between them. Spreaders between the profiles kept them aligned and maintained the correct level of tension in the seat. The saran fabric of the 'indoor-outdoor group', as it was called at the time, was soon discontinued and replaced with leather. The group included a series of tables, and in 1969 the Soft Pad version was developed, with leather cushions for added comfort.

Photoshoot of Aluminium Group chairs, 1958

Marvin Rand
Eames Office staff working on the Aluminium Group chair, 1957
Gelatin silver print, 26 × 21 cm (10 ¼ × 8 ¼ in.)

The Work of Charles and Ray Eames, Prints & Photographs Division, Library of Congress, Washington DC

Art of Living

Tandem Sling Seating at O'Hare
Airport, Chicago, 1962

Tandem Sling Seating in
a museum setting, 1962

The Tandem Sling Seating system
was first developed for Dulles
and O'Hare airports and went into
production in 1962. The modular
single- or double-row system
proved highly successful and is
still widely used in public spaces.

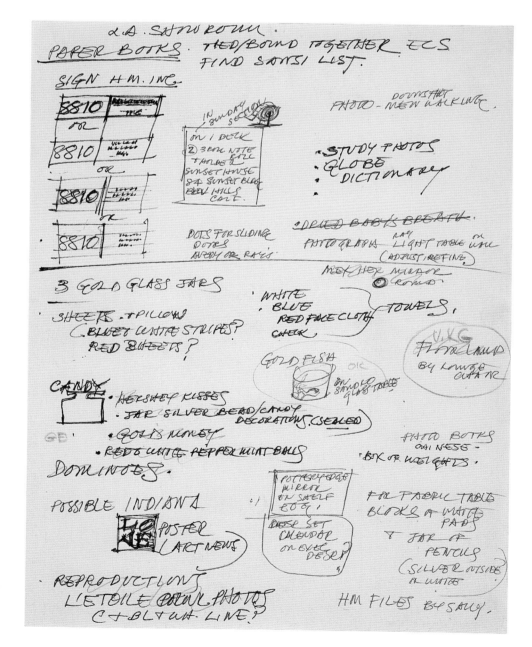

Herman Miller showroom, Los Angeles,
California, 1949

Ray Eames
Display notes and prop list for Herman Miller
showroom, Los Angeles, c.1950
Ink, graphite and coloured pencil on paper,
28 × 22 cm (11 × 8 ⅝ in.)

The Work of Charles and Ray Eames, Prints
& Photographs Division, Library of Congress,
Washington DC

Art of Living

Plan of Herman Miller showroom, Los Angeles, c.1950
Ink, coloured pencil and coloured adhesive film on diazo, 51 × 38 cm (20⅛ × 15 in.)
The Work of Charles and Ray Eames, Prints & Photographs Division, Library of Congress, Washington DC

Interior of Herman Miller showroom, Los Angeles, 1950

Interior of Herman Miller showroom, Los Angeles, 1949

The Eameses designed Herman Miller's first West Coast showroom, at 8806 Beverley Boulevard in Los Angeles. The 465-square-metre (5,000 sq. ft) showroom bore a marked resemblance to the couple's own house, completed a few months after the showroom opened in the autumn of 1949. The Eames Office arranged displays throughout the 1950s and 1960s in Los Angeles and in showrooms in New York and Chicago. The individual, eclectic and, at times, playful installations were carefully conceived, as Ray's illustrated list of props (opposite) attests.

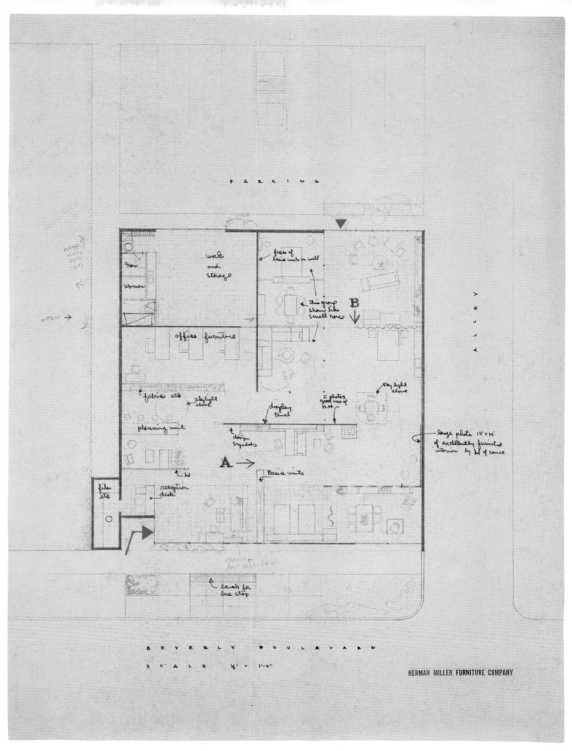

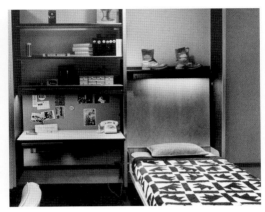

Interiors of Herman Miller
showrooms, Los Angeles
and New York, 1949–66

Sometimes, objects used in
the Herman Miller showroom
displays were borrowed
from galleries, such as the
Giacometti sculpture seen
opposite. Murals were
another regular feature, and
the blown-up photograph
adjacent to the Giacometti
figure is of the inner courtyard
of Richard Neutra's Van der
Leeuw Research House I
in Silver Lake, Los Angeles.

Ray Eames
Draft of instructions for using
the Revell Toy House
Graphite and ink on paper,
each sheet 27.7 × 21.6 cm
(10 ⅞ × 8 ½ in.)
The Papers of Charles and
Ray Eames, Manuscript
Division, Library of Congress,
Washington DC

In the late 1950s, Charles and
Ray Eames were asked to create
a model 'modern house' for the toy
manufacturer Revell Company.
The Office devised the Revell Toy
House (1959), a ¾-inch-scale
prototype kit of injection-moulded
plastic parts. The structural grids
and panels that made up the kit
could be constructed in different
configurations of one, two, three
or four levels and then furnished
with miniature Eames furniture and
home accessories. The aesthetic
and flexible modular system of
the toy was clearly modelled on
the Eameses' own house and their
approach to domestic life. Herman
Miller had planned to use the toy
as a sales tool in its showrooms;
however, owing to unresolved
manufacturing issues, the toy never
went into production.

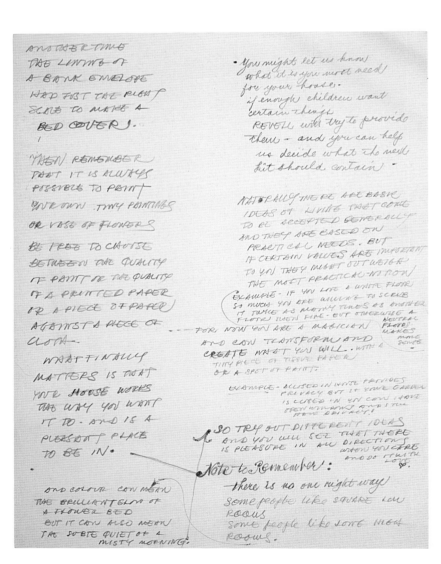

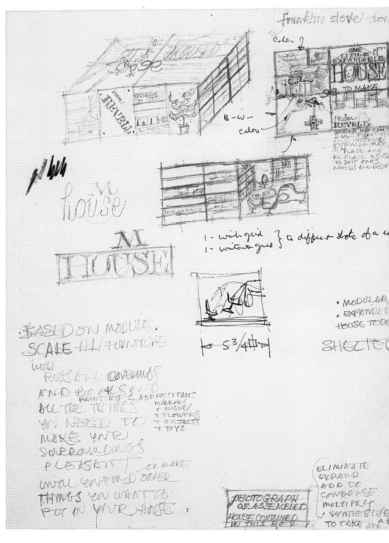

Contact sheet of configurations of the Revell Toy House

Deborah Sussman and another Eames Office staff member assembling the Revell Toy House, 1961

A proposed configuration of the Revell Toy House

The shift in Eames furniture design from the low-cost furniture of the late 1940s and early 1950s to the later, more expensive executive chairs was accompanied by a rise in copycat designs. Herman Miller's promotion of the furniture began to emphasize authenticity, asserting the supremacy of official Eames designs over their many imitators. In 1962 the Eames Office designed the well-known 'Beware of Imitations' advertisement. The witty use of a whimsical, vernacular idiom is typical of the Office's graphic design during that period, influenced by staff member Deborah Sussman.

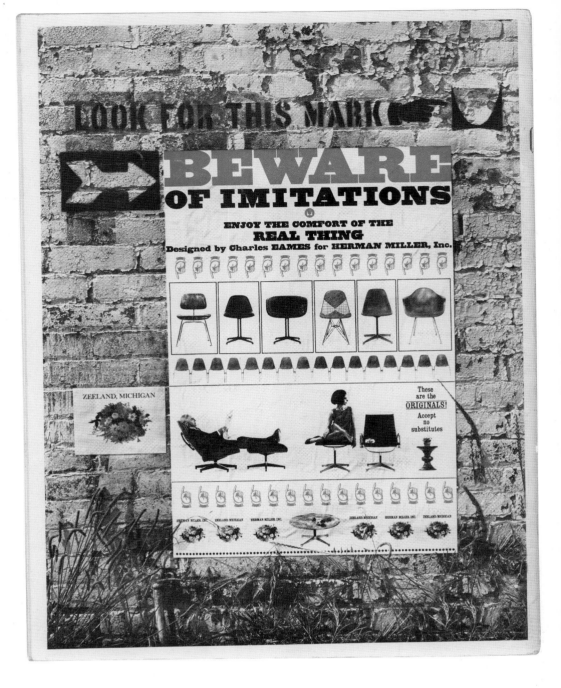

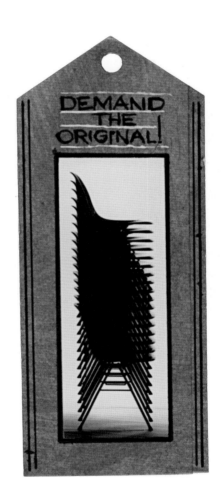

*Opposite, far left and top*

Deborah Sussman and another Eames Office staff member shooting the 'Beware of Imitations' advertisement for Herman Miller

*Above, right*

'Beware of Imitations' advertisement for Herman Miller on back cover of *Arts & Architecture*, December 1963
Offset lithograph on paper, 32.2 × 24.7 cm (12 ⅝ × 9 ¾ in.)
Collection of Dr Steve Parnell

*Opposite, bottom; above, left; and right*

Studies for Herman Miller sales material

Ink, photograph and paper on card, 8.9 × 12.4 cm (3 ½ × 4 ⅞ in.)

Ink and photograph on card, 11.4 × 5 cm (4 ½ × 2 in.)

Ink, pencil, photograph and paper on card, 14 × 10.5 cm (5 ½ × 4 ⅛ in.)

The Papers of Charles and Ray Eames, Manuscript Division, Library of Congress, Washington DC

# Context as Destiny: The Eameses from Californian Dreams to the Californiafication of Everywhere

Sam Jacob

In Shakespearean tragedy, character is destiny. Credulity, indecision and ambition are the flaws from which the calamities of Lear, Hamlet and Macbeth flow, the source of their eventual destruction. For designers, though, we might argue that it is context, not character, that is destiny. That is to say, the time and place from which they emerge is the thing more than anything that shapes a designer's world. And the worlds that they in turn create.

It is impossible to think of Charles and Ray Eames without thinking of mid-century California. Equally, it is hard to imagine California without the Eameses. Their design practice channelled the West Coast zeitgeist into tangible objects and images of ways of life that still resonate in such mantras as Apple's 'Designed in California'. Indeed, the very notion of 'California' as contemporary design idea might be the fullest legacy of the Eameses' own practice.

California was the Eameses' geographic location and an idea absolutely central to their design project. At that moment, California was the epitome of the New World, a place suffused with a new kind of modernity – with prosperity, opportunity, sunshine, technology and glamour. To understand just how different Charles and Ray and their Californian context were, we only have to look at how they were viewed by the still Eurocentric culture of architecture and design of the time.

The British architect Peter Smithson, who, along with his wife, Alison, was a leading figure in the twin British post-war avant-gardes of Brutalism and the proto-Pop of the Independent Group, wrote with a kind of envious wonder about Charles Eames: '[He] is a natural Californian Man, using his native resources and know-how – of the film-making, the aircraft and the advertising industries – as others drink water; that is almost without thinking.'[1] The Eameses were designers native to a world that could only just be glimpsed from this side of the Atlantic (this side of the Rockies too, for that matter) through the keyhole of media – through products, films, magazines and music. It was a world that fascinated the Smithsons and the Independent Group, who together were interrogating the legacy of modernism and recognizing that '… Today We Collect Ads'.[2]

For architects and designers like the Smithsons, the Eameses' Californian-ness opened a dazzlingly bright window into another world, a sun-kissed world far from the origins of European modernism weighed down by all that Old World baggage – by history, politics and war, by notions of an avant-garde, by post-war reconstruction and the serious politics of the welfare state.

To the Smithsons and their ilk, the Eameses appeared as if designers from the near future. They saw in the American couple a 'light-hearted thinking in featherweight climate-bits-and-pieces seeming off-the-peg-architecture … [a] do-it-yourself out of gorgeous catalogues, the Sears-Roebuck thinking … [a] whole blow-up, plug-in, camp-out, dump-digging type of thinking and living'.[3] They saw in Charles and Ray the kind of design practice that they themselves were struggling to imagine – a form of design practice that combined the modernist legacy of social improvement with new sensibilities of popular, mass-produced modernity. They saw a lightness of touch, with a direct connection to lifestyle and an easy ability to reach out across the traditional boundaries of design and out into the wider world.

One of the Eameses' most famous films, *Powers of Ten*, acts as a manifesto for this new relationship between design and the world.[4] Made for IBM, the film zooms out from the surface of the earth into deep space, then bungees back to the nucleus of an atom. It shows us the vastness of the universe through helium-filled lightness, as if design had been released from its traditional material weight. But it also shows us design's place within these extremes of scale. The datum between these two

*Opposite*

Charles Eames directing a photoshoot for Aluminium Group furniture outside 901, February 1960

*Above*

Artwork for *Powers of Ten: A Film Dealing with the Relative Size of Things in the Universe and the Effect of Adding Another Zero*, 1977

points is a couple picnicking on the Chicago lakeshore with a blanket spread out, a basket, an apple pie, a copy of *Scientific American* and J. T. Fraser's *The Voices of Time* (1966).[5] Objects, buildings, cities and people are placed within a vast continuum that the camera glides through with astonishing ease. Design, the film says, exists as part of this huge spectrum between the cosmos and the atom. Books, fields, lakes, cities – the things design makes – are part of a continuum that extends to planets and to atoms.

*Powers of Ten* used the possibilities of film as a medium to explore a vast, vertical depth of the universe. The Eameses' design practice, however, is more often characterized by its easy, wide horizontal sweep.

We see this in the breadth of their interests and influences. The Eameses' world stretched from high design all the way to such vernacular, 'non-design' things as folk objects, tin toys and all the other items they arranged to create new suggestions of how the world might be. All of this, the Eameses' work argued, was the world of the designer. Design could be – should be – the plenty of product catalogues, the lens of Hollywood, the imagination of the sound stage, the glossy page of the magazine and, for the Eameses most of all, the glow of the silver screen, the beam of a projector, the flicker of a TV screen.

The Eameses' lightness is literal: a house frame assembled in a day from steel components off the back of a truck.[6] Chairs formed from wire mesh and thin moulded plywood. Things arranged in space rather than fixed, where the physical stuff becomes a gossamer-light world of heightened aesthetic lifestyle. But Eames lightness is also the light of films, slideshows, projections and photographs. Their lightness extended to the invisible ends of the spectrum, where the electromagnetic wavelengths of broadcast often became the site of their operation. The Eameses' work existed in the glowing space of media as much as it did in the heavy, physical world of traditional design. Its lightness was practical, conceptual and metaphorical, a way of figuring design within the post-war cultural and technological experience.

Yet for all the Eameses' domestic lightness, it was America's military-industrial complex that was arguably their most generous patron. Think of their experiments with plywood that found fertile ground with the US military. Or their films communicating ideas for corporate America and exhibitions promoting governmental departments.

As a consequence, the Eameses' work exists in very different worlds simultaneously. It is part of their own constructed image of domesticity, within the popular world of lifestyle and entertainment, but it is also the public face of corporate communication. The continuum of their practice forms a kind of *Powers of Ten* of post-war America. Instead of a vertical zoom, their practice comprised a wide pan, from the living room to the battle field, from the picnic to the Cold War. Did the Eameses design for the domestic freedoms of consumer capitalism? Or did their work manifest a plausible myth for ideological imperialism? More likely, we should understand them as designers able to connect one with the other, able to frame the corporate and governmental in domestic terms and reframe domestic possibilities with the technologies, efficiencies and breakthroughs of advanced capitalism.

Likewise, their own studio is difficult to delaminate. Should we think of it as an experimental design atelier dedicated to material and formal experiments with social ambitions, a tradition stretching back through the Bauhaus to William Morris? Or was it a practice that provided a blueprint for the corporate-communication design agencies that followed them? Again, perhaps their practice was both. Their construction of the image of contemporary domestic bliss was inseparable from their role in constructing the image of corporate America. Each was the promise of the other, bonded by the glue of media.

It should come as no surprise that the Eameses' design products continue to flourish in the context from which they emerged. They are objects that, like their designers, seem 'native' to the worlds of film-making and advertising. Eames furniture, more than most signature design, is a staple of television, film, advertising shoots and more. It is as though, somehow, their furniture is more finely tuned to the construction of image, narrative and character than the work of other designers. By comparison, think of the Smithsons. Their large-scale housing estate in east London, Robin Hood Gardens (1972), for example, acts as a backdrop only to gritty television crime drama.

Sometimes, the Eameses' designs are a marker of an era, a visual timestamp, such as on the sets of *Mad Men* (2007–15) or in Beyoncé's *Countdown* video (2011), where their mid-century-ness signals history. Yet the same pieces are just as able to act as signs of the future – think of the Lounge Chairs in *Space 1999* (1975–7), *Iron Man 2* (2010) and *Tron: Legacy* (2010) – as if their original modern-ness is embedded within them, transporting them to a perennial near future. At other times, the chairs communicate a classy kind of modern efficiency – on Wolf Blitzer's CNN studio set, say. This efficiency is at the heart of the quiz show *Mastermind*, in which a Soft Pad Lounge Chair acts as the 'hot seat', the centrepiece of a lonely landscape of examination, suggesting the precision and exactitude expected of the show's contestants. We also see the chairs in the office of smarmy corporate lawyer Howard Hamlin in the television series *Better Call Saul* (2015– ), where they form part of a world of professional success far beyond the means of the show's struggling protagonist, whose own office is in the storeroom of a nail bar. Elsewhere, these objects indicate the intricacies of taste and culture, as in the sitcom *Frasier* (1993–2004), in particular the way in which psychiatrist Frasier Crane's Lounge Chair and Ottoman contrasts with his ex-cop father's Lazy Boy ('You think I don't want to pick you up right now, carry you over to that Eames classic and show you why it's the best-engineered chair in the world?').[7]

If the Eameses were masters of their own curated lifestyle and the placed object, it is exactly this sensibility that still, through contemporary art directors and production designers, lives on in the carefully constructed screen images just discussed. It is as though the furniture itself possesses a particular ability to act within media space. This inherent stagecraft of Eames furniture is even present in the real world. Think of how the Eameses' furniture seems somehow to remain always slightly apart from

the space it inhabits – how its form creates space around it, how it meets the ground as if touching down. Their work sits in this world as if somehow simultaneously apart from it, as if picked out by a spotlight, as if to amplify its sensation of placed significance.

But another Eamesian legacy is one that extends in an entirely different direction, spinning out from their own interest in the popular and the vernacular – in the things beyond the narrow definitions of design.

Search for 'Eames' on eBay and you will be rewarded with thousands of results. Take your pick. Maybe you fancy a 'Large Retro chair in faux lizard skin heals eames'. Or a 'Brass Gladiator Chariot Sculpture Mid-Century Eames'. Or a 'Globe Hidden Ashtray Space Age Mid-Century Modern Eames Era 1960s'. Or a 'PIN UP & DESIGN SOEUR AURELLE Kinky Nun Stephan Saint Emett/Eames SCULPTURE'; or a 'vintage 3 EAMES ERA MID-CENTURY NATURE BOY CAVEMAN REAL RABBIT FUR'.

The format of eBay's website has led to sellers developing a search-friendly way of writing listings. Kinky nuns, cavemen, Aztecs, Denmark, Brutalism, Regency, Sputnik – all are alchemized by the prefix 'Eames' to perform within the site's algorithms. In this context, 'Eames' has nothing to do with original authorship, nor with design scholarship or showroom authenticity. Yet perhaps it recalls instead that openness of spirit that first dazzled the Smithsons, the spirit that led them to write, 'the Eameses have made it respectable to like pretty things'.[8] eBay Eamesification could be the contemporary, vernacular equivalent of the Eameses' collections of ordinary decorative objects that once fascinated the Smithsons.

The medium through which all this flows is not the traditional junkshop but, to quote eBay's tagline, 'the world's online marketplace'. It is a vernacular design-cult born of the Internet itself, born within the networked culture of communication. It is as if the world of objects and the media that communicates them – so integral to the Eameses' own practice – has interbred to produce a virulent offspring of mediated objects that exist in the California-everywhere space of the Internet.

If this is an afterlife of the Eameses, it is an appropriate one. The technologies and culture of the Internet are descendants of the Eameses' mid-century California. Their media of TV, films and magazines became digital. Their 'gorgeous catalogues' of Sears, Roebuck & Co. became, for the baby boomers, that bible of tune-in, drop-out living, the *Whole Earth Catalog*.[9] Their experiments in freedoms of lifestyle segued into the counterculture movements of the 1960s and 1970s that bloomed on the West Coast. These movements merged with entrepreneurialism and corporate culture to become the tech behemoths of the twenty-first century, driven by experiment, design culture and lifestyle, just as the Eameses had been. Could we even draw a line from the Eameses' Venice studio to the Googleplex or to Apple's Infinite Loop? Is Apple's 'Designed in California' a contemporary version of the promise the Smithsons once saw in the Eameses' 'natural' Californian design project?

We remain as fixated on the Eameses as exemplars of a specific Californian context as the Smithsons once were. The time and place they articulated remains a powerful cultural moment, a permanent mid-century-ness that their name has come to define. But just as their furniture provides films and TV sets with an ability to represent both that moment and an endless near future, the Eameses also remain important in the construction of contemporary design contexts.

Indeed, thanks to the Internet, in the twenty-first century we all inhabit an idea of California that the Eameses helped to invent. Their context – or at least a version of it – has become ours. Their ideas of individuality, of freedom, the pleasures of lifestyle and the significance of media are now part of a global culture. And their

formation of design practice as operating between the domestic and the corporate has become the paradigm of how we now make work.

In the Shakespearean sense of the word, we could see the context of both the Smithsons' and the Eameses' practice as a form of tragedy. The European post-war welfare state – so integral to the Smithsons' practice – has, since the late 1970s, been more or less dismantled thanks to a political narrative intent on describing its perceived failures. On the other hand, the Eameses' context has grown so successful as to overshadow their original intent. If the Smithsons could glimpse the 'California everywhere' we now all inhabit, would they still admire its innocence and easiness? According to some, the 'Californian Ideology' – a belief in the power of a knowledge-based economy to drive growth while simultaneously bringing about a more egalitarian society – has in fact strengthened corporate and governmental control.[10] The liberties and lightness that so dazzled the Eameses' European counterparts have, say critics of the ideology, now taken on a darker, heavier hue.

Beyond all the chairs, objects, images and films, and distinct from their place in time and space, Charles and Ray Eames remain optimistic figures in design culture. Their work argues for forms of design practice that are able to manufacture their own kind of context, that can take the world one finds oneself in and reshape it. Indeed, the Eameses' own career demonstrates what we could call the Shakespearean design doctrine – that the construction of context is the primary act of design, from which everything else then flows.

*Opposite*

Still from *Frasier* (Episode 1, Series 8, 2000)

*Above*

The 'hot seat' from the BBC television programme *Mastermind*

*Overleaf*

Furniture with drawings by Saul Steinberg at 901, 1950 Photograph by Peter Stackpole for *Life*

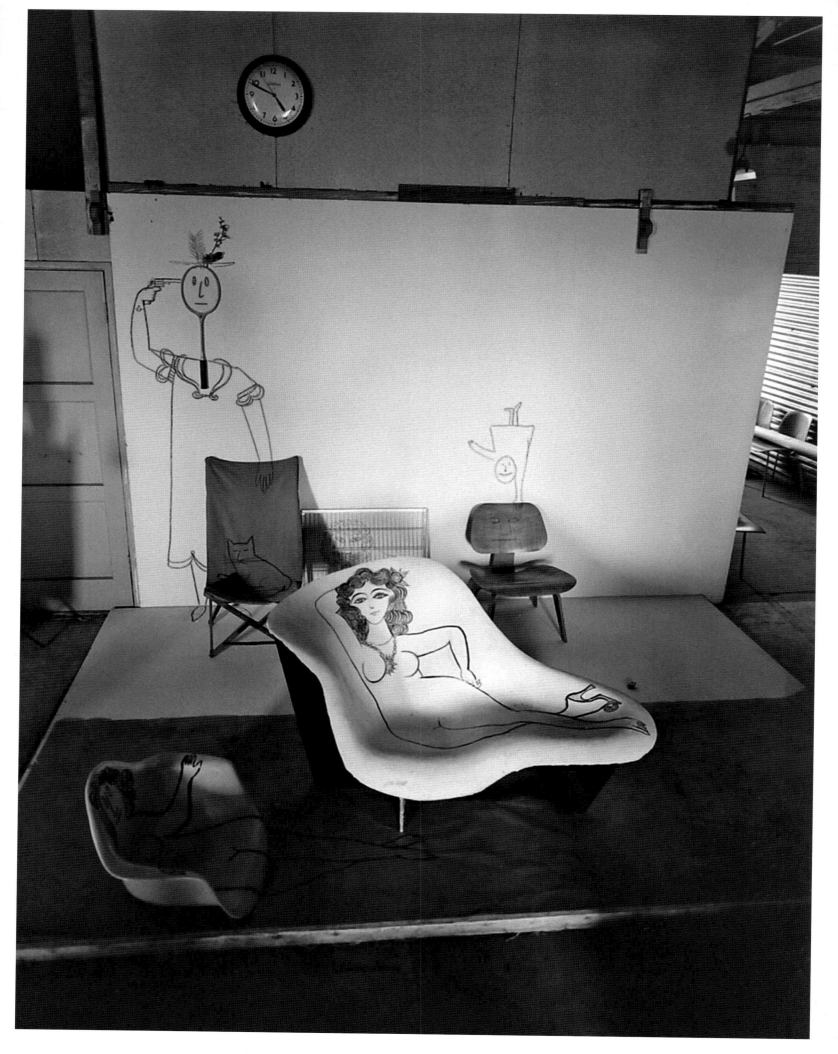

*Opposite*

Frames from *Circus*

3-screen slideshow consisting of images of the circus taken by Charles Eames from the 1940s onwards

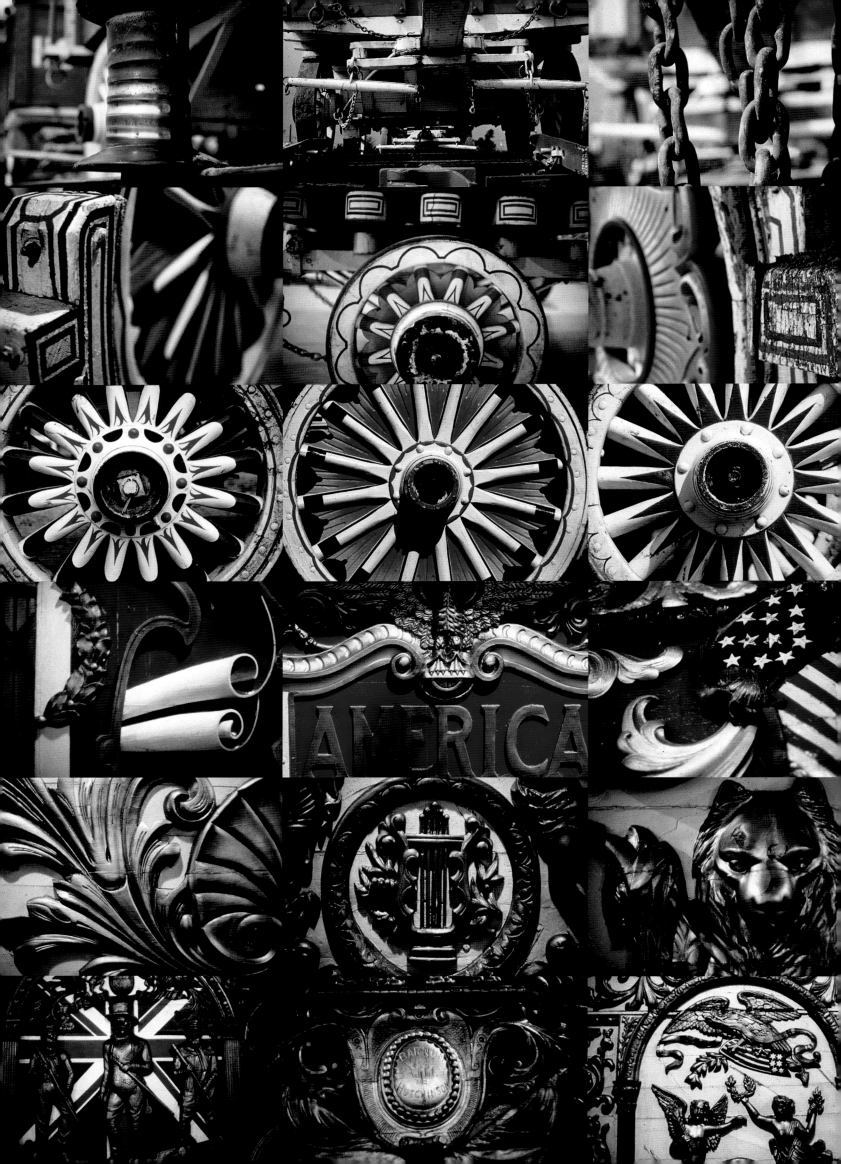

# CELEBRATION AS A HUMAN NEED

*Celebration is a human need that we must not, and cannot deny ...*
*Celebration is not exclusive – it is the most inclusive human act.*
—Corita Kent

At the beginning of 1954, the art department at the Immaculate Heart College (IHC), Los Angeles, decided on its annual theme: 'Celebration as a Human Need'. As stated two years later in the college's *Irregular Bulletin*, the theme had been 'the core of the work done here ... It was intended as a year's study but has proved to be such a rich source that it has been adopted for an indefinite period – we are beginning to suspect that it is tied with the forever that gives significance to the now.'[1] The bulletin was sent to Charles and Ray Eames by Corita Kent, a nun of the order of the Sisters of the Immaculate Heart of Mary and, at that time, a teacher in the art department at the college.[2] Kent was great friends with the Eameses; she shared their love of craftsmanship and the joy they found in beauty, and she often showed their films to her students. The sentiment of the college bulletin was redolent of the Eameses' own attitude towards both life and work, with celebration and play being integral to their practice.

In the Eameses' eyes, even the most ordinary object was potential source material; they saw endless possibilities for creativity in the world around them. They amassed an array of everyday objects, decorative ornaments and toys over their lifetimes, both gifts from friends and objects picked up on their own travels to such varied countries as Mexico, India and Japan. They admired the meticulous craftsmanship and attention to materials often involved in the making of such objects. Despite the diversity of their collections, specific thematic strands could be picked out, including masks, kites, tops, boats and trains. From accurate scale models to whimsical toys, these objects found themselves as stars in the narratives of the Eameses' films, including *Traveling Boy* (1950), *Toccata for Toy Trains* (1957) and *Tops* (1969). Their interest in such objects was not for the sake of their authorship, but rather their form and meaning.

The Eameses were sensitive to the idea of anonymous design in material culture. From the Indian lota to the folk object, they were interested in traditional forms that were passed down through generations, continually evolving but universally understood and celebrated. Charles and Ray were both prolific photographers, and their work found its way into such diverse publications as the architecture and design journal *Domus* and the *Everyday Art* magazine published by the American Crayon Company, in which Charles's photos of Alexander and Susan Girard's collection of folk objects were featured.[3] The Eameses were fascinated by the rituals and ceremonies of other cultures, as well as their material manifestations. The festivals and everyday customs specific to these cultures became the foundation of poetic films and slideshows. The circus was a particular source of inspiration; the slideshow *Circus* evokes the aura of magic and joyful vitality of the circus while also revealing the crafted showmanship and rigorous discipline involved in such a spectacle.[4] Charles often noted that the circus related to their own work and interests, in that it epitomized the maxim of 'taking pleasure *seriously* in one's everyday work'.[5]

*Previous page*
Charles and Ray Eames in the studio at the Eames House with toys and props used in *Toccata for Toy Trains*, 1957
Photograph by Allan Grant for *Life*

Eames Office staff outside 901 wearing Independence Day sunglasses designed by Deborah Sussman, 4 July 1965. Staff include Sussman, Mairea Poole, Parke Meek and Glen Fleck

*Opposite page*
Immaculate Heart College
Envelope addressed to the Eameses announcing the art department's focus on the theme 'Celebration as a Human Need', Thanksgiving 1956
Collage on paper, 44 × 32.5 cm (17 ⅜ × 12 ¾ in.)
The Papers of Charles and Ray Eames, Manuscript Division, Library of Congress, Washington DC

*Overleaf*
Corita Kent, 'Sources', in Kent and Jan Steward, *Learning by Heart: Teachings to Free the Creative Spirit* (New York: Bantam Books, 1992)

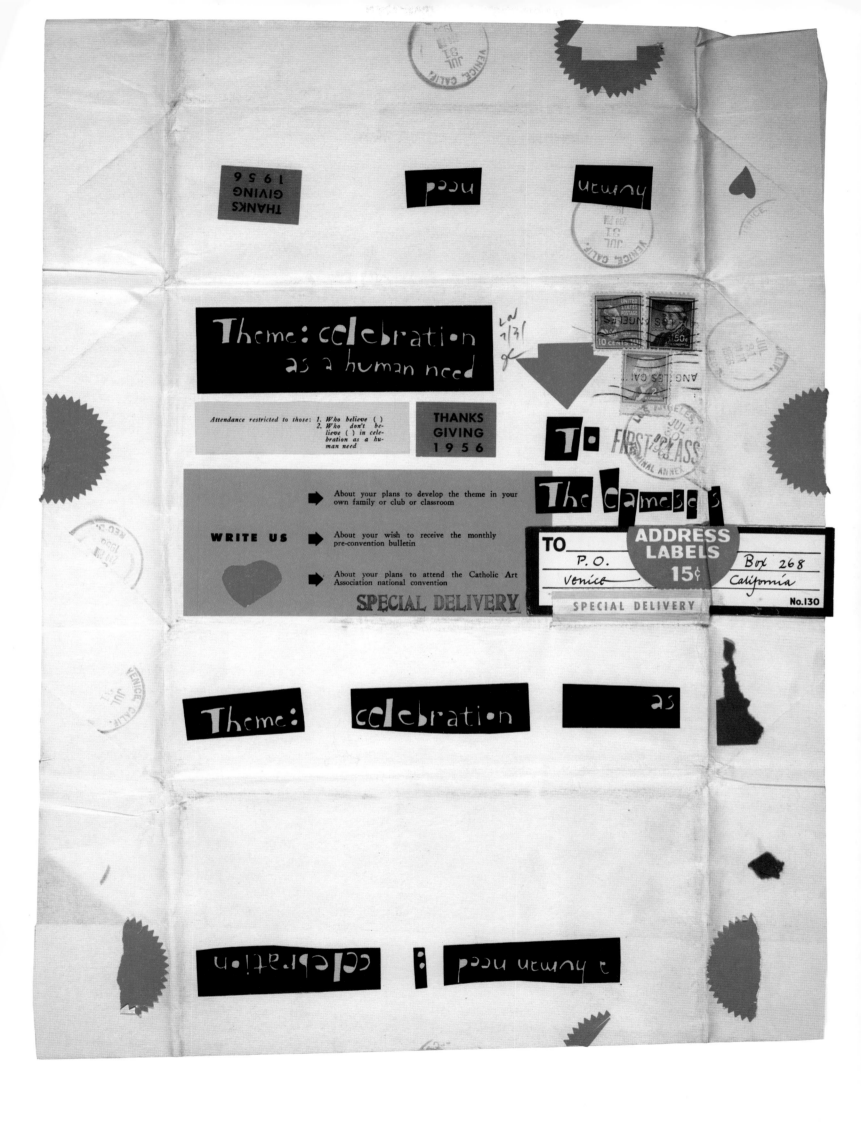

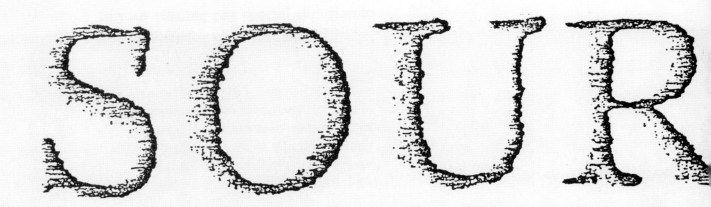

# SOUR

*Charles Eames*

## 40

*SOURCE: from the Latin surgere, "to spring up, to lift." The beginning of a stream of water or the like; a spring, a fountain. The origin; the first or ultimate cause. A person, book, or document that supplies information. A source is a point of departure.*

*I had already finished school when I met my real teacher, Charles Eames. He was not an art teacher; he was an artist who taught— taught by words, films, exhibits, buildings, classes, visits, phone conversations, and furniture. He dropped out or was dropped out of college before graduation. When he was asked for credentials for a teaching job, he got his friend Saul Steinberg to draw a diploma that had lots of writing but no words, complete with seal and red ribbons. Charles had great style in all he did.*

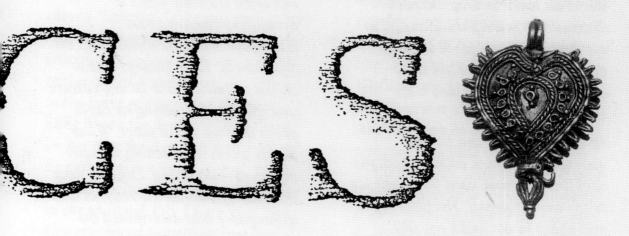

For this country's first cultural exchange with Russia he made a seven-screen film—each screen showing still and moving images simultaneously—that explained the American way of life to the Russians. Seven screens, he said, to present more fully the complexities of our problems (and delights) so that all might benefit from our experience without having to repeat our mistakes. After that, one screen was never enough.

When he talked, he often made long pauses in his sentences. It was as if he was stopping midway because new relationships and connections had come in since he had started the sentence and he needed to form the next phrase to include those new ideas. He used words that were simple and almost absolutely appropriate.

Charles said that the first step in designing a lamp (or anything) was not to ask how it should look—but whether it should even be. He always started fresh at the beginning. He showed us how to develop principles rather than follow formulas.

When I taught, I could show any one of several of his films to introduce any new project to my students. I have shown and seen some of his films literally hundreds of times. Like Spring, they never bore. The first film Charles ever gave our school was Parade (seven minutes). We showed it that morning seven times in a row, stopping only long enough to rewind. He spoke always with the light touch evident in Parade, in simple words; but his lightest touch was somehow principle. His films will go on teaching forever.

41

From Eames or from any of his works we learn to drop outworn distinctions and separations and to see new relationships–to see that there is no line where art stops and life begins. He talked a lot about connections.

Of his teachings I can hardly distinguish between what he actually said and did from what he taught me to say and do myself. His teaching is still living in me and I am still learning from that life in me, as well as from students and friends and every single contact with people and things. He taught me that too.

At Berkeley he and his wife, Ray, taught an introductory class to all architecture students. Overhearing one of the students make a derogatory remark about Renaissance art, he constructed an assignment. Each student was to choose a limited time in one culture and find out everything he could about that time and place. What people wore, what eating utensils they used–everything. Digging deep this way opened up the reasons and atmosphere that determined the shape of the things that were made.

I borrowed this assignment for an interior design class. I began the class by asking each student to say what "style" she wanted her home to be done in. Then came the Eames

the Eames office

Ray Eames

*assignment. I will never forget the reaction of the student who had chosen "colonial." She was giving her report with great enthusiasm—describing the look and contents of a real colonial home—when she came to the point of describing the guns hung above the fireplace. It dawned on her that the lived life had a lot to do with how her home looked. I can still see the look coming over her face as she spat out,* Oh, I hate you! *She had convinced herself against her early choice. She had taught herself a lot. A good assignment can make the student do just that.*

*Some good sources come naturally out of what the teacher is filling*

*herself with and become part of the bombardment of materials that are a regular part of giving a new assignment or starting a class. Books like* Spinster *by Sylvia Ashton Warner, which is a splendid novel that describes an inspired kind of teaching, can be quoted from or assigned.* Magical Child *by Joseph Chilton Pearce, with its plan of how to grow up well, is another excellent source. Enthusiasms of the teacher flow into the class—a sharing takes place and rich ideas are sparked. We are each other's sources.*

Corita

*a wall in the Eames office*

The 93-square-metre (1,000 sq. ft) studio at the Eames House played many different roles for Charles and Ray Eames. At various points, the space functioned as a testing ground for experimentation, a workshop, a storage space, a film studio, a space for play and a living area. For their earliest films, in which toys were the protagonists, Charles, Ray and Eames Office staff would set up a makeshift film set on the lower level (see page 177). On at least one occasion they set up towering constructions of cardboard boxes that could be demolished by swinging into them from the mezzanine level. The studio became a repository for source material, from everyday objects, toys and folk art to paper kites, books and posters of favourite artists, including Corita Kent and Henri Matisse. It was a space that was continually activated for both work and play.

Celebration as a Human Need

Opposite and above
The studio at the Eames House, July 1958
and November 1952

*Right*
Ray Eames with Jill Mitchell, who studied under
Charles at Cranbrook and worked at the Eames
Office, 10 November 1951

*Overleaf*
The studio at the Eames House

## And now Dhamas are dying out in Japan

Alison Smithson

I can see the part played by Ray Eames in all that they do: the attention to the last detail of the collected material, the perseverance in finding what exactly is wanted; although the seeker may not know the exact object until it is finally seen. The stoic pleasantness that jollies along everyone to the bitter end; for there is no doubt that assistants and clients go out of their mind towards the end, if not at stages in between. The principal does, him or herself, but yet cannot afford to; particularly over assistants, if the job really has to be done to the perfection imagined.

The prettiness of our lives now I attribute to Ray even more than Charles; we would not be buying flower-patterned ties but for the Eames card game. Ourselves and Eduardo Paolozzi know where it came from. It is possible Nigel Henderson alone could have led us to steam engines and the ephemera of life via old boots, bits of sacking, ancient postcards magicked

over by photography, but I like to think i[?] Ray and Charles Eames we owe the debt [?] extravagance of the new purchase. The [?] whistle, the Woolworth's plastic Chri[?] decoration and toy, on to the German pr[?] metal toy and the walking robots: fresh, [?] colourful ephemera.

Does Peter Blake's generation at the [?] know[1] the people who made so much of [?] ephemera acceptable[2]—Henderson woul[?] do *that*. Certainly I think it is not clear t[?] Tilson generation and evades entirely [?] generation younger who buy the floral p[?] bunches of dried flowers, Mexican col[?] furniture, rag dolls, and so on.

The Eames allowed us to know Girard ar[?] the cheap Mexicana and candles availab[?] American tourists. The Eames' made G[?] respectable-pop for habitat and Enid C[?]

he clashing pink colours aboard as house
s.

ames films gave new life to our inherited
so that they did not have that peculiar
parlour-collection chill of Black eyes and
nade (Barbara Jones). Our generation
as children reborn from post-war Britain
ve objects of a particular international
r. The Eames gave us courage to make
of anything that attracted.

an what became suddenly very clear was
panese influence on the West Coast, the
y of the spotlessly clean simple interior,
ful wrappings, Kleenex.

fluence of the West Coast comes to us
gh Eames. We see Eames in his films
ting from the round-the-corner facilities,
eveloped technology of the film world.

nfluenced who out west?

Eames influence help create Disneyland
as there another influence creating both
and the historical collection perfection
got into coloured westerns mid-50s —the
period enamelled coffee can and cup,
s Stewart or Burt Lancaster drink out of,
etc.?

West Coast world supports the Eames.

ames support the West coast world for us
help support our European dream of
ica as a great free place to be in.

me way they are the other extreme of the
a bums who live off the bottom of the
Coast literary world. The Eames are the
g Dhamas who live in the clouds about
Angelos. They are our Los Angelos— who
dentially provided us with the furniture[3] to
n perspectives of buildings. Again it all
s to us because of the available-round-
rner technology of America.

know that before Eames furniture, if you
a perspective of an interior there was no
after the Thonet Le Corbusier used, or
rst period modern furniture made by Le
usier—for the same reason—that you
draw in: and none of this could be bought
40s and 50s. The British Thonet available
cond-hand shops is altogether different
the Paris flea market Thonet. Reproduction
rn is a mid-60s phenomena.

was the British Rourkee or Bengal safari
available still at the Army and Navy.

s the world of the horrors of the Festival of
n and so on.

Eames chair was like a message of hope
another planet.

naiveté of, and practised by, Peter Blake does
clude awareness of other phenomena; just as
ng' about cribbable objects (say by designers)
an awareness.

rican painters may get all the credit.

er to the blackbird and post blackbird era frame
. The early plywood and adjustable shelving,
tables, do not speak in any way for us.

1
Wire chairs. (See also page 445)

2
A selection of cards from the House of Cards picture deck and pattern deck.
(See also pages 443, 462)

The House of Cards is currently being published by Otto Maier Verlag, Ravensberg/
Germany. © Tintarella S.A.

*Pages 188–9*
Alison Smithson, 'And Now Dhamas Are Dying Out in Japan', *Architectural Design*, September 1966

Stills from *Traveling Boy*, 1950
Film, 12 min.

*Traveling Boy* was Charles and Ray Eames's first film, made in the studio at the Eames House. It charts the journey of a mechanical boy as he embarks on a voyage through a landscape of toys, shot against a backdrop of circus graphics and drawings by Saul Steinberg. Three

endings were filmed, but no final choice was made, leaving the film unfinished. *Traveling Boy* paved the way for the Eameses' second film featuring a cast of toys, *Parade, or Here They Come Down Our Street* (1952), which won an award at the Edinburgh Film Festival in 1954.

Celebration as a Human Need

Stills from *Day of the Dead*, 1957
Film, 14:25 min.

This film celebrates the Mexican festival Día de los Muertos. Alexander Girard had persuaded the Museum of International Folk Art in Santa Fe to support the project, and the museum funded the Eameses' research trip to Mexico to make the film. They were accompanied by the Girards and Eames Office staffer Deborah Sussman. The final result is a poetic insight into the rituals and traditions associated with the festival through the objects made each year to celebrate it.

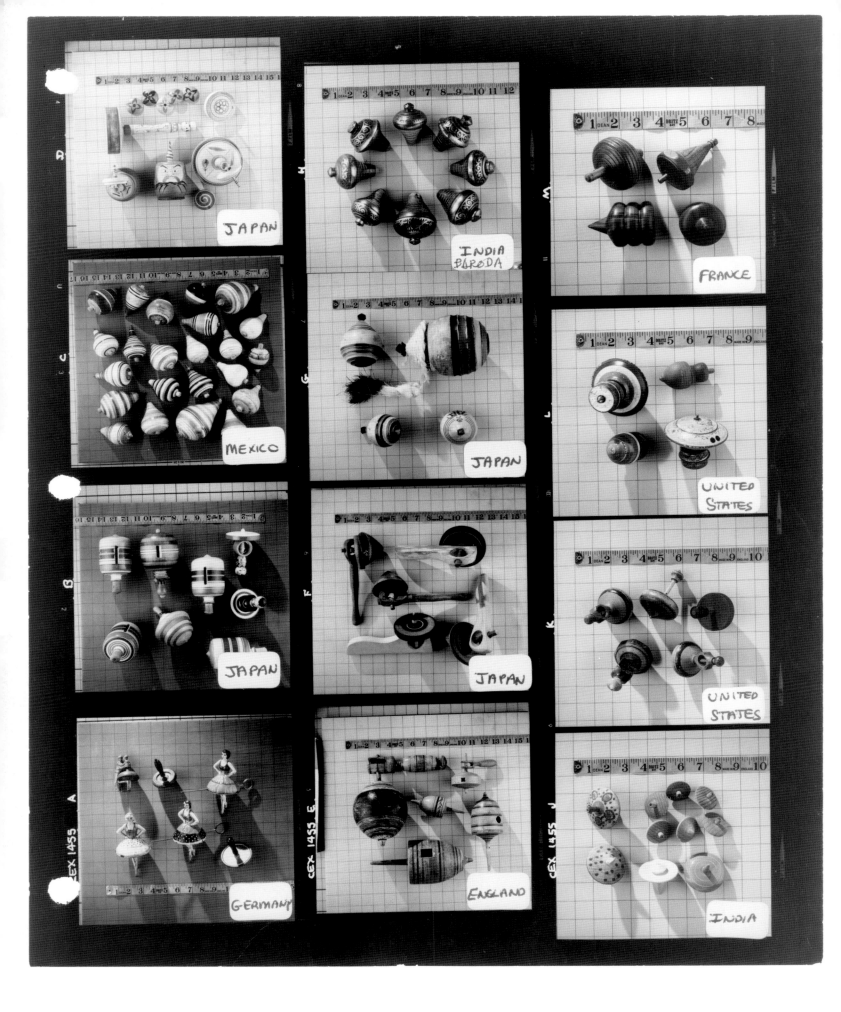

Tops arranged by origin, 1956
Black-and-white photograph,
26 × 21 cm (10 ¼ × 8 ¼ in.)
The Work of Charles and Ray
Eames, Prints & Photographs
Division, Library of Congress,
Washington DC

1970

25

# FILM
## QUARTERLY

PAUL SCHRADE

# Poetry of Ideas:
# The Films of Charles Eames

*Although many important artists have used film outside the usu*
*theatrical-feature conventions, critics have too seldom found ways*
*discussing their work. Considering the great amount of creati*
*energy going into short films of all kinds at present, t*
*neglect needs to be remedied. The study below is an attempt to come*
*terms with the output of an immensely talented man whose films—whi*
*are only a part of his creative work—represent a peculiar*
*contemporary synthesis of film with science and technolog*

*They're not experimental films, they're not*
*really films. They're just attempts to get*
*across an idea.*
— CHARLES EAMES

Charles Eames was baffled by the fact that anyone would want to write an article about his
films. "When asked a question like that, about
'my approach to film,'" Eames said, "I would
almost reply, 'Who me, film?' I don't think of it
that way. I view film a little bit as a cheat; I'm
sort of using a tool someone else has developed."
Because of his casual attitude toward "Film"
—his debunking of the romantic myth of the
"artist personality" and his concept of film as
a primarily informational medium—Charles
Eames has been able, in his recent films, to
give "Film" what it needs most: a new way of
perceiving ideas. As films move away from a
period in which they were content to only show
what they felt, and attempt little by little to
also tell what they think, many of the most
talented film-makers, young and old, are trying
to graft onto movies the cerebral sensibility they
have so long resisted. Eames personifies this
sensibility, a sensibility so synonymous with his
life and work that he cannot conceive of himself as only a "film-maker."

There are many ways one can think abo
Charles Eames. He defies categorization; he
architect, inventor, designer, craftsman, s
entist, film-maker, professor. Yet in all his
versity Eames is one creator, and his creati
is not a series of separate achievements, but
unified aesthetic with many branch-like ma
festations. Eames's films do not function ind
pendently, but like branches; they do not d
rive from film history or tradition, but from
culminant culture with roots in many fiel
A capsulized biography can give, in the m
vulgar way, the scope of his career; but,
always, Eames remains greater than the su
of his avocations.
Born in St. Louis in 1907, Eames studi
architecture at Washington University, in 19
started his own practice, and in 1940 marrie
Ray Kaiser, a painter with whom he subs
quently shared credit for all his work. In 19
Eames and Eero Saarinen collaborated on d
signs for the Museum of Modern Art's Organ
Furniture Competition. From these desig
came a generation of Eames chairs: from t
luxurious black leather Eames lounge chair
the omnipresent molded fiberglass stackir
chairs, which, within twenty years, had r

*Charles and Ray Eames in their studio.*

ceived such mass acceptance that Eames's way of sitting was, in a fundamental sense, everybody's way of sitting. In 1941, to encourage the wartime production of their first chair prototypes, Charles and Ray perfected an inexpensive lamination process for wood veneers, and in the same year Charles went to work, temporarily, for the art department of MGM. In between chairs, the Charles Eames Workshop produced toys, furniture, gliders, leg splints, and magazine covers. In 1949 Eames designed the Santa Monica House (where he still lives), which, like the chairs, was a model of simplicity and variety, and soon became a standard textbook illustration.

The Eames films commenced in 1950 and over the next fifteen years they won awards at Edinburgh, Melbourne, San Francisco, American, Mannheim, Montreal, and London film festivals. "A Rough Sketch for a Sample Lesson for a Hypothetical Course," presented by Charles and Ray (with George Nelson and Alexander Girard) in 1953 at the University of Georgia and UCLA, was the first public presentation of multi-media techniques. In 1960 Eames's rapid cutting experiments in the CBS "Fabulous Fifties" special won him an Emmy

for graphic design. During this period Eames designed a series of World's Fair presentations: in 1959 the multi-screen presentation for the US exhibit at Moscow, in 1962 a multi-screen introduction to the US Science Exhibit at Seattle (where it is still shown), in 1964 the IBM Ovoid Pavilion and the film presentations in it, at the New York Fair. Over the years Eames has prepared courses and lectured across the world, and will this fall hold the Charles Eliot Norton Chair of Poetry at Harvard.

Charles Eames can weave in and out of these diverse occupations because he is not committed to any of them. He is, in the final account, committed to a way of life which encompasses them all. The toys, chairs, films are the available tools through which Eames can actualize his life-style. The common denominator of Eames's occupations is that he is, elementally, one thing: a problem-solver, with aesthetic and social considerations. He approaches life as a set of problems, each of which must be defined, delineated, abstracted, and solved. His architect's mind visualizes complex social patterns twisting and folding like a three-dimensional blueprint. He respects the "problem" not only as a means to an end, but as an aesthetic pleasure in itself. Although Eames rarely rhapsodizes about anything, his most "emotional" prose is saved for a description of the problem-solving process:

*The ability to make decisions is a proper function of problem solving. Computer problems, philosophical problems, homely ones: the steps in solving each are essentially the same, some methods being elaborate variations of others. But homely or complex, the specific answers we get are not the only rewards or even the greatest. It is in preparing the problem for solution, in the necessary steps of simplification, that we often gain the richest rewards. It is in this process that we are apt to get a true insight into the nature of the problem. Such insight is of great and lasting value to us as individuals and to us as a society.*

    —from *Think*,
      the IBM New York Fair presentation

For Eames, problem solving is one of the answers to the problem of contemporary civilization. Not only does his problem-solving process provide beauty and order, but it constitutes the only *optimistic* approach to the future. He is currently working for the Head Start program, a task he feels vital because "you have to teach children to have a genuine respect for a large number of events and objects which are not of immediate gain to them. It is the only thing which puts a human being in situation where he can promptly assess the ne step. Whether it is in the ghetto or Appalach kids get their beginning having respect only things which have an immediate payoff, a this is no way to run a railroad, particula when you don't know what the next proble will be." Eames will not indulge in the desp of a complete overview, not because it is illeg mate, but because it can't solve the problem "You can't take too broad a perspective," says, quoting Nobel Prize winning physic Richard Feynman; "you have to find a corn and pick away at it."

Charles Eames is, in the broadest sense the word, a scientist. In his film introduction the US Science Exhibit at the Seattle Fa Eames prescribed what that rare creature, t true scientist, should be, and it is a descriptio of Charles Eames:

*Science is essentially an artistic or phil sophical enterprise carried on for its own sak*

*US Exhibit, Moscow World's Fair, 1959*

*In this it is more akin to play than to work. But it is quite a sophisticated play in which the scientist views nature as a system of interlocking puzzles. He assumes that the puzzles have a solution, that they will be fair. He holds to a faith in the underlying order of the universe. His motivation is his fascination with the puzzle itself—his method a curious interplay between idea and experiment. His pleasures are those of any artist. High on the list of prerequisites for being a scientist is a quality that defines the rich human being as much as it does the man of science, that is, his ability and his desire to reach out with his mind and his imagination to something outside himself.*

*—from House of Science*

To counter that the puzzles don't have a solution and are not fair is to beg the question, because the scientist does not admit these possibilities into his working definition. Because his pleasures "are those of any artist" the scientist sustains his world not necessarily by empirical proof, but by his "faith in the underlying order

of the universe." In this way Eames's scientist may seem similar to the scientists of the Enlightenment who constructed elaborate fictions of order, only to have them collapse with the next wave of data. But unlike the Newtonian cosmologist Eames does not state that the solvable problem is necessarily a microcosm for the universe, which may have no solution. Eames is describing a *Weltanschauung*, not the universe. A corollary argument leveled (often by artists) against Eames's scientist accuses him of being shallowly optimistic, unaware of man's condition. C. P. Snow defended scientists against this charge in his "Two Cultures" lecture: "Nearly all of them [the scientists]—and this is where the color of hope genuinely comes in—would see no reason why, just because the individual condition is tragic, so must the social condition be." It is a fallacy of men of letters to equate contemporaneity with pessimism—as if Beckett's "it" crawling in the mud was unavoidably the man of the future. One of the exciting

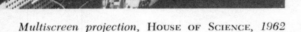

*Multiscreen projection,* HOUSE OF SCIENCE, *1962*

things about Eames's film-maker, like his scientist, is that he challenges the hegemony of pessimism in the contemporary arts.

Although Eames's structuring of the problem may seem antiquated (and this is debatable), his solutions are undeniably modern. His statement about the designing of a chair is not only a remarkable account of the creative process, but also a pioneering approach to art in a society in which the individual has become progressively functionalized and collectivized:

"How do you design a chair for acceptance by another person? By not thinking of what the other guy wants, but by coming to terms with the fact that while we may think we are different from other people in some ways at some moments, the fact of the matter is that we're a hell of a lot more like each other than we're different, and that we're certainly more like each other than we're like a tree or a stone. So then you relax back into the position of trying to satisfy yourself—except for a real trap, that is, what part of yourself do you try to satisfy? The trap is that if you try to satisfy your idiosyncrasies, those little things on the surface, you're dead, because it is in those idiosyncrasies that you're different from other people. And in a sense what gives a work of craft its personal style is usually where it failed to solve the problem rather than where it solved it. That's what gives it the Noguchi touch, or whatever. What you try to do is satisfy your real gut instincts and work your way through your idiosyncrasies, as we have tried in the stuff we've done, the furniture or the ideas. You know it's tough

enough just to make the first step of unde standing without trying to introduce our pe sonality or trying to outguess what the othe guy's thinking."

The Eameses have constructed structures— a house, chair, film—in which people can de fine themselves not by their idiosyncrasies bu by their similarities. These structures perm problem-solving—and therefore give the scien tist hope. To some these structures will seen artificial and solipsistic, but in an age whic has so ruthlessly degraded man's individualit any attempt to restructure the concept of hu manism will necessarily seem artificial.

From Eames's sensibility have come two con tributions: one pertaining primarily to archi tecture and design, which has already been in corporated into the international cultural main stream, and another most applicable to film which is being developed and exists only a potential for mass audiences.

Eames's first contribution concerns what British critic Peter Smithson calls "object-in tegrity." The Eames aesthetic respects an ob ject for what it is, whether machine-made o hand-crafted, and is based on "careful selectio with extra-cultural surprise, rather than har mony of profile, as its criteria—a kind of wide eyed wonder of seeing the culturally disparate together and so happy with each other." Smith son goes on, "This sounds like whimsy, but the vehicles are ordinary to culture." Eames's vehicles, his "structures," make it possible for an object to have integrity.

The Eames aesthetic brought art into the marketplace through the assembly line. There was neither fear of nor blind obedience toward the machine. The machine, like its heir the computer, are tools which must be used by the artist as well as the entrepreneur. It is pro letarian art: "We want to get the most of the best to the most for the least," Eames has said; "in the final analysis I want to try to reach the greatest number of people." The Eames chair stands as a tribute to the universality of his aesthetic; at the same time beautiful and func tional, it is being manufactured in every con tinent except Africa. "By the late 50's," writes

Smithson, "the Eames way of seeing things had in a sense become everybody's style."

Eames's aesthetic is in opposition to one of the older canons of art criticism, Ruskin's theory of "invention." In "The Nature of the Gothic" Ruskin instructed customers to purchase only goods which showed the hand of the inventor, rejecting anything copied or undistinctive, even to the point of preferring the rough to the smooth. The Eames aesthetic contends that the customer, who organizes the life context in which objects exist, is as much a creative agent as the artist, and that it is his creative imperative to organize and respect the "inventive" as well as the commonplace objects. "If people would only realize," Eames said, "that they have the real stuff in their hand, in their back yards, their lives could be richer. They are afraid to get involved."

The second Eames contribution results when the Eames aesthetic of object-integrity is carried into the electronic age. There are two reasons: first of all, a computer cannot have object-integrity the way a chair or a toy train does. A chair is essentially shape, color, and movement, but a computer is much more. To respect a computer one must understand how it thinks, must appreciate Boolean Logic. As Eames's objects became more complex, his approach necessarily became more cerebral.

Secondly, the object-integrity aesthetic is now confronted by an objectless society. "The conscious covetors are growing tremendously," Eames has said, "and the covetables in our society are shrinking tremendously. There's not much worth coveting. I feel that a lot of this vacuum is going to be beautifully filled by certain mastery of concepts, mastery of, say, the French or Russian language. And the beauty of this is that the coin of the realm is real. It means involvement on the part of the guy that's getting it. He's got it, all he has to do is give of himself. A lot of this is going to have to come through film."

Eames's second contribution, then, concerns the presentation of ideas through film. His method is information-overload. Eames's films give the viewer more data than he can possibly process. The host at the IBM Pavilion succinctly forewarned his audience:

*Ladies and gentlemen, welcome to the IBM information machine. And the information machine is just that—a machine designed to help me give you a lot of information in a very short time.* —from *Thing*

Eames's information machine dispenses a lot of data, but only one idea. All the data must pertain directly to the fundamental idea; the data are not superfluous, simply superabundant. Eames's innovation, it seems to me, is a hypothesis about audience perception which, so far, is only proved by the effectiveness of his films. His films pursue an Idea (Time, Space, Symmetry, Topology) which in the final accounting must stand alone, apart from any psychological, social, or moral implications. The viewer must rapidly sort out and prune the superabundant data if he is to follow the swift progression of thought. This process of elimination continues until the viewer has pruned away everything but the disembodied Idea. By giving the viewer more information than he can assimilate, information-overload short-circuits the normal conduits of inductive reasoning. The classic movie staple is the chase, and Eames's films present a new kind of chase, a chase through a set of information in search of an Idea.

To be most effective the information cannot be random, as in a multi-media light show, or simply "astounding," as in the multi-media displays at Expo '67 which Ray described as "rather frivolous." The Idea conveyed by the information must have integrity, as evidenced by its problem-solving potential, intellectual stimulation, and beauty of form. The multi-media "experience" is a corruption of information-overload in the same way that the Barbara Jones and Peter Blake "found-art" collages are corruptions of object-integrity—they present the innovation without the aesthetic. Through information-overload, the Idea becomes the new covetable, the object which has integrity in an objectless society. To paraphrase Eames, it is in the quest of the Idea that we often gain the richest rewards.

The films of Charles and Ray Eames fall into two categories. The first, the "Toy Films," primarily use the first Eames contribution, object-integrity; the second, the "Idea Films," use the second Eames contribution, information-overload.

Through precise, visual, non-narrative examination the toy films reveal the definitive characteristics of commonplace objects. The toy films were the natural place for the Eameses to begin in film, for they found in simple, photographed objects—soap-water running over blacktop, toy towns and soldiers, bread—the characteristics they were trying to bring out in the furniture design:

*In a good old toy there is apt to be nothing self-conscious about the use of materials—what is wood is wood; what is tin is tin; and what is cast is beautifully cast.*

—from *Toccata for Toy Trains*

Eames's film career is often equated with his toy films. Because of this mistaken assumption, the Eames films have already seen a critical rise and fall. Eames's films received their initial recognition during the heyday of the Norman McLaren pixillation, the early fifties, when the Museum of Modern Art and the Edinburgh Film Festival acclaimed the early toy films, *Bread, Blacktop, Parade.* Eames's reputation rose with McLaren's, and fell with it. The Eameses became typed as the toy film-makers, and critical interest died off.

The Eameses continued to make films, toy films as well as idea films. The toy films have progressed throughout the intervening years, using "toys" of varied complexity, the Santa Monica House, baroque churches, toy trains, the Schuetz calculating machine, the Lick Observatory. Each toy film presents a structure in which objects can "be themselves," can act like "toys" in the same way that humans, given a certain structure, can act like children. The object need not be only functional; it can assume a number of positions. The Lick telescope is at one time practical, cumbersome, odd, and beautiful. One feels the same respect for the telescope that the Lick astronomer must feel after years of collaboration with the instrument.

It cohabits the same structure, has meanin both functional and aesthetic, and, in brief, h integrity.

The latest toy film, and the best, is *Tops,* seven-minute study of just what the title say tops. *Tops* is a refinement of the toy film tech nique. The structures are simplified: there is n narration, scantier backdrops, less plot; and th object assumes a greater importance within th structure. Tops of every variety are presented The viewer studies the ethnic impulses, th form variations, the coloration, and the spinnin methods of tops. The first half of *Tops* presen tops in all their diversity, gradually narrowin the scope of its investigation to simpler an simpler forms: a jack, a carrom, and, finally,

spinning tack. This is a moment of object-integrity: all the complexity and variation of tops have resolved into the basic form of two planes, one of them suspended by the balanced forces of gravity and gyroscopic momentum. The unaware viewer realizes that he has never really understood even an insignificant creation like a top, never accepted it on its own terms, never *enjoyed* it. The second half of *Tops*, which depicts the "fall" of the tops, moves back to more complex tops, against blank backgrounds, giving the viewer a chance to see the same tops again, but with the new eyes of insight and sensitivity.

Eames feels that the toy films are as essential as the idea films. "I don't think it's an over-

statement," he remarked "to say that without a film like *Tops* there would be no idea films. It's all part of the same process, and I think I could convince IBM of that, if necessary."

From the outset of their film-making, the Eameses were also making another sort of film, a film which dealt with objects with cerebral integrity. Eames's first idea film, *A Communications Primer*, resulted from a problem Eames realized he had to state before he could solve. He says, "I had the feeling that in the world of architecture they were going to get nowhere unless the process of information was going to come and enter city planning in general. You could not really anticipate a strategy that would solve the increase in population or the social changes which were going on unless you had some way of handling this information. And so help me, this was the reason for making the first film, because we looked for some material on communications. We went to Bell Labs and they showed us pictures of a man with a beard and somebody says, 'You will invent the telephone,' or something. And this is about all you get. So we made a film called *Communications Primer*, essentially for architects."

Innovation is often a by-product of Eames's problem solving, as when Charles and Ray developed a lamination process for wood veneers to permit mass manufacture of their chairs. Similarly, Eames, in his desire to solve the complex, non-immediate problems of the city, and in his desire to bring integrity to the computer, developed a revolutionary method of information presentation. In 1953 Charles and Ray presented "A Rough Sketch for a Sample Lesson for a Hypothetical Course," the first multimedia demonstration. "A Rough Sketch" not only featured three concurrent images, but also a live narrator, a long board of printed visual information, and complimentary smells piped through the ventilation system.

Eames's technique of information-overload has progressed just as his toy film technique has, and some of the first "revolutionary" films look rather primitive compared to his recent work. Eames has developed several methods of information overload. The most basic, of course,

is fast cutting (*Two Baroque Churches* has 296 still shots, roughly one every two seconds). He often has several screens (the most being twenty-two at the N.Y. Fair, although not all the images were projected simultaneously), but has realized that a multiplicity of action on one screen can often have more impact than a single action on several separate screens. He has often used animation to simplify data, so that it can be delivered faster with clarity. One of Eames's most successful techniques is to split the screen between live action and animation, each of which affects the mental process differently. Eames also counterpoints narration, sound effects, music, and images to present several related bits of data simultaneously.

These techniques will certainly fade, just as did the McLaren aspects of his earlier films. Multi-media projections are a bit passé just now, and Eames isn't designing any at the moment. But, nonetheless, Eames's films hold up phenomenally well, because they are based on an aesthetic, not just an innovation. (Eames's specific techniques have several competent practitioners: Wheaton Galentine's 1954 *Treadle and Bobbin* corresponds to Eames's toy films, Don Levy's 1964 *Time Is* corresponds to Eames's idea films.) Even though the specific techniques and in some cases the very ideas of his earlier films may become antiquated, Eames's way of living seems as immediate today as ever. The solutions may no longer seem pressing, but his problem-solving process still offers beauty and intellectual stimulation.

Two of Eames's recent films, *Powers of Ten* and *National Aquarium Presentation,* are re-

finements of the idea-film technique just a *Tops* is a refinement of the toy films. These tw films represent the two sorts of ideas Eames de signs, the single or the environmental concep and are more universal than Eames's earlie computer ideas. Because of the richness of th aesthetic Eames brings to these films, the idea they portray inevitably strike deeper tha originally intended.

*Powers of Ten* was a "sketch film" to be pre sented at an assembly of one thousand of Am erica's top physicists. The sketch should, Eame decided, appeal to a ten-year-old as well as physicist; it should contain a "gut feeling" abou dimensions in time and space as well as a soun theoretical approach to those dimensions. Th solution was a continuous zoom from the far thest known point in space to the nucleus of carbon atom resting in a man's wrist lying o Miami Beach. The camera zooms from the man's wrist to a hypothetical point in space and zooms back again, going through the man' wrist to the frontier of the inner atom.

Going out, the speed of the trip was $10^{t/1}$ meters per second°—that is, in each 10 sec onds of travel the imaginary voyager covered 10 times the distance he had traveled in the previous 10 seconds. In this schema a trip from the nucleus of the carbon atom to the farthest known reaches of the universe takes 350 sec onds. This information is presented in several

° Time divided by 10 is the "power"—in other words, after 40 seconds, you are 10-to-the-fourth meters away, or one followed by four zeros (10,-000).

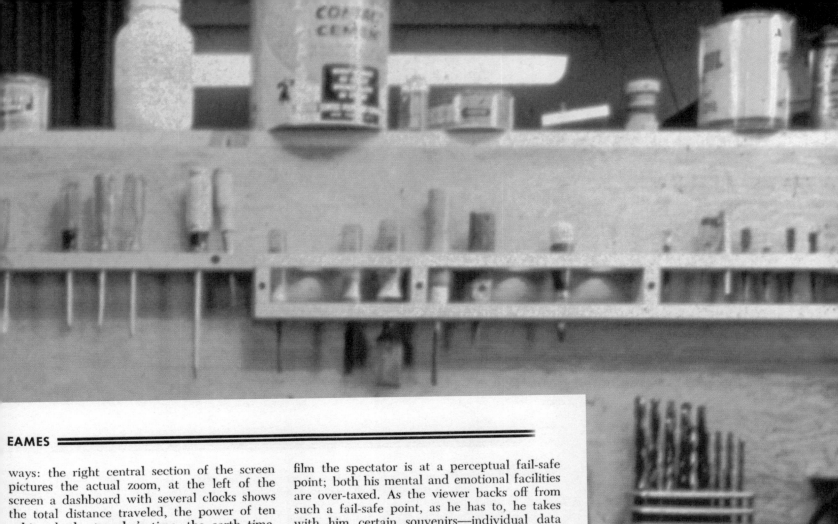

ways: the right central section of the screen pictures the actual zoom, at the left of the screen a dashboard with several clocks shows the total distance traveled, the power of ten achieved, the traveler's time, the earth time, and the percentage of the speed of light. A dispassionate female voice—a robot stewardess—describes every second of the journey in full, rapid detail. The narrator also supplies extraneous, unexpected information. "We have now reached the point where we can see the distance light travels in one minute," she says, and a short burst of light, one minute long, passes before our eyes. In addition, there is an eerie score supplied by Elmer Bernstein on a miniature Japanese organ.

Handling information in such a way, *Powers of Ten* is able to give more data more densely than a multi-screen presentation. The pictorial area of the screen in itself has more visual information than the mind can assimilate. Every spot on the image is a continuous transformation: skin becomes a wrist, wrist a man, man a beach, beach a peninsula, and so on, each change the square of the previous change, and each faster than the viewer can adjust his equilibrium. The zooming image, in itself, is only an "experience" and could easily be used in a light show (as it has been at the Whiskey A Go Go in Los Angeles). But the irony of *Powers of Ten* is that the narration and the dashboard demand exactly what the viewer is unable to do: make cerebral sense of the fantastic voyage. The monotone narration and animated dashboard affect the other side of perception; they use the conventional methods of appealing to reason. From the first frame of this eight-minute

film the spectator is at a perceptual fail-safe point; both his mental and emotional facilities are over-taxed. As the viewer backs off from such a fail-safe point, as he has to, he takes with him certain souvenirs—individual data which in each case will be different, but mostly an Idea which in this case is about the dimensions of time and space.

The interstellar roller-coaster ride of *Powers of Ten* does what the analogous sequence in *2001: A Space Odyssey* should have: it gives the full impact—instinctual as well as cerebral—of contemporary scientific theories. (In comparison *2001*, like Expo '67 seems "astounding.") It popularizes (in the best sense of the word) post-Einsteinian thought the way the telescope popularized Copernicus; and the effect is almost as upsetting. The spectator is in perspectiveless space; there is no one place where he can objectively judge another place. Just as the vacationing hayseed begins to think of himself as a citizen of the country rather than of just Sioux Center, and the jet-setter begins to think of himself as a citizen of the world rather than of just the United States, so the time-space traveler of *Powers of Ten* thinks of himself as a citizen of the universe, an unbounded territory.

Eames approached the problem in universal terms (to please the ten year-old as well as the nuclear physicist) and, as in designing a chair, sought to find what was most common to their experience. Sophisticated scientific data was not the denominator (although the film had to handle such matters with complete accuracy to maintain credibility), but it was that inchoate "gut feeling" of new physics which even the

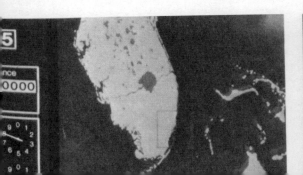

most jaded scientist, as Eames says, "had never quite seen in this way before." Just as it took a more complex and intellectual structure to give a computer integrity than a toy train, so it took a more complex and intellectual structure to give the powers-of-ten-extended-through-space-and time-idea integrity than Boolean Logic. *Powers of Ten* goes beyond a simple explanation of the powers of ten (which Eames had done in his *IBM Mathematics Peep Show* by using the parable of the chess board and sacks of grain), and concretizes a concept of the universe true to contemporary experience. And that Idea is covetable.

*National Aquarium Presentation* resulted from a more earthly problem. *Aquarium* is, simply enough, a report to the Department of Interior on a proposed National Aquarium. After two years of research and design, the Eames office presented the Department of the Interior not a voluminous sheath of blueprints, but a ten-minute color film and an illustrative booklet. The problem was not only to develop the design and rationale for the Aquarium, but also to persuade an economy-minded Congress to lay out the cash for such a project. When dealing with the government, film is the petitioner's ideal medium: "I've discovered," says Eames, "that not even a senator dares to stand up and interrupt a film."

Again Eames had to state the problem before he could solve it: "*Aquarium* wasn't a selling job, it was a report. Mike Kerwin, a venerable member of Congress, was interested in this and this was to be Mike Kerwin's monument. But Mike Kerwin didn't have any idea really of what an aquarium should be. As he or someone else said, 'Anything to keep those little children from peeing in the Capitol.' This is about the level these projects get started. The only thing you can do is try to create a level someone else would be embarrassed to fall below."

*National Aquarium Presentation* constructs the Aquarium in ten minutes, from overall conception to minute detail. Step by rapid step the film discusses the rationale, decides on a location, landscapes the environment, constructs the

building, details the departments, and takes th[e] viewer on a guided tour of the finished institu[-]tion. Diverse methods of information presen[-]tation are used: graphs, animation, models, live[?] action, narration, music.

The guiding principles of the Aquarium ar[e] not simply aquatic curiosity or research. Lik[e] all of Eames's creations, the Aquarium is found[-]ed on organization, practicality, intelligence[,] and enjoyment. *Aquarium* makes sure that th[e] viewer doesn't mistake those fish for somethin[g] inessential to man. One who wishes to attac[k] the Aquarium must attack the principles it [is] based on. The true function of the Aquarium [is] stated in the concluding lines of narration:

*Still the greatest souvenirs of the Aquariu[m] may be the beauty and intellectual stimulatio[n] it holds. The principal goal is much the sam[e] as science, to give the visitor some understan[d]ing of the natural world. If the National Aquar[-]ium is as good as it can be, it will do just tha[t]*
—from *National Aquarium Presentatio[n]*

Even though Congress has yet to give fina[l] approval, the National Aquarium exists. It exist[s] not only to the architects, to whom it alway[s] exists, but also to those who have seen Eames'[s] film. After seeing the film, viewers speak of th[e] Aquarium in the present; the fact that the[y] cannot go the Washington and experience th[e] Aquarium tactilely is only a chronological mis[-]fortune. The viewer has already experienced th[e] full delights of the Aquarium, its beauty and in[-]tellectual stimulation. When the Aquarium i[s] finally built, it seems to me, it will not be be[-]cause the government really felt that it wa[s] needed, but because the Aquarium has alread[y] existed in so many minds—Congressmen, sci[-]entists, bureaucrats—that a physical structur[e] was necessary to concretize the cinematic ex[-]perience. And, if the Aquarium is built, it wil[l] be a rare demonstration of the *Realpolitik* pow[-]er of an idea.

The irony and power of *National Aquariu[m]* is that it is greater than the Aquarium ever ca[n] be. In its finest form the Aquarium exists in th[e] mind, and the physical structure can only b[e] a pale imitation of the dream. Eames calls *Na[-]tional Aquarium* a "fiction of reality," and lik[e]

*Ecological greenhouse*, NATIONAL AQUARIUM, *1967*

the best fictions it is more meaningful than its reality. Eames has constructed the Aquarium like Borges constructed the Library of Babel, in his short story of that title. Like the Aquarium the Library is real because it is definitive, it can encompass all reality. Just as the writer of "Library of Babel" was able to define himself as a member of the Library, it is possible to define oneself as a member of the Aquarium. The Aquarium has all the virtues of a meaningful existence; it offers a way of perceiving the outside world, one's neighbor, and one's self. And even if one is only a visitor to the Aquarium, as we all must be, the Aquarium presents the virtues of beauty and intellectual stimulation that one would be embarrassed to fall below.

The radical, wonderful thing about Eames's Aquarium is that you *can* live there. One of the pleasures and limitations of Traditional cinema is that it is idiosyncratic: only Fellini can fully live in Fellini's world, Godard in Godard's, Hawks in Hawks's (great films transcend these limitations to varying degrees). Like an architect, Charles Eames builds film-structures in which many people can live, solve their problems, and respect their environment.

The three films discussed, *Tops, Powers of Ten*, and *National Aquarium Presentation*, total less than twenty-five minutes of screen time. To extrapolate an environmental aesthetic from a ten-minute sponsored film like *National Aquarium* may seem like the height of critical mannerism to some, and it is certainly possible that Eames's first films are not as important as I think they are. But in examining his films in detail, one finds the essential qualities of contemporary art. The Eames aesthetic personalizes assembly-line art, gives creator power to the consumer, permits individual integrity within a dehumanized collective, and allows the field to have as much value as the items within it.

In film, the Eames aesthetic introduces a new way of perceiving ideas into a medium which has been surprisingly anti-intellectual. Cinema threw every other art into the twentieth century, Wylie Cypher contends in *Rococo to Cubism*, and remained woefully in the nineteenth itself. Much of the upheaval in contemporary films has been the protest of the romantic-idiosyncratic tradition against itself. Even the best of recent

films, like *Persona, Belle de Jour, The Wild Bunch*, are too inherently a part of the tradition they protest to posit an alternative cinema. The few film-makers handling ideas today, Robbe-Grillet, Rohmer, Godard, Resnais, seem to fail because they cannot escape the romantic perspective. The French intellectual cinema (the *only* intellectual cinema) verges on bankruptcy; its failures are as disastrous as Godard's *One Plus One*, its successes as minimal as Robbe-Grillet's *Trans-Europe Express*. Because Eames comes from another discipline with a pre-existing aesthetic he is able to bring innovation to an art which in the area of ideas is only spinning its wheels. It is Eames's aesthetic which is ultimately the innovation.

Eames returns to film in a limited and exploratory manner what Cubism took from it in the early 1900's. What Sypher wrote of the cubist art of Cézanne, Eliot, Pirandello, and Gide is now true of Eames's films:

"Have we not been misled by the nineteenth-century romantic belief that the imagination means either emotional power or the concrete image, the metaphor alone. We have not supposed there is a poetry of ideas."

### INTERVIEW

*I spoke with Charles Eames on several occasions during January, 1970, and the quotes in the preceding article are excerpted from those conversations. Afterward, I posed written questions to Eames, intended to capsulize and explore many of the discussions we had had, to which he responded in writing.*

*Your career has seen many permutations. At times you have been an architect, furniture designer, a craftsman, an inventor, a film-maker, and a professor. Do you see a sense of design in your own career, or does it appear to be more accidental or haphazard?*

Looking back on our work, I see no design —certainly nothing haphazard, and not much that could really be called accidental. What I think I see is a natural, though not predictable, growth toward a goal that has not ever been specified.

*Given an empty blank, say, about the size of an IBM card, how would you characterize your current occupation?*

I am occupied mostly by things that I have to fight my way through in order to get some work done.

*How does an Eames film originate? What do the discussions with the producer(s) entail? What determines whether you and Ray will accept or reject a proposed film?*

A film comes as a result of one of two situations. It is either a logical extension of some immediate problem we are working on, or it is something we have been wanting to do for a long time and can't put off any longer.

*On several occasions you have stated that you regard film simply as the medium through which you solve problems and explain concepts. What, for you, has made film so uniquely suited to this task?*

We have fallen for the illusion that film is a perfectly controlled medium; that after the mess of production, when it is all in the can, nothing can erode it—the image, the color, the timing, the sound, everything is under control. It is just an illusion— thoughtless reproduction, projection and presentation turn it into a mess again. Still, putting an idea on film provides the ideal discipline for whittling that idea down to size.

*One of the most consistent techniques in your films is information-overload, that is, you habitually give more data than the mind can assimilate. What do you think is the effect of this cascading level of information on the viewer? Do you think this effect can be conditioning, that it can expand the ability to perceive? In other words, will a viewer learn more from the fifth Eames film he sees than the first, assuming they are of equal complexity?*

I don't really believe we overload, but if that is what it is, we try to use it in a way that heightens the reality of the subject, and where, if the viewer is reduced to only a sampling, that sampling will be true to the spirit of the subject. Maybe after seeing one or two the viewer learns to relax.

*Concerning* Day of the Deed *and* Two Baroque Churches in Germany, *films which utilize*

*a rapid succession of still views,* Michael *Brawne wrote in* Architectual Design *that "the interesting point about this method of film making is not only that it is relatively simple to produce and that rather more information can be conveyed than when there is movement on the screen, but that it corresponds surprisingly closely with the way in which the brain normally records the images it receives." Do you feel this is actually the way the brain works, and is that why you used that technique?*

Because the viewer is being led at the cutter's pace, it can, over a long period, be exhausting. But this technique can deliver a great amount of information in much the same way we naturally perceive it—we did this pretty consciously.

*Alison Smithson, another British critic, has written of your furniture, "The influence of the West Coast comes to us through Eames." To what extent do you think Mrs. Smithson is correct? This question may imply that Los Angeles is the prototype for America, as some city-planners have said, and I certainly wouldn't hold you responsible for that.*

Los Angeles is the prototype for any city built by any people from anywhere, who have been removed from their native constraints. We have perhaps carried with us a few more constraints than most, and this may be what the Smithsons choose to recognize.

*You have never handled a fictional situation in your films, and I assume this is by choice rather than accident. I would like to ask if there might arise a problem which you felt could best be solved in a fictional manner—but this is incumbent upon an understanding of what is "fiction." The* IBM Puppet Shows *segment "Sherlock Holmes in 'The Singular Case of the Plural Green Mustache'" would seem to be a fiction in conventional terms, yet its plot is nothing but an exercise in Boolean Logic. The outstanding feature of* National Aquarium Presentation *is that it seems to be a fiction more real—more immediate—than the object it portrays. Perhaps it would be more accurate to ask what you would consider a "fiction" in the framework of your films, and if you feel or have*

*felt any aspects of fictionality creeping into your work?*

I think the meaning of fiction that you ascribed to the Aquarium is quite accurate. Fiction in this case is used as a model or simulation against which to try out possible reactions. I suppose it is true that none of our films has had any trace of plot, in most of them it is structure that takes the place of plot.

*One definition of fiction which might be applied to your films is anything which violates the scientific verities of the universe. Yet one of the thrusts of modern science is the truth that science considered from any one perspective is in itself a fiction. Would you consider making a fiction of science, that is, either criticizing a particular theory-fiction because it is too limited, or positing a multi-faceted conception of perceiving the universe, just as you posited the Aquarium?*

I believe it would be possible to build in film a conception/a fiction of science—but it would probably be bound by the same constraints as any scientific hypothesis.

*Relevant to this discussion is the fact that you have never explicated philosophical or psychological problems, only scientific ones. You have never attempted a film like, say, an adaptation of Cassirer's* Philosophy of the Enlightenment, *although such a film made in your style could be extraordinary. A philosophical theory cannot be empirically limited in the way a scientific one can, yet I think your best "science" film,* Powers of Ten, *works in that area where modern science and philosophy converge in outer space. You once mentioned the possibility of making a film illustration of one of Richard Feynman's lectures. Would not such a project bring you even further away from the comfortable ground of computer logic and into the nebulous sphere of modern philosophy?*

I have never looked upon any of our films as being scientific, but at the same time I have never considered them less philosophical than scientific.

When dealing with some fairly elaborate problems, such as the computer, the city, the Aquarium, etc., we have usually tried to re-

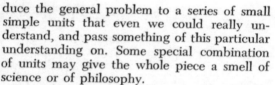

duce the general problem to a series of small simple units that even we could really understand, and pass something of this particular understanding on. Some special combination of units may give the whole piece a smell of science or of philosophy.

*Several years ago, C. P. Snow's* Two Cultures *revived the science-art debate in England, and to a lesser extent in this country. Are there two cultures in the way Snow describes, and is this necessarily dangerous? Science and art seem to have merged completely in the lives of yourself and Ray, but others have a difficulty integrating these spheres.*

If there are two cultures, as Snow suggests, it is probably no more or less dangerous than the ignorance that goes with polarized training and thinking ever was—but, at this time in particular, it seems unnecessary.

*You once expressed concern over Feynman's involvement with local artists. You said the tendency for a collision with a sculptor or a painter who is preoccupied with certain personality idiosyncrasies could derail him (Feynman) and you want to protect him because something great could happen. Is this statement simply altruistic, or perhaps are you reacting to a certain voguishness or lack of thought on the part of the artists, or even that scientists shouldn't truck with "idiosyncratic" methods of expression?*

Naturally, I would not think that any exposure to the art types would really derail Feynman. I am super-impatient with those, who, with the object of somehow heightening the aesthetic values of the community, seek to bring painters and sculptors together with scientists in a conscious effort to affect the aesthetic climate.

I have a conviction, no matter how unlikely it sometimes seems, that somehow, sometime, out of the world engaged in problem-structuring and scientific pursuits, will come a sharpening and a new awareness of aesthetic values.

The danger is that this world can be prematurely contaminated by a virus that results in preoccupation with self-expression. When a scientist, engineer, mathematician (with natural

resistance less than that of Feynman) collid with the painter, sculptor, they catch the bu to which the painter, sculptor have develope an immunity. Little moves toward self-expres sion, a self-conscious attitude toward "Art" an a numbing of the sense that would allow ther to recognize aesthetics as an extension of thei own discipline.

*In* House of Science, *the scientist is define as one who "assumes that the puzzles have solution, that they will be fair." What woul your scientist say if someone countered that th puzzles had no solution, and weren't fair?*

He could give one scientist's reaction, Ein stein's. When asked a question similar to that he replied, "God may be subtle, but he's no malicious."

Stills from *Tops*,
1966–9
Film, 7:15 min.

*Tops* began as a short montage of spinning tops made for the television programme *Stars of Jazz* in 1957. Charles and Ray continued to work on the excerpt and expanded it into a longer, colour version in the late 1960s. The final film, with a score by Elmer Bernstein, features a total of 123 spinning tops of all shapes, sizes and origins, including China, England, France, India, Japan and the United States. Each is set into motion, prompting a reflection on the universality of their form and the physics of their movement.

## The Travelling Eameses

Charles and Ray enjoyed travelling. Unlike many Americans in the jet age, however, they did not travel abroad as tourists, in the sense of deciding to visit specific places as a leisure treat and paying for the travel themselves. For the most part they travelled for work, for instance at the invitation of a business client, foundation or government, or, to a lesser extent, as part of a cultural exchange. On to those trips they piggybacked sightseeing, including in neighbouring cities or countries, always seeking out toys and other objects of the kind they enjoyed collecting. Whenever possible, they took the opportunity to link up with friends, particularly in England. Among those they visited there were the costume and set designer Margaret Harris, who worked for them in the early to mid-1940s; film and television actors Alexander Knox and Doris Nolan, victims of the 'Red Scare' and Hollywood black- and grey-listing who moved to London in the early 1950s; and Labour MP and government minister Tony Benn.

During their long partnership (1941–78), Charles and Ray travelled to twenty-three foreign countries. Some visits, however, were only for brief periods en route to other destinations, and the oft-given impression that they were constantly travelling all over the world needs some qualification. In comparison with their friends Alexander Girard and his wife, Susan, who collected objects from 100 countries in six continents, for example, their travels and collecting were relatively modest.

Charles spent three months in Europe in 1929 on an extended honeymoon with his first wife, and took an eight-month road trip in Mexico on his own in 1933–4. Ray had not previously travelled abroad when she met Charles, but her interest in foreign cultures, especially those of India and Mexico, is evident from documents relating to her life as a young artist in New York in the 1930s. Despite their common interest in other 'pre-industrial' cultures, a lack of money, the Second World War and the time they spent establishing and developing their early projects meant that they did not travel abroad in their first thirteen years together. They travelled for pleasure locally, especially in California, Nevada, Arizona and New Mexico, visiting sites of outstanding natural beauty and/or of architectural and archaeological interest. Along the way, they visited Native American trading posts and attended the famous Native American celebratory parade and dances at Gallup, New Mexico.

Native American cultures, along with those of Mexico, constituted their main geo-cultural imaginaries in the 1940s and 1950s, and their conceptions of other cultures led them to accept the first of two commissions in India in 1958 (see pages 242–6). When they did visit other countries, fruitful exchanges often occurred between their imagination, their accumulated knowledge, and what they saw and experienced there. Travel offered an opportunity to collect souvenirs, and items brought or shipped home included two chairs from India and masks and celebratory headwear from Mexico. When they visited West Germany in 1954 (Charles was funded by a cultural-exchange programme sponsored by the West German government), they showed more interest in old toys and games, folk art and Baroque churches – about which they made a beautiful film[1] – than in contemporary German art and design. Another result of that visit was *Konditorei*, a slideshow about one of the pastry shops that their friend Billy Wilder, the film director, had encouraged them to visit. Their fascination with ornament in both of these German projects signalled the distance they had travelled – visually and intellectually – from orthodox modernism, as did the Baroque-style Christmas ornament they hung from their staircase at home.

The sheer amount of work undertaken by the Eameses meant that it was difficult for them to be away from the Office for too long, or too often. Notable exceptions included Charles's work during the making of the film *The Spirit of St. Louis* (1957, directed by Wilder), which in 1955 took him to locations around the world while Ray managed the Office. They visited India for fifteen weeks from late December 1957 to 11 April 1958, working on what became the *India Report* (April 1958). But when preparing an exhibition on the life of India's first prime minister, Jawaharlal Nehru, in 1964, it was Ray who got to spend months at a time there while Charles was based in Los Angeles. Together they spent about six weeks in the USSR after delivering their *Glimpses of the U.S.A.* presentation to the American National Exhibition when it opened in July 1959.

The Eameses knew so much about Japanese culture in the early 1950s that fellow designer Henry Dreyfuss assumed they must have been there. The National Museum of Modern Art in Tokyo asked the US State Department to fund a one- to two-month visit by Charles in 1957, to coincide with the exhibition *20th Century Design* (curated by The Museum of Modern Art, New York), but despite him explaining that he and Ray worked as 'a team', there was no funding forthcoming for Ray. The Eameses' first trip to Japan appears to have been five days en route to India in late 1957. They met up with the noted industrial designer Isamu Kenmochi, one of several friends and contacts who sought out unusual objects for them, including rare kites and papier mâché animals. Japan remained special for them, and, despite his failing health, Charles accepted an invitation to speak in Tokyo in July 1978. Too tired to make the trip, Ray went in his stead, as if preparing herself for the widowhood that would come the following month.

Pat Kirkham and Elizabeth St George

*Opposite*

Frames from *Konditorei*
3-screen slideshow

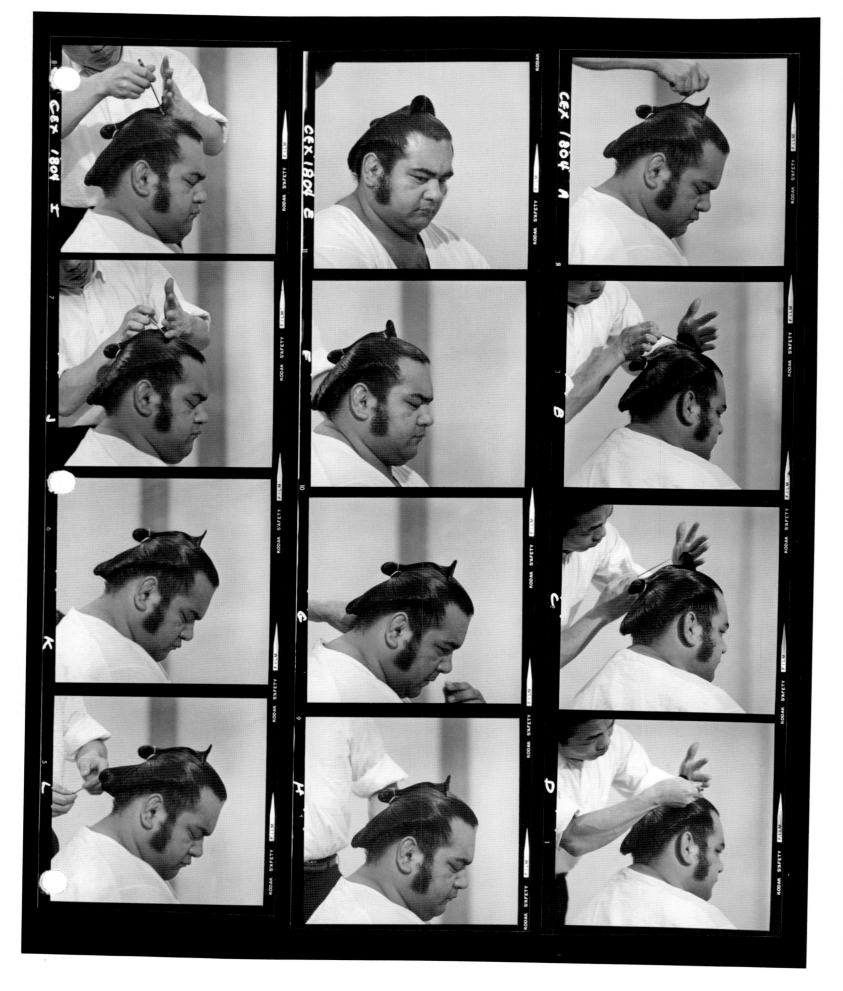

Photographs of sumo wrestler Takamiyama Daigoro at 901, 1972
Black-and-white photographs, each 26 × 21 cm (10 ¼ × 8 ¼ in.)

The Work of Charles and Ray Eames, Prints & Photographs Division, Library of Congress, Washington DC

In 1972 the Hawaiian-born sumo wrestler Takamiyama Daigoro (born Jesse Kuhaulua) and his hairdresser accompanied Miyoko Sasaki, a former Eames Office staff member, on a visit to the Eames House and Office. Takamiyama had that year earned the honour of becoming the

first foreign-born sumo wrestler to win the top-division championship. During his visit, Charles and Ray made a spontaneous film, *Sumo Wrestler* (4 min., unfinished), documenting step by step the ritual of preparing his traditional hairstyle for wrestling.

Celebration as a Human Need

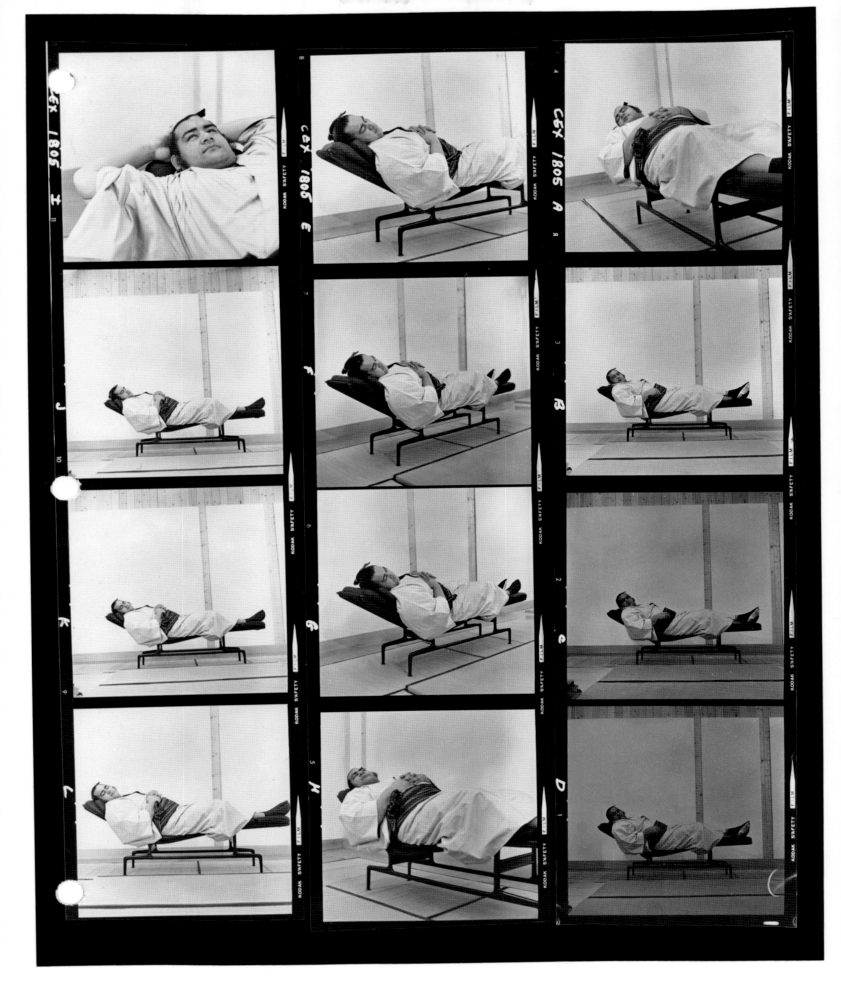

213

Celebrating Connections: From Aby Warburg's
'Iconology of the Interval' to the 'New Kinds of
Models' of Charles and Ray Eames

Lotte Johnson

In 1924 Aby Warburg, the influential German art historian and cultural theorist, began compiling and continually reorganizing a vast array of images into a kind of picture map: the *Mnemosyne Atlas*.[1] The *Atlas* consisted of a series of wood panels covered with black cloth, to which were attached thousands of images and clippings, often with no captions. Taken from books, magazines, newspapers and everyday sources, this visual material was arranged according to various categories and sequences. The idea for the project, which remained unfinished when Warburg died in 1929, sprang from the method of using images mounted on large boards for lectures and exhibitions; Warburg expanded this practice into a mode through which he could present his ideas in a novel way. The panels suggested startling new relationships between images, proposing what Warburg termed the 'iconology of the interval'. It was the symbolic connections between these fragments that fascinated Warburg – the reappearances of forms, gestures and thought throughout history.

Looking at the surviving black-and-white photographs of Warburg's *Atlas*, one cannot help but recall Charles and Ray Eames's own pin-up exercise several decades later, in which they traced the development of the computer for the exhibition *A Computer Perspective* (1971) with a densely layered three-dimensional timeline. Their 'atlas' of the computer incorporated a range of source material, including computer components, documents and photographs. Each item was brought together to convey a complex history of the machine, connecting the scientific and technological discoveries that led to its conception and development. Whether the Eameses knew about Warburg's *Atlas* is unclear; what is certain, however, is that they would have been aware of his written work, for Warburg's notion of 'iconology' dominated the theoretical discourse of the second half of the twentieth century.[2] Formal analogies aside, Warburg's unfinished project provides us with a point of departure for placing the Eameses within a trajectory of twentieth-century thinkers who looked at the spaces *between* things, who probed the possibility that meaning was embedded in the relationships between images, things and ideas as they recurred across time and place.

The Eameses' fascination with the importance of connections was not something detached from the intellectual climate of the time. In the middle decades of the twentieth century, there was an academic turn towards modes of thought that foregrounded the role of relationships over that of essences, and to those that championed the importance of differences over fixed identities. These intellectual tropes were characteristic of a broad movement in cultural and critical theory that can be traced in the simultaneous transitions from modernism to postmodernism and from structuralism to post-structuralism. The Eameses may not have been directly influenced by these academic movements, which were mainly confined to continental Europe until the works of such thinkers as Michel Foucault, Jacques Derrida and Gilles Deleuze were translated into English in the 1970s and 1980s, but the similarities are not merely coincidental. One can see both the Eameses' interest in connections and the importance of connections to the leading figures of such movements as post-structuralism as products of their time. These practitioners, the Eameses among them, were direct followers of those early twentieth-century critics, including Warburg, who challenged the orthodoxy of classical art theory by drawing attention away from the work of art as an isolated object and directing it towards the many and disparate connections that the work maintains with the world around it.

The Eameses repeatedly stressed the importance of 'connections' to their practice as designers, and sought new and provocative ways in which to communicate information.[3] Writing in the mid-1950s, the English art critic and curator Lawrence Alloway noted that Charles 'thinks in terms of relationships rather than aesthetic standards of form', and that he is interested in 'design as a process of transmission rather than design as approximation to a canon'.[4] Charles himself stated that 'the real current problems for architects now – the problems that a Brunelleschi, say, would gravitate to – are problems of organization of information ... *Communications Primer* was a recommendation to architects to recognize the need for more complex information ... for new kinds of models of information.'[5] The Eameses' film *A Communications Primer* (1953) proposed new kinds of cross-disciplinary communications systems and underlined that meaning is determined in the transfer of information, that symbols carry meaning that is filtered and shaped by the mode and context in which they are communicated.

Warburg's notion that ideas and forms recur across time and place, and that the connections between them are meaningful, resonates with the Eameses' own approach to image-making. Charles and Ray took thousands of photographs: of their work; of everyday life, at home and in the Eames Office; of exhibitions they visited; of objects and people they encountered; and of places they travelled to around the world. Rather than merely documentary in nature, this persistent image-making was integral to their work. Drawing on their library of thousands of slides, for example, the Eameses created numerous slideshows for a wide variety of audiences, including friends, colleagues, students and such corporations as IBM and Herman Miller. For many of these presentations, the slides were sequenced and arranged so that they could be displayed on up to three screens at once. The slideshows encompassed an extraordinary range of subject matter, from various events and aspects of the environment (*Road Race*, *Railroad*, *Townscape* and *Seascape*, shown to architecture students at the University of California, Berkeley, in 1953 and 1954) to the inner workings of a pastry shop in Munich (*Konditorei*), a detailed study of a circus accompanied by the sounds of the big top (*Circus*, shown as part of the lecture series Charles delivered as the Charles Eliot Norton Professor of Poetry at Harvard University in 1970), and a sequence of 345 images prompting the viewer to look at the world with a fresh perspective and addressing the meaning of 'quality' through such diverse items as highways, ruins, spinning tops and coins (*G.E.M.*).

These slideshows explored the connections and continuities in everyday life, often using close-ups and details to celebrate overlooked aspects of our surroundings and illuminate recurring themes and ideas. The double- or triple-channel format of each presentation allowed for striking conjunctions of images, highlighting unexpected but repeated relationships between things, and connecting objects and ideas across time, places and cultures. According to Charles, showing multiple images simultaneously produced a 'depth of view', to the extent that 'we found that everything we encountered needed the multiple-image technique'.[6] Many of the Eameses' slideshows were seen as ever-evolving works, constantly reordered and reconfigured by staff at the Eames Office for presentations in new contexts. Interestingly, Warburg's *Atlas* was also seen as a work in progress; the content of each panel went through several rounds of reselection and rearrangement to reflect the thinker's evolving ideas.

The physical objects designed by the Eameses were a further manifestation of their expansive approach to visual meaning. Their House of Cards (1952) is a prime example, the packaging for which describes the enclosed deck of cards as featuring 'pictures gathered from sources all over the world. Familiar and nostalgic objects.' These objects were selected and photographed by the Eameses but then offered up to the user-player to be reselected, reconfigured and reordered. As well as functioning as a playful

It was rare that these objects would be displayed in their house according to type; rather, the Eameses would place seemingly disparate objects next to one another in surprising tableaux. As the British architect Peter Smithson noted, there was 'a kind of wide-eyed wonder of seeing the culturally disparate together and so happy with each other'.[8] Objects were grouped together and rearranged in the manner of a paste-up exercise played out in three dimensions.

The Eameses' collections of objects served a purpose beyond forming an integral part of their domestic realm. The objects amassed would often assume the role of protagonist in their experimental films. *Tops* (1966–9), for example, is composed of repeated shots of different types of spinning top from around the world, both traditional and contemporary. Through the repetition of a single form and its variations, a myriad of possible meanings and connections are offered up to the viewer, from the simplicity of the toy's functional design to the physics of motion, the celebration of play and the idea of rebirth in the top's seemingly infinite spin. In a tribute to Charles Eames given in 1978, the British politician Tony Benn reflected that, in the film, 'the unity of humanity comes through in a way that is utterly pleasurable and absolutely unforgettable'.[9] It was not the spinning top in and of itself that fascinated the Eameses, but the meaning, function and design that it carries; it is a symbol whose meaning is embedded in the relationships between its many iterations.

In the second of his Norton Lectures, Charles echoed the observations of the Hungarian artist and theorist György Kepes when he said that there was a necessity to devise 'visual models for matters of practical concern where linear description can't cope'.[10] This mode of thinking can be seen in all areas of the Eameses' universal approach to design. Their practice was distinguished by a persistent challenge to linearity, looking to the connections within constellations of images and ideas in order to find solutions to problems, and thus blurring the boundaries between the fields in which they operated. Just as Warburg's *Atlas* served as a vehicle for the expression of his ideas about meaning, offering an expansive reading not only of the history of art but also of the symbolism of the everyday world, the Eameses' continual configuring and reconfiguring of groups of images and objects epitomized an expansive attitude towards the field of design. This practice of making and analysing connections, which runs through all of the Eameses' work, was not simply a tool for the practice of design; rather, it constituted a radical and original method for exploring the visual language of meaning that surrounds us.

modular structure, House of Cards illuminated the recurring symbols, forms, patterns and shapes that are apparent in everyday objects. In fact, the Eameses saw objects as solutions to problems in the world, reflecting the values they held. This was carried through to their creation of interiors, such as the room they designed for the exhibition *For Modern Living* (Detroit Institute of Arts, 1949). In the catalogue for the exhibition, E. P. Richardson notes that, for the Eameses, objects and images could be ideas in themselves, and that in their room the 'enjoyment of any two objects is increased proportionately by their proper relation to each other'.[7] In other words, it is through the relationships between objects that they can be fully understood and appreciated. Likewise, in House of Cards, everyday items are photographed both in multiples and as single objects, allowing the player to find numerous parallels and connections to other cards within the deck. The Eameses never neglected to offer up connections between things, and, through their designs, prompted others to do so too.

The Eameses' celebration of connections was evident not only in the model living environments and products they designed for others, but also in their own domestic arrangements. Charles and Ray endlessly rearranged the interior of their house, including the many objects on display. The Eameses amassed an extensive array of objects over their lifetimes, collecting things wherever they went, from countries as diverse as Japan, Mexico, India, Germany and England. They were interested in the many variations and expressions of particular forms and functions; they often collected thematically, focusing, for example, on such objects as masks, boats, spinning tops and figurines. Their collections spanned both history and different cultures, and ranged from the simplest examples to the most intricate they could find. There seemed to be little hierarchy in their collecting, and they found endless types of buttons just as fascinating as model trains or ceremonial masks.

*Page 214*

Detail of the 'History Wall' for *A Computer Perspective*, IBM Corporate Exhibit Center, New York, 1971–5

*Above*

Aby Warburg
*Mnemosyne Atlas*, Panel 79, 1929

*Opposite*

Frames from *India*
3-screen slideshow consisting of images taken by Charles during the Eameses' numerous trips to India from 1958 onwards

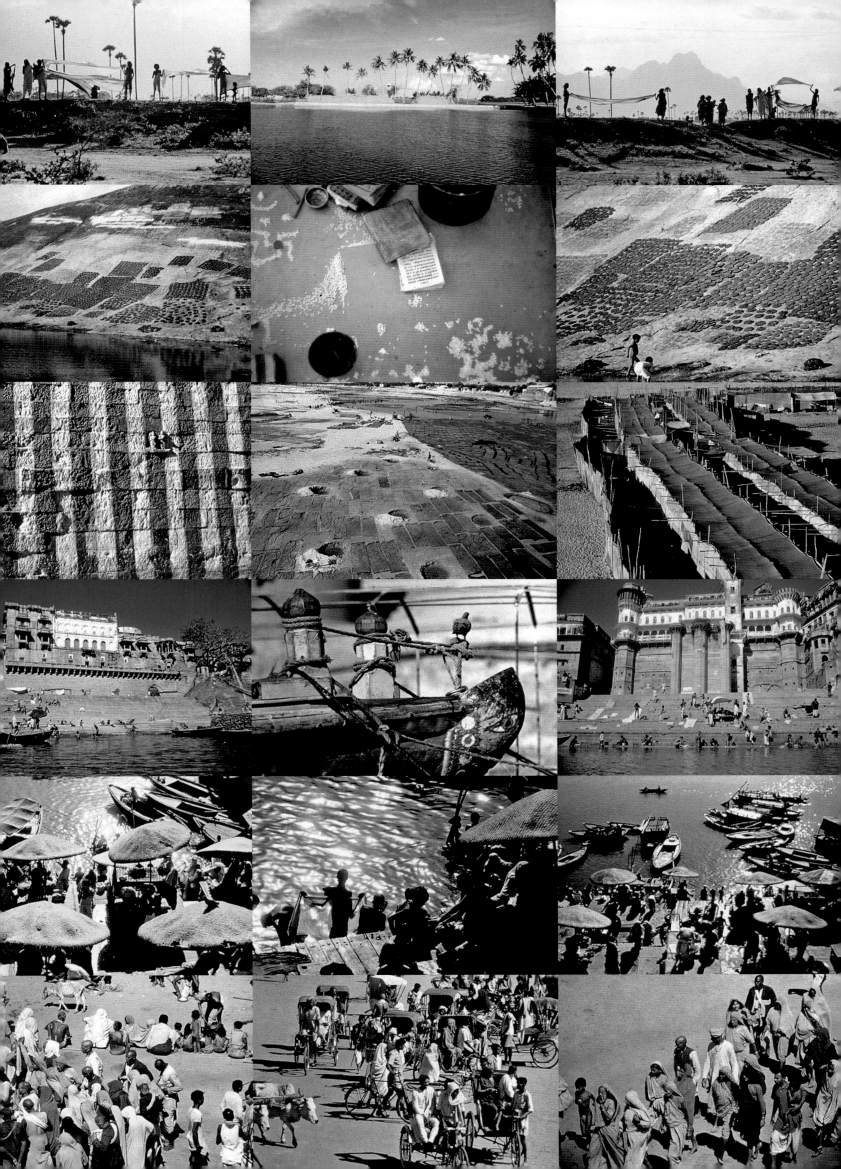

# SAMPLE LESSONS

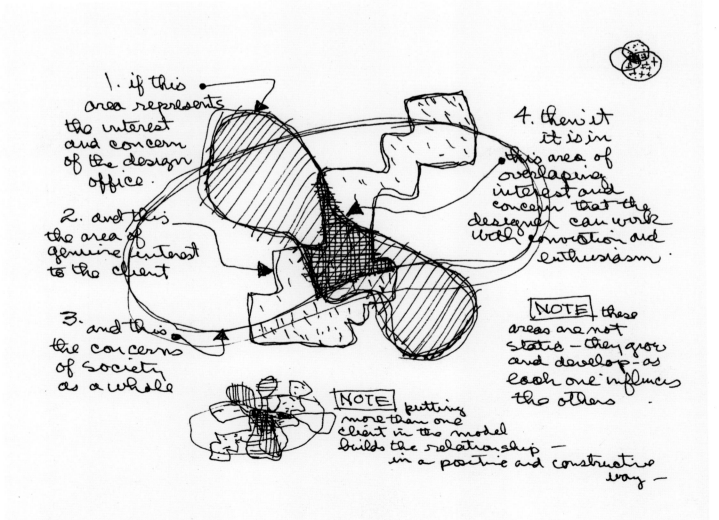

*Communication is what links any living organism together.*
—Charles Eames

In 1952 the Department of Fine Arts at the University of Georgia in Athens invited George Nelson to review its curriculum and help develop a new programme for the faculty. Nelson joined forces with Charles Eames and together they devised a 'sample lesson' to demonstrate their proposed course, founded on 'breaking down the barriers between fields of learning'.[1] With the help of Alexander Girard, they prepared what was perhaps the first public multimedia presentation in the United States, incorporating graphics, film, music, slides, smells and commentaries to augment the experience; as Charles remarked, 'we wanted to heighten awareness'.[2] Although too costly to be adopted by the faculty, *A Rough Sketch for a Sample Lesson for a Hypothetical Course*[3] was a pioneering experiment in interdisciplinary teaching.[4] Initially conceived with a focus on 'art as a kind of communication', it put forward a radical pedagogical model for expanded attitudes towards learning. The Eameses repeatedly returned to this philosophy and approach in their work, consistently employing multimedia techniques to condense complex ideas. They remained actively involved in educational contexts, sought after for their conception of design as an enquiry into problem-solving and the transmission of ideas. Among other engagements, they led a monthly seminar for architecture students at the University of California, Berkeley, from 1953 to 1954; Charles was appointed Charles Eliot Norton Professor of Poetry at Harvard University for 1970–71;[5] and in 1977 he was made Regents' Professor at the University of California, Los Angeles.[6] Charles and Ray were also frequent attendees at the International Design Conference in Aspen, Colorado, which provided an opportunity for industry professionals to come together to discuss the expanding realm of design.[7]

The medium of film provided another means of pedagogical expression. *A Communications Primer* (1953) addressed 'the need for a broader concept of what communication means and how it operates', advocating new information theories as useful tools.[8] *Powers of Ten* (1968 and 1977), a series of films exploring the mathematical principle of the title, are remarkable investigations into how we understand and process information about the changing world around us. Perhaps the Eameses' most tangible contribution to the field of education was their role in the formation of the National Institute of Design (NID) in Ahmedabad, India. Commissioned by the Indian government, Charles and Ray submitted their *India Report* in 1958, responding to the challenges that India was facing in the light of Western design and technology. They recommended a new educational model that could bridge tradition and modernity, proposing an interdisciplinary board of governors.[9] Their study provided the basis for NID, which remains one of the foremost schools of design today. The *India Report* begins with a 'sample lesson' from the early Sanskrit poem the *Bhagavad Gita*, which resonates with the Eameses' own ethos: 'You have the right to work, but for the work's sake only; you have no right to the fruits of work. Desire for the fruits of work must never be your motive in working.' For the Eameses, process was everything.

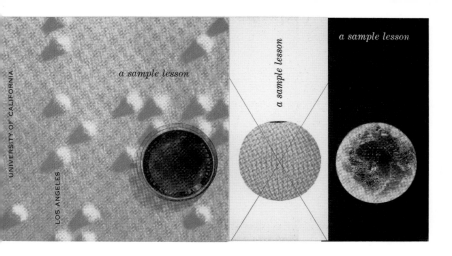

...thing new is happening ... a
...progression, perhaps, toward
...wn the barriers between fields
...of learning ... toward making
...little more intuitive ... toward
...asing communication between
people and things.

...e called it a sample lesson ...
...have called it the first step or
...s or the initial experiment ...
...tever it is called, this is news
...not a trend yet ... just new.

*let's look at it !*

six months ago, George Nelson and Charles
Eames, two of America's top
architectural and industrial designers,
were called to the University of
Georgia by art chairman Lamar Dodd.
their job: to study and suggest curriculum
revision in that University's Department of
Fine Arts. they found many things
... but the important things were barriers ...
between art and engineering, for instance
... or engineering and business ... and business and
art in technique and art in appreciation.

by virtue of their backgrounds and talents which
had already broken through these barriers,

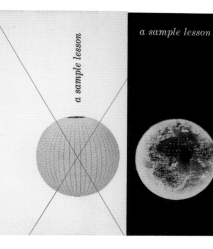

*a sample lesson*

*a sample lesson*

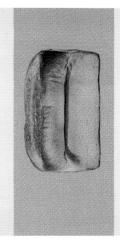

...d Eames knew that art is not just paint and a frame or stone
...e ... art is a building, a house, a machine ... art is a chair, a
...a loaf of bread ... art is a mathematician's formula, a philoso-
...y of life, any man's dreams ... art is sight and sound and touch
...even smell.

...and Eames set out to break down these barriers for other
...UT HOW? they prepared and assembled *a sample lesson* in
...and we ... hope will soon be a complete course of intense

instruction. aided by architect-designer Alexander Girard, they have interrelated art to all
things. the choice of art as a basic subject
matter was accidental, unpremeditated ... it
could just as well have been meteorology or
home economics or arithmetic or psychology
or ... the list is limited only by what man knows.

beyond this, lies deep water. because a
*sample lesson* is more of an experience than
a tangible solid ... because it is more of an
emotion than an action ... it is difficult to explain. *a sample lesson* must be seen and heard
and felt and smelled.

on May 27, 28 and 29, Mr. Nelson and Mr.

Eames will present *a sample lesson* to select,
invited audiences. *there is no fee.* the avowed
interest is getting your reaction ... and your
action.

since demand for attendance is huge and the
capacity of our classroom is small, your immediate application for tickets is vital. admission
is by ticket only.

### the schedule

two performances daily — from 4-6 p.m. and
from 8-10 p.m. on three consecutive days
Wednesday, May 27, Thursday, May 28,
Friday, May 29, 1953 in Old
Chemistry Building 19 on the Los Angeles
campus of the University of California

*a sample lesson*

### how to apply for tickets

Individuals may obtain tickets (limit: 2 to a person) by writing or coming in person to University Extension Ticket Office,
10851 Le Conte Avenue, Los Angeles 24, California. If you
write, enclose a stamped, self-addressed envelope. No telephone reservations will be accepted. Indicate preferred day
and time of attendance in order of preference. Tickets will be
assigned according to your first preference only if space permits.
If you represent an organization, club or association and you
want a group of tickets, write or call: Dr. Sam Houston, Department of Conferences, University Extension, University of
California, Los Angeles 24, BR. 2-6161, AR. 3-0971, Ext. 721.

Second presentation of *A Rough Sketch for a Sample Lesson for a Hypothetical Course*, University of California, Los Angeles, May 1953

*Opposite*

'Score' for *A Rough Sketch for a Sample Lesson for a Hypothetical Course*, 1952–3
Ink and pencil on paper, 54.3 × 43.2 cm (21⅜ × 17 in.)

The Papers of Charles and Ray Eames, Manuscript Division, Library of Congress, Washington DC

Sample Lessons

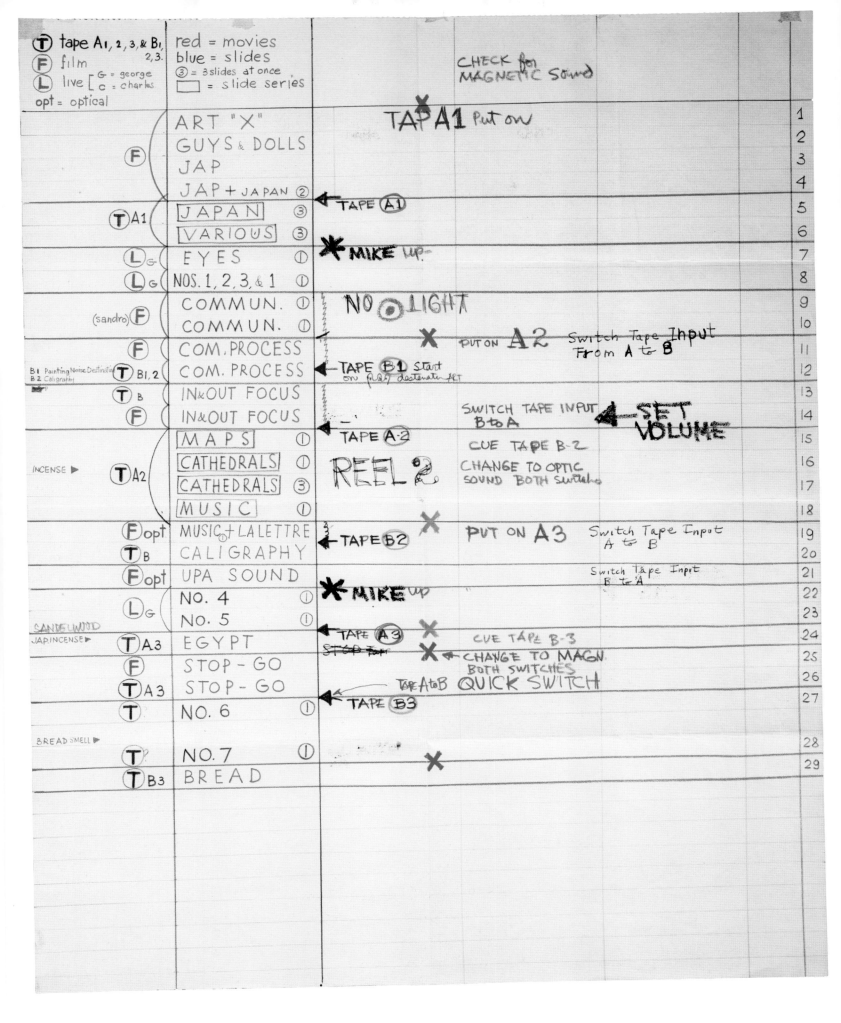

| | | | | | |
|---|---|---|---|---|---|
| (T) tape A1, 2, 3, & B1, 2, 3. | red = movies | | | | |
| (F) film | blue = slides | | | | |
| (L) live [ G = george / C = charles | ③ = 3 slides at once | | CHECK for MAGNETIC SOUND | | |
| opt = optical | ▭ = slide series | | | | |

| | Label | Item | | Annotations | No. |
|---|---|---|---|---|---|
| | (F) | ART "X" | | ✖ TAPE A1 Put on | 1 |
| | | GUYS & DOLLS | | | 2 |
| | | JAP | | | 3 |
| | | JAP + JAPAN ② | ◄ TAPE (A1) | | 4 |
| | (T) A1 | JAPAN ③ | | | 5 |
| | | VARIOUS ③ | | ✳ MIKE up | 6 |
| | (L) G | EYES ① | | | 7 |
| | (L) G | NOS. 1, 2, 3, & 1 ① | | | 8 |
| (sandro) | (F) | COMMUN. ① | | NO ⊙ LIGHT | 9 |
| | | COMMUN. ① | | | 10 |
| | (F) | COM. PROCESS | | ✖ PUT ON A2 Switch Tape Input From A to B | 11 |
| B1 Painting Noise Destination / B2 Caligraphy | (T) B1, 2 | COM. PROCESS | ◄ TAPE B1 start on (PLAY) destination ART | | 12 |
| | (T) B | IN & OUT FOCUS | | | 13 |
| | (F) | IN & OUT FOCUS | ◄ TAPE A-2 | SWITCH TAPE INPUT B to A ◄ SET VOLUME | 14 |
| | (T) A2 | MAPS ① | | CUE TAPE B-2 | 15 |
| INCENSE ▶ | | CATHEDRALS ① | | REEL 2 CHANGE TO OPTIC | 16 |
| | | CATHEDRALS ③ | | SOUND BOTH Switches | 17 |
| | | MUSIC ① | | | 18 |
| | (F) opt | MUSIC + LA LETTRE ① | ◄ TAPE B2 | ✖ PUT ON A3 Switch Tape Input A to B | 19 |
| | (T) B | CALIGRAPHY | | | 20 |
| | (F) opt | UPA SOUND | | Switch Tape Input B to A | 21 |
| | (L) G | NO. 4 ① | | ✳ MIKE up | 22 |
| | | NO. 5 ① | | | 23 |
| SANDLEWOOD / JAP. INCENSE ▶ | (T) A3 | EGYPT | ◄ TAPE (A3) | ✖ CUE TAPE B-3 | 24 |
| | (F) | STOP - GO | STOP for | ✖ ◄ CHANGE TO MAGN. BOTH SWITCHES | 25 |
| | (T) A3 | STOP - GO | | Tape A to B QUICK SWITCH | 26 |
| | (T) | NO. 6 ① | ◄ TAPE B3 | | 27 |
| BREAD SMELL ▶ | (T) | NO. 7 ① | | ✖ | 28 |
| | (T) B3 | BREAD | | | 29 |

*A Rough Sketch for a Sample Lesson for a Hypothetical Course* was a two-hour 'lecture performance' utilizing a range of audiovisual aids – a three-screen slide presentation, film, live narration, sound and music – to communicate effectively complex course material in a short period of time. The overload of ideas was intended to stimulate the student's imagination to a much larger degree than was possible with a single image. Synthetic smells, such as incense and bread, were pumped into the lecture theatre via the air-conditioning system to further heighten the multi-sensory effect.

Brochure for *A Communications Primer*, 1953
Photomechanical print on paper,
55.9 × 21.6 cm (22 × 8 ½ in.)
Eames Collections LLC

*A Communications Primer* grew out of work completed while developing *A Sample Lesson* and marked a turning point in the Eameses' film-making, as it was their first project to combine live footage, animation and still photography. It also signalled the start of their long-term collaboration with composer Elmer Bernstein. Conceived as an introduction to communication, the film begins with an analysis of Claude Shannon's schematic diagram of signal processing.[1] As with many Eames Office 'information' films, an array of beautiful visual examples are assembled to convey complex ideas in a meaningful and accessible way. Charles felt that the pioneering theories developed by such thinkers as Shannon, Norbert Wiener[2] and John von Neumann[3] were particularly resonant with the challenges faced by architects and planners, and could provide useful tools for the profession to model and evaluate information for effective decision-making.[4] The film was supported by the Rockefeller Foundation and introduced the Eameses' work to IBM, which used the film to familiarize their staff with Shannon's ideas.

a 16 mm film

## A COMMUNICATIONS PRIMER

in color and sound: running time 22 minutes

### MADE BY CHARLES AND RAY EAMES

WITH MUSIC ESPECIALLY COMPOSED BY ELMER BERNSTEIN

The intention of this film is to open some doors to the many and various aspects of the subject of communication which is becoming increasingly important to all of us.

The need for a broader concept of what communication means and how it operates has been simultaneously felt in many areas.

organization

regional planning   natural science

medicine   government   music   graphic arts

material programming   sociology   military research

painting   labor   merchandising   business   physical sciences

political science   production   economics   tooling

logistics   design   psychology   architecture

physiology   mechanics   philosophy

literature

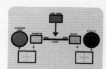

This need so commonly felt may lead to the first definite step in breaking down the barriers that have grown up between fields of learning.

## A COMMUNICATIONS PRIMER

does not pretend to teach the subject, but we hope that seeing it will help discourage ever thinking of communication in a limited way.

The requests for rental and purchase of

## A COMMUNICATIONS PRIMER

have come from a broad cross section of the areas indicated above—from the fields of

business, education, of science and of art.

## A COMMUNICATIONS PRIMER

16 mm: in color and sound: running time 22 minutes

LIFE-LEASE PURCHASE: from
CINE SERVICE
1350 WESTWOOD BOULEVARD
LOS ANGELES 24, CALIFORNIA

SALES PRICE including reel, can and vapor processing: **$200**

PREVIEW PRINTS are available to individuals or organizations interested in considering purchase. The only charge for such previews is for transportation.

RESTRICTIONS: life lease purchasers may not use this film for rental, commercial, theatrical or television purposes.

Inquiries for rental should be directed to the
MUSEUM OF MODERN ART, New York City, or the
UNIVERSITY OF CALIFORNIA, Los Angeles

## A COMMUNICATIONS PRIMER

WITH MUSIC ESPECIALLY COMPOSED BY ELMER BERNSTEIN

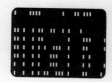

### MADE BY CHARLES AND RAY EAMES

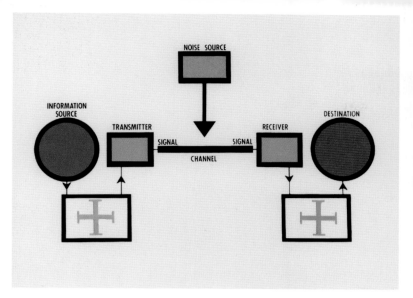

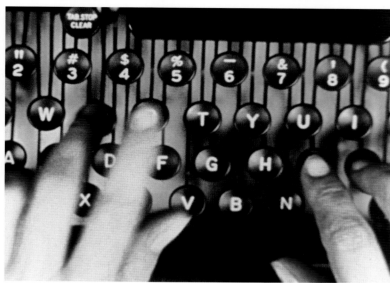

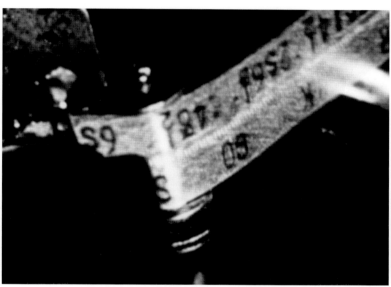

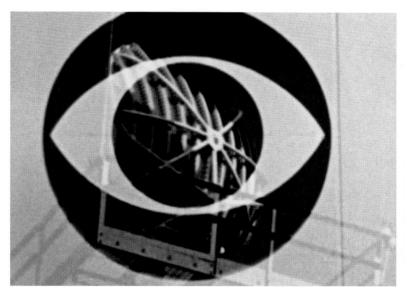

Images and stills from *A Communications Primer*, 1953
Film, 22:14 min.

*This page and page 241*

Charles Eames, 'Architecture
1 and 2', *Ark Annual* (University
of California, Berkeley, 1954)
Printed paper, 25.4 × 19 cm
(10 × 7 ½ in.)
The Papers of Charles and
Ray Eames, Manuscript
Division, Library of Congress,
Washington DC

In the early 1950s William
W. Wurster, the new dean of the
architecture department at the
University of California, Berkeley,
invited architects to rethink the
institution's curriculum. Charles
and Ray Eames were asked to
teach a design course for first-
year architecture students for
the academic year of 1953/4. In
response, they devised a series
of experimental monthly seminars
in which they showed such multi-
screen slideshows as *Railroad*,
*Townscape*, *Seascape* and *Road
Race* alongside excerpts from their
films, poetry and other readings,
in order to introduce key ideas that
they wanted to address with the
students. Lecture topics ranged
from 'visual and intellectual
awareness' and problem-solving
to 'the importance of associations';
the Eameses would then set their
125 students workshop problems
to tackle over the following month.[1]
As is illustrated here, the students
documented some of the outcomes
of the course in the School of
Architecture's *Ark Annual* (1954,
pp. 29–31), inviting Charles to
contribute his own short reflection.

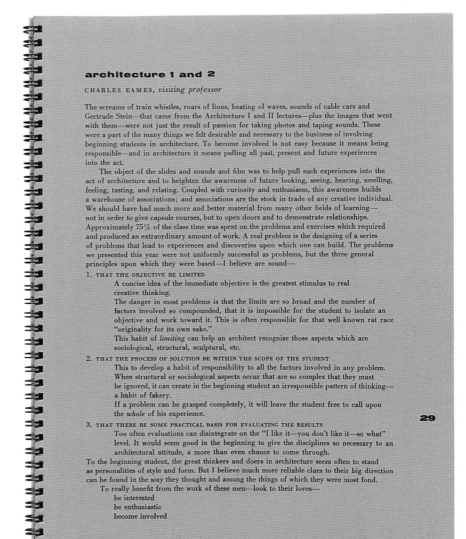

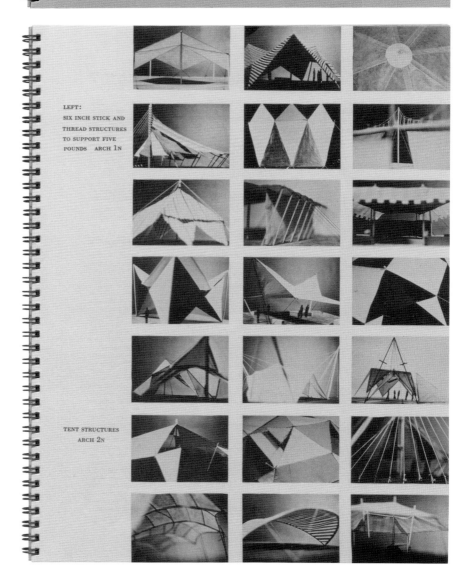

plying

dustrial methods

education

uld be

education

r industry:

# Art X =

rge Nelson

yone who has ever meddled with activities outside
own specialty knows that the amateur approach
tains two sets of possibilities: there is always the
nce that its fresh view of a problem may open un-
pected avenues of thought; there is also the likeli-
od of its leading the enthusiast up blind alleys long
ce explored and abandoned by the professionals.
e experience I am going to describe was initiated
amateurs in the field of education, and the ideas
ich developed from it may turn out to be valid—
they may not. I suspect that they are by no means
familiar to workers in the field. The reason for
senting the story to an audience concerned with
oblems of business and industry rather than educa-
n is in part the steadily growing evidence that the
rriers between these two areas are not as solid as
have led ourselves to believe; also because I have
me to believe that the industrial approach can play
ital role in helping education cope with the difficul-
s that currently beset it.

The experience that led to this conclusion began at
e University of Georgia. Early in the summer of
52 the phone rang and the caller identified himself
Lamar Dodd, head of the university's department
fine arts. His reason for calling was an invitation
fly down and give a lecture. I declined. It was June,
ere had been too much talking at schools the past
inter, and it was sure to be uncomfortably hot in
thens.

As things turned out, it was. Two days later the
ersistent Mr. Dodd was again on the phone. It seemed
at what they wanted wasn't really a lecture, but
nsultation with the faculty on some problems of
ucational policy. This was a ready-made opportunity
get out from under, and I quickly explained that
obody could possibly know less about educational
licy. "I know," drawled the voice at the other end
the wire. "That's why we want you."

## reground

eorgia's department of fine arts is a large one, and
ke similar departments at other universities its func-

tions are widely varied. The majority of the student
group consists of undergraduates taking art as a
major, not as a rule with any intention of making it a
career, but simply because they like it. Many of them
are girls who believe it will help them as future home-
makers, presumably by improving their taste in decoration. Each year a sizable group comes in from the
department of home economics, no doubt for the same
reason. A small percentage of the students, particularly those in textiles and ceramics, go on to establish
careers in these fields. But essentially the department
is one which turns out laymen interested in the arts
rather than professionals.

As a necessary part of the discussions I was to have
with the faculty, a tour through the various classes
was arranged. Everything I saw was familiar: courses
in theory, classes in drawing and painting, classes in
design, craft workshops for weaving, screen painting,
ceramics and so on. At this point several uneasy
thoughts came to mind. Here was a place functioning
exactly like any art school, but it was supposed to turn
out non-professionals. All art schools, obviously, turn
out one or the other, but what seemed a little odd was
the lack of visible differences between the two kinds
of instruction. To the outside observer, it seemed that
there was possibly a confusion in both methods and
objectives. Does it make sense for a girl whose main
ambition is to become a homemaker to pretend for
four years that she is aiming for a career in sculpture
or painting? Perhaps it does, but isn't the real problem to foster understanding and creative capacity so
that these qualities could be employed in any situation?
And if this were the real problem, how would a school
go about meeting it? Is intensive instruction in drawing and modeling the best way? Or is this method used
simply because it has always been the art school
method?

In the discussions which followed, these questions
were put to the faculty rather tentatively. The response was quick and intelligent. A feeling gradually
developed that it might be worth re-examining objectives and perhaps trying some experiments in educa-

# the Georgia experimen[t]

tional techniques—though at the time no one had any very clear idea of what the experiments might be. We decided to have another session in the fall and Lamar Dodd, who had guided the discussions with an extraordinary combination of firmness and sensitivity, suggested the formation of a small advisory committee. I asked him to invite Charles Eames.

## Battleground

At the beginning of the fall meeting we again went through the routine of visiting the various classes. Now that we had asked the basic questions, it was perfectly clear that much time was being wasted through methods originally developed for other purposes. For example, one class was finishing a two-week exercise demonstrating that a given color is not a fixed quantity to the eye but appears to change according to the colors around it. In a physics class such a point would have been made in about five minutes with a simple apparatus, and just as effectively.

We cited this example in an effort to establish a principle by which teaching effectiveness could be evaluated. We suggested that if a school knew fairly precisely what it wanted to communicate, a yardstick could be used for checking its methods. The yardstick was a clock. In other words, given the intention of communicating something specific, the shortest time taken to do this—*without loss of comprehension or retention*—represented the best method.

At this point storm warnings began to go up. Were we proposing to apply time-motion studies in the painting studio? Maybe, we retorted, such schools as this had no business teaching painting. The discussion became an argument, then a free-for-all.

From the faculty's point of view, there were good reasons for opposing mass educational techniques at a college level. For many of them college is the last stronghold of individualized instruction, where the student-teacher relationship is the vital core of education. Others, we realized, were exasperated by proposals which would mean new burdens on the school budget and their own scarce time. There exists in the

art professions, a strong feeling that their probl[em] are unique and that methods sanctioned by tradi[tion] need not be questioned too closely. All of this was [per]fectly understandable, for in education, standard[s of] performance are not under the same pressure a[s in] industry, and the price of inefficiency is not exa[cted] as swiftly or as ruthlessly.

That night Eames and I discussed the turmoil [cre]ated by what we had believed were innocuous pr[opo]sals. It was our feeling that the most important th[ing] to communicate to undergraduates was an awarene[ss] of relationships. Education, like the thinking of [the] man in the street, was sealed off into too many c[om]partments. If a girl wanted to know something ab[out] decorating her future home and what she got w[ith a] class in painting, this might make perfectly g[ood] sense, but perhaps it was up to the school to bui[ld a] bridge between the two so that she might see how t[hey] were related. Whether this was accomplished [by] personal or impersonal methods seemed of little [con]sequence.

## Preparation

It occurred to us that if the faculty was confused [and] uncertain about what we wanted, it might be bec[ause] we were too. The following day, in an atmospher[e of] interested cooperation, we proposed that we pre[pare] a specific example of our thinking in the form [of a] sample lesson for an imaginary course (the co[urse] was promptly labelled "Art X"). We asked, too, [that] Alexander Girard be invited as the third membe[r of] the committee during preparation of the lesson.

It was a relief to have our part in this explora[tion] now placed on a "put up or shut up" basis, but it [was] only after leaving Athens that we realized what [we] had let ourselves in for. The idea was to develop h[igh] speed techniques for exposing the relationships [be]tween seemingly unrelated phenomena. This me[ant] films, slides, sounds, music, narration—the fami[liar] world of audio-visual aids—and it soon became c[lear] that we were committed to a job which might ea[sily] demand the resources of a Hollywood production u[nit.]

There was also the problem of how the three "producers" were going to work together: Girard lived in Michigan, I worked in New York, and Eames, in California.

Problems are made to be solved. We solved ours by outlining the lesson and dividing it into "packages" which could be produced separately. Girard agreed to make a facsimile exhibit which was supposed to accompany each of the canned lectures. Eames and I divided the one-hour lesson between us. Slides were to be made as needed and movies were to be made or, if possible, borrowed. The subject of the lesson was "Communication," and if anyone should ask why we started with so impossibly difficult a theme I can only answer that at the time we did everything the hard way. We wanted a subject permitting the exploration of relationships and "Communication" offered plenty of opportunities. And there was the easily comprehended starting idea, that art was a kind of communication.

**Presentation**

Five months later the "Art X" company met in Athens, burdened with as much equipment as a traveling medicine show. There was a 16-mm. projector handling both film and magnetic sound. There were several tape recorders. There were three slide projectors, three screens which filled the end of the auditorium, cans of film, boxes of slides, reels of magnetic tape. Girard's exhibit arrived in a series of mammoth packing cases and he also brought a collection of bottles of synthetic smells, to be introduced into the room via the air conditioning system at various points in the show. Seventy-two hours later when we had staggered through the first creaky performance, we found that it took eight people to run it.

What had happened during the months of work was that our ideas had outstripped technical resources. As an example, while running off some slide sequences, it occurred to us that two slides run at once could illustrate certain contrasts. We liked the simultaneous projection so much that we tried three slides and found ourselves with a kind of poor-man's Cinerama on our hands. But to carry out this simple notion required three projectors, three screens and a magnetic tape playback.

The reason for the complexity was lack of money. Technical means for wide-screen projection already existed, but they were out of reach. Our dream had been to produce a one-hour lecture which could be transported in a few small cans; ultimately we decided that it was more important on the first try to explore as many possibilities as we could and to worry later, if the need should arise, about making the results portable.

What was the show about? The illustrated chart gives an idea of the subjects touched upon, but any audio-visual presentation that is more than a series of stills strung together cannot be described except in its own terms. Take, for instance, the small section which relates to the idea of "abstraction":

A slide goes on the screen, showing a still life by Picasso. A narrator's voice identifies it, adds that it is a type of painting known as "abstract," which is correct in the dictionary sense of the word, since the painter abstracted from the data in front of him only what he wanted and arranged it as he saw fit. The next slide shows a section of London. The dry voice identifies this as an abstraction too, since of all possible data about this area, only the street pattern was selected. Then follow other maps of the same area, but each presents different data—routes of subways, location of garages, etc. The voice observes that each time the information is changed, the picture changes. The camera closes in on the maps until only a few bright color patches show; the communication is now useless to the geographer, but there is something new in the residue of colors and shapes. Then a shift to a distant view of Notre Dame, followed by a series which takes you closer and closer. The narrator cites the cathedral as an abstraction—the result of a filtering-out process which has gone on for centuries. The single slide sequence becomes a triple-slide projection. Simultaneous exterior views change to interior views. Organ music crashes in as the narration stops. The interior becomes a close-up of a stained glass window. Incense drifts into the auditorium. The entire space dissolves into sound, space and color.

What I have tried to describe is a fragment which may have taken four minutes in its entirety. But even in this flash presentation a very complex communication was completed. The students were shown a modern painting to which they reacted with feelings ranging from hostility to exaggerated reverence. They were then forced to make a swift adjustment to the unexpected idea that maps and cathedrals were also kinds of abstractions, and finally introduced to a sample of medieval architecture in a way which tried to communicate atmosphere rather than fact.

To describe all this with anything approaching adequacy might take a competent lecturer an hour, and still the emotional impact would be lacking. The degree to which learning can be accelerated through audio-visual methods is perhaps its best known characteristic: what may be even more significant is the extraordinary force with which it can be used to relate idea and concepts. Its significance lies in the extreme delicacy and complexity of relationships which go to make up the modern world. The success of leadership, even in relatively small ventures, depends to an ever-increasing extent on comprehension of these relationships. Industry, in recent years, has shown an awareness of the problem by sending off more and more of its most talented young executives —not only to the business schools—but to the liberal arts departments of the universities. Superior performance as a specialist is no longer enough. And dependence on the traditional tools of communication is no longer enough either.

## Money

The first thing one learns about audio-visual techniques is that they are expensive, and our own experience with the "Art X" show quickly taught us that a course prepared in this way could add up to a fantastic total. The cost of film-making in a commercial studio (16 mm. color with sound) rarely averages out at less than $1,500 per minute—and a lecture takes fifty minutes. Even assuming every possible economy, a full course on almost any subject, prepared for wide distribution, could easily cost $1,000,000.

At first blush it may seem idiotic even to consider this kind of thing for institutions so chronically short of funds as schools, but the industrial designer has a somewhat different viewpoint than the professional educator. The sum of $1,000,000, for instance, is not large if it is the new tooling for a refrigerator which is being considered; $50,000,000 is a modest sum if the product is to be a new line of cars. To an educataor such comparisons might seem meaningless, since the two kinds of investment are totally different. But for us it brought up a question: are they so different? With the question came a new picture of education as a "handicraft" process in a society geared to other methods. With the picture, a hypothesis: many of the difficulties facing education today are related to the persistence of outmoded methods.

If, by some miracle in reverse, two men could make one automobile by hand in a year, the industry would require a working force of 10 to 12 millions. There would be a labor shortage, as there is in teaching today, and cars would be very expensive.

Two or three centuries ago in the European universities there existed a numerical ratio between faculty and students which may have been on the order of one to fifteen, or perhaps one to five. This could be described as a production ratio: it took $x$ faculty members to produce $y$ graduates. Today's ratios are: University of Illinois, five to six students per faculty member; Iowa, nine; Harvard, three or four; Michigan, sixteen. Now it is possible that education is one activity immune to the effects of the Industrial Revolution, and that nothing will ever change its production ratios. But I wonder.

Let us consider something else. There are listed the World Almanac some 1,000 colleges and univers ties. Let us assume that certain common denominat courses, such as physics, biology, art appreciatio etc., are taught in all of them. Let us also assume th in each institution an average of $1,500 is budget for the instructor's time and other costs. If th figure were accurate (it is probably low) you wou have a recurring annual bill of $1,500,000 for i structing the nation's undergraduates in, say, elemer ary biology. This is hardly low-cost production, industrial standards. Nor can it possibly be claim that the present "handicraft" method results in pi duction of a uniformly high level.

With what has already been said, the contrasti industrial approach to this problem needs no detail explanation. The big investment would be made on at the beginning. The most gifted teachers in t field would be retained, and they would be backed with all needed technical facilities. The result: series of "packages" available to students everywhe The cost per student: a fraction of what it is tod I cannot say that this procedure would solve the fina cial problems of the schools, but it seems reasonal to hope that it might relieve them. And much mc than money is involved.

## Time

One of the most irksome problems confronting t educator is the competition for the student's tin On the one hand are the pressures for a more high specialized education-training which covers mc ground more intensively than ever. (Consider wl a physicist has to learn today.) On the other is t insistence that everyone have a liberal dose of t liberal arts. Both pressures, moreover, will increa The demands of business, science and industry w become more exacting, not less. Public awareness the dangers of a society run by half-educated speci ists is also greater.

It is hard to see how, with present teaching met ods, the schools can hope to turn out the compete technician who is *also* a mature, educated individu A clear distinction between the two objectives, ho ever, might open the way to improved methods. Wh a school turns out a professional, his capacity perform is of crucial importance. To date, the be way to learn to do something is to *do* it, preferab under expert guidance. This is time-consuming, a there are few short-cuts. The procedures involved a general liberal education, however, are different. is not necessary for the student to be able to wr Latin poetry, remember the date of the battle Thermopylae or the name of the barroom where I

## A sample lesson: subject "COMMUNICATION"

Excerpts from a visual lesson prepared by Charles Eames and George Nelson from original and borrowed films and slides, presented at the University of Georgia and U.C.L.A.

### 1 Introduction

Opening film (10 minutes) makes one point: the completion of a communication requires not only a message and a transmitter, but a receiver capable of tuning in.

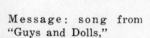

Message: song from "Guys and Dolls,"

constructed in the form of a fugue.

"Receivers" include student in American history (not used to thinking of Paul Revere as a horse).

bookie, who knows all about race horses, nothing about fugues,

specialist in oriental literature, who does not speak English.

Each can receive only a portion of the apparently simple message.

### 2 Visual Communication

Film dissolves in triple color slide sequences, simultaneously projected. The sequences (about 50) cover an extreme variety of visual communications: painting, artifacts, sculpture, equipment, landscape design, structures, type faces, etc.

Here again the intention is to show that comprehension of a message varies with the capacity of receiver. Music background, no narration. Running time, about 10 minutes. Both sections by Nelson.

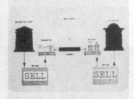

### 3 Communications Process

picks up the opening idea of the transmitter-message receiver relationship and develops it.

There is the example of a stockbroker's office, with transmissions of the simplest message: "Buy" or "Sell."

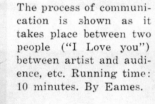

"Noise" is described as a factor in message distortion.

The process of communication is shown as it takes place between two people ("I Love you") between artist and audience, etc. Running time: 10 minutes. By Eames.

### 4 Abstraction

The point: The use of abstraction is necessary in communications, since it is rarely possible to send a *total* message. Examples: a Picasso still life, maps of a section of London ("change the information and you change the picture") and cathedrals in England and France.

Presentation of abstraction in communication changes from single slides (above) to simultaneous triple projections shown below. Smell effects (incense) accompanied slides of cathedral interiors. Detailed description is given in text. Slides, 35 mm color. Running time, 8 minutes. By Nelson.

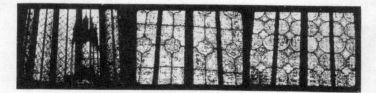

### 5 La Lettre

### 6 UPA

← *La Lettre*

Excerpts from a French film on the evolution of lettering and calligraphy. 16 mm black and white. 4 minutes.

→

## 7 Egypt

A 10-minute 16 mm film in color, taken from the magnificent footage shot by Ray Garner, generously made available for the lesson. Here a dead civilization is shown as a live transmitter. Its ruined architecture, sculpture, jewelry, hieroglyphics add up to a communication on a variety of levels. Again the success of the transmission depends on the ability of the receiver to decode the silent messages. Edited by Nelson.

← *UPA*

"The animated calligraphy of sound" — a 3-minute fragment taken from a 16 mm color film made by UPA for CBS. Edited by Eames.

→

*Communications Method*

An extension of the "Process" film, which penetrates still more deeply into the procedures used in communication. It shows, primarily, how the most complex of messages can be broken down into myriads of individual on-off, yes-no, stop-go decisions.

## 8 Communications Method

*Communications method (continued)*

Example of ways messages may be broken individual decisions: half-tone photograph of a face is made up of several hundred thousand black-or-white decisions.

An electronic computer presents as many possible decisions as the half-tone.

"The simplest human-act" — picking a flower — takes infinitely more stop-go decisions than the most complex computer or printing plate.

Mosaic and pointilliste paintings are examples of complex productions visibly based on great numbers of separate, decisive acts.

Note: Both the "Process" and "Method" films, by Eames, have been merged into a single 16 mm color films which runs about 20 minutes, entitled "A Communications Primer." The film is available for distribution.

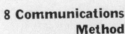

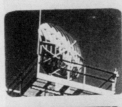

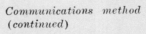

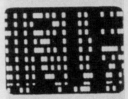

Marlowe got into his final brawl. The objective is to help him form a coherent picture of human activity, a capacity to understand its great achievements, an ability to form independent judgements, and above all, to learn to relate isolated bits of information in terms of a large context.

To meet the second of these objectives, the approach tried in the sample lesson offers rich possibilities. It can communicate with great force and tremendous speed; it can establish relationships in minutes which would take a classroom lecturer hours. If the "briefings" such a method makes possible were substituted for many current elective courses, whole sections of time would be freed, and the specialist student could be powerfully exposed, during his undergraduate years, to many important areas of human activity.

We are aware of the widespread feeling that canned education destroys the value of the personal contacts that schools and colleges make possible. People used to be suspicious of food out of cans. One cannot deny the inspirational value of direct contact with a great teacher but how many great teachers are there? And why shouldn't a great teacher, in addition to inspiring one small group of students, be passed on to students in other schools?

Interestingly enough, the audio-visual methods, so rich in educative potential have been confined largely, to date, to the teaching of trade skills and to conveying isolated bits of information. And the best of the experiments in education—as distinguished from training—have appeared in television.

## Results

If the result of work on the Art X lesson was to give us a new insight into some aspects of education, it does not follow that the result at the University of Georgia was the prompt allocation of a million dollars for the production of a course in art appreciation. What happened was far more constructive.

The Art X sample lesson was run through six times before the demands of students and faculty were satisfied. It produced both confusion and enlightenment, generated enthusiasm and hostility, and a rather depressed conviction that this kind of project was simply out of the grasp of a single school. Then one faculty member happened to remark, "Well, if we had about $25,000 for equipment. . ." and Eames and I both erupted in unrehearsed but perfect unanimity. We pointed out that nobody had given us $25,000, or fancy equipment, or a staff of technicians, and that we had offices to run while making Art X. It apparently made the point. The weekend following the showings, a number of faculty members descended upon one of the larger classrooms and began ripping out its insides with their own hands. That summer

they ripped down the barriers between courses wh had previously been rigidly separated. In the fall, students walked in on a new kind of learning exp ence, one which gave them drawing, modeling, pa ing, carving and automatically projected lectures a single integrated activity. Miraculously, two fac members have managed to turn out over thirty these presentations in one school year, and tho there are immense obstacles to overcome, I doubt v much that it will stop.

It is early to draw conclusions but two things quite clear: (1) given the determination, a school produce its own audio-visual material with limi resources. The results are far from technically peccable, but it doesn't matter; (2) creative use the industrial approach does not eliminate the teac —it upgrades him. It also gives an entirely new di tion to the curriculum.

## Prospects

The emergence of a valid new concept is like sudde turning on a light in a dark room. One no longer fe one's way from one separate object to another: room and its contents become visible as a unity. Art X lesson was innocently undertaken as a dev for the clarification of certain ideas about teaching ended up by illuminating some of the immense enri ment which could come about through application the industrial method to education. Its costs, by vance calculation, were prohibitive—so it goes ahe anyway. It presents all the dangers which stem fr centralized production and control—but in practice takes form at the grass roots level as an activity which any institution can participate. The speed communication is so great that the conventional cou can be compressed into a kind of briefing. This, turn, suggests one kind of answer to the educati needs of industry, and to the growing demand f general adult education. It relates automatically the emergence of non-commercial television. It su gests the merging, in a future not too far off, of t many current experiments in communication into new pattern of continuing education.

Art X said its piece in an industrial vernacular b cause industry has given us more and better ways say things than we had before. The pictures whi flickered across the multiple screens were made machines, developed by machines and projected machines. The voices, music and sounds were ele tronically recorded, amplified and played back. But was people who said the words, wrote the music, a made the final statement. This is why there is r need to be afraid of our tools—even in education. Th teacher may become less visible in the new classroo but he will still be there.

CARDBOARD TOWERS   ARCH 1n

LEFT: FORM SEQUENCE AND COLOR STUDIES   ARCH 1n

# Towards a Communication-Oriented Society: The Eameses' *India Report*

Anthony Acciavatti

'The change India is undergoing is a change in *kind* not a change of degree', declared Charles and Ray Eames in their 1958 report to the Government of India and the Ford Foundation. After touring India for three months to devise a programme of instruction for village and small-scale industries, they professed: 'The medium that is producing this change is communication; not some influence of the West on the East. The phenomena of communication is something that affects a world not a country.'[1] An unsurprising declaration, perhaps, by two California-based designers whose work treated everything, from films and furniture to toys and exhibitions, as technologies of communication and instruction. It was also a prophetic vision of communication not as a tool of domination, as the telegraph system and railways had been under British colonialism, but as a global agent of change.[2]

However, a simple change in kind this was not. Rather, in a rural nation of some 558,000 villages, the Eameses saw communication having a major impact on a region divided by myriad languages, rooted in a handicraft-based economy and isolated by centuries of colonial rule.[3] In such a heterogeneous country as India, with no common language, religion or sense of nationhood, the village served as a common, unifying social unit.[4] How best to change

village behaviour, in the home and on the street, was an unprecedented communications challenge. Yet it was here, within India's republic of villages, that the Eameses envisioned an evolving, self-conscious, modern nation geared towards altering behaviour patterns through retraining and technological literacy: a 'communication-oriented society', that post-war dream of a world held together by exchanges of information.[5] India was thus entering a larger, global conversation – the communication of information.

Labelled a report for 'professional design training in India', the *India Report* was at once heroic and practical, much like its authors. Its conclusions had more to do with India transitioning to a communication-oriented society, and institution building, than with vocational training. In order to bring about this transition, Charles and Ray Eames proposed the establishment of India's first design school. Amid a series of economic observations and pedagogical recommendations, which take the form of a treatise on nation building and design education, the Eameses imagined the school as a kind of communications hub or national broadcast centre. This broadcast centre would strive to make a case for an 'alert and impatient national conscience – a conscience concerned with the quality and ultimate values of the environment'. Exhibitions, printed material, photography, film, demonstrations – all modes of information exchange were to be combined with research, training and service to the government and industry so that the school would effectively 'communicate with itself and the nation'.[6]

Ultimately, the institutional and curricular recommendations of the *India Report* served as the blueprint for the establishment of the National Institute of Design (NID). Founded in 1961 in the industrial city of Ahmedabad, home to textile mills and Mahatma Gandhi's ashram, NID was the first institute of design in the so-called developing world. The 1950s was a decade of rapid institution-building in India, and the Eameses' report was just one of many institutional recommendations written by foreign technical experts and funded by the Ford Foundation.[7] Established within India's Ministry of Commerce and Industry – rather than the Ministry of Education or bureaus dealing with community development – NID was to be part of a larger effort to mobilize India's 'human and material resources through industrialisation'. And this was to be done on a scientific basis. As stated in the Government of India's *Scientific Policy Resolution* of 1958, 'The use of human material for industrialisation demands its education in science and training in technical skills ... India's enormous resources of manpower can only become an asset in the modern world when trained and educated.'[8] NID was expected to play as important a role in training a new cadre of experts as it was in helping to industrialize the rural masses and assist them in helping them help themselves.[9]

How did the Eameses come to be involved in crafting such an institution? And why did the Indian government and Ford Foundation believe that small industries would profit from the couple's design expertise? Answers to both these questions are at once biographical and geopolitical. The *India Report* allows us not only to explore the Eameses' work in communications and visual education, but also to understand why the couple's experiments in design education were crucial to India's economic and industrial future.

The *India Report* emerged from two unlikely sources: India's attempts to industrialize its small-scale and village industries in order to shore up its national economy, and the Eameses' innovative experiments in visual education and product design. First, on the matter of India's economy. In the mid-1950s, unable to produce either consumer or industrial goods in factories, the Indian government officially adopted a plan of industrial decentralization. Indian leaders looked to small industries, such as handicrafts, metalwork, weaving and leatherwork, to produce consumer goods. The thinking was straightforward enough: by encouraging 'labour-intensive small-scale and household industries to create as much employment as possible', the government would be free to release funds for such heavy industry as steel plants.[10] The Eameses were surely aware of this, for three years earlier Charles had been commissioned to make a film of the *Textiles and Ornamental Arts of India* exhibition at The Museum of Modern Art in New York. Opened in April 1955, the show was made to look like a bazaar or marketplace, while the film, in the words of the director of exhibitions and publications at the museum, Monroe Wheeler, was intended to 'enrich American esthetic experience' and act as a 'stimulus to the great crafts of India'.[11]

Yet with regards to stimulating the Indian economy, Wheeler's words and Charles's images were framed by larger geopolitical concerns: namely, the significant role that small-scale and village industries played in the history of the Cold War, a history now largely forgotten. As India embarked on an economic strategy that integrated national industrialization with rural development, the United States government and its cadre of wealthy philanthropic organizations competed for influence with another world power, the Soviet Union. Both saw India as a potential pawn in their very different endgames of domination: while the Americans saw India as a model Asian nation capable of following a different path from Stalin's planned industrialization in the USSR and Mao's Great Leap Forward in China, the Soviets saw India as a young neighbour with ambitions of establishing a socialist state.[12]

India's first prime minister, Jawaharlal Nehru, believed that the country's economic development depended on industrialization. Despite his involvement in establishing the Non-Aligned Movement, a group of mostly developing nations committed to siding neither with nor against the major powers of the Cold War, Nehru courted technical assistance from the Americans and the Soviets.[13] In 1955, while the Soviets were investing millions of dollars in the Bhilai Steel Plant in eastern India, the New York-based Ford Foundation provided a $1.3 million grant to aid the 'development of village and small-scale industries'. The grant was intended to address the 'scarcity of employment opportunities', an issue that had become 'the nation's major economic concern'.[14] As part of the grant, the Ford Foundation financed the purchase of equipment, the services of technical consultants and four new regional design centres across the country tasked with improving the quality of small-scale and village industries. As far as the Ford Foundation was concerned, the development of heavy industry would do little to combat the economic stagnation of rural India. In short, factories would lead to a more centralized economy, providing fewer jobs than a decentralized one based on village and small-scale industries. Furthermore, India's Industrial Policy Resolution of 1956, as well as its Second Five Year Plan (1956–61), favoured decentralization as the best way to ensure even economic development and minimize 'unplanned urbanization'.[15] India's 'revitalization' of village and small-scale industries represented a radical experiment in nation-building.

It is not an overstatement, therefore, to say that a new India was taking shape in the middle of the twentieth century, introducing, in the process, new complications of governance and finance; new encounters with technology, foreign experts and overseas markets; and new opportunities for production, distribution and consumption. Yet, how to go about implementing a system of training and education that would improve the quality and increase the output of goods produced by small-scale and village industries remained a challenge of staggering proportions.

In 1957, following Monroe Wheeler's recommendation that 'no effort should be spared in obtaining' the Eameses, the Ford Foundation hired the couple as technical experts for the training and modernization of small-scale industries in India.[16] The Ford Foundation had already enlisted economists, buyers from Macy's department store in New York and fashion designers to make

recommendations for improving the quality of India's consumer goods. The Eameses, however, were able to offer something that none of these foundation-financed advisers could: pedagogical expertise.

The *India Report* was not the Eameses' first attempt at design education. By the mid-1950s Charles and Ray were recognized as having made 'a significant contribution to visual education techniques'.[17] This was due in large part to the success of their film *A Communications Primer* (1953). As a visual exploration of Claude Shannon and Norbert Wiener's theories of message transmission,[18] the film developed out of the Eameses' earlier experiments with the designers George Nelson and Alexander Girard to retool a 'handicrafts'-based art education at the University of Georgia.[19] As the academic and writer Fred Turner has pointed out, the Eameses, both in the film and at the university, envisioned audiences as 'information processors' in a world where 'information systems ranging from computers to societies were held together by individuals in interaction with each other'.[20] The *India Report* drew from these notions of interaction and human processing, but also framed these as aspirational pedagogical virtues on which the proposed design school ought to be evaluated.

Part I of the *India Report* recognized that the largest issues facing India had to do with 'problems of environment and shelter'.[21] Always looking to combine economic concepts with design objectives, the Eameses emphasized the role design should play in defining the elements of a 'standard of living', as opposed to industrial standardization.[22] Moreover, they believed that such living standards should be qualities important to Indians in terms of services and everyday objects. In an effort to make this work culturally as well as functionally useful, they recommended starting at the scale of the village so as 'to explore the evolving symbols of India'.[23]

*Pages 242–3*

India, 1958

Charles and Ray Eames with painter and cultural anthropologist Haku Shah and family in India, *c.*1965

*Above*

Ray Eames in India, 1958

*Opposite*

Indira Gandhi and Ray Eames at the National Institute of Design, Ahmedabad, during the production of *Jawaharlal Nehru: His Life and His India*, 1965

Installation view of *Nehru*, 1965

Sample Lessons

Of all the objects the Eameses encountered in India, none symbolized the evolution of Indian design more than the lota, a round water pot typically made of polished brass. Throughout their trip, Charles photographed the lota obsessively. In their report, they lauded 'its sculpture as it fits the palm of the hand, the curve of the hip', and asked, 'How does it feel to possess it, to sell it, to give it?'[24] But what most impressed them was that 'no one man designed the lota but many men over many generations'.[25] Given that the Eameses were credited with coupling 'vernacular materials and industrial processes' to create 'new generic forms' in their own work,[26] it should come as no surprise to learn that they celebrated the pot's collective familiarity and authorship.

Beyond being a celebration of anonymity, the lota provided an object lesson in designing something for reasons other than beauty or leisure: it was designed not to be looked at, but rather to work well. Most importantly, the lota embodied a sensibility – what we might call a form of knowledge – that was not communicated through writing or speaking. This form of non-verbal or tacit knowledge was crafted by many hands, was perfected across generations, and achieved an aesthetic that was not self-conscious. For the Eameses, the lota communicated without speaking.[27]

To their Indian hosts, however, the lota communicated something quite different, for it is also customarily used to cleanse oneself after defecating. Did Indians scrunch their noses at the valorization of the lota? Did its hygienic function elude the American couple, as some have fairly suggested?[28] We might wish to speculate that the Eameses' believed that tacit knowledge could be best conveyed by means of an object with which everyone had some intimate experience. What we can say, however, is that the lota communicated to the Eameses a special kind of concurrence that embodied their own consolidation of artistic and generic, design and function. What they hoped a new generation of designers would take from the lota is the idea that beauty could emerge from the designer's hands-on approach to design.

Part II of the *India Report* outlined a curriculum dedicated to just such an approach, covering everything from the disciplinary backgrounds of the students and teachers to the design of the physical plant (building) and four hypothetical lessons. Each of these lessons, from designing a 'package of services and effects which will be the most essential to salvage from a city about to be destroyed' (a lesson borrowed from the American architect and inventor Buckminster Fuller) to the design of a parade, festival or other kind of temporary event, demanded a mixture of artistic and generic form. In this regard, the lota was a mythopoeic object lesson in how to go about crafting a modern Indian institute of design. It follows, therefore, that the Eameses advised that India's new institute of design should 'hasten the production of the "lotas" of our time. It is not a self-conscious effort to develop an esthetic', they insisted. 'It is a relentless search for quality that must be maintained if this new republic is to survive.'[29]

Yet the survival of the republic was a heavy burden to place on the shoulders of whoever was chosen to lead the new institute. Two people in particular were capable of integrating such practical and philosophical questions of design education in India: Gautam and Gira Sarabhai, two of the eight children of the leading industrialist and textile-mill owner Ambalal Sarabhai. Both Gautam and Gira had an abiding interest in industrial design and handicrafts, no doubt shaped by their unique upbringing. In common with all of Ambalal's children, they had been home-schooled using the Montessori method. Gautam eventually graduated from the University of Cambridge with degrees in mathematics and philosophy before he and Gira studied with the American architect Frank Lloyd Wright at Taliesin East, Wright's home and estate in Wisconsin, in the 1940s.[30] Shortly thereafter, the brother-and-sister team established the Calico Museum of Textiles in their hometown of Ahmedabad in 1949. This 'wonderhouse', as it was known, exhibited both handmade and mass-produced textiles from the family's personal collection. Credited with launching 'Ahmedabad's renaissance in independent India',[31] the museum was the first post-independence institution devoted to the 'interdependence of design and technology'. Fundamentally concerned with shortcomings in art education, the museum was intended to inform producers and consumers about ways in which to 'integrate function and materials'.[32]

In 1961 Gautam was appointed chairman of the governing council of NID, while Gira was eventually appointed chairwoman of its board of directors. The 1960s were formative years for NID. Before moving into the 'physical plant' that Gira and Gautam were designing to house the institute, NID spent most of the decade on the mezzanine floor of Sanskar Kendra, the then unfinished city museum of Ahmedabad designed by Le Corbusier in 1951. There, in 1962, Gira and Gautam began the task of staffing NID, beginning with just two designers: Dashrath Patel and, later, H. Kumar Vyas.[33] With these two foreign-educated designers, and a growing number of foreign consultants from Europe and the United States, NID began the process of identifying and training future faculty members to instruct students in postgraduate studies.

Founding a design institute in a country with no history of establishing such bodies was no easy task. Throughout their tenure at NID, Gautam and Gira struggled with their pedagogical

programme. In addition to drawing on their background in the Montessori method and time at Taliesin, they came to rely on foreign expertise and institutions to frame the pedagogy of the institute. As the writer Alexander Keefe has noted, with Ford Foundation dollars and the Sarabhais' international connections, Ahmedabad in the 1960s 'became a kind of outpost of the New York downtown scene'.[34] With funding from the Rockefeller Foundation, such figures of the arts as John Cage, David Tudor, George Nakashima and Yvonne Rainer visited the institute to lead short workshops. At the same time, the Sarabhais established ties with the newly founded Hochschule für Gestaltung (HfG) in Ulm, West Germany.[35]

Instead of becoming a broadcast centre from which to communicate with the nation's villages, NID adopted a curriculum that mirrored the HfG's method of instruction.[36] Likewise, the student projects published in NID's first catalogue in 1969 resembled work produced by European and North American schools of design.[37] In his unsolicited report sent to the Eameses in 1970, J. S. Sandhu, a designer and professor at the Royal College of Art in London, harshly criticized NID. He contended not only that the institute was producing knock-offs of Western designs, but also that it had nothing to do with the focus of Charles and Ray's *India Report*: aiding village industries and communication. 'A Bauhaus or [HfG] or Charles Eames Associates can only flourish in a particular place and period, and are often the result of the general development of the country rather than the cause', noted Sandhu. 'Injudicious and ill-considered borrowing of such organizations', he continued, 'will not help development but will more likely hinder it.'[38] What most displeased Sandhu was the lack of empirical investigation into the most pressing physical and social factors affecting India. All of this led Sandhu to conclude that NID was unable to communicate in any meaningful way with India's rural masses.[39]

Although there were some successes at NID in the 1960s, such as its collaboration with the Eames Office on the design of the exhibition *Jawaharlal Nehru: His Life and His India*, which opened at the Union Carbide Building in New York in 1965, the majority of the institute's work fell short of the expectations of government officials and the Ford Foundation alike. It did not look, in the words of Ford Foundation representative Douglas Ensminger, as though NID was 'evolving as an indigenous Indian institution'.[40] Given that the Ford Foundation had financed two American designers to write the report that had given rise to the institute and two European designers to produce a follow-up report,[41] not to mention the foundation's $1.1 million in grants to NID in its first ten years, Ensminger's comments can be seen as rather ironic.[42] In 1969 the Ford Foundation re-hired the Eameses to evaluate whether or not NID had lived up to the ideals of the *India Report*. While the Eameses were supportive of Gira and Gautam, Charles, in private correspondence with officials in New Delhi, eventually shared his concern 'that so few simple-homely-down-to-earth-Indian design problems were attacked' at the institute.[43] In October 1970, in an effort to stymie criticism and improve relations with New Delhi and the Ford Foundation, Gautam and Gira hired Vice Admiral A. B. Soman (retired) as the institute's administrative director.[44]

Perhaps as a consequence of Sandhu's report, and awaiting the results of the national elections in India, the Eameses did not submit their new report to the Ford Foundation until May 1971. Just one page long, the report began:

The institute and our feelings about it have been much in our thoughts – we look on it rather as our grandchild … More than ever, it would seem terribly important that the Ford Foundation share the responsibility with the Indian government for this national institution – to guard its autonomy and guide its direction, – to make it function at the highest possible level for the good of the country as a whole as well as the students, as a working model for future institutions, – all that we hoped for when the first report was put together.[45]

Due in large measure to the Eameses' tepid report, the Ford Foundation chose to terminate all funding to NID in 1971.[46] Meanwhile, circumstances at the institute only worsened.[47] In July 1972, after spending less than two years at NID, Vice Admiral Soman had his contract terminated by the Sarabhais and the institute's board of directors.[48]

Soman's dismissal provoked a scandal. The vice admiral chose to denounce the Sarabhais publicly, accusing them of nepotism and of lining their own pockets from research undertaken at the institute. Opposition parties to Indira Gandhi's government seized on the scandal, using it to criticize her policies and appointments. A committee, led by the journalist Romesh Thaper, was appointed in 1973 to investigate. The Sarabhais were ultimately absolved of all wrongdoing; however, both Gautam and Gira decided to leave the institute in 1974 and devote themselves to their family businesses and the Calico Museum. NID remained open, and significant reforms ensued. One of the first major changes was to the status of the institution. By the mid-1970s, NID was at long last able to award diplomas to its graduates. Over time, it became a recognizably more conventional school of design, with a list of alumni that included some of India's most celebrated designers.

In spite of the Eameses' desire to create a trans-disciplinary educational environment, as expressed in the *India Report*, NID suffered a fundamental structural problem: how to bridge institutionally the gap between industrial design and small-scale industries, how to set new standards. The difficulty of establishing such a techno-scientific project of collectivization goes without saying; expecting a single institution to fulfil this role for a newly independent nation approached absurdity.

While NID's attempts to link industry with small-scale and village enterprises did not survive beyond the pages of the *India Report*, the space that was thereby created for a 'communication-oriented society' did not disappear. It was but a single iteration of a larger economic project to integrate national industrialization with rural development. The limits of design pedagogy were observed, but the belief in the power of design to assist in India's nation-building programmes did not suffer. As Romesh Thaper noted in his report on NID, published in 1974, design 'enhance[s] communication … It is not a luxury or cosmetic addition, nor is it "art". It is our environment.'[49] Although Thaper and his committee echoed the tenets of the *India Report*, they recommended that the institute focus on increasing the number of qualified designers it produced, as opposed to hastening the production of 'new lotas of our time'.

By the mid-1970s the lota was rendered, to all intents and purposes, uncommunicative.

*something about*

**TRANSFORMATIONS and REDISCOVERY**

Stills from *Banana Leaf: Something about Transformations and Rediscovery*, 1972
Film, 2:29 min., unfinished

This film was originally intended as one of the IBM *Mathematica* 'Peep Shows' to explain the concept of relative values. It explores the cyclical role of the banana leaf in Indian culture, revealing its use as a tool for eating by both extremes of society, from the very poor to the very wealthy. Charles often used this parable in his lectures to elucidate his ideas on continuity and process.

The influential films known as *Powers of Ten* – about 'the relative size of things in the universe', linking microcosm to macrocosm – were inspired by *Cosmic View: The Universe in 40 Jumps* (1957), a book by the Dutch educator Kees Boeke. In 1963 the Eameses filmed *Cosmic View*'s illustrated panels[1] and made a short technical test of camera acceleration;[2] by 1968 they had realized their first full translation of Boeke's journey into and out of space: a 'sketch' film worked out in the making and produced on a small budget for the annual meeting of the Commission on College Physics. A small team worked with Charles and Ray on the production, including Parke Meek, Ted Orlan, Antti Paatero, Dick Donges and Judith Bronowski, who also provided the narration. In 1977 the film was updated to reflect advances in research; two powers were added to each end of the journey and the site of focus was moved from a Florida golf course to a park near Lake Michigan in Chicago.

*This page*

Ray Eames outside 901 dressing the picnic set for *A Rough Sketch for a Proposed Film Dealing with the Powers of Ten and the Relative Size of Things in the Universe*, 1968

Production of *A Rough Sketch*, 1968. From left: Ray Eames, Charles Eames (in crane), Judith Bronowski, Parke Meek and Dick Donges

*Opposite, clockwise from top left*

Production of *Powers of Ten: A Film Dealing with the Relative Size of Things in the Universe, and the Effect of Adding Another Zero*, 1977

Charles Eames photographing Paul Brühwiler's hand for *A Rough Sketch*, 1968

Eames Office staff member photographing globe for a production panel for *Powers of Ten*, 1977

Eames Office staff member working on production panel for *Powers of Ten*, 1977

Production of *Powers of Ten*, 1977

Sample Lessons

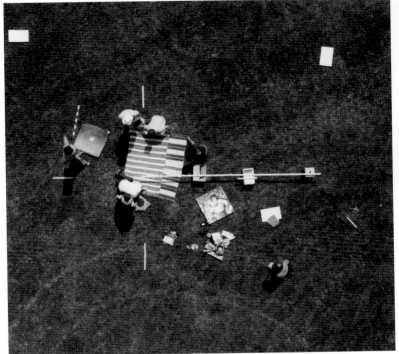

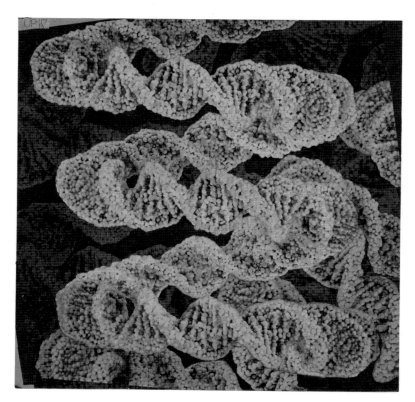

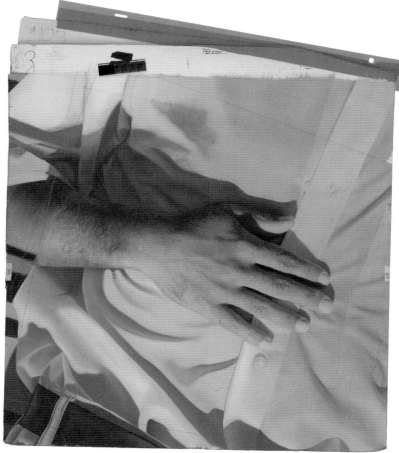

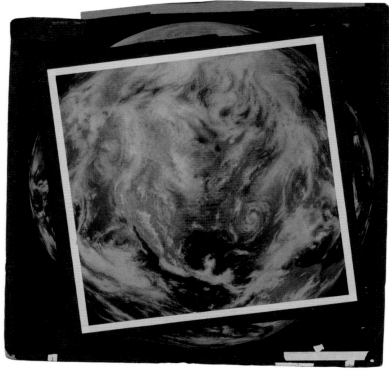

Production panels for *Powers of Ten: A Film Dealing with the Relative Size of Things in the Universe, and the Effect of Adding Another Zero*, 1977

The Work of Charles and Ray Eames, Prints & Photographs Division, Library of Congress, Washington DC

*Clockwise from top left*

Mixed media on Masonite, 92 × 92 cm (36 ¼ × 36 ¼ in.)

Mixed media on foamcore with metal bar, 110 × 102 cm (43 ¼ × 40 ⅛ in.)

Mixed media on foamcore with taped photo overlay, 102 × 97 cm (40 ⅛ × 38 ¼ in.)

Mixed media on foamcore with taped photo overlay, 107 × 107 cm (42 ⅛ × 42 ⅛ in.)

Mixed media on foamcore with metal bar, 105 × 93 cm (41 ⅜ × 36 ⅝ in.)

Sample Lessons

The 1977 version of *Powers of Ten* was a much larger endeavour. The project was led by Alex Funke, who joined the Eames Office shortly after the completion of the 1968 film. The opening picnic sequence is live action, but the camera then zooms out from shots of such production panels as those seen here, which were meticulously prepared for filming from a selection of photographic sources. Funke, assisted by Michael Weiner, shot the panels precisely, frame by frame, to produce the animated motion seen in the final film. Funke and Weiner kept an exposure log, which after a year of filming numbered some fourteen thousand frames.[1]

Final artwork from *Powers of Ten: A Film Dealing with the Relative Size of Things in the Universe, and the Effect of Adding Another Zero*, 1977 Film, 9 min.

The 1977 version of *Powers of Ten* is arguably the most widely viewed and influential Eames Office production and a much-cherished teaching tool. The Eameses were actively engaged with science research and education, and collaborated on the film with their long-term friends the scientist Philip

Morrison and his wife, Phylis, an education specialist. As well as advising on the film, Morrison narrates this version. The couple subsequently worked with Ray and the Office on the *Powers of Ten* publication, which included these images of the film's 42 powers.

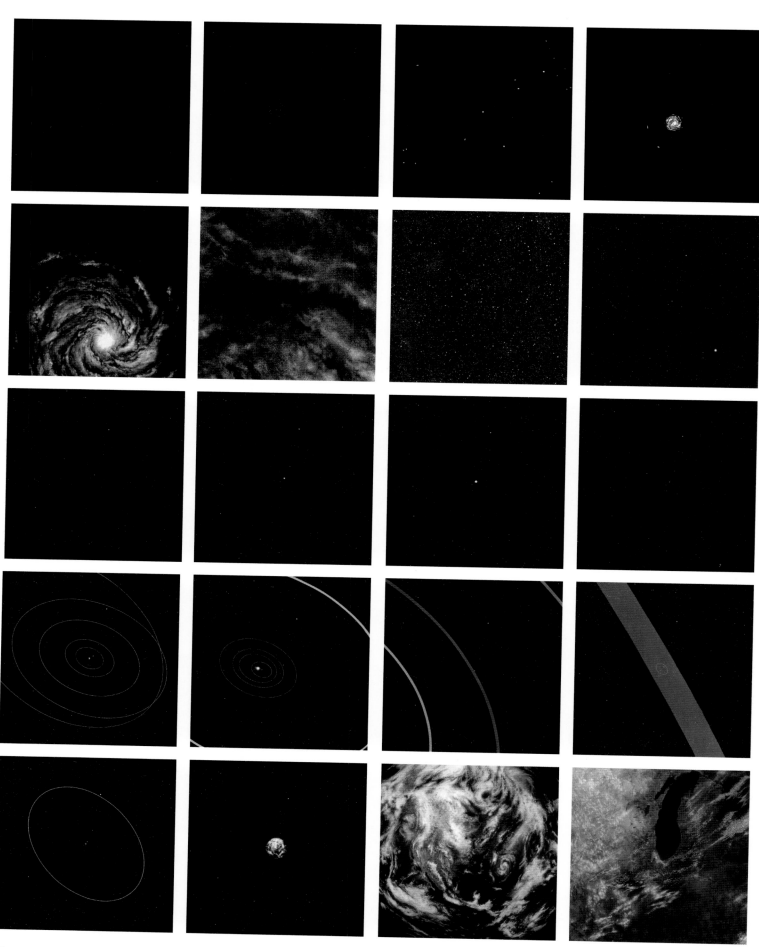

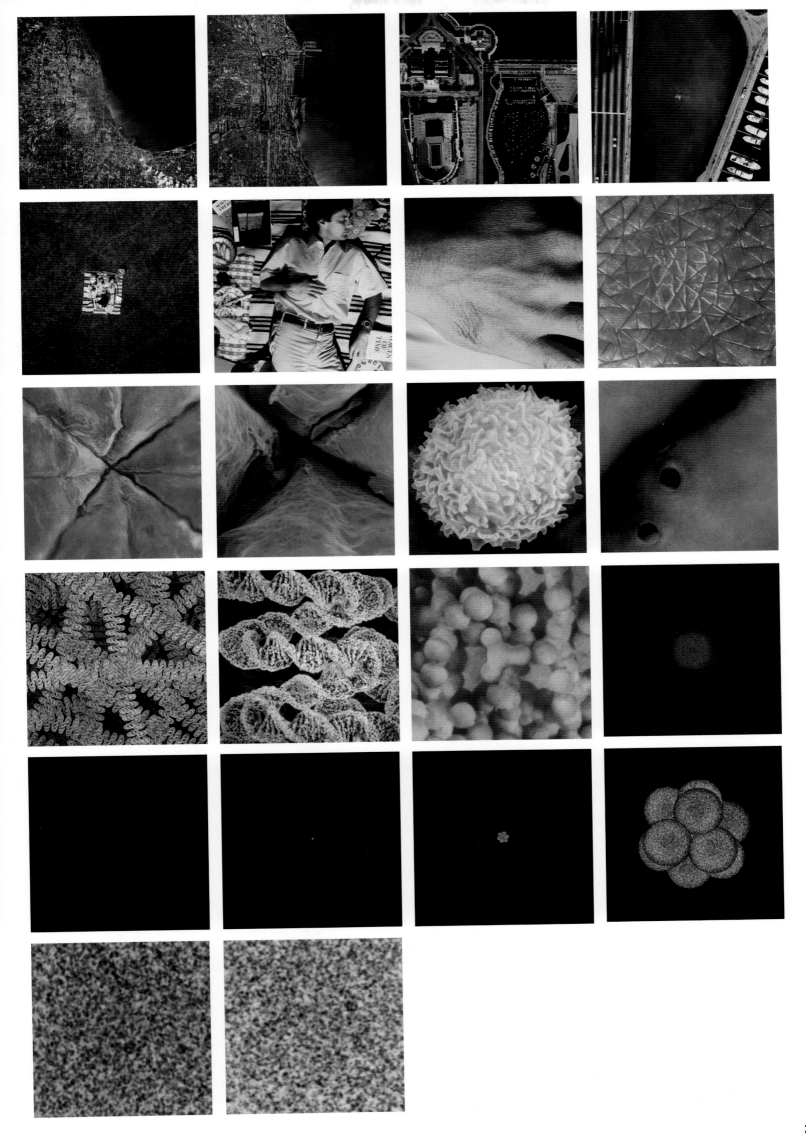

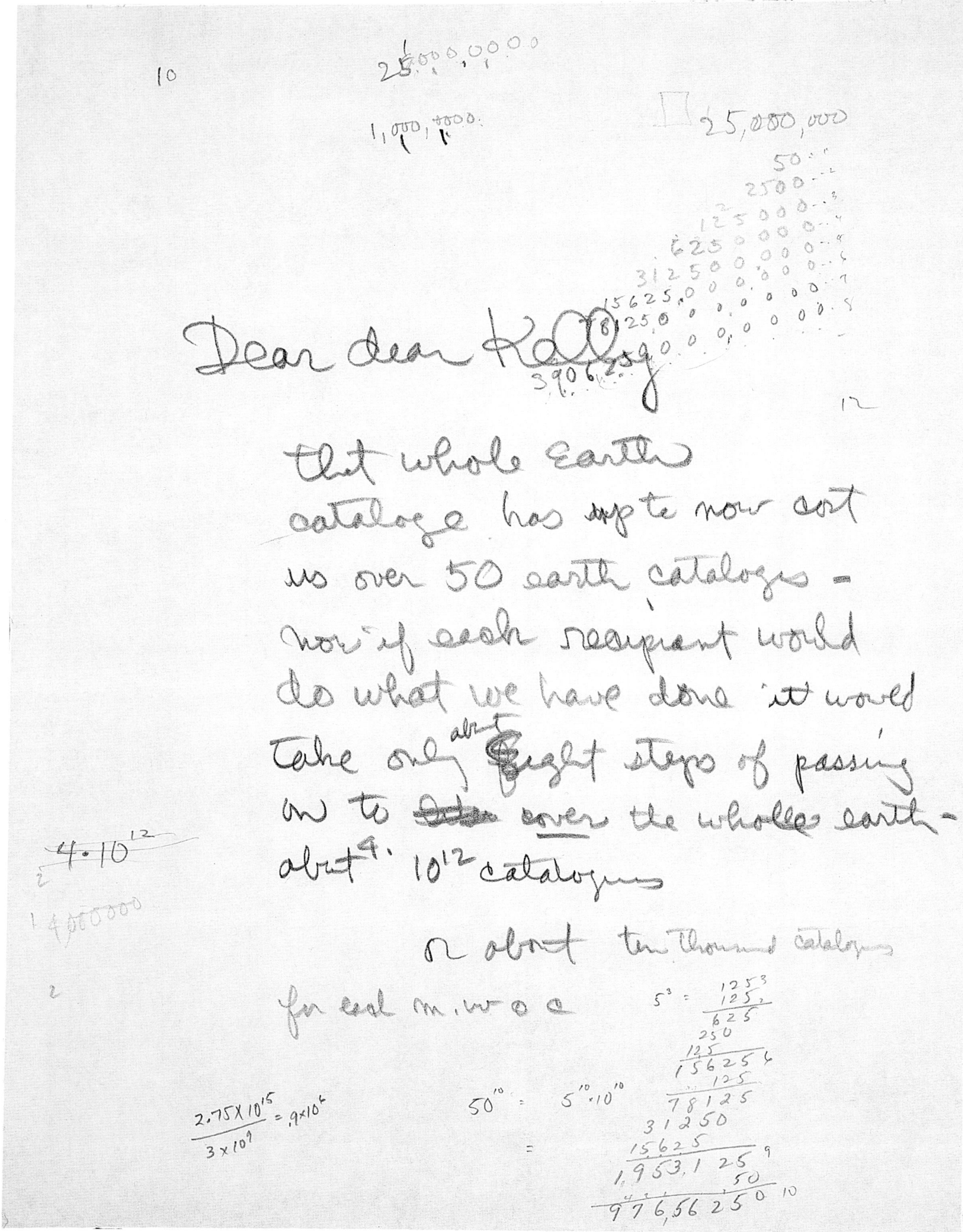

10

25,000,0000

1,000,000

25,000,000

50
2500
125000
625000
3125000
15625,0000
3906,250,000

12

$\frac{4 \cdot 10^{12}}{2}$

1,000000

2

Dear dear Kellogg

that whole Earth
catalog e has up te now cost
us over 50 earth catalogs —
now if each recipient would
do what we have done it would
take only about eight steps of passing
on to cover the whole earth —
about 4 · $10^{12}$ catalogues

or about ten thousand catalogs
for each m. w o e

$\frac{2.75 \times 10^{15}}{3 \times 10^9} = .9 \times 10^6$

$5^3 =$ 1253
125
625
250
125
15625
125
$50^{10} = 5^{10} \cdot 10^{10}$
78125
31250
15625
$=$ 1,953,125
50
976,56 250

The *Whole Earth Catalog*, a rich compendium of information providing 'access to tools' for the countercultural community and innovators in the fields of design and technology, was as important to Charles and Ray Eames as the Sears catalogue had been nearly three decades earlier. *Whole Earth* first appeared in the autumn of 1968 and featured on its inaugural cover the first full-colour photograph of the earth, taken on the Apollo space missions and released by NASA earlier that year. On 27 October 1969, Charles drafted a letter to Sister Helen Kelley, president of the Immaculate Heart College in Los Angeles from 1963 to 1977, stating his desire for others to share the catalogue just as they had done at the Eames Office. The final transcript reads:

Dear, dear Sister Kelley:
That Whole Earth Catalog has, up to now, cost us over 50 Earth Catalogs – now if each recipient would do what we have done, it would take only about nine steps of passing on to <u>cover</u> the whole earth ($5.5 \times 10^{15}$ square feet).

About $3 \times 10^{15}$ catalogs,
Or
About one million catalogs for each man, woman and child.

Charles Eames

*Handwritten calculations:*

LAND — LAND + WATER

$$\text{AREA IN SQ. MILES} \quad 59 \times 10^6 \quad 197 \times 10^6$$
$$\times (5.3 \times 10^3)^2 \text{ SQ. FEET} \Big\} \quad 1.65 \times 10^{15} \quad 5.5 \times 10^{15}$$
$$= 28 \times 10^6 = \text{SQ FEET}$$

POPULATION $3 \times 10^9$

$$\text{SQ.FT/PEOPLE} = \frac{5.5 \times 10^{15}}{3 \times 10^9} = 1.8 \times 10^6 = 1,800,000$$

AREA OR CATALOG ≈ 2 SQ.FT.
CATALOGS/PEOPLE = 900,000
CATALOGS/WHOLE EARTH = $2.75 \times 10^{15}$
$50^9 ≈ 2 \times 10^{15}$

---

*Scanned almanac page:*

452 — Information Please Almanac — World Geography and Miscellaneous

**Population, Land Areas of the World, and World Elevations**

| Area | Estimated population, in thousands, 1963 | Approximate area, in thousands of sq. mi. | Per cent of total land area | Population density per sq. mi. | Elevation, feet Highest | Elevation, feet Lowest | Dimensions, miles East-West | Dimensions, miles North-South |
|---|---|---|---|---|---|---|---|---|
| WORLD | 3,160,000 | 58,417 | 100.0 | 60.3 | Mt. Everest, Asia, 29,028 | Dead Sea, Asia, 1,290 below sea level | 24,902 | 24,860 |
| ASIA, incl. Philippines, Indonesia, and European and Asiatic Turkey; excl. Asiatic U.S.S.R. | 1,748,000 | 10,665 | 18.3 | 163.9 | Mt. Everest, Tibet-Nepal, 29,028 | Dead Sea, Israel-Jordan, 1,290 below sea level | 5,400 | 5,300 |
| AFRICA | 294,000 | 11,671 | 19.9 | 25.1 | Mt. Kilimanjaro, Tanzania, 19,340 | Qattara Depression, Egypt, 440 below sea level | 4,600 | 5,000 |
| NORTH AMERICA, including Hawaii, Central America, and Caribbean region | 281,000 | 9,365 | 16.0 | 30.0 | Mt. McKinley, Alaska, 20,320 | Death Valley, Calif., 282 below sea level | 3,200 | 4,000 |
| SOUTH AMERICA | 158,000 | 6,870 | 11.8 | 23.0 | Mt. Aconcagua, Arg-Chile, 22,834 | Sea level | 3,200 | 4,600 |
| ANTARCTICA | Uninhabited | 6,000 | 10.3 | ... | Fridtjof Nansen, 15,781 | Sea level | ... | ... |
| EUROPE, incl. Iceland; excl. European U.S.S.R. and European Turkey | 437,000 | 1,903 | 3.3 | 229.6 | Mt. Blanc, France, 15,781 | Sea level | 3,300 | 2,400 |
| OCEANIA, incl. Australia, New Zealand, Melanesia, Micronesia, and Polynesia | 17,000 | 3,294 | 5.8 | 5.2 | Mauna Kea, Hawaii, 13,796 | Lake Eyre, Australia, 38 below sea level | ... | ... |
| U.S.S.R., both European and Asiatic | 225,000 | 8,649 | 14.8 | 26.0 | Mt. Elbrus, 18,481 | Caspian Sea, 96 below sea level | 5,000 | 2,500 |

**High Population Densities (per square mile)**

| | |
|---|---|
| Singapore | 7,028.5 |
| Malta | 2,665.5 |
| Netherlands | 981.9 |
| Belgium | 819.1 |

| | |
|---|---|
| Japan | 682.1 |
| Germany (West) | 608.8 |
| United Kingdom | 577.4 |

| | |
|---|---|
| Trinidad and Tobago | 478.3 |
| Italy | 438.1 |
| Haiti | 424.7 |

---

*(Right column, almanac)*

**World Ext...**

Highest recorded shade temperature:
World: 136.4° F. at Azizia, Libya, North...
United States: 134° F. at Death Va...
Lowest recorded temperature:
World: −126.9° F. at Vostok, near sou...
In Siberia, −89.9° F. at Oimekon,* F... February 5 and 7, 1892.
United States: −69.7° F. at Rogers Pass...

**Universities—Me...**

Universities, in the modern sense of the term, sprang up in the 12th and 13th centuries in response to the resurgence of learning that preceded the Renaissance in Europe...

---

*Opposite and above*

Initial calculations by Charles Eames for his letter to Sister Helen Kelley, 1969

Pencil on paper, 27.9 × 21.3 cm (11 × 8 ⅜ in.)

Photomechanical print and pencil on paper, 27.9 × 21.6 cm (11 × 8 ½ in.)

The Papers of Charles and Ray Eames, Manuscript Division, Library of Congress, Washington DC

*Right*
*Whole Earth Catalog*, Fall 1968

Page 257

Frames from *Tanks*
3-screen slideshow consisting of images of the marine animals kept in tanks set up at 901 during work on the National Aquarium project, 1966–9

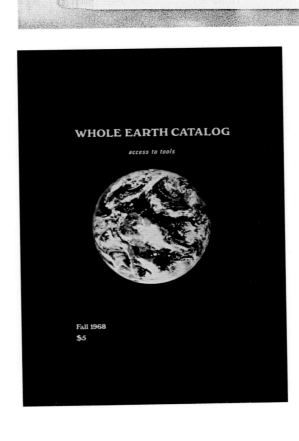

WHOLE EARTH CATALOG

*access to tools*

Fall 1968
$5

## 'What is Design?'
## Madame L. Amic and Charles Eames
## From the film *Design Q&A*, 1972

Madame L. Amic: What is your definition of design, Monsieur Eames?

Charles Eames: One could describe design as a plan for arranging elements to accomplish a particular purpose.

Is design an expression of art?

I would rather say it's an expression of purpose. It may, if it is good enough, later be judged as art.

Is design a craft for industrial purposes?

No, but design may be a solution to some industrial problems.

What are the boundaries of design?

What are the boundaries of problems?

Is design a discipline that concerns itself with only one part of the environment?

No.

Is it a method of general expression?

No. It is a method of action.

Is design a creation of an individual?

No, because to be realistic, one must always recognize the influence of those that have gone before.

Is design a creation of a group?

Very often.

Is there a design ethic?

There are always design constraints, and these often imply an ethic.

Does design imply the idea of products that are necessarily useful?

Yes, even though the use might be very subtle.

Is it able to cooperate in the creation of works reserved solely for pleasure?

Who would say that pleasure is not useful?

Ought form to derive from the analysis of function?

The great risk here is that the analysis may be incomplete.

Can the computer substitute for the designer?

Probably, in some special cases, but usually the computer is an aid to the designer.

Does design imply industrial manufacture?

Not necessarily.

Is design used to modify an old object through new techniques?

This is one kind of design problem.

Is design used to fit up an existing model so that it is more attractive?

One doesn't usually think of design in this way.

Is design an element of industrial policy?

If design constraints imply an ethic, and if industrial policy includes ethical principles, then yes – design is an element in industrial policy.

Does the creation of design admit constraint?

Design depends largely on constraints.

What constraints?

The sum of all constraints. Here is one of the few effective keys to the design problem: the ability of the designer to recognize as many of the constraints as possible; his willingness and enthusiasm for working within these constraints. Constraints of price, of size, of strength, of balance, of surface, of time and so forth. Each problem has its own peculiar list.

Does design obey laws?

Aren't constraints enough?

Are there tendencies and schools in design?

Yes, but these are more a measure of human limitations than of ideals.

Is design ephemeral?

Some needs are ephemeral. Most designs are ephemeral.

Ought design to tend towards the ephemeral or towards permanence?

Those needs and designs that have a more universal quality tend toward relative permanence.

How would you define yourself with respect to a decorator? An interior architect? A stylist?

I wouldn't.

To whom does design address itself: to the greatest number? To the specialists or the enlightened amateur? To a privileged social class?

Design addresses itself to the need.

After having answered all these questions, do you feel you have been able to practise the profession of design under satisfactory conditions, or even optimum conditions?

Yes.

Have you been forced to accept compromises?

I don't remember ever being forced to accept compromises, but I have willingly accepted constraints.

What do you feel is the primary condition for the practice of design and for its propagation?

A recognition of need.

What is the future of design?

Still from *Design Q&A*, 1972. Film, 5:20 min. The Eameses' answer to the final question was not spoken but answered with a montage of flowers.

# INFORMATION MACHINES

The 'Information Machine' was a multimedia experience conceived by the Eames Office for the IBM Pavilion at the 1964–5 New York World's Fair. But its title can also serve as a metaphor for the Office itself, neatly encapsulating the Eameses' approach to work, especially those large-scale, communications-led projects undertaken from the 1960s onwards. Charles and Ray Eames and their team tackled a range of topics, from history, the sciences and philosophy to architecture, urban planning and economics, and took a great deal of time – and care – to understand deeply the subjects on which they were working. At times, specialist consultants from a wide field of disciplines were engaged to complement the research carried out by Eames Office staff, and although certain themes appeared with regularity – information theory or the history of science, for example – no project was the same. Throughout their development, ideas were modelled in a range of ways for different purposes. While planning the IBM Pavilion, for example, the project was outlined in two 'film models' as the Office evolved and defined the pavilion's overarching concept. Physical models of varying scales were also produced, to test ideas or to communicate the project to the client or visitors to 901. These working models were valuable tools that enabled Charles, Ray and their team to maintain focus on the concept driving the whole endeavour. In their final form, ideas were communicated in a medium best suited to the project's requirements, whether that be a short film, a multi-image or multimedia presentation, a three-screen slide lecture, an exhibition, a report or interactive display devices.

In 1975, twenty-two years after the Eameses, George Nelson and Alexander Girard first presented their *Rough Sketch for a Sample Lesson for a Hypothetical Course*, Charles was back in Atlanta, Georgia, to deliver a talk entitled 'An Architectural Model is an Information Device'. Notes for the talk provide valuable insight into his thinking and the methods the Eames Office developed to communicate ideas. 'We have the capacity to absorb large numbers of impressions quickly. What we need to do is take greater advantage of this capacity. In this way we can get more information out to people effectively. This is a challenge that faces us as designers, as architects, as businessmen and as people who want to get some of the problems of the world ironed out.'[1]

The *Sample Lesson* was in many ways a test run for the Eameses' first attempt to communicate a wealth of information quickly and at a monumental scale. Their seven-screen immersive film, *Glimpses of the U.S.A.* (1959), was made for the American National Exhibition in Moscow and incorporated some two thousand images in a filmic montage. The film did indeed impart impressions quickly – the 'glimpses' of an American way of life of the title – but the visual experience did not leave viewers confused or alienated. Rather, the overall effect was absorbing and impressive, communicating a narrative greater than the sum of its parts. The information-overload tactic was successful because the film's fundamental idea was simple and direct, and orchestrated with precision. This approach was employed again for the six-screen film presentation *House of Science*, a project devised for the United States Science Exhibit at the Seattle World's Fair in 1962, and on a much greater scale two years later for the IBM Pavilion. Exhibitions were also abundant with information; *A Computer Perspective* (1971–5) and *The World of Franklin and Jefferson* (1975–6) were dense chronological displays, rich in detail and objects.

Tony Benn, the British politician and friend of Charles and Ray Eames, captured the essence of the Eameses' legacy in his tribute to Charles given at the American Embassy in London in 1978: 'that quality of analysis was, and is, very much needed at this time in history when the human race has to come to terms with, and get used to, a completely new set of tools. He introduced us to the tools of our generation.'[2]

*Previous page*

Charles and Ray Eames selecting images for *Photography and the City: The Evolution of an Art and a Science* in the slide room at 901, 1968

Installation view of *Think*, IBM Pavilion, New York World's Fair, 1964–5

*Opposite*

Charles Eames and Deborah Sussman working on a mock-up of the 'History Wall' for *Mathematica: A World of Numbers … and Beyond* at 901, 1961

## Communicating America: Moscow, 1959

In January 1958 the USSR and the USA signed an agreement inaugurating a period of cultural exchange. The first fruits of this agreement were the Soviet Exhibition of Science, Technology and Culture in New York (30 June – 10 August 1959) and the American National Exhibition in Moscow's Sokolniki Park (25 July – 4 September 1959). For the American government, the latter was an unprecedented opportunity to assert the merits of capitalism to a Soviet audience. George Nelson was enlisted to mastermind the exhibition design and immediately invited the Eames Office to participate. Nelson, the Eameses and Jack Masey, coordinator of design at the United States Information Agency (USIA),[1] developed the exhibition's design strategy, and the Eameses' commission – the immersive seven-screen, 12-minute film *Glimpses of the U.S.A.* – formed one of the principal exhibits.

Recent Soviet innovations in technology, particularly the successful launch of Sputnik 1 in 1957, had received significant international coverage. The Soviet Exhibition in New York, accordingly, emphasized scientific and technological advancements. Acknowledging their potential weakness in this field, the Americans placed commodities, rather than industrial or military technologies, centre stage. Nelson designed an expansive, colourful glass structure known as the 'Jungle Gym' to house a display of American products, including both his own and Eames furniture by Herman Miller. The structure was conceived as a 'kind of bazaar stuffed full of things', a consumer landscape through which visitors wandered as if in a supermarket.[2] Elsewhere were fashion shows, demonstrations of kitchen appliances, a library and free samples of Pepsi Cola, reinforcing a picture of the United States as a nation rich in possessions.[3]

For some visitors to the exhibition this was a point of criticism, and they were quick to point out the relative lack of science and technology. Others suggested that the products on display were prototypes, fantasies of future achievements, rather than mass-produced commodities accessible to the majority. This was the accusation levelled by Soviet Premier Nikita Khrushchev during the famous 'Kitchen Debate' with American Vice President Richard Nixon. The supposedly impromptu televised debate, staged in the kitchen of a model suburban home, was chiefly concerned with the relative advantages of the capitalist and communist systems in everyday life. Nixon insisted that much of what could be seen in the exhibition, including the house in which they stood, was affordable to the average working-class family.

Nelson acknowledged that the displays could provide only a partial representation of the United States, and were not sufficient to persuade visitors of the benefits of capitalism. Various exhibits were introduced to provide a more holistic portrait of American society. Visitors brought their questions about the United States either to a team of young Russian-speaking guides or to IBM's RAMAC computer, which was programmed with the answers to more than 4,000 queries.

One of the most popular attractions at the exhibition, *Glimpses of the U.S.A.* was a key contribution to this broader narrative. The Eameses projected a montage portraying life in the United States on to seven screens, each measuring 6 × 9 metres (20 × 30 ft), suspended from the ceiling of a geodesic dome based on designs by Buckminster Fuller. The narrative was structured around the everyday week, and featured daily meals, commutes, work, education and leisure. Images were grouped so that instead of seeing one photograph of a suburban kitchen, viewers saw seven. The automobile was a recurring motif, shown at first in isolation but subsequently in the context of the car park or highway, where its prevalence was made clear. If visitors were sceptical about the objects they saw in the exhibition, the film assured them that not only did they exist in America, they were *widespread*. The sequence was precisely orchestrated: images of children playing in a school playground were followed by those of universities, laboratories and, finally, industrial manufacture. In this way, montage was employed to suggest connections between domestic comfort, material wealth, and the systems and institutions of American society. The American way of life was represented as a coherent and productive system, American citizens as industrious and content. Ignoring a request from USIA officials to end with images of jet aircraft, the Eameses finished the film with moments of familial love and, as the final shot, a bunch of forget-me-nots.[4] The Eameses cannily chose to avoid the competitive stance of much Cold War propaganda, striking instead a characteristically hospitable tone.

Luke Naessens

АМЕРИКАНСКАЯ ВЫСТАВКА В МОСКВЕ
СОКОЛЬНИКИ, ЛЕТО 1959 г.

ГЕОДЕЗИЧЕСК
ные здесь экспон
образовании, пр
стве, здравоохра
всей жизни Сое
купола помещае
дающихся амери
павильон, в стр
мали участие и с
нутся в Сокольн
ставки.

2

Charles and Ray Eames at the American
National Exhibition, Moscow, 1959
Photograph by Jack Masey

Artist unknown
Brochure for the American National Exhibition,
Moscow, 1959, cover (left, with logo by
George Nelson Office) and interior (right)
Photomechanical print on paper,
13 × 20.8 cm (5 ⅛ × 8 ¼ in.) closed, 13 × 41.6 cm
(5 ⅛ × 16 ½ in.) open
Private collection

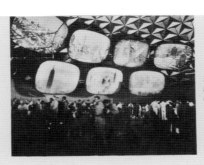

На семи огромных экранах,
прикрепленных к потолку купола,
показаны Соединенные Штаты.

ПЛАСТМАССОВЫЕ ПАВИЛЬОНЫ.
В трех павильонах из пластических масс
демонстрируются экспонаты архитектуры,
фотографии и мод.
Широкое применение
пластических масс наглядно
показывает быстрый рост этой новой
отрасли промышленности в США.

*Clockwise from top left*

Fashion show staged beneath the fibreglass umbrella canopies designed by George Nelson Office at the American National Exhibition, Moscow, 1959

Visitors inspecting a refrigerator Photograph by Dan I. Slobin

Replica supermarket installation

Visitors looking at a shoe display

The 'Jungle Gym' designed by
George Nelson Office

Visitors watching a demonstration
of the IBM RAMAC computer
Photograph by Elliott Erwitt

Furniture display, including Eames
Aluminium Group side chair

December 11, 1958

Mr. Charles Eames
901 Washington Boulevard
Venice, California


Dear Charlie:

Naturally, one cannot help being fond of one's own ideas, and, as of this moment, I am violently infatuated with my tic-tac-toe device. There are two aspects of the idea which appear to go beyond author's ego. One, I have been continuously uneasy about our ring of screens since we thought of it. I defended the scheme as strongly as I could in Washington, but I think what I was really defending was the idea of conveying bits of information.
In the second place, the persistent confusion of Circarama with the dome show finally got to look less like bureaucratic stupidity and more like a red light.
I think it is possible that we made a fundamental error in setting up the original ring of screens, which was influenced not only by the dome, but also, I suspect, by Circarama. I think you will agree that there is a fundamental difference between the two ideas and that the continuous ring of screens does work for Circarama and might, quite possibly, not work for the dome show. In Circarama, one is in a cylindrical vehicle. It is going somewhere. You can see what is ahead. You know what is behind. You only turn around for amusement or to get a fleeting glimpse of something already seen. Now this is not at all the case in our own show. If one is looking at the Milwaukee supermarket up front, there is every reason in the world to look at the Fort Lauderdale supermarket directly behind. This means, I think, that the audience must perpetually twirl to get all the facts being thrown at it. This, essentially, is why I think that the tic-tac-toe device is actually a clearer and better solution to the problem of doing what we think we want to do.
On the phone yesterday, we just began to touch on the fantastically exciting possibility of images going on the nine screens in all kinds of ways and in all sorts of orders. I get slightly dizzy just thinking of the things that could now be done to really convey the information we have.
After our phone conversation, I got some of the crew together, and we kicked this around. Their review of it appears to suggest that there would be other plusses. For instance, we could now allocate about half of the floor space to viewing of the screened information, and we could very well use the other half for exhibits of whatever appropriate kind. This, of course, throws out the doughnut, but there is no way of having the doughnut anyway, unless they allow us to put it on a mezzanine. The reason, of course, is that if it were located on the ground floor, there would be no way for the people in the dome to get to any of the exits. They have already told me there will be no mezzanines because there will be no money. (We are going ahead with a mezzanine in the glass building, anyway.) Unless you and Ray suddenly blow a big whistle, we are going ahead with finishing our preliminary presentation, using the new idea as the dome proposal. Instead of acknowledging the dome by concentric rings, we will now acknowledge it by setting up the most drastic contrasts possible. The plan will follow the 'inside of a watch' scheme. The screens will be the huge visual element they have been looking for. Incidentally, we set up a quick model last night, and the thing looks like the devil with rectangular screens. We are therefore – again, unless you blow a whistle – going to try for square screens, each with rounded corners. This wastes some of the film, but as a Hasselblad owner, you don't have a leg to stand on.
If we can persuade Washington to accept this new configuration as the final scheme for the dome show, I am dying to have this work out as a genuine three-way collaboration. If Billy [Wilder] is in (wonderful!) it would be four-way. Considering how much we accomplished in our last three-day stint, I don't see why it would not be possible for us to get together, either on one coast or the other, for a couple of sessions. I wish I could come out and work as your handyman, but this, alas, cannot be.

React!

Best,
George Nelson

The Eameses worked closely with George Nelson, Jack Masey and – in the early stages – film director Billy Wilder to plan the *Glimpses of the U.S.A.* screen configuration. They modelled several variations before arriving at a solution they felt provided the optimum viewer experience and gave the film's subject credibility. The Eames Office was responsible for the film itself. The 12-minute montage brought together more than two thousand images, many selected from the Eameses' own collection or shot by the Eames Office team especially for the production. Additional sources included *Life*, *Time* and *Fortune* magazines and Magnum Photos, as well as friends and collaborators whom they had asked to take photographs of specific subjects. The Eameses maintained total control of the film's content, and according to Charles Eames the final cut was not seen by any government representatives until they landed in Moscow.[1]

*Opposite*

Transcript of a letter from George Nelson to Charles Eames, 11 December 1958

II:135, Folder 6, The Papers of Charles and Ray Eames, Manuscript Division, Library of Congress, Washington DC

*This page*

Charles Eames, George Nelson and Jack Masey working on an early screen configuration for *Glimpses of the U.S.A.*, 1959

View of a ½-inch scale model of an early screen configuration for *Glimpses of the U.S.A.*, 1959

John Whitney, Nick Chaparos, Peter Pearce, Nancy Kane, Parke Meek, Miyoko Sasaki, Ray Eames, Charles Eames, John Neuhart, Lucia Capacchione and an unidentified Eames Office staff member standing in a ⅕-scale projection model of the screen configuration for *Glimpses of the U.S.A.*, 1959

*Overleaf*

Installation view of *Glimpses of the U.S.A.*, American National Exhibition, Moscow, 1959

# Squaring the Hypothetical Circle: Getting Around *Mathematica*

Kristen Gallerneaux

It must have required many ages to discover that a brace of pheasants and a couple of days were both instances of the number two.
—Bertrand Russell

*Growing Geometries*

At Case Study House No. 8, that icon of modern architecture built by Charles and Ray Eames in the Pacific Palisades neighbourhood of Los Angeles, there is a fuzzy-edged interplay of plant life: the rectilinear geometry of the steel Kaiser beams framing the house captures a collaboration of industrial materials *within* nature, rather than simply *slicing into* nature. Likewise, the meadow below the Eames House overlooking the Pacific Ocean has its own story to tell: how it demanded and won its sovereignty when the house was pushed to the side of the property to preserve the grassy middle. Inside the house, an echo of a tumbleweed hangs from the ceiling by a string; outside, huge split-leaf philodendrons (*Monstera deliciosa*) yawn towards the windows from the living-room garden. After the deaths of Charles and Ray, the house became an arrested space; everything remained the same. Everything, that is, except the plants. They continued to grow – as did the legacy of the Eameses.

Yet at the moment when it seems as though a complete compendium has been formed of all of the examples of the Eameses working in tandem with nature – of their love of exposing the hidden orders of natural philosophy – another example presents itself where it is least expected. In March 2015, during a tour of the Eames House, a guide could be seen pointing to a blueprint and explaining to a group of visitors:

> This circle is the eucalyptus tree known as 'Tree Number One'. Not because there are two, three, four, five trees, but because [the Eameses] just *chose* to identify it that way. And see this hypothetical centre line? It's 444 inches off to this corner, 9 feet up to this corner and then vertically 2 feet up to the slab. So the x-y-z dimension for planning the Eames House was based off the supposed centre of this – Tree Number One. Can you visualize that?

The guide's reverence for this one particular eucalyptus tree, in combination with how he had drawn out mathematical principles in the air with words, urging his audience to visualize the connection of hidden geometries between the house and nature, was well timed. The encounter seemed especially charged to one member of the group, a visiting curator from the Henry Ford Museum – and the author of this essay – whose home institution in Dearborn, Michigan, had just that day announced its official acquisition of the Eames Office's interactive exhibition *Mathematica: A World of Numbers ... and Beyond*.

*Interactivity, in Action*
There are three extant versions of *Mathematica*, each of which developed out of the symbiotic relationship between the Eames Office and IBM. Two versions were created in 1961: the first for the California Museum of Science and Industry in Los Angeles (now at the New York Hall of Science), the second for the Museum of Science and Industry in Chicago (now at the Museum of Science in Boston). The third version is well travelled. In the form of several interactive devices, it made its first appearance in the IBM Pavilion at the 1964–5 New York World's Fair. It was then installed at the Time-Life Building in New York from 1965 until 1966, when it went to the Pacific Science Center in Seattle. In the 1990s it was purchased by SciTrek, the Science & Technology Museum of Atlanta, where it was on view until the museum's closure in 2004. For most of the past decade, the exhibition has been in storage with the Eames Office. In April 2015, however, it arrived at its new permanent home, the Henry Ford Museum.

*Mathematica* is true to its namesake – Sir Isaac Newton's *Philosophiæ Naturalis Principia Mathematica* (1687) – presenting ideas and situations that demonstrate the entwined relationship between the natural world and mathematics. Those unfamiliar with the Eameses' exhibition may well be wondering exactly how displays of arithmetic problems could possibly be entertaining. In truth, however, the exhibition contains very few numbers.

At its core, *Mathematica* endeavours to teach visitors about mathematics in a non-mathematical way. Maths is exposed as something that permeates the natural world – from the mirrored parity of a snowflake to the logarithmic spiral of a nautilus shell. In the exhibition, graphics of fern fronds, tornadoes, seashells and an egg are all associated with mathematical principles.

The networked veins of a birch leaf or mud flat, for example, are used to demonstrate the theories of topology.

The heart of *Mathematica* is populated by a group of large, mechanical, interactive devices. And it is these devices that give rise to Newton's ideal learning environment: a place in which an observer can come to an understanding of a process through direct demonstration, in action.[1] The 'Minimal Surfaces' device features six specially formed wire wands that dip in and out of a soapy bath to create delicate cubic, tetrahedral and other atypical bubble-forms. The bubbles render the invisible nature of surface tension visible, if only briefly. When a button is pressed on the 'Celestial Mechanics' device, metal ball bearings are released and travel around and down its vortex-like funnel, demonstrating the orbital relationship between heavenly bodies. Gravity ends the ball bearings' slow, downwards waltz as they disappear into a hole at the bottom.

The clockwork clink of thousands of plastic balls dropping through a grid of pegs, finally to settle into a perfect bell curve, marks out the 'Probability Machine'. A sustained 30 seconds of silence precedes the racket of the balls being released into the bowels of the machine, for the whole process to begin again. Probability, according to the American mathematician and mathematical historian James R. Newman, 'is a measure of our degree of confidence that a thing will happen'.[2] A graphic residing close to the machine depicts a two-panel cartoon of a hand holding out a teacup under a raincloud. In one version, with the words 'unpredictable' written below, the cloud has released only a single drop; in the second panel, the words 'more predictable' accompany the same drawing, only now the cloud is unleashing a torrent of rain. Such amazingly succinct graphics can be found throughout *Mathematica*.[3]

The legacy of Charles and Ray Eames is most often celebrated in terms of their contribution to furniture design, but there is an extended and rich territory to be discovered beyond this. *Mathematica* is one of the most cohesive examples of exhibition technology ever produced by the Eameses, and one of the first so thoroughly to take on ideas of interactive technology for educative purposes in a museum context. It cleverly blends the museological with the carnivalesque: interactive stations, dense signage and objects under glass vitrines mix with peepshows, optical wonders, delight in discovery and the vivid palettes of circus tents. The concentration of potential experience offered by *Mathematica*, directed at each and every sense, was never intended to be absorbed in one take; rather, the aim was to encourage return visits.

Despite the playful chaos of *Mathematica*, a constant sense of utter precision runs throughout the exhibition, the product of a perfect union between aesthetics and refined information design. The interactive devices are beautifully thought out, providing flash and fodder from a distance, but coming into focus as well-ordered tools for communication the closer one gets.

Words and disembodied numbers, free of context, floating on large banners, become subjects of aesthetic scrutiny. Jokes scattered throughout the exhibition carry deeper weight than they imply on the surface. And for all its asides and anecdotes, the smallest quip in *Mathematica* might serve as a powerful lure inwards, enfolding a visitor into its networks of complex principles.

### Frames within Frames

Just as there are connections between the Eames House and landscape, and between nature and mathematics, the papers of the Eames Office at the Library of Congress in Washington DC reveal deep thinking about the science–nature continuum among Office staff during the time of *Mathematica*'s production. Snapshots of prototyping and production coexist happily with entire rolls of film depicting interlocking rings of water, crystalline structures and magnified snowflakes. These images are the alternatives to the final versions that appeared on the exhibition's 'Image Wall'. Other lines of visual thought include views of abstracted petroglyphs, aerial topology shots and a massive oil fire in El Segundo, California, filling the sky with rolling black clouds.

While the exhibition was being developed, an Eames Office researcher put together a photographic reference file of material held in rare-book libraries. A contemporary researcher might find themselves hunched over a table with a digital camera – capturing images of the 35mm images that the Eames Office had gathered in much the same way in 1960. Occasionally in these original materials, a historic hand strays into shot, holding down a book to flatten it. In the physical act of viewing these materials now, one is often forced to do the same. This action emulates a portion of *Mathematica*'s 'Image Wall'. In an illustration of geometrical progression – a similar sense of nestled infinity – the image of a boy holding a picture frame is repeated within the frame ad infinitum.

A glimpse of the *Mathematica* research and production files at the Library of Congress reveals early ideas, scribbled on crisp squares of paper, marked up with whatever was at hand before they passed out of mind. A typographic paste-up for the 'Celestial Mechanics' device, spelling out the words 'To Start', letter by letter; a collection of hurried notes: 'Ray remembers a model like this', 'Method: turn lathe', 'Bucky – rigidity of spheres … The model is a building!'; snapshots of pages from books about mathematicians, marked up with red grease pencil delineating crop

boundaries, ready for reproduction on the 'History Wall'; a photograph of Ray smiling, crawling on her hands and knees, helping with the installation of the exhibition at the Pacific Science Center – the same version of *Mathematica* acquired by the Henry Ford Museum. There is also evidence of things that did not come to pass, such as a drawing of a Rube Goldberg/Heath Robinson device involving levers, chains and, according to a note on the drawing, a 4,000-pound (1,800-kg) weight.

### Mathematica Now

While the Henry Ford is not the only museum to be the steward of a version of *Mathematica*, the iteration to be housed at this institution is the fullest expression of the exhibition there is, with unique components demonstrating the concepts of conic projection and random walks. The voices of museum artefacts change depending on the environment in which they are displayed, and the collision of *Mathematica* with the Henry Ford's robust industrial and design collections is a distinctive one. The values instilled at the Eames Office, and the outcomes of *Mathematica* as an exhibition, are well aligned with those of Henry Ford himself: to 'learn by doing', to never stop learning. As museum staff rehabilitate the interactive devices to operational order once more, visitors, in turn, will be given the hands-on opportunity to poke, prod, observe and bond with the lessons they provide.

As one considers the history of *Mathematica* and begins to absorb the wealth of archival material around its creation, a realization comes to pass: no matter how large a magnifying glass one holds over the historic images, one can never fully meld with the experience of visitors to the original installations of the exhibition, such as those at the 1964–5 New York World's Fair and the Pacific Science Center circa 1966. But these histories, while partially recoverable, are not our own to relive. We need to become enveloped in the unified fields of mathematics, science and nature in our own time. To accompany the installation of the exhibition at the Henry Ford Museum, contemporary portals – and new futures for visitors – will be created, opening up the world that is *Mathematica*.

THE THEORY OF PROBABILITIES IS NOTHING MORE THAN GOOD SENSE CONFIRMED BY CALCULATION.

:LAPLACE 1796·

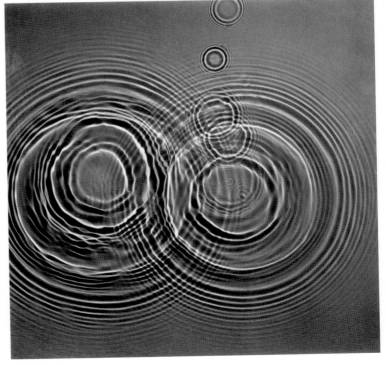

*Pages 276–7*
Installation view of *Mathematica: A World of Numbers ... and Beyond*, California Museum of Science and Industry, Los Angeles, 1961

Section of the *Mathematica* 'Image Wall' installed at the New York World's Fair, 1964–5

*Opposite*
Installation view of the 'Celestial Mechanics' device in *Mathematica*, California Museum of Science and Industry, Los Angeles, 1961

Detail from the *Mathematica* 'Image Wall' demonstrating geometrical progression, 1961

*This page*
Installation view of the 'Probability Machine' in *Mathematica*, California Museum of Science and Industry, Los Angeles, 1961

Detail from the *Mathematica* 'Image Wall', 1961

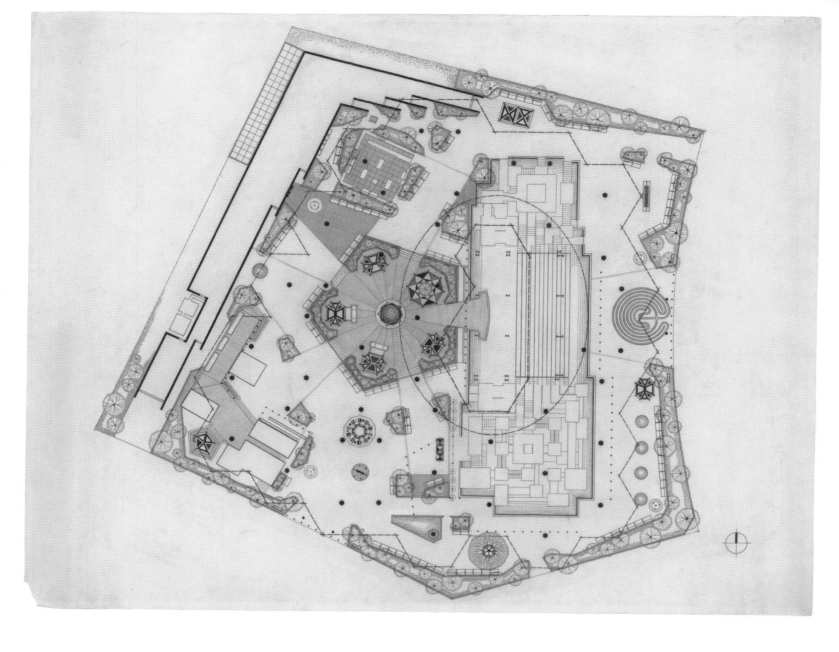

Plan of the IBM Pavilion,
New York World's Fair, 1964–5
Graphite on paper, 92 × 118 cm
(36 ¼ × 46 ½ in.)

The Work of Charles and Ray
Eames, Prints & Photographs
Division, Library of Congress,
Washington DC

'To take the curse off the image
of the soulless giant computer,
the late Eero Saarinen, architect,
and Charles Eames, designer,
created for International Business
Machines, not a building but a
grove.'[1] Part garden of delights, part
vision of the future, the IBM Pavilion
at the 1964–5 New York World's
Fair was a compelling spectacle.

Formal work on the pavilion,
which was conceived by the Eames
Office and Eero Saarinen and
Associates, began in 1962. Saarinen
– a friend of Charles and Ray's since
their days together at Cranbrook
Academy of Art – had passed away
in September 1961, as plans for the
pavilion were taking shape, so his
associates, Kevin Roche and John

Dinkeloo, saw the project to fruition.
The architects were responsible
for the overall site planning and
architecture – the Ovoid Theater
(home to the 'Information Machine'),
the plastic roof canopy supported
by Cor-Ten steel 'trees' and other
infrastructure – while the Eames
Office concentrated on the design
of exhibits, film presentations and
signage. The design of the pavilion
was welcoming and carnival-like,
allowing IBM to introduce the
latest automated technologies to
the public in a relaxed atmosphere;
the setting emphasized IBM's
business strategy, which sought
to communicate that, contrary
to popular belief, advances in
computer technologies were not
sinister or dangerous, but a force
for positive change.

The fair ran for two six-month
seasons (22 April – 18 October 1964
and 21 April – 17 October 1965) and
received more than 185,000 visitors
a day. For many people, a trip to the
pavilion gave them their first direct
interaction with a computer.

*Opposite*

View of the IBM Pavilion,
New York World's Fair, 1964–5

Artist unknown
Brochure for the IBM Automatic
Language Translation Machine
at the IBM Pavilion, New York
World's Fair, 1964
Photomechanical print on paper,
29.7 × 21 cm (11 ¾ × 8 ¼ in.)

From the Collections of The Henry
Ford, Dearborn, Michigan

Demonstration of the Automatic
Language Translation Machine,
1964

**IBM** Automatic Language Translation   New York World's Fair 1964/65

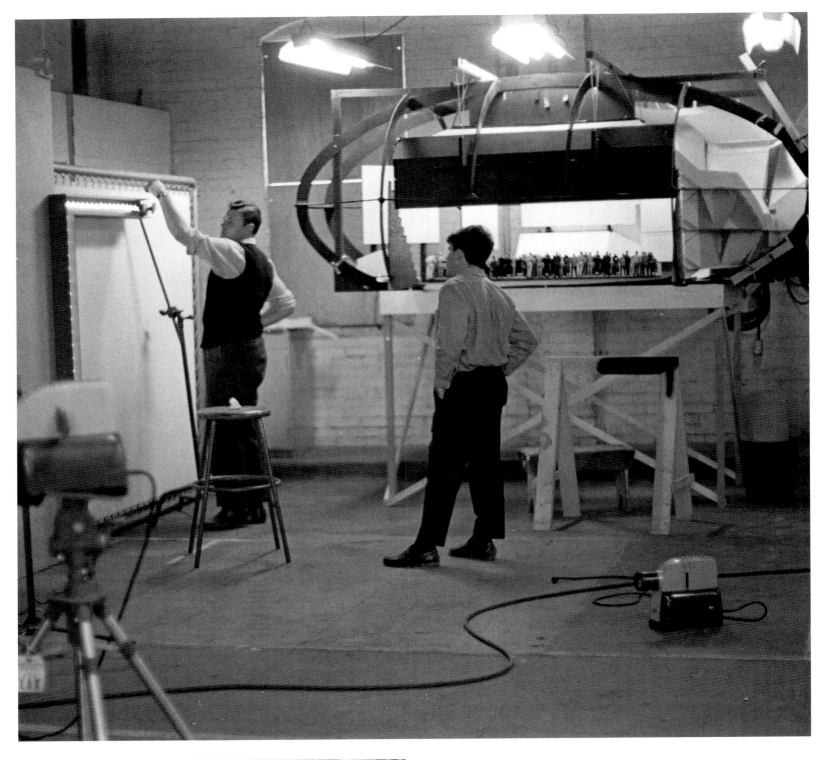

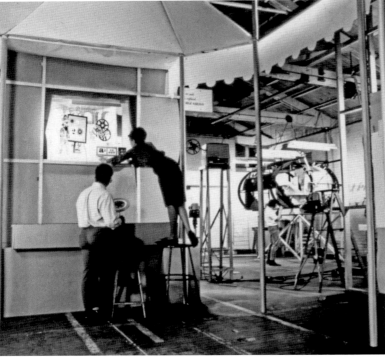

Eames Office staff members at 901 working on a scale model of the Ovoid Theater for the IBM Pavilion, 1964

Deborah Sussman and another Eames Office staff member at 901 working on an early mock-up of the Sherlock Holmes puppet show for the IBM Pavilion, 1964

The Eames Office produced a number of models of the pavilion and its different elements in order to work through such concepts as the screen configuration for the Ovoid Theater and the design of the puppet theatre. The Office made two short films, *IBM Presentation #1* (1962) and *IBM Presentation #2* (1963), using footage of drawings, plans and models to communicate the whole project to senior IBM executives at various stages in the planning process.

*Top left*
Charles Eames showing Antony
Armstrong-Jones a scale model
of the IBM Pavilion, 1964

*Top right, right and below*
Scale models of the IBM Pavilion

**Here's how handwritten numerals are recognized by the IBM Character Recognition System.** A spot of light from a cathode tube "looks" at the card  and traverses the area *3* until it strikes a portion of a written numeral. *3* It then follows around its contour until it returns to the starting point. *3* A comparison of this pattern is made with a stored computer pattern *3333333833* and it is then recognized. *3 1234567890*

The spot of light then moves on to the next number at the rate of 200 characters per second. When the entire date is read, it is relayed to the IBM 1460 computer system which searches its disk files for the news of that day. The IBM 1404 printer is then instructed to print the news on this card.

2013.93.3 *cco*

---

6/14/1965                                                                 18

THE FOLLOWING NEWS EVENT WAS REPORTED IN THE NEW YORK TIMES ON THE DATE THAT YOU REQUESTED:

NOV. 30, 1960:    SOVIETS DEMAND RECALL OF UN FORCE FROM CONGO; CITE FINANCIAL DRAIN ON UN BUDGET.

---

*Opposite*

Demonstration of IBM's Optical Scanning and Information Retrieval System in the IBM Pavilion, 1964

Visitors to the pavilion were able to request a specific news headline from this exhibit by feeding a handwritten date into the computer. IBM had anticipated visitors trying to outwit the machine by entering a date in the future. When this occurred, the souvenir card was printed with a special message calculating the number of days until the information was available.

View of the IBM Pavilion, 1964

*This page*

Souvenir card from the Optical Scanning and Information Retrieval System, 1965, back (top) and front (above)
Photomechanical print on paper, 8.3 × 18.7 cm (3 ¼ × 7 ⅜ in.)
From the Collections of The Henry Ford, Dearborn, Michigan

Paul Rand
Brochure for the IBM Pavilion, New York World's Fair, 1964
Photomechanical print on paper, 25 × 25 cm (9 ⅞ × 9 ⅞ in.)
From the Collections of The Henry Ford, Dearborn, Michigan

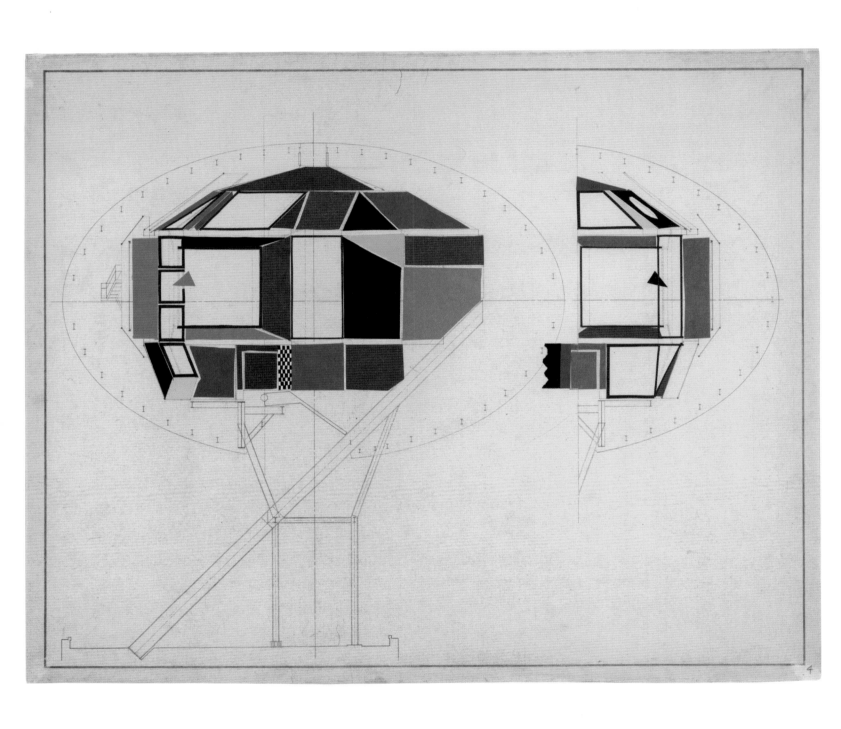

For visitors to the 1964–5 New York World's Fair, one of the main attractions was the 'Information Machine', a multisensory experience. It took place in the Ovoid Theater: a spheroid building made of structural steel and concrete plaster, clad with 3,000 vacuum-formed letters spelling 'IBM', each 0.76 metres (2 ½ ft) tall. The theatre itself was 35 metres (115 ft) long and 17.7 metres (58 ft) tall, and was suspended 9.8 metres (32 ft) above the ground. In order to enter the Information Machine, visitors had to navigate a maze of suspended walkways, which could accommodate more than a thousand people at any one time. At the end of the walkways, a gate led to a grandstand-style seating structure with long, narrow benches, foot rests and handrails. Although the structure afforded views of the fair's other attractions, including the IBM Pavilion's reflecting pool, wandering musicians and, in the distance, the Pool of Industry and Fountain of the Planets, it was not only a place to sit and enjoy the sights. Known as the 'People Wall', it also served as the entrance to the Ovoid Theater.

After filing through the gate, visitors would take a seat in one of the Wall's twelve rows, each holding approximately thirty-five people. Once the maximum capacity had been reached, a man in bow tie and tails would descend on a platform from the roof of the pavilion and hover over the audience. This was the live-action portion of the show: a host to welcome visitors to the Information Machine. The host would begin by explaining to the audience how the People Wall worked, ensuring that no one would be surprised by what they were about to experience. After the explanation, a door in the floor of the Ovoid Theater would open, and the entire 29.5-ton (65,000-lb) People Wall – operated by a hydraulic lift, in a similar manner to an elevator – would rise with its 420-plus occupants at a 45-degree angle into a large, air-conditioned space. The door below would close shut, blocking out the sights and sounds of the fair, and leaving the audience to face a curved theatre full of screens, twenty-two in total. Most of these screens were rectangular, but some were circular, triangular or trapezoidal.

The host, who would rise on his platform into the theatre along with the audience, would begin the show with the words: 'Welcome, Ladies and Gentlemen, to the Information Machine!' The presentation that followed was titled *Think*, and was shown on fifteen of the theatre's larger screens (the largest of which measured 5.2 × 7.3 metres / 17 × 24 ft). Moving-image films were projected on to nine of these screens, and slides on to six. The remaining seven screens in the theatre were used to complement the show by displaying lights and colours. The presentation's

soundtrack was composed by Elmer Bernstein (who provided film scores for many Eames Office productions), with narration by Charles Eames. The presentation was designed such that, at times, only one or two screens showed images, while at others all nine film screens featured images that together made up a single picture.

The theme of the presentation was problem-solving – more specifically, the similar ways in which computers and the human brain solve problems. The presentation attempted to illustrate these parallels in a simple yet effective manner by portraying a variety of pertinent events and phenomena, such as a road race, railways, city planning, weather systems and a dinner party. American actress Joan Shawlee, well known to the audience from her roles in *Some Like it Hot* (1959) and *The Apartment* (1960), portrayed the dinner party's hostess, who used logic to solve her seating-arrangement conundrum. The guests at the dinner party had no speaking lines, but were played by an interesting mix of Los Angeles personalities and friends of the Eameses, including:

John Houseman, veteran actor, acting teacher and early Orson Welles collaborator

Virginia Dwan (credited as Virginia Kondratiev), art collector, philanthropist and owner of Dwan Galleries in London and New York

Dr Stuart and Lucia Bailey, owners of the Stuart Bailey House, or Case Study House No. 20A, designed by Richard Neutra

Philip Dunne, a screenwriter, and his wife, the actress Amanda Dunne

Melinda Hurst, wife of Samuel Hurst, former dean of the USC School of Architecture and Fine Arts

Frank Pierson, a screenwriter and director whose credits included, as screenwriter, *Cool Hand Luke* (1967) and *Dog Day Afternoon* (1975) and, as director, *A Star is Born* (1976),

Ray Eames, Glen Fleck and Charles Eames developing the script for *Think*, 1964

Installation view of *Think*, 1964

together with his wife, Polly; both lived in a house designed
by the architect Craig Ellwood

Crombie Taylor, an architect

Dr Irwin Shiell, a dentist from Los Angeles whose wife also
appears in *Think* (cracking eggs in the breakfast scene);
both were friends of an Eames Office employee, who
recommended them for the film

Frederick A. Usher, a designer and artist and former Eames
Office staff member

Audrey Young (credited as Audrey Wilder), an actress and the wife
of long-time friend and collaborator of the Eameses Billy Wilder

The host of *Think* did not narrate the entire show, but rather
reappeared throughout to provide context for the audience.
To accommodate the many overseas visitors to the fair,
translations in French, Italian, German, Japanese and Spanish
were made available via headset.

The synchronization of the People Wall, the host and the
projection system made the Information Machine one of the most
complicated presentations at the fair. Planning documents written
by the Eames Office stated that the show needed to be timed to
within a twenty-fifth of a second. Attendants were located on the
entrance and exit gates of the Wall to escort a new audience into
their seats as the previous one departed. One attendant operated
the Wall and provided visual cues to the projectionist to start
the show. An interconnected system of seven moving-image
projectors and six slide projectors was employed. The projectors
were located in two booths, and the projectionist was able to
operate them remotely. The films were run on a constant loop
to avoid the rewinding that would normally be required between
shows. The entire sequence was designed to take 20 minutes:
5 minutes for the simultaneous on- and offloading of the audience,
1 minute for the introduction, 1 minute each for the ascent and
descent of the People Wall, and 12 minutes for the presentation.

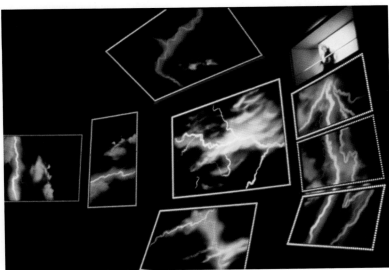

It is estimated that, during the fair's open seasons, the
Ovoid Theater showed *Think* to 16,000 people every day. The
presentation was updated in 1965, with slight changes to the
overall content, although the main theme remained the same.
These changes, for the most part, were reflected in the film *View
from the People Wall* (1966), a single-screen version of *Think*
created by the Eames Office to preserve the presentation for those
who did not attend the fair, as well as future audiences. The 1965
version of *Think* was also captured in the Eames film *IBM at the
Fair* (1965), in a time-lapsed sequence. The original 1964 version
has now been digitally preserved from the original interpositives,
projection prints and soundtrack – items that can be found in the
Eames Collection at the Library of Congress in Washington DC, in
the Motion Picture, Broadcasting and Recorded Sound Division.

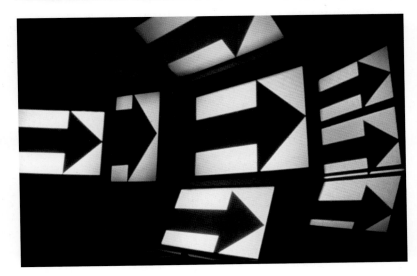

*Above*
Installation views of *Think*, 1964

*Left*
Ray Eames arranging the table setting for
the 'Dinner Party' sequence of *Think*, 1964

Charles Eames admired the circus as a highly structured, moveable city that functioned on precision, discipline and imagination. It showed 'apparent license on the surface ... Everything in the circus is pushing the possible beyond the limit.'[1] Filled with visual riches and focused staff, 901 Washington Boulevard was the Eameses' three-ring circus: furniture, films, exhibitions. By the 1960s, exhibitions were in centre ring (death-defying acts not required, time-defying ones certainly). Charles was impresario and ringmaster; Ray, his 'artistic conscience'.[2]

What we might call the Eameses' 'exhibition era' began in 1961 with *Mathematica: A World of Numbers ... and Beyond*, installed first in Los Angeles, then Chicago and, five years later, Seattle, all three iterations sponsored and maintained for years by IBM. *Mathematica* was followed by the IBM Pavilion at the 1964–5 New York World's Fair; *Jawaharlal Nehru: His Life and His India*, which started its global travels in 1965; *Photography and the City*, which opened at the Smithsonian Institution in Washington DC in 1968; and *A Computer Perspective*, presented in early 1971 at IBM's Madison Avenue showroom in New York with changing corner-window displays on astronomy. The era came to an end when *The World of Franklin and Jefferson* commenced its international tour in Paris in early 1975. A prodigious output.

Exhibitions are inherently ephemeral, yet more than fifty years after its first installation *Mathematica* continues to delight at two American museums, soon to be three.[3] It is a brilliant visualization of mathematical theories and a classic manifestation of the intense Eames design process. Reflecting on its making, Charles observed: 'For the better part of a year we have been working, trying, building, talking and battling with mathematics – and with a patient mathematical consultant. It has been much the same hair-raising experience that accompanies any design problem, but with the added exhaustion that comes from perpetual excitement peaks.'[4] The 'patient consultant' was Raymond Redheffer, mathematics professor at the University of California, Los Angeles (UCLA). In Redheffer, Charles found an intellectual sparring partner with infectious enthusiasm and an endless ability to brainstorm ways in which to present abstract ideas. On occasion, to make a point or ease tension, Redheffer, an able gymnast, would grab the office wall ladder and flip himself horizontally into a human flag.

In the spring of 1973, more than a decade after *Mathematica*'s opening, concept work on *Franklin and Jefferson* was burgeoning. Writing to his superiors at the United States Information Agency (USIA) after an exhaustive six-day, four-city photographic research trip with Charles and two Eames Office staffers, programme officer David Paul expressed the commitment required of an Eames client:

> Eames' attack on a subject seems to be that of a discoverer – an inductive amassing and shifting and re-shifting of the data to find a meaningful pattern. It is the opposite of the more usual deductive approach – choose a thesis and then set out to document it, to build a case to prove it. This difference in approach makes some difficulties for us, for USIA. Discovery is hard to schedule, and the price of discovery is hard to quantify in the usual units. But if there was any logic in USIA's original choice of Charles Eames to do this exhibit ... we ought to make every effort, within the limits of our contractual process, to allow Eames to do his work in his way. I don't minimize the heroic patience this may entail.[5]

Ultimately, Charles convinced the USIA to transfer the project to the American Revolution Bicentennial Administration and secured the imprimatur of the Metropolitan Museum of Art, New York, with funding from IBM.

In creating exhibitions, one is often asked to grapple with such questions as: who is the audience? What do they want to experience? What will this hypothetical 'they' understand and find interesting? For Charles, these questions were irrelevant. He would typically respond, 'Don't tell me what you think others will find interesting or will understand, what do you find interesting?'[6] Thus, those of us creating the exhibitions had to be personally excited about an idea, or we should not advocate its inclusion. At the same time, there was an underlying goal to serve all comers – 'to convey *our own* understanding, limited though it may be, in such a way that it has meaning for a non-specialist but isn't trivial or embarrassing for the person who knows most about the subject'.[7]

A formula that began with *Mathematica* – personal enthusiasm for a subject; a belief that, through the right design,

the Eameses', especially Charles's, excitement would be infectious to the exhibition's visitors; creative consultants with whom the Office could explore ideas and wrestle out solutions; and a willingness on the part of Charles and Ray to commit virtually the whole staff, not to mention clients and colleagues, to investigating myriad aspects of the topic at hand from diverse angles – was inherent in the development of all subsequent exhibitions. Three projects from the very heart of the centre ring – the National Aquarium, *Photography and the City* and *Nehru*, each commissioned by government agencies and developed without IBM patronage – offer different windows into the Eameses' exhibition-making process.

In the spring of 1966, the United States Department of the Interior, under the leadership of the pioneering environmentalist Stewart Udall, commissioned the architectural practice of Kevin Roche John Dinkeloo and Associates (KRJDA) to create a National Fisheries Center and Aquarium in Washington DC on an island in the Potomac located to the south of the National Mall. Roche invited Charles to develop the visitor experience. 'He had an ability to address the heart of the problem as he saw it. He dealt with process always, very carefully and methodically; he searched and searched. He had no preconceptions.'[8] Malcolm S. Gordon, a specialist in marine locomotion at UCLA, was enlisted as scientific consultant. Gordon stressed the importance of research at the future institution, as well as aquatic environments that would educate as much as they would entertain. Conservation should be an underlying theme. Gordon's ideas were embraced by Charles and the team at 901 Washington Boulevard, as were the challenges Gordon noted – one of the most significant being how to dispose of large volumes of seawater without affecting the Potomac's ecosystem. 'If the Aquarium comes off well, it should produce a revolution in the nature of public aquarium.'[9]

To better understand the challenge (and provide images for the filmed concept report), saltwater tanks with more than seventy-five species of marine life were set up in the back of the Office, normally the domain of furniture design. Lights and a movie camera stood by, ready to take quick shots of interesting developments, such as the delicate movements of the tiny *Polyorchis haplus* or the antics of a small octopus. Numerous models also had to be built – at a scale of 1:12 for the main interiors and tanks, and still larger for specific elements, such as the multilevel coral reef and the rooftop 'ecological greenhouse', which Roche likened to the spine of a sleeping cat.[10] In the spring of 1967, those of us making the models could barely stay ahead of the demanding shooting schedule to complete the film in time for Udall to present it to Congress later that year, just after its summer recess.

The National Aquarium was arguably the most ambitious project ever undertaken by the Eames Office. The answering of queries and the sharing of details with the office of KRJDA as it finalized construction documents continued periodically into 1970. In total, $3 million of the $10 million authorized by Congress was spent on planning, research, design and engineering. President Nixon recommended that the project be abandoned, however, and impounded the balance in early 1971. The National Aquarium survives today only as a small booklet and the concept film, a 'fiction of reality', created as a report to gain congressional approval.[11] If funding were forthcoming, it was hoped that the Aquarium would embody 'the virtues of beauty and intellectual stimulation that one would be embarrassed to fall below';[12] and if it were not, wrote Charles, the film would serve 'to document our concept and to set a term of comparison for any further attempts'.[13] Although never built in Washington DC, the project succeeded in influencing a generation of aquariums and gave

Pages 290–91
Barbara Fahs Charles and Charles Eames discussing the installation of *Photography and the City*, May 1968
Photograph by Margaret Thomas for the *Washington Post*

Glen Fleck and Ray Eames working on the model for the National Fisheries Center and Aquarium, June 1966

*This page*
1-inch scale model of the National Aquarium, 1967
Photograph by Charles Brittin

School students visit *Photography and the City*, Smithsonian Institution, Washington DC, 1968

*Opposite*
Installation view of *Photography and the City*, 1968

Graphic design by Paul Brühwiler for Eames Office
Poster for *Photography and the City*, 1968
Photomechanical print on paper, 88.9 × 58.4 cm (35 × 23 in.)
Collection of Robert Staples and Barbara Fahs Charles

Information Machines

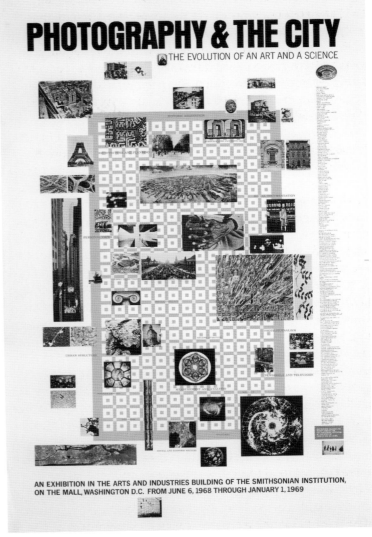

Charles and staff at the Office a brief, intense opportunity to explore the natural world and advocate for its protection.

During the summer of 1967, with the Office working frantically to complete the film report for the Aquarium, Charles learned that Frank Taylor, director of museums for the Smithsonian Institution, was seeking the ideal consultant to develop *The Changing City*, an exhibition of 250 to 350 photographs exploring photography's relationship to the city – as a recorder of moods and tempos, as a tool for planning, as a reflection of the city's human inhabitants.[14] It was planned as the first of six photographic exhibitions, precursors to a new museum of photography.

Initially, Taylor did not have Eames in mind for the role, but Charles's enthusiasm for the concept was infectious. It embraced three of his primary interests: photography in all its forms, architecture and urban planning, and science applied to understanding the environment. Despite an extremely tight budget of $45,000 to research, design and produce the exhibition, the Office took it on with gusto. 'You know, of course, that this will have to be just about the best photographic show ever', Charles effused as we started our research.[15] It was tempting to imagine an urban equivalent of *The Family of Man*, Edward Steichen's landmark photography exhibition at The Museum of Modern Art, New York, twelve years earlier.

By December 1967, the exhibition had a new title: *Photography and the City: The Evolution of an Art and a Science*. 'It is not a catchy title,' Charles noted to Frank Taylor, 'but we feel great enthusiasm for the way the material supports it.'[16] Taylor's original concept of 250 to 350 photographs exploded to 1,500 as we gathered original negatives, first-generation copy negatives or fine prints from more than one hundred institutions and individuals in eleven countries.[17] Charles searched the files of news agencies, and met with urban planners in London, New York and Boston. Newsreels, televised news reports and computer analyses expanded the visualization of urban activities and concerns. Images spanned both technique and time, from the first in-camera photograph, taken by Nicéphore Niépce in about 1827, to the most current events. Days before opening, photos were still coming in from Paris, showing the student protests, and from Resurrection City, the encampment of the Poor People's Campaign on the National Mall, just a short distance from the exhibition's venue.[18] The vast majority of prints were made in the darkroom of the Eames Office.

Charles wrote all the accompanying texts, some in the last few days of preparation, dropping them down from his desk on the balcony overlooking the exhibition to our workstation below to be marked up and sent off to the typesetter. The poster for the show states: 'Photographs selected and exhibit designed for the Smithsonian Institution by the Office of Charles and Ray Eames' – a direct assertion by the Eameses that they and their staff were as capable as any museum curator, and that they were proving it at one of America's most prestigious museums.

A gala opening in the Smithsonian's Arts and Industries Building was planned for the evening of 5 June 1968. Early that morning Robert Kennedy was shot in Los Angeles. The party was cancelled. *Photography and the City* opened quietly to the public the following day, not long after we learned that Kennedy had died, and would be on display until 1 January 1969. There was no newspaper coverage. To those of us who had worked so hard to create the exhibition, it felt like a non-event. Nearly four weeks later spirits were lifted when Wolf Von Eckardt, architecture critic for the *Washington Post*, wrote a review – the only review – praising the show for making 'an already interesting subject positively exciting … [The Eameses] have made exhibition design a new art form, much as documentary films have become a new art form.'[19]

Von Eckardt's endorsement was extremely gratifying, but Charles's own assessment also rang true: 'The show is too large – we started it on too broad a front and became perhaps overzealous in trying to upgrade material in areas that were not familiar to us. Still I feel it is a needed show.'[20] In the months that followed, Charles and Office staffer Glen Fleck reprised the material as a film, *The Image of the City*, with increased emphasis on recent analytical technologies, including the latest images of earth taken from space, which Fleck had negotiated to receive from NASA shortly after the return of Apollo 7. In linear format, even with the Eameses' affection for rapid-fire images, the film presents a focused message that often eluded visitors immersed in the towering visual overload of the exhibition. Later, the Smithsonian toured an abbreviated version of the show, but pursued neither an ongoing series of photographic exhibitions nor a museum of photography. Despite its faults, *Photography and the City* was a loving salute to photography, an insightful statement on urban planning, and a prescient look at the urban environment and the new tools for its analysis.

*The India Report*, compiled by Charles and Ray Eames in 1958, led to the foundation three years later of the National Institute of Design (NID), India's first national design school. There, students and instructors working together on real projects would be a core aspect of learning. In August 1964 Indira Gandhi, at that time India's minister of information and broadcasting, commissioned the fledgling institute to prepare a biographical exhibition about her recently deceased father, Jawaharlal Nehru, India's first prime minister. The show would open in New York City less than six months later. It was a huge challenge – their first major exhibition – for NID's young faculty and initial batch of students. 'Our first thought was to reach Charles as our godfather', Dashrath Patel, NID Design Director for Visual Communication, reported.[21]

It was uniquely challenging for the Eameses, too. All their other projects were created by staff and consultants working in the insular world of 901 Washington Boulevard, and built by established fabrication firms. Now, the Eameses and key members of the Office would be working day and night, half a world away, with instructors, newly graduated architects and beginning design students – two dozen or so in total – in the pigeon-occupied upper levels of the recently built Sanskar Kendra, the city museum in Ahmedabad designed by Le Corbusier. Ray spent nearly three months in India, searching for images and objects and considering layouts. Deborah Sussman, the first Office staff member on site, stayed the longest, orchestrating the graphics. Glen Fleck flew out for a short while, for research and content development. Robert Staples, the last of the Eames team to make the journey, was sent for ten days in late October 1964 with a plan and model photographs to help finalize the three-dimensional designs. Ten days turned into two months as he and H. Kumar Vyas, NID Design Director for Product Design, worked closely together to convert the designs into elegant teak and brass structures, upholstered in a kaleidoscope of traditional Indian fabrics. The majority of these structures were crafted at NID under master carpenter Haribhai Panchasara, with brass castings and larger panels fabricated in small workshops around Ahmedabad, a city with strong traditions of craftsmanship. Alexander Girard, designer of the exhibition *Textiles and Ornamental Arts of India* (MoMA, 1955), responded to the Eameses' call for assistance and spent three weeks helping to source fabrics and many of the other elements that would add to the visual feast. Charles, who had negotiated the agreement with NID and discussed initial ideas during a two-week visit in August before developing concepts and spatial layouts with Office staff in Venice, California, was back in Ahmedabad by mid-November, having researched photos along the way in New York and London.

As its title suggests, *Jawaharlal Nehru: His Life and His India* told the story not only of Nehru, one of the architects of India's independence, but of India itself. Clearly, the design intent of the exhibition was to reflect the country's visual intensity. Rich textures and colours underscored a dramatic storyline told in 1,200 photographs and 30,000 words, mostly quotations from Nehru, many taken from the books he had written during his nine imprisonments for the cause of independence. H. Y. Sharada Prasad, editorial adviser to the project, media adviser to Indira Ghandi, brilliant journalist and freedom fighter with personal experience of the struggle that Nehru had led, selected the

quotations and crafted the texts. Indeed, Sharada Prasad's role in shaping *Nehru* should not be underestimated. One visitor to the exhibition described it as 'a spiritual exploration of a great man and the monumental challenge he faced';[22] another remembered it as 'an overwhelming experience ... it engulfed you with emotion'.[23]

More than fifty years old and part of the DNA of hands-on science centres everywhere, *Mathematica* is arguably the most influential exhibition the Eames Office created. *Jawaharlal Nehru: His Life and His India* still resonates strongly as a model for exhibition design and, perhaps more importantly, as a lesson in what it means to be a designer. Vikas Satwalekar, one of the young postgraduate students who worked with Deborah Sussman on the *Nehru* timeline, notes that his 'first experience of exhibition design became an invaluable lesson in how a conductor extracts the best out of each musician in the orchestra without compromising the harmony of the whole' – a lesson that would serve him well when he was named executive director of NID in 1989.[24] Like Satwalekar, that first generation of Indian designers and design students who created *Nehru* have, in turn, influenced subsequent generations of designers. It was H. Y. Sharada Prasad who articulated the message that many of those involved in the exhibition, if not all, would take with them as they moved forward in their careers: 'The secret of design, Eames used to say, is to care. The more you care, the more you find within yourself.'[25]

Sam Passalacqua photographing one of the live aquarium tanks at 901
Photograph by Charles Brittin

Following a 1962 act of Congress requiring the development of a National Fisheries Center and Aquarium in Washington DC, appointed architects Kevin Roche John Dinkeloo and Associates commissioned the Eames Office to work with them on the proposal. The progressive initiative was intended to house educational exhibitions, live-specimen galleries, an aquatic garden, a 30-metre-high (100 ft) greenhouse, research facilities and administrative offices; the Eames Office was asked to design the exhibitions, graphics, films and other material. Assisted by Malcolm Gordon, a member of the biology department at the University of California, Los Angeles, Office staff immersed themselves in research for the project. Tanks with marine habitats were set up at 901 so that staff could study behavioural patterns and understand how to convey them to visitors. They took numerous photographs and live footage, compiling them into a poetic three-screen slideshow, *Tanks* (see pages 257–64), and a short film, *A Small Hydromedusan: Polyorchis Haplus* (1970), which follows the movements of a diaphanous jellyfish. As part of the formal proposal to Congress, the Office produced graphic panels and a meticulously executed scale model of the centre. They also created a film (1967) and a booklet (1969), each explaining the features of the centre and underlining the importance of such a project in terms of increasing the public's understanding of the natural world and the urgent need to protect the environment.

*Below and opposite*
Pages from the *National Fisheries Center and Aquarium* booklet, 1969
Photomechanical print on paper, 14 × 28 cm (5 ½ × 11 in.)
Private collection

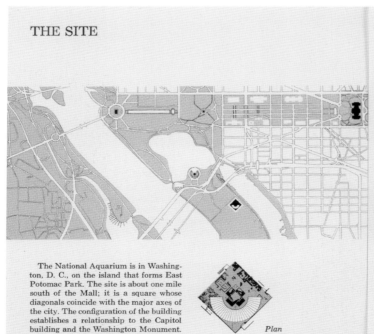

## THE SITE

The National Aquarium is in Washington, D. C., on the island that forms East Potomac Park. The site is about one mile south of the Mall; it is a square whose diagonals coincide with the major axes of the city. The configuration of the building establishes a relationship to the Capitol building and the Washington Monument.

*Plan*

2

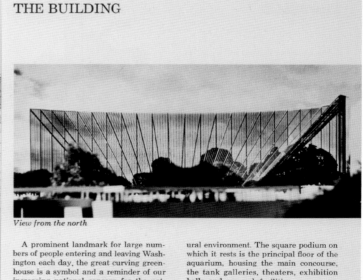

## THE BUILDING

*View from the north*

A prominent landmark for large numbers of people entering and leaving Washington each day, the great curving greenhouse is a symbol and a reminder of our increasing national concern for the natural environment. The square podium on which it rests is the principal floor of the aquarium, housing the main concourse, the tank galleries, theaters, exhibition halls, and research facilities.

3

## THE SPACE

The Aquarium Building will house, in approximately 166,000 square feet, five different kinds of activity:

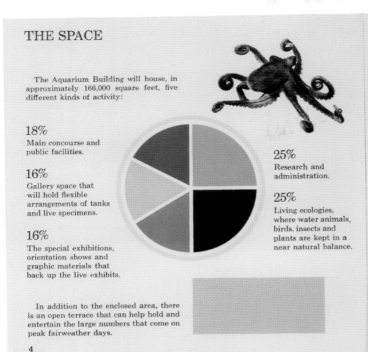

**18%**
Main concourse and public facilities.

**16%**
Gallery space that will hold flexible arrangements of tanks and live specimens.

**16%**
The special exhibitions, orientation shows and graphic materials that back up the live exhibits.

**25%**
Research and administration.

**25%**
Living ecologies, where water animals, birds, insects and plants are kept in a near natural balance.

In addition to the enclosed area, there is an open terrace that can help hold and entertain the large numbers that come on peak fairweather days.

4

## THE PURPOSE

The authorizing Act of Congress of October 9, 1962, commits the National Fisheries Center and Aquarium to a high level of scientific research, and to the display of aquatic organisms and environments for "educational, recreational, cultural and scientific purposes."

The fulfillment of these goals could bring to the word "aquarium" a broader meaning than it has normally held. The display of aquatic life will include birds, insects, amphibians, and growing plants, with special stress on the delicate balance among them. The educational and recreational aspects will be built on a framework of scientific discipline.

Our present national environmental crisis gives a new sense of urgency to this commitment. To the millions of students, citizens, lawmakers and businessmen who visit the capital each year, the Aquarium will dramatically present the principles on which the biological world operates. It will introduce these visitors to the pleasures that come from an understanding of the great aquatic environment—they will be shown much of what can be done to preserve and protect it; and they may come to have a more informed respect for it.

5

---

*A close-up look*

*Sea anemone tentacles*

*Nudibranch*

*Tube blenny*

## SMALL TANKS AND INTIMATE VIEWS

Much of the drama and the beauty of aquatic life occurs at a scale best experienced with a magnifying glass or a microscope. This is the scale of the fantastic and the colorful—at this size, the normal living functions are performed with equipment and configurations that are unfamiliar and with action that can be both hairraising and beautiful.

*Burrowing sea anemone*

*Sun starfish*

This experience includes isolated views of biological functions and some good lessons on the appropriate size of things. The National Aquarium will attempt to bring the great rewards of the micro world to the attention of the interested viewer.

22

23

---

*The earth*

## MAINTAINING THE WORLD'S ECOLOGY

The theme of conservation is implicit in the whole aquarium program; the experience, and the exhibits, are designed to foster the kind of personal involvement and responsible interest which effective conservation presupposes.

A strategically placed area is given over to presenting and discussing some of the aesthetic and functional aspects of conservation:

—the problems of management of aquatic resources;

—the urgency of the restoration of degraded environments;

—the techniques being developed to study environments — (infra-red and radar photography, sonar, satellite observations);

—the global effects of water pollution; man's direct and indirect encroachment on aquatic habitats.

*Colorado river delta*

*Dry lake bed*

35

Barbara Fahs Charles, Henry Beer and Robert Staples working on a full-scale mock-up of the 'History Wall' for *A Computer Perspective* at 901, 1970

Installation view of *A Computer Perspective*, IBM Corporate Exhibit Center, New York, 1971

*Opposite*
Computer House of Cards, 1971
Printed card, each 8.9 × 5.9 cm (3 ½ × 2 ⅜ in.)

*A Computer Perspective* (1971–5) was the first of many exhibitions designed by the Eames Office for the IBM Corporate Exhibition Center in New York. The exhibition traced the evolution of those inventions that had led to the modern computer. The main feature was the 15-metre-long (50 ft) 'History Wall', a complex, 3D timeline made up of documents, artefacts and photographs, as well as both vintage and modern machines. Other exhibits included the 'Audiovisual Rack', a multi-screen slideshow of the latest advances in computer applications, and an interactive computer game, 'Twenty Questions'. The project took two years to devise and was organized and designed by Eames Office staff member Robert Staples working with Barbara Fahs Charles, Glen Fleck and Bill Tondreau, among others.

Information Machines

Jehane Burns and Jeannine Oppewall at 901, researching for the exhibition *Moveable Feasts and Changing Calendars*, 1973

Installation view of *Moveable Feasts*, IBM Corporate Exhibit Center, New York, 1973

Charles and Ray Eames at *Isaac Newton: Physics for a Moving Earth*, IBM Corporate Exhibit Center, New York, 1973

Between 1972 and 1977 IBM commissioned the Eames Office to research and produce a series of small, travelling exhibitions exploring the people and ideas that had shaped modern science. The Office developed a distinct vocabulary for the exhibitions. Visitors were confronted with a dense array of information – text, photographs, diagrams and objects – mounted on free-standing portable panels. Decorative elements were introduced according to the season in which the exhibition opened: potted plants for spring exhibitions, for example, and eighteenth-century festive artefacts for a Christmas exhibition on Isaac Newton.

This multimedia approach was continued on a larger scale in *The World of Franklin and Jefferson*, produced for the American Revolution Bicentennial in 1976. This expansive exhibition toured both in the United States and internationally. Information was clustered on free-standing structures, which stood among dense displays of varied and sometimes surprising artefacts, including instruments, dress and even a stuffed bison.

*Right*
Graphic design by Paul Brühwiler for Eames Office
Poster for *The World of Franklin and Jefferson*, Grand Palais, Paris, 1975
Photomechanical print on paper, 160 × 119.4 cm (63 × 47 in.)
Collection of Robert Staples and Barbara Fahs Charles

*Below*
Installation views of *The World of Franklin and Jefferson*, British Museum, London, 1975 (top left), and The Metropolitan Museum of Art, New York, 1976

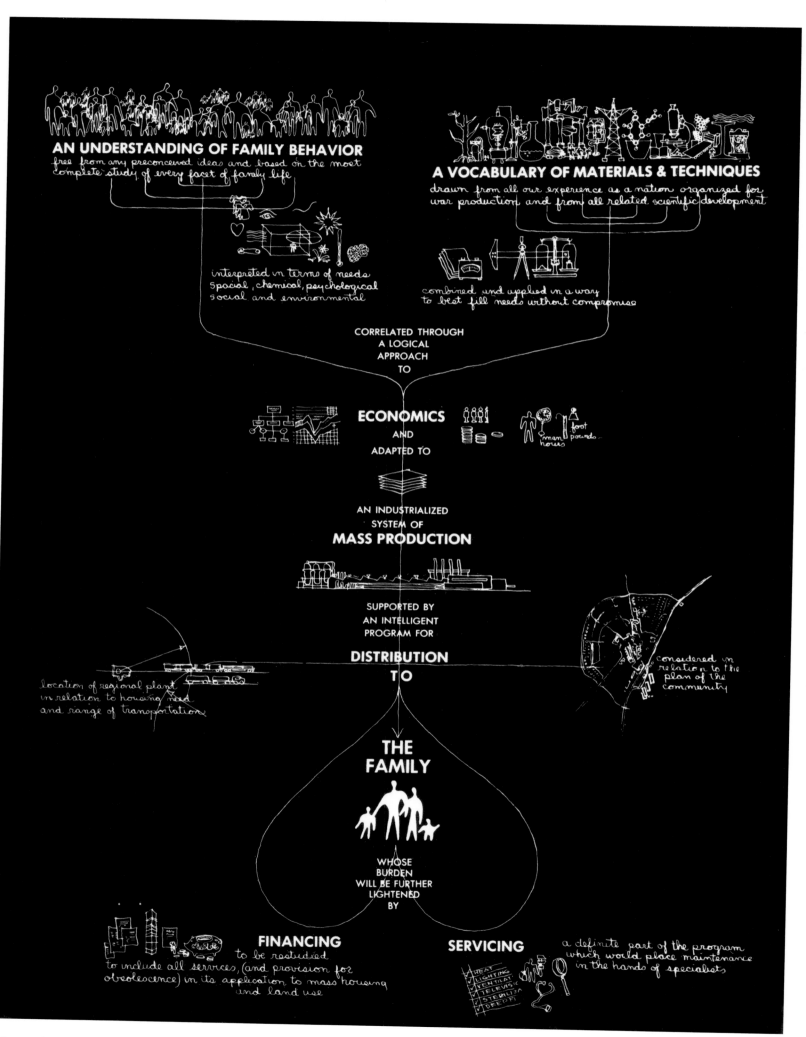

**AN UNDERSTANDING OF FAMILY BEHAVIOR**
free from any preconceived ideas and based on the most complete study of every facet of family life

**A VOCABULARY OF MATERIALS & TECHNIQUES**
drawn from all our experience as a nation organized for war production and from all related scientific development

interpreted in terms of needs
spacial, chemical, psychological
social and environmental

combined and applied in a way
to best fill needs without compromise

CORRELATED THROUGH
A LOGICAL
APPROACH
TO

**ECONOMICS**
AND
ADAPTED TO

man hours    foot pounds

AN INDUSTRIALIZED
SYSTEM OF
**MASS PRODUCTION**

SUPPORTED BY
AN INTELLIGENT
PROGRAM FOR

**DISTRIBUTION**
**TO**

location of regional plant
in relation to housing need
and range of transportation.

considered in
relation to the
plan of the
community

**THE**
**FAMILY**

WHOSE
BURDEN
WILL BE FURTHER
LIGHTENED
BY

**FINANCING**
to be restudied
to include all services, (and provision for
obsolescence) in its application to mass housing
and land use

**SERVICING**
a definite part of the program
which would place maintenance
in the hands of specialists

The last major Eames project, 'Inventions: The Artifacts of Innovation' (1977–8), was to have included short films, an exhibition and a book. The unfinished project would have shown the history of invention from a global perspective, demonstrating how greater communication led to specific discoveries.[1] Illustrating how knowledge was disseminated, the inventions to be featured were to show the dependence on an openness of information between nations, business and institutions. The Eameses pointed out that the future depended on 'a new level of understanding', rather than simply 'heaping-up more information', to form 'an understanding of the effects of innovation on interconnected living systems'.[2] Formulating a framework to speed the global transmission of knowledge, Charles and Ray saw 'information as the accelerator' for innovation.[3] After all, they had already successfully applied knowledge developed in other industries to their design work, from techniques for shock mounting and plywood moulding to building their own home by assembling off-the-shelf components. Incrementally applying significant technological advances to an existing body of knowledge, the Eameses categorized innovative techniques already in use and improved on them.

More than any other Eames project, 'Inventions' provided insight into the Eameses' vision of the way in which social, commercial and political interests might align in order to promote greater cooperation. Funded by IBM, the exhibition was to tour America and be displayed in sixteen foreign capitals by the United States Information Agency (USIA).[4] In the exhibition agreement, IBM and the USIA jointly stated, 'Implicit in the exhibition would be the notion that central to the progress of innovation are the tools, discoveries, and techniques of science and technology and that the search for betterment truly transcends temporal as well as ideological and national boundaries.'[5] Beyond the idea of innovation as serving the immediate present, the project was intended to show the exponential growth of discoveries – how a single technological advancement could initiate a succession of subsequent innovations. One example of this process described by the Eameses was the pacemaker, which originated from an electrical experiment in Italy in 1791, with further development in India and Australia during the 1920s, leading to the first surgical implant in the United States in 1960.[6] The invention relied on research conducted over 169 years on multiple continents, with clear lines of communication required to make the various innovations known to all. Through such examples as the pacemaker, the Eameses sought to emphasize 'significant technological innovations of high social impact', so the advantages of open societies could be made obvious.[7]

Included in the notes for the 'Inventions' exhibition was an explanation of the 'art of leapfrog', the potential advantages gained when two distant cultures meet for the first time.[8] According to the Eameses, the Japanese were able to skip successive stages in their technological development and modernize rapidly thanks to knowledge gained from another culture. In their film *The Black Ships* (1970), the Eameses examine how technology served as a means of communication in 1852, as advanced American commodities were used to entice the Japanese to open their borders after two hundred years of self-imposed isolation. The technologies presented contained a message, with such inventions as the steamship, the locomotive and the telegraph system improving the transmission of information. The extraordinary pace with which Japan modernized in subsequent years supported the concept that technological leapfrogging in the contemporary world could occur through greater cross-cultural interaction.

Examples in the exhibition were to highlight inventions that had served society as a whole, rather than the individual. One instance noted that 'in 1620, Francis Bacon – counsellor to Queen Elizabeth – called for a program of applied scientific inquiry – experiment

and publication', which changed the procedure for research and the mode of its communication in a manner that benefited the entire society.[9] Furthering the social ideals of the Enlightenment, the Eameses went beyond simply exhibiting how they believed inventions occurred by actively seeking to make existing public resources serve a larger population. In a report submitted to the Librarian of Congress in 1977, they recommended distributing computer terminals to every major city in the United States, making access to the American national library readily available. The Eameses wrote: 'The Library of Congress has a special responsibility … a responsibility to the citizen at large, in pursuit of any of those activities for which there's a broadening need for information – sales, planning, electing one's representatives, learning for the pleasure of it, writing, film-making, theater, "consumerism"'; that is, 'a responsibility to the young, born to "universal expectations" but not yet sure what goods their society offers'.[10] In this context, the 'consumerism' they sought was related to knowledge, rather than products or resources – the exchange of ideas, rather than the exchange of material goods. Extending the United Nations' Universal Declaration of Human Rights, the 'universal expectations' described by the Eameses recognized access to intellectual material as a basic right of every citizen.

In addition to government participation, the Eameses anticipated that cultural institutions would need to distribute their collections by investing in the infrastructure necessary to reach a broad audience. In a lecture delivered at the Smithsonian Institution in Washington DC in 1977, Charles emphasized that 'each of these institutions also recognizes the importance of systems which will make their services available in places far distant from headquarters: regional storefronts, tape and video libraries, on-line "congenial" terminals, cable TV picking up programs by satellite. And lastly, each recognizes the need for all of them to have on-line access to some at least of each other's data.'[11] When introducing these ideas, the Eameses described the need for a network of information that efficiently connected institutions together, so that when visiting one institution the knowledge contained in all the others would be available.

In a study for an arts centre associated with the Metropolitan Museum of Art in New York, the Eameses suggested an analogous line of reasoning: 'The Center could provide (for the use of the Museum, for visiting scholars and to all those engaging in research and teaching in the visual arts) an archive of photographic documentation … It should negotiate with phototheques [picture libraries] in other art-historical institutions for the right to copy their material selectively onto microfiche or video disc.'[12] Following approaches developed earlier to extend the use of existing collections, the Eameses suggested that the museum create 'packets of information' to be made available '1) to the Museum,

2) to public television, 3) to schools, university departments, and anyone else'.[13] Here, cultural institutions were presented as public instruments available to aid the production of new work, rather than simply serve as depositories of information.

This manner of thinking extended into the realm of education, and in 1969 the Eameses prepared a report for Howard Johnson, president of the Massachusetts Institute of Technology (MIT). In the *MIT Report*, as it became known, the Eameses recommended that students create packets of information in their own areas of expertise – in the form of films, slides, audiotapes and other media – to be distributed to the wider community. Moreover, they suggested that students be required to teach at local elementary schools using educational materials, such as 'films, demonstrations, words, experiences, pictures, plays, models – anything that would help the central idea have meaning to the children', drawn from the students' own academic disciplines.[14] Instead of maintaining a strict divide between the arts and the sciences, the *MIT Report* brought the subjects closer together, the idea being that MIT should have 'film-makers in the departments'.[15] According to the Eameses, the films needed to be expository, with the students directly involved in the film-making process so as to improve their visual literacy and communications skills. To ensure that the best work reached the largest audience, the Eameses proposed a self-optimizing distribution system, whereby the information packets would be distributed first within a department, then the best of those shared across MIT, and the very best disseminated to other institutions and the mass media. In 1978, in notes made for the 'Making Connections'-themed 28th annual International Design Conference in Aspen (IDCA), Charles summarized their concerns: 'most scholars, scientists, curators, aren't trained to want to face the process of re-understanding a subject that they know, in any terms except the written word.'[16] Their intention was for the creation of a film to function 'more as a research tool than a teaching tool – testing/refining/upsetting one's own view of one's own area'.[17] Methods of communication served as means to visualize and understand one's own thinking.

The Eameses expressed one of their most critical theories for the alignment of the arts with society in the film *Exponents* (1973), which was created at the Eames Office by the American mathematician Raymond Redheffer. Charles wrote in his notes, 'EXPONENTS Made by the mathematician who needed it. Ideally you want to turn everybody into [a] Consumer/Producer.'[18] The importance of the 'Consumer/Producer' resonated throughout the Eameses' later work, as they advocated for every citizen's participation in the generation of information. As producers of more than a hundred films, the Eameses constantly examined the ways in which a society accumulates, filters and shares knowledge. Educational ideals were not conceived as definitive lesson plans, but as approaches to amassing, editing and distributing information. Here, the emphasis on the larger structural issues revealed an overarching framework to bring about social change through greater connectivity.

In 1972 the Eames Office made the film *Cable: The Immediate Future* with a grant from the National Science Foundation. They proposed using cable television as a means of sharing ideas through simultaneous two-way transmission: 'Two decades of television and the beginnings of a communication revolution have helped to generate in our society a new mood of universal expectancy, much of which centers around information, education, and the opportunity to be involved in the process. Cable television systems, with their immense capacity and flexibility, could fulfil this expectancy.'[19] Offering the potential for an almost unlimited number of channels connecting people, the vision is remarkable in its delineation of social advances provided by technology: the Eameses describe cable television serving as a 'two-way interactive system with

computers in line'. Foreseeing 'electronic mail delivery, facsimile reproduction, social services, community forums', they envisioned a networked society with 'wired schools and universities linked directly to the wired cities', comprehending that the transformative effects of the information age were already occurring.[20] Continuing to research alternative communications methods, they searched for techniques that would maximize existing resources. Following 'What is a House?', a 1944 diagram by the Eameses centred on industry and framed by the greater social, cultural and economic conditions that influence mass production, *Cable* describes similar ideas but bases its argument on the flow of information, rather than the flow of material.[21] Dissatisfied with the culture of consumerism in America to which they had contributed, the Eameses sought a shift in ambition to make everyone an active producer and consumer of intellectual material, instead of an avid consumer of goods and products.

As the Eameses acknowledged in 1977, 'The "problem" our society faces is not so much a lack of scientific, or technical, or even sociological knowledge – it's a lack of ways of transmitting existing knowledge to people as they need it, in forms they can readily grasp and use.'[22] And although a wide range of digital information is accessible today, the uniquely held information found in archives, specialist libraries and cultural institutions remains difficult to obtain. Elaborating on the problem, the Eameses wrote: 'Innovations now appear (and start to interact) faster than we as a society can evaluate them … Learning to make choices among alternatives already available may now be more urgent, for us as a society, than increasing our rate of innovation. Certainly one of the essentials is good communicative models of what we know – so that all those involved in decisions share the best possible basis for discussion. Our capacity to gather data has outstripped our capacity to model it.'[23] As a society, we need to develop innovative methods to visualize our existing knowledge in order to expand it. To shift from a consumer culture to a communicative culture entails a shift in emphasis towards acknowledging the importance of intellectual capital and refining the structures required to captivate and inspire.

*Pages 302–3*
Charles Eames
Diagram for 'What is a House?',
article by Charles Eames and John
Entenza on prefabricated housing,
*Arts & Architecture*, July 1944

Still from *The Black Ships: The Story of Commodore Perry's Expedition to Japan told with Japanese Pictures of the Time*, 1970
Film, 7:40 min.

*Above*
Still from *Cable: The Immediate Future*, 1972
Film, 10 min.

*Opposite*
Charles and Ray Eames working on an early ½-inch scale model of *Mathematica*

# Selected Chronology

**1907**
Charles Eames born in St Louis, Missouri – 17 June

**1912**
Bernice Alexandra 'Ray' Kaiser born in Sacramento, California – 15 December

**1925**
Charles enrols in Washington University, St Louis, studying architecture

**1929**
Charles marries Catherine Dewey Woermann

**1930**
Charles and Catherine's daughter, Lucia Dewey Eames, is born – 11 October

Charles opens his own architectural office, Gray & Eames, in St Louis, with partner Charles Gray

**1933**
Ray finishes her studies at May Friend Bennett School in Millbrook, New York. While living in New York she attends dance classes led by Martha Graham and studies with artist Hans Hofmann until 1939

**1935**
Charles opens a new architectural firm with Robert T. Walsh, Eames and Walsh

**1936**
Ray becomes a founding member of American Abstract Artists

**1938**
Eliel Saarinen offers Charles a fellowship to resume his architecture and design studies at Cranbrook Academy of Art, Michigan

**1939**
Charles begins teaching at Cranbrook

**1940**
Charles is appointed head of the new Department of Experimental Design at Cranbrook; he works part-time on architectural projects with Eliel and Eero Saarinen

Ray attends Cranbrook for 4 months

Charles and Eero Saarinen win first prize in the storage and seating categories in the 'Organic Design in Home Furnishings' competition at The Museum of Modern Art, New York; Ray and Don Albinson (a future Eames Office staff member) assist with presentation drawings and models

**1941**
Charles and Catherine Woermann Eames are divorced – May

Charles and Ray marry – 20 June

Charles Eames and Eero Saarinen at Cranbrook Academy of Art, c. 1940

Ray Eames with friend Lee Krasner in New York, April 1941

Charles and Ray move to California – July; they live in the Richard Neutra-designed Strathmore Apartments until 1949

Charles works in the art department of MGM Studios

Charles and Ray begin experiments with compound-curved moulded-plywood furniture in their apartment

**1942**
Plyformed Wood Company is established

First moulded-plywood sculpture

Plyformed Wood Company receives US Navy commission to produce moulded-plywood splints and stretchers; stretcher does not progress beyond prototype stage

Ray designs first cover for *Arts & Architecture*; Charles becomes editorial associate and Ray joins the editorial advisory board

**1943**
Plyformed Wood Company becomes Molded Plywood Division of the Evans Products Company; moves to new premises at 901 Washington Boulevard, Venice, California

Molded Plywood Division contracted to produce nose section of military glider and other aircraft parts

Continued plywood-chair experiments

Charles and John Entenza develop plans for a city hall for *Architectural Forum*'s 'New Buildings for 194X' May issue

Ray designs 10 covers for *Arts & Architecture*

**1944**
Ray designs 8 covers for *Arts & Architecture*

Charles and Ray contribute to July issue of *Arts & Architecture* on prefabricated housing, with John Entenza and Herbert Matter

**1945**
Case Study House No. 8 by Charles Eames and No. 9 by Eames and Eero Saarinen announced as part of the *Arts & Architecture* magazine Case Study House Program

Slideshow: *Lecture 1*

Plywood Chair, Children's Chairs, Tables, Stools and Elephant

Ray designs Crosspatch fabric

Eames furniture included in presentation at Barclay Hotel, New York – December

**1946**
Plywood Lounge Chair, Folding Screen, Table and Radio Enclosures

Case Goods

*New Furniture Designed by Charles Eames*, The Museum of Modern Art, New York

Herman Miller begins mass production of Eames furniture designs, following George Nelson's recommendation

**1947**
Folding Tables

'Jefferson National Expansion Memorial' competition

Ray produces fabric designs, and designs 2 covers for *Arts & Architecture*

**1948**
'International Competition for Low-Cost Furniture Design', The Museum of Modern Art, New York

Billy and Audrey Wilder marry; Charles and Ray join them on their honeymoon

**1949**
Herman Miller Furniture Company Showroom, Los Angeles; the Eames Office designs interiors and settings for Herman Miller showrooms in Los Angeles, Chicago and New York until 1976

Charles and Ray move into Case Study House No. 8 – December

Eames Office produces room set for the exhibition *For Modern Living*, Detroit Institute of Arts

**1950**
Case Study House No. 9 completed

Eames Storage Units (ESU)

*Good Design* exhibition programme, Merchandise Mart, Chicago; The Museum of Modern Art, New York

Carson Pirie Scott department store windows, Chicago

Eames Office begins work on graphics for Herman Miller Furniture Company

Film: *Traveling Boy*

Design for house for Audrey and Billy Wilder

Plastic Armchair and Side Chair

Toy Masks

Low Table Wire (or Rod) Base (LTR)

Saul Steinberg completes series of drawings on furniture and in Office on a visit to 901

**1951**
Elliptical Table Rod Base (ETR)

Wire Chair and Sofa

Design for Kwikset House

The Toy, manufactured by Tigrett Enterprises

Macy's 4-Room Display

Charles speaks at International Design Conference in Aspen

Charles and Ray host a Japanese tea ceremony at the Eames House

**1952**
The Little Toy

Films: *Blacktop*; *Parade* (both win Edinburgh International Film Festival awards in 1954)

Philip Dunne Office

House of Cards, pattern and picture decks

Ray designs robes for Herman Miller Mixed Chorus; donated to chapel choir of Hope College, Michigan, in 1960

**1953**
*A Rough Sketch for a Sample Lesson for a Hypothetical Course* presented at the University of Georgia, Athens, and the University of California, Los Angeles, in collaboration with George Nelson and Alexander Girard

Films: *Bread*; *A Communications Primer*

Giant House of Cards

Hang-It-All

Course for architecture students at University of California, Berkeley

Slideshows: *Railroad*; *Road Race*; *Seascape*; *Townscape*

Publicity image for the Hang-It-All, September 1953

**1954**
Sears Compact Storage

Max De Pree House

Sofa Compact

Film: *S-73 (Sofa Compact)*

Stadium Seating

Charles travels to Germany as part of the German State Department cultural exchange programme

**1955**
Stacking Chairs

Films: *House: After Five Years of Living*; *Textiles and Ornamental Arts of India*; *Two Baroque Churches in Germany*

Slideshow: *Konditorei*

The Coloring Toy

Charles works on Billy Wilder's film *The Spirit of St Louis*

**1956**
Lounge Chair and Ottoman

Film: *Lounge Chair*

Stephens Speaker

**1957**
Films: *The Spirit of St Louis* (montage); *Stars of Jazz*; *Day of the Dead*; *Toccata for Toy Trains* (Edinburgh International Film Festival award); *The Information Machine*

Griffith Park Railroad

Alcoa Solar Do-Nothing Machine

Charles and Ray visit India to begin research for a report commissioned by the Indian government – December

### 1958
Aluminium Group furniture

Films: *Herman Miller at the Brussels Fair*; *The Expanding Airport*; *De Gaulle Sketch*

*India Report* submitted to Indian government (forms basis for the National Institute of Design, Ahmedabad, established in 1961)

### 1959
Revell Toy House

Films: *Kaleidoscope Shop*; *Time & Life Building International Lobby*

Multi-screen installation: *Glimpses of the U.S.A.*, American National Exhibition, Moscow

Charles delivers Annual Discourse for Royal Institute of British Architects and the Royal College of Art Lethaby Lectures at the Victoria and Albert Museum, London

### 1960
Time-Life Building Lobbies, Chair and Stools

Films: *The Fabulous Fifties*; *Kaleidoscope Jazz Chair*; *Introduction to Feedback*

### 1961
Furniture design for La Fonda restaurant

Exhibition: *Mathematica: A World of Numbers ... and Beyond*, California Museum of Science and Industry, Los Angeles

Eames Contract Storage

Films: *ECS*; *Mathematica* 'Peep Shows' (win Outstanding Film of the Year Award at the London Film Festival in 1963)

Slideshow: *Tivoli*

Charles receives Diploma of Honorary Royal Designer for Industry from the Royal Society of Arts, London

### 1962
Multi-screen installation: *The House of Science*, Seattle World's Fair

Films: *The Good Years*; *Before the Fair*; *IBM Fair Presentation #1 and #2*

Tandem Sling Seating

### 1963
Tandem Shell Seating

### 1964
School Seating

Installation view of *House of Science*, United States Science Exhibit, Seattle World's Fair, 1962

3473 Sofa

IBM Pavilion for New York World's Fair; includes multi-screen installation *Think*

Film: *The House of Science*

Segmented Base Tables

### 1965
Exhibition: *Jawaharlal Nehru: His Life and His India*, with National Institute of Design, Ahmedabad, India; Union Carbide Building, New York; Royal Festival Hall, London; Smithsonian Institution, Washington DC; Museum of Science and Industry, Los Angeles; Delhi, India

Films: *Westinghouse in Alphabetical Order*; *The Smithsonian Institution*; *Computer Day at Midvale*; *Sherlock Holmes and the Singular Case of the Plural Green Mustache*; *IBM at the Fair*

### 1966
Films: *View from the People Wall*; *The Leading Edge*

Smithsonian Carousel

National Aquarium Proposal

### 1967
Films: *National Fisheries Center and Aquarium*; *The Scheutz Machine*

Slideshows: *G.E.M.*; *Herman Miller International*; *Picasso*

Eames House is awarded Grand Prix Award by American Institute of Architects

### 1968
Films: *A Computer Glossary*; *Babbage's Calculating Machine*; *IBM Museum*; *The Lick Observatory*; *A Rough Sketch for a Proposed Film Dealing with the Powers of Ten and the Relative Size of Things in the Universe*

Intermediate Desk Chair

Exhibition: *Photography and the City: An Evolution of an Art and a Science*, Smithsonian Institution

Washington Presentation Center for IBM

Chaise

### 1969
Soft Pad Aluminium Group furniture

Films: *Image of the City*; *Tops*

Exhibition: *What is Design?*, Musée des Arts Décoratifs, Louvre, Paris

PBS TV special *Profile of Charles Eames*

Charles and Ray begin preparing the *MIT Report*, suggesting new approaches to learning

### 1970
Films: *Soft Pad*; *The Fiberglass Chairs*; *A Small Hydromedusan: Polyorchis Haplus*; *The Black Ships*

IBM Computer House of Cards

Drafting Chair

Charles appointed to National Council of the Arts by President Richard Nixon; Charles Eliot Norton Professor of Poetry, Harvard University; and Honorary Fellow at Manchester Polytechnic, UK

### 1971
Two-Piece Plastic Chair and Two-Piece Secretarial Chair

An Eames Office staff member working in the graphics room at 901, early 1970s

Loose Cushion Armchair

Exhibition: *A Computer Perspective*, IBM Exhibit Center, New York

Films: *Computer Landscape*; *Clown Face*

### 1972
Films: *Computer Perspective*; *Sumo Wrestler*; *Cable: The Immediate Future*; *Alpha*; *Banana Leaf*; *SX-70*; *Design Q&A*

Exhibitions at IBM Exhibit Center, New York: *Wallace J. Eckert: Celestial Mechanic*; *Fibonacci: Growth and Form*; *Copernicus*

### 1973
Films: *Exponents: A Study in Generalization*; *Franklin & Jefferson*; *Two Laws of Algebra: Distributive and Associative*; *Copernicus*

Still from *SX-70*, 1972. Film, 11 min.

Exhibitions at IBM Exhibit Center, New York: *Moveable Feasts and Changing Calendars*; *On the Shoulders of Giants*; *Isaac Newton*

*Furniture by Charles Eames*, The Museum of Modern Art, New York

### 1974
Film: *Newton's Method*; *Kepler's Laws*; *Callot*

Newton Cards

Exhibition: *Philosophical Gardens*, IBM Exhibit Center, New York

### 1975
Film: *Metropolitan Overview*

Exhibition: *The World of Franklin and Jefferson*, Grand Palais, Paris; National Museum of Poland, Warsaw; British Museum, London

*An Eames Celebration – Several Worlds of Charles and Ray Eames* film, produced and directed by Perry Miller Adato

*Nelson/Eameses/Girard/Propst: The Design Process at Herman Miller*, Walker Art Center, Minneapolis

### 1976
Films: *The World of Franklin and Jefferson*; *Atlas*; *Something About Photography*; *The Look of America*

Exhibitions: *The World of Franklin and Jefferson*, The Metropolitan Museum of Art, New York; Art Institute of Chicago; Los Angeles County Museum of Art; *Images of Early America*, Herman Miller showroom, Los Angeles

Slideshow: *Tall Ships*

*Connections: The Work of Charles and Ray Eames*; exhibition tours the United States, United Kingdom and Europe

### 1977
Slideshows: *Innovations*; *Innovations II*

Films: *Daumier: Paris and the Spectator*; *Powers of Ten: A Film Dealing with the Relative Size of Things in the Universe, and the Effect of Adding Another Zero*; *Polavision*

Exhibition: *The World of Franklin and Jefferson*, National Museum of Anthropology, Mexico City

IBM 590 Corporate Exhibit Center Proposal

Ray receives Woman of the Year award from California Museum of Science and Industry Muses

Charles and Ray are made members of Alliance Graphique Internationale

### 1978
Films: *Sonar One-Step*; *Art Game*; *Merlin and the Time Mobile*; *Cézanne: The Late Work*; *Degas in the Metropolitan*

Charles delivers 'Making Connections' lecture at the International Design Conference in Aspen

Charles dies, St Louis, Missouri – 21 August

### 1979
Film: *A Report on the IBM Exhibition Center*

Ray accepts the Royal Institute of British Architects Gold Medal on behalf of her and Charles

### 1984
Leather and Teak Sofa

Ray receives Honorary Doctorate of Fine Arts, Otis Art Institute of Parsons School of Design, part of the New School for Social Research

### 1988
Ray dies, Los Angeles, California – 21 August

# Notes

*Something about the World of Charles and Ray Eames*

1 Charles Eames, Charles Eliot Norton Lecture No. 1, Loeb Theater, Harvard University, Cambridge, MA, 26 October 1970, quoted in E. W. Seay, 'Ideas and Words of Charles Eames', unpublished manuscript, 1981, p. 32, Eames Office Archives, Los Angeles, California.

2 Their first film, *Traveling Boy*, was made in 1950 and was never finished; their next films, *Blacktop* and *Parade: or Here They Come Down Our Street* (both 1952), won awards at the Edinburgh International Film Festival in 1954. See pages 312–13.

3 In 1970 Charles Eames was appointed Charles Eliot Norton Professor of Poetry at Harvard University, a prestigious position offered to those individuals who have made a significant contribution to the arts. Previous Norton professors include T. S. Eliot, Robert Frost, Igor Stravinsky, Sigfried Giedion, E. E. Cummings (a poet greatly admired by the Eameses), Herbert Read and Pier Luigi Nervi. The topic of Charles's series of six lectures delivered between October 1970 and April 1971 was announced as 'Problems Relating to Visual Communication and the Visual Environment'. See John and Marilyn Neuhart, and Ray Eames, *Eames Design* (New York: Abrams, 1989), p. 355.

4 Charles Eames, Charles Eliot Norton Lecture No. 1, p. 32.

5 *Ibid.*

6 See 'Life in Work', pages 17–52.

7 See Eames Demetrios essay in 'Life in Work', pages 20–23.

8 Jehane R. Burns, 'Did You Get the Pictures?', *Close-Up*, vol. 12, no. 3, 1981, p. 6 (published by the Polaroid Corporation, Cambridge, MA).

9 'We painted the sidewalk out in front of the shop, and Charles and Don were up top moving furniture about so that the shadows would fall in the right place, because it just happened that we saw it, and it looked so wonderful that we decided we should use it for a good photograph. And at the end of the afternoon, just being so tired, we just stretched out, and Don said … you know, we had another one. We put chairs on top of us and shot it up on the roof and we took several. And we let it happen just because we were so tired, instead of arguing about it.' Ray Eames, interview with Ralph Caplan, 24 February 1981, conducted on behalf of the Herman Miller Furniture Company, Herman Miller Archives, Zeeland, Michigan.

10 Charles Eames to the interviewer in a 1951–2 television interview about his work, 'Union Station' television interview, c. 1951, courtesy Eames Office Archives, Los Angeles, California.

11 The architect Kevin Roche worked with Eero Saarinen from 1950 until Saarinen's death in 1961 and collaborated with the Eames Office on several projects, including the IBM Pavilion at the 1964–5 New York World's Fair (see pages 280–85) and the National Aquarium and Fisheries Center proposal (see pages 296–7). 'The first time I really collaborated with Charles was on a slide presentation he was preparing. He was especially interested in the Northland shopping centre in Detroit, one of the very first large-scale shopping centres in the US, designed by Victor Gruen, and so with a crew of people from the Office we went down there and took about 300 photographs. Charles then collaged these into his presentation, some of which later appeared in his *Glimpses of the U.S.A.* film in Moscow.' Kevin Roche, 'Thomas Weaver in Conversation with Kevin Roche', *AA Files*, 71, Winter 2015.

12 See 'At Home with the Eameses', pages 61–128; and Pat Kirkham, *Charles and Ray Eames: Designers of the Twentieth Century* (Cambridge, MA: MIT Press, 1995).

13 MoMA's 'International Competition for Low-Cost Furniture Design' was announced in 1948 and received nearly 3,000 entries from thirty-one countries. Winners were announced in January 1949. The Eames Office and the University of California, Los Angeles, were awarded second prize in the seating category; British designers Robin Day and Clive Latimer received first prize in the storage unit category. An exhibition about the competition was on display at MoMA between 17 May and 16 July 1950. See press releases, The Museum of Modern Art, 19 January 1949 and 1 May 1950; and The Museum of Modern Art collection online, www.moma.org/collection/works/2133 (accessed 28 August 2015).

14 See Mary Anne Staniszewski, *The Power of Display: A History of Exhibition Installations at the Museum of Modern Art* (Cambridge, MA: MIT Press, 1998) p. 176.

15 See '3 Judgements: Good Design at the Merchandise Mart', *Interiors + Industrial Design*, vol. 109, no. 8, March 1950, pp. 86–90.

16 Richard Hamilton, quoted in 'FoB+10', *Design*, no. 149, May 1961, p. 51.

17 In answer to the question, 'Is it [design] a method of general expression?' posed to Charles Eames by Madame L. Amic and recorded in the film *What is Design?* (1972), Charles states: 'No. It is a method of action'. See page 256.

18 Charles Eames, 'Union Station' television interview.

19 *Ibid.*

20 See, for example, 'A Prediction: Less Self-Expression for the Designer', *Print*, vol. 14, no. 1, January 1960, pp. 77–9.

21 Charles Eames, 'Design, Designer and Industry', *Magazine of Art*, December 1951, pp. 320–21.

22 Charles Eames is quoted as saying, 'The objective is the simple thing of getting the best to the greatest number of people for the least'. In 'Sympathetic Seat', *Time*, no. 7, 10 July 1950.

23 See Hamilton, in 'FoB+10', p. 46.

24 Deborah Sussman oral history (with Eames Demetrios), 5 February 1992, Eames Archive, Los Angeles, California.

25 George Nelson, 'Art X: The Georgia Experiment', *Industrial Design*, no. 5, October 1954, pp. 44–51.

26 Charles Eames, 'On Reducing Discontinuity', *Bulletin of the American Academy of Arts and Sciences*, vol. 30, no. 6, March 1977, p. 24.

27 The Eameses were greatly influenced by György Kepes's book *Language of Vision* (Chicago: Paul Theobald, 1944).

28 Charles Eames, 'Language of Vision: The Nuts and Bolts', *Bulletin of the American Academy of Arts and Sciences*, vol. 28, no. 1, October 1974, p. 17 (emphasis in original). For more information about the project, see 'Information Machines', pages 265–304.

29 Charles Eames, 'Advice for Students', handwritten notes on talks to students at University of California, Los Angeles, January 1949, cited in Daniel Ostroff, ed., *An Eames Anthology: Articles, Film Scripts, Interviews, Letters, Notes, and Speeches* (New Haven and London: Yale University Press, 2015), p. 35.


## LIFE IN WORK

*Introduction*

1 Pat Kirkham, *Charles and Ray Eames: Designers of the Twentieth Century* (Cambridge, MA: MIT Press, 1995), p. 35.

2 See Perry Miller Adato, dir., *An Eames Celebration – Several Worlds of Charles and Ray Eames*, 1973, 90 min.

3 Ray Kaiser's Cranbrook application form, dated 23 August 1940, Alumni Records, Archives of Cranbrook Academy of Art, Bloomfield Hills, Michigan.


*A Contemporary Practice: The Eameses in the 1940s*

1 Charles Eames, unpublished notes for 'Making Connections', International Design Conference in Aspen, June 1978, I:58, Folder 3, The Papers of Charles and Ray Eames, Manuscript Division, Library of Congress, Washington DC (hereafter cited as Eames Papers).

2 Charles Eames, Charles Eliot Norton Lecture No. 1, Loeb Theater, Harvard University, Cambridge, MA, 26 October 1970, quoted in E. W. Seay, 'Ideas and Words of Charles Eames', unpublished manuscript, 1981, p. 32, Eames Office Archives, Los Angeles, California.

3 Ray Eames, interview with Ralph Caplan, 24 February 1981, conducted on behalf of the Herman Miller Furniture Company, Herman Miller Archives, Zeeland, Michigan.

4 A term of art is a word or phrase that has a precise, specialized meaning within a particular field or profession. In this case, the film industry describes any continuous zoom shot that goes dramatically in or out from a great distance as 'a Powers of Ten shot'.

5 Personal conversation with the author, Lucia Eames and Alex Funke. In his notes for a lecture given in 1974, Charles made a note to say, 'This-is-how-it-should-be-ness'. Charles Eames, lecture notes, Penrose Memorial Lecture, American Philosophical Society, Philadelphia, April 1974, II:218, Eames Papers.

6 'Every time I lay a table I am designing something.' Charles Eames, quoted in Keith Colquhoun, 'Innovator in Earth Shoes', in Daniel Ostroff, ed., *An Eames Anthology: Articles, Film Scripts, Interviews, Letters, Notes, Speeches by Charles and Ray Eames* (New Haven and London: Yale University Press, 2015), p. 340.

7 Ray worked on the competition boards, but was not involved directly with the designs; she and Charles had just met. They married in June 1941 and moved to Los Angeles the following month.

8 'Museum of Modern Art Announces Winners in Industrial Design Competitions for Twenty-One American Republics', press release, The Museum of Modern Art, 1 February 1941, p. 2.

9 Charles Eames to Eliot Noyes, 1941, quoted from copy of letter in Eames Office Archives, Los Angeles, California.

10 Ray Eames, interview with Ralph Caplan, 24 February 1981, conducted on behalf of the Herman Miller Furniture Company, Herman Miller Archives, Zeeland, Michigan.

11 In the autumn of 1941 Charles Eames was employed by the art department of Metro-Goldwyn-Mayer, in order to fund the Eameses' early experiments in moulded plywood manufacture. He principally assisted the set designers as a draughtsman, and spent time on the sets of such films as *Mrs. Miniver* and *I Married an Angel* (both 1942).

12 Anthony G. Bowman, 'Charles Eames: The Designer as Renaissance Man', *Ameryka*, 19 October 1971, pp. 41–2.

13 In 1956 Chinese-born physicists Chen Ning Yang (b. 1922) and Tsung-Dao Lee (b. 1926) discovered violations in the principle of parity conservation, which had incorrectly been assumed to be a universal law of physics (a discovery fairly summarized as proving that the universe is left-handed). In 1957, while still in their thirties, they were jointly awarded a Nobel Prize for their work in particle physics.

14 Owner of the Ford Motor Company, Henry Ford (1863–1947) was an American industrialist best known for his innovations in mass production and the organization of labour. He was also a collector of industrial and everyday objects, and in 1929 established the Edison Institute in Greenfield, Michigan, in order to preserve his collection for the public. The institution remains open today as The Henry Ford.

15 On 7 December 1941, Japan launched a surprise aerial attack on the US naval base at Pearl Harbor in Hawaii. The attack galvanized American support for the Second World War, and led directly to the US government's decision to join the Allied forces.

16 Charles Eames to Richard Raseman, letter on wood veneer, 8 June 1942, Archives of Cranbrook Academy of Art, Bloomfield Hills, Michigan. Charles's outstanding debt of $158.48 to the Cranbrook Academy is noted as overdue for payment in a letter from Raseman to Charles dated 19 November 1941, Cranbrook Archives.

17 Ray Eames, interview with Ralph Caplan, 24 February 1981, conducted on behalf of the Herman Miller Furniture Company, Herman Miller Archives, Zeeland, Michigan.

18 The Skunk Works is the common alias for Lockheed Martin's Advanced Development Division. In the 1940s the division implemented an unconventional organizational system with minimal bureaucratic interference, and gained a reputation for producing highly innovative aircraft designs under severe time constraints and with limited resources. Today, the term is often used to refer to a small group of thinkers, designers or engineers given a large amount of autonomy by an organization in order to experiment and innovate.

19 By this point, however, Charles's mother lived with his sister, Adele, and her family.

20 In December 1945 Evans Products organized a press and trade preview of their Molded Plywood Division designs at the Barclay Hotel in New York.

21 Herman Miller was first introduced to the Eameses' work by the American industrial designer George Nelson, who saw their designs at the Barclay Hotel exhibition of 1945. Herman Miller distributed Eames chairs the following year, and eventually went on to purchase the wood-moulding division of Evans Products and manufacture Eames designs. Today, Vitra makes Eames furniture in Europe and the Middle East, while Herman Miller produces it in the United States and the rest of the world.

22 'The Best of the Century', Time, 31 December 1999, pp. 73–7.

23 Interview with the author, East Grenville, Pennsylvania, 14 March 1992.

24 Silicon Valley is a comedy series first broadcast in 2014 on HBO. It follows the attempts of a programmer to establish a start-up in the eponymous area of Northern Californian, the heartland of America's computing and electronics industries.

25 George Nelson, interview with Mickey Friedman, 1974, Herman Miller Archives, Zeeland, Michigan.

26 Interestingly, Ray recalled that they first utilized the material when they made the sliding screens for the Eames House.

27 From An Eames Primer: 'In 1947, John Wills had developed a way to cure fiberglass at room temperature … He recalled how Charles arrived "out of the blue" in a beat-up Ford at his (Wills') workshop in Arcadia, California, in 1948 or 1949. Charles had with him a craft paper mockup of the armshell and asked Wills to make a fiberglass shell of it … The charge: $25. Wills made two just in case. When Charles came back a week or so later, Charles looked at the fiberglass shells very carefully, circling them, sitting in them, taking them in … When it came time to pay, Wills asked if he wanted both. Charles replied, "I can't really afford it – maybe some other time."' The one left behind remained in Wills's workshop for almost half a century, and is now in the permanent collection of The Henry Ford. Eames Demetrios, An Eames Primer (New York: Universe, 2001), pp. 116–17.

28 Charles Eames to Eero Saarinen, 19 November 1949, quoted from copy of letter in Eames Office Archives, Los Angeles, California.

29 Charles Eames, in Perry Miller Adato, dir., An Eames Celebration – Several Worlds of Charles and Ray Eames, 1973, 90 min.

30 During his time at Cranbrook, Charles shot film of the campus and the academy, including footage of Maija Grotell (1899–1973) at work. Grotell was a Finnish-born ceramicist, and held the position of Instructor of Ceramics and Pottery at Cranbrook.

31 The Good Design exhibitions were staged annually between 1950 and 1955 by The Museum of Modern Art and the Merchandise Mart, a wholesale merchandising centre in Chicago. Showcasing contemporary product design, the displays were limited to mass-produced, purchasable objects, rather than prototypes or unique artefacts. Versions of each exhibition were shown at both venues. Charles and Ray Eames were responsible for designing the first exhibition in 1950.

32 Charles Eames, Charles Eliot Norton Lecture No. 1.

33 Ibid.

34 Charles Eames, in 'If I Could Tell a Woman One Thing about Furnishing a Home …', Family Circle, vol. 52, no. 3, March 1958, pp. 27–33.

### Page 26

1 The Plyformed Wood Company was established in late 1942 by Charles and Ray Eames with the architects Gregory Ain and Griswald Raetze and the set designer Margaret Harris; Raetze and Harris were former associates of Charles's from MGM Studios. Harry Bertoia and photographer Herbert Matter joined the group the following year. Other key staff included Norman Bruns and Marion Overby.

### Page 46

1 Eliot Noyes, 'Charles Eames', Arts & Architecture, September 1946, p. 26.

### Page 49

1 Charles Eames, narration for 'The Development of the Molded Plywood Chair', film made for Discovery television programme, San Francisco Museum of Art, 1953, cited in Daniel Ostroff, ed., An Eames Anthology (New Haven and London: Yale University Press, 2015), p. 117.

### Page 52

1 The exhibition ran from 13 March to 31 March 1946.

2 Hugh De Pree, Business as Unusual (Zeeland, MI: Herman Miller, 1986), p. 44.

## AT HOME WITH THE EAMESES

### Introduction

1 Quoted in the announcement of Case Study House Nos. 8 and 9 in Arts & Architecture, December 1945.

2 Alison and Peter Smithson, 'The New Brutalism: An Editorial', Architectural Design, January 1955, p. 1.

3 Charles Eames, in Perry Miller Adato, dir., An Eames Celebration – Several Worlds of Charles and Ray Eames, 1973, 90 min.

### Charles and Ray Eames, the Proto-Brutalists

1 II:23, The Papers of Charles and Ray Eames, Manuscript Division, Library of Congress, Washington DC. Philip Johnson was one of America's most prominent, longest practising and best-connected architects of the twentieth century. In 1932, as the first director of the Department of Architecture at The Museum of Modern Art in New York, he co-curated the influential exhibition Modern Architecture: International Exhibition, thereby giving rise to the term 'International Style'. He was also an early acolyte of Ludwig Mies van der Rohe. Douglas Haskell was an American architecture critic, an early proponent of modern architecture in the United States and editor of Architectural Forum from 1949 until 1964.

2 Ibid. The CIAM (Congrès Internationaux d'Architecture Moderne), active between 1928 and 1959, was an organization composed of the most prominent architects of the interwar years that promoted the use of modern architecture internationally. Team X (or Team 10) was a group of modern architects, unofficially headed by Alison and Peter Smithson, that got together during the 9th CIAM congress and was charged with organizing the 10th in 1956 (hence the name). The group subsequently disbanded and CIAM and continued as a more informal outfit from 1960 until around 1981.

3 Reyner Banham, Los Angeles: The Architecture of Four Ecologies (London: Allen Lane, 1971), p. 223.

4 See, for example, 'Life in a Chinese Kite: Standard Industrial Products Assembled in a Spacious Wonderland', Architectural Forum, September 1950; John Entenza and Charles Eames, 'Case Study House for 1949', Arts & Architecture, December 1949; 'A Designer's Home of His Own', Life, 11 September 1950; 'House at Santa Monica California', Architectural Review, October 1951; Frank Newby, 'The Work of Charles Eames', Architectural Design, February 1954. The architect and teacher Michael Brawne, for instance, said that he first came across the house in the September 1950 issue of Architectural Forum. Michael Brawne, 'The Wit of Technology', Architectural Design, September 1966, p. 449.

5 Mark Girouard, Big Jim: The Life and Work of James Stirling (London: Pimlico, 2000), pp. 51–2.

6 Anne Massey, The Independent Group: Modernism and Mass Culture in Britain 1945–59 (Manchester: Manchester University Press, 1995), p. 84. Active in the 1950s, the Independent Group was a small and informal group of artists, writers and architects who met at the Institute of Contemporary Arts and sought to challenge what they perceived to be the dominant and elitist modernist culture of the period.

7 According to Peter Smithson, 'As far as I can remember, we heard about it in the 1950s.' Peter Smithson and Hans Ulrich Obrist, Smithson Time: A Dialogue/Ein Gespräch (Cologne: König, 2005), p. 8.

8 On the influence of the Eames House, see Beatriz Colomina, 'Couplings', OASE, June 1999; Francisco González de Canales, Experiments with Life Itself (Barcelona: Actar, 2013); Peter Smithson, 'Just a Few Chairs and a House: An Essay on the Eames-Aesthetic', Architectural Design, September 1966; Dirk van den Heuvel and Max Risselada, '"Just a Few Houses …"', in Dirk van den Heuvel and Max Risselada, eds, Alison and Peter Smithson: From the House of the Future to a House of Today (Rotterdam: 010 Publishers, 2004), pp. 9–11.

9 Anthony Vidler, 'Troubles in Theory V: The Brutalist Moment(s)', Architectural Review, February 2014; Anthony Vidler, 'Re-writing the History of the Recent Present: From the New Empiricism to the New Brutalism', lecture, AA PhD Open Seminar Series, Architectural Association, London, 26 November 2012, available to view online at www.aaschool.ac.uk/VIDEO/lecture.php?ID=2017 (accessed 9 July 2015); Anthony Vidler, 'Another Brick in the Wall', October, no. 136, Spring 2011, pp. 105–32; Anthony Vidler, 'Brutalism, Ethic or Aesthetic?', in Kyle May, ed., CLOG: Brutalism (Brooklyn: CLOG, 2013).

10 Reyner Banham, The New Brutalism: Ethic or Aesthetic? (London: Architectural Press, 1966), p. 134.

11 'Secundum' translates as 'according to'. Banham was cloyingly rather fond of his Latin phrases.

12 Robin Middleton, 'The New Brutalism or a Clean, Well-Lighted Place', Architectural Design, January 1967, p. 7. This is in fact an alternative provenance of the New Brutalism, as compared to Banham's rather one-sided version.

13 Reyner Banham, 'The New Brutalism', Architectural Review, December 1955, p. 355.

14 Alison Smithson, 'Beatrix Potter's Places', Architectural Design, December 1967, p. 573. See also Dirk van den Heuvel, 'Alison and Peter Smithson: A Brutalist Story, Involving the House, the City and the Everyday (plus a Couple of Other Things)', PhD dissertation, Delft University of Technology, 2013, pp. 57–103.

15 Alison Smithson and Peter Smithson, 'The New Brutalism', Architectural Design, January 1955, p. 1.

16 Incidentally, the Smithsons credit Alvar Aalto's Baker Dormitory at MIT (1947–8) as being the first Brutalist building, and, in their scathing review of Banham's book, blast him for missing it. See Alison Smithson and Peter Smithson, 'Banham's Bumper Book on Brutalism', Architects' Journal, 28 December 1966, p. 1591.

17 See, for example, Pat Kirkham, 'Architecture', in Charles and Ray Eames: Designers of the Twentieth Century (Cambridge, MA: MIT Press, 1995), pp. 97–141; Elizabeth A. T. Smith, Case Study Houses: The Complete CSH Program 1945–1966 (Cologne: Taschen, 2009); Elizabeth A. T. Smith, ed., Blueprints for Modern Living: History and Legacy of the Case Study Houses (Cambridge, MA: MIT Press, 1999); Barbara Goldstein, ed., Arts & Architecture: The Entenza Years (Santa Monica, CA: Hennessey & Ingalls, 1998); Ethel Buisson, 'In the Shade of the Eucalyptus', in Ethel Buisson and Thomas Billard, The Presence of the Case Study Houses (Basel: Birkhäuser, 2004), pp. 58–69.

18 Entenza and Eames, 'Case Study House for 1949'.

19 Ibid., p. 27.

20 Cited in Beatriz Colomina, 'The Gift: Reflections on the Eames House', in Pamela Matthews and David McWhirter, eds, Aesthetic Subjects (Minneapolis: University of Minnesota Press, 2003), pp. 347–65.

21 Ray Eames, quoted in Esther McCoy, Case Study Houses 1945–1962 (Santa Monica: Hennessey & Ingalls, 1977), p. 54.

22 Van den Heuvel, 'Alison and Peter Smithson: A Brutalist Story', p. 178.

23 Brawne, 'The Wit of Technology', p. 453.

24 Alison + Peter Smithson: The Shift, Architectural Monographs 7 (London: Academy Editions, 1982), p. 14.

25 Dirk van den Heuvel, '"Picking Up, Turning Over and Putting With …"', in Van den Heuvel and Risselada, Alison and Peter Smithson, pp. 12–28; Van den Heuvel, 'Alison and Peter Smithson: A Brutalist Story', pp. 185–7.

26 Van den Heuvel, 'Alison and Peter Smithson: A Brutalist Story', p. 319.

27 Brawne, 'The Wit of Technology'; Smithson, 'Just a Few Chairs and a House'.

28 Van den Heuvel, 'Alison and Peter Smithson: A Brutalist Story', pp. 182, 237.

29 Banham, 'The New Brutalism', p. 361. The other
two were 'clear exhibition of structure' and 'valuation
of materials "as found"'.
30 Alison Smithson and Peter Smithson, *Changing
the Art of Inhabitation* (London: Ellipsis, 1994).
31 *Ibid.*, pp. 33–7, 141–3.
32 *Ibid.*, p. 141.

**'At Home' with the Eameses: Performance, Hosting
and Hospitality**

1 'Log', II:227, Folder 3, The Papers of Charles and
Ray Eames, Manuscipt Division, Library of Congress,
Washington DC (hereafter cited as Eames Papers).
2 'Log', II:227, Folder 3, Eames Papers.
3 Elmer Bernstein oral history (with Eames Demetrios),
13 January 1992, Eames Office Archives, Los Angeles,
California.
4 Stanley Abercrombie, *George Nelson: The Design
of Modern Design* (Cambridge, MA: MIT Press, 1995),
p. 163, cited in Pat Kirkham, *Charles and Ray Eames:
Designers of the Twentieth Century* (Cambridge,
MA: MIT Press, 1995), p. 320.
5 The photographs show Charles, Nelson, Masey
and Wilder discussing the exhibition. For Eames–
Nelson correspondence, see Eames Papers.
6 Deborah Sussman to her parents, 1 November 1954,
facsimile in collection of the author. See also Mimi
Zeiger, 'History Has Become a Trove of Artefacts
Ready for Appropriation', *Dezeen Magazine Online*,
16 October 2014, www.dezeen.com/2014/10/16/
mimi-zeiger-opinion-deborah-sussman-design-
history (accessed 14 May 2015).
7 'Log', II:227, Folder 3, Eames Papers.
8 *Ibid.*
9 For 1952 see *ibid.*; for 1988 see Elaine Sewell
Jones, conversation with the author, Los Angeles,
August 1991.
10 John Neuhart *et al.*, *Eames Design: The Work of the
Office of Charles and Ray Eames* (New York: Abrams,
1989), p. 137; William Morris, 'The Beauty of Life',
lecture given to the Birmingham Society of Arts and
School of Design, 19 February 1880, later published
in William Morris, *Hopes and Fears for Art: Five
Lectures Delivered in Birmingham, London, and
Nottingham, 1878–1881* (London: Ellis & White, 1882),
p. 108.
11 See Pat Kirkham, '*Humanizing Modernism*': The
Crafts, "Functioning Decoration" and the Eameses',
*Journal of Design History*, vol. 11, no. 1, 1998, pp. 15–29.
'Functioning decoration' was central to several
aspects of the Eameses' life and work, including
the 'at home' hospitality, the Eames room at the
exhibition *For Modern Living* (1949), the showrooms
and the dinner-party sequence from the multi-screen
presentation *Think* (1964).
12 For mask-making, see Neuhart *et al.*, *Eames Design*,
pp. 144–5; for Vincent Price, see Victoria Price,
*Vincent Price: A Daughter's Biography* (New York:
St. Martin's Press, 1999), pp. 193–4, 200.
13 Donald Albinson, conversation with the author
following an interview, Pennsylvania, September
2004.
14 Neuhart *et al.*, *Eames Design*, p. 87.
15 *Eames Demetrios, An Eames Primer* (New York:
Universe, 2001), p. 66. For modern dance, see
Kirkham, *Charles and Ray Eames*, pp. 35, 159.
16 Neuhart *et al.*, *Eames Design*, pp. 57, 145.
17 For 'functioning decoration', see Edward K.
Carpenter, 'A Tribute to Charles Eames', *Industrial
Design 25th Annual Design Review* (1979), pp. 12–13.
For the rest, see Kirkham, *Charles and Ray Eames*,
pp. 143–9; Kirkham, '*Humanizing Modernism*', pp.
15–29; Pat Kirkham, 'New Environments for Modern
Living: "At Home" with the Eameses', in Penny
Sparke, ed., *Designing the Modern Interior: From
the Victorians to Today* (Oxford and New York:
Berg, 2009), pp. 173–4.
18 Deborah Sussman, conversation with the author,
Los Angeles, March 2014.
19 *Ibid.*; Kirkham, *Charles and Ray Eames*, pp. 143–99.
20 Peter Smithson, 'Just a Few Chairs and a House: An
Essay on the Eames-Aesthetic', *Architectural Design*,
September 1966, p. 443, cited in Kirkham, *Charles
and Ray Eames*, pp. 143–99. See also Kirkham,
'New Environments for Modern Living', pp. 172–4.
21 Tina Beebe, conversation with the author, Los
Angeles, February 2012.

22 Kirkham, *Charles and Ray Eames*, pp. 143–99;
Kirkham, 'Humanizing Modernism', pp. 16–27.
23 Digby Diehl, 'Q & A: Charles Eames', *Los Angeles
Times West Magazine*, 8 October 1972, p. 14,
reprinted in Daniel Ostroff, ed., *An Eames Anthology:
Articles, Film Scripts, Interviews, Letters, Notes,
and Speeches* (New Haven and London: Yale
University Press, 2015), pp. 313–17.
24 Diehl, 'Q & A', p. 14. See also 'The Guest/Host
Relationship', *Eames Office Official Site*, www.
eamesoffice.com/the-work/the-guest-host-
relationship (accessed 14 May 2015).
25 'Photo Friday: Dinner at the Saarinens'', *Cranbrook
Kitchen Sink*, Cranbrook Center for Collections
and Research, 25 October 2013, https://
cranbrookkitchensink.wordpress.com/2013/10/25/
photo-friday-dinner-at-the-saarinens (accessed 14
May 2015).
26 Albinson, conversation with the author following
an interview, September 2004. See also Carpenter,
'A Tribute to Charles Eames', p. 12.
27 Albinson, conversation with the author following an
interview, September 2004. Given that the Wilders
were Charles and Ray's guests for an evening 'at
home' that was to be photographed for *Look*
magazine (see main text), I asked Albinson if his story
related to that particular night. He was adamant that
it did not, that this was normal practice. Nancy
Albinson confirmed that, even though they had first
got to know the Eameses when they were students
in Charles's industrial design class at Cranbrook,
and Don was an employee, and regardless of the fact
that they were 'nowhere as glamorous a couple
as the Wilders', Charles and Ray went to almost as
much bother when she and Don visited for dinner
or, if their three sons were with them, a picnic lunch
out of doors. Although Nancy did not learn that the
Eameses thought about design and good hosting
as connected until fifty years later, she immediately
remarked, 'That makes perfect sense.' Nancy
Albinson, conversation with the author,
Pennsylvania, September 2004.
28 For Ray and 'larger picture', see her comments
during the television launch in 1956 of the Eames
Lounge Chair and Ottoman, 'Eames Lounge Chair
Debut in 1956 on NBC', YouTube video, 11:31, posted
by 'Omidimo', 18 April 2011, www.youtube.com/
watch?v=z_X6RsN-HFw. See also Kirkham,
*Charles and Ray Eames*, pp. 143–66; Esther McCoy,
'An Affection for Objects', *Progressive Architecture*,
August 1973, p. 67.
29 For 'super simple ... scrumptious', see Sussman,
conversation with the author, March 2014; for
enormous platters of fruit and other food, see Art
Seidenbaum, 'Sitting Room Only at an Eames Film
Festival', *Los Angeles Times*, 3 October 1976, p. R32.
For the Eameses and good food in general, see Billy
Wilder, conversation with the author and Saul Bass,
Los Angeles, August 1994.
30 W. R. Lethaby, 'Art and Workmanship', *The Imprint*,
vol. 1, January 1913, reprinted in *Form in Civilization:
Collected Papers on Art and Labour* (London:
Oxford University Press, 1922), pp. 208–13.
31 Kirkham, *Charles and Ray Eames*, p. 157. For cocktail
parties, see 'A Designer's Home of His Own', *Life*,
11 September 1950, p. 148; for inauguration, see
Sussman, conversation with the author, March 2014.
32 Sussman, conversation with the author, March 2014.
33 Billy Wilder, conversation with the author,
Los Angeles, August 1994; Carpenter, 'A Tribute
to Charles Eames', p. 12.
34 Audrey Wilder, telephone conversation with
the author, 1993.
35 Billy Wilder, conversation with the author, August
1994; Carpenter, 'A Tribute to Charles Eames', p. 12.
36 Audrey Wilder, telephone conversation with the
author, 1993.
37 Images taken by Noguchi at the event bear the
date of 24 July 1951. See reproduction numbers
LC-USZ6-2279, LC-USZ6-2280, LC-USZ6-2281,
LC-USZ6-2282, LC-USZ6-2283 and
LC-USZ6-2284, The Work of Charles and Ray
Eames, Prints and Photographs Division, Library
of Congress, Washington DC.
38 For the Eameses and Japan, see Neuhart *et al.*,
pp. 154, 170; Kirkham, *Charles and Ray Eames*, pp.
115–17 and *passim*; Kirkham, 'New Environments for
Modern Living', pp. 177–81; Pat Kirkham, 'At Home

with California Modern, 1945–65', in Wendy Kaplan,
ed., *Living in a Modern Way: California Design,
1930–65* (Cambridge, MA: MIT Press/Los Angeles
County Museum of Art, 2011), pp. 146–76; Barbara
Lynne Rowland Mori, 'The Tea Ceremony:
A Transformed Japanese Ritual', *Gender & Society*,
vol. 5, 1991, pp. 86–8. For Chaplin and Japan, see Bruce
Wallace, 'Mr. Kono and the Tramp', *Los Angeles Times*,
16 April 2006, available online at http://articles.latimes.
com/2006/apr/16/entertainment/ca-chaplin16
(accessed 14 May 2015); see also the Chaplin Society
of Japan: www.chaplinjapan.com/english.html
(accessed 14 May 2015). For Noguchi, see Masayo
Duus, *The Life of Isamu Noguchi: Journey Without
Borders*, trans. Peter Duus (Princeton, NJ: Princeton
University Press, 2004).
39 For another photograph of Yamaguchi and Chaplin,
see Sakuya Fujiwara and Yoshiko Yamaguchi, *Ri Koran
watakushi no hansei* (Tokyo: Shinchosha, 1987).
I am grateful to the late Barbara J. Brooks for
photocopies of images from this book. See also
'Charlie with Japanese actress Shirley Yamaguchi,
1953', *Discovering Chaplin*, 3 February 2014, www.
discoveringchaplin.com/2014/02/charlie-with-
japanese-actress-shirley.html (accessed 14 May
2015). The image on the *Discovering Chaplin* website
is dated 1953, but it may have been taken during
Chaplin's visit to Japan of 1961.
40 'NEA National Heritage Fellowships – Sosei Shizuye
Matsumoto', *National Endowment for the Arts*, 1994,
http://arts.gov/honors/heritage/fellows/sosei-
shizuye-matsumoto (accessed 14 May 2015); Mori,
'The Tea Ceremony', pp. 86–97. See also Kirkham,
'New Environments for Modern Living', pp. 177–81.
41 Duus, *The Life of Isamu Noguchi*, p. 223.
42 Other Japanese visitors welcomed at the Eames
House included the famous potters Shoji Hamada
and Soetsu Yanagi, who came with the British potter
Bernard Leach (the three men were on a lecture tour
of the United States, 1953); 'Tiger' Saito, editor of *Japan
Today*; the industrial deisgner Isamu Kenmochi; and
Sokosen, later the grand tea master Soshitsu Sen XV.
See Neuhart *et al.*, *Eames Design, passim*.
43 II:6, Dreyfuss Folder, Eames Papers.
44 'Log', II:227, Folder 3, Eames Papers.

This essay is dedicated to Lucia Eames (1930–2014)
and Barbara J. Brooks (1953–2013), scholar of
Japanese history and culture (see also note 39, above).

*Page 122*

1 Charles Eames to Eero and Lily Saarinen, 29 August
1950, Eames Office Archives, Los Angeles, California.
Buckminster 'Bucky' Fuller (1895–1983) was an
American inventor, designer, architect and theorist
best known for his description of the principles
behind the construction of geodesic domes.

**ART OF LIVING**

*Introduction*

1 'Sympathetic Seat', *Time*, 10 July 1950, pp. 45–6.
2 'Once in discussing the design of Herman Miller's
New York showroom, the words "good design"
were used. Charles Eames said, "Don't give us that
good design crap. You never hear us talk about that.
The real questions are: Does it solve a problem?
Is it serviceable? How is it going to look in ten years?"'
Hugh de Pree, *Business as Unusual* (Zeeland, MI:
Herman Miller, 1986), p. 34.

*Page 141*

1 '$30,000 In Grants, $20,000 In Prizes In International
Competition For Design Of Low-Cost Furniture.
Announcement Of Terms And Conditions', press
release, The Museum of Modern Art, 5 January 1948.

*Page 143*

1 *For Modern Living*, promotional brochure,
Detroit Institute of Arts, 1949.

*Page 146*

1 Alison Smithson, 'And Now Dhamas Are Dying Out
in Japan', *Architectural Design*, September 1966,
pp. 16–17.

*The Dress of Charles and Ray Eames*

1 Rebecca Arnold, *The American Look: Fashion, Sportswear and the Image of Women in 1930s and 1940s New York* (London: I.B. Tauris, 2009), p. 89.

2 Design Museum, 'Charles + Ray Eames', *Design at the Design Museum*, www.designmuseum.org/design/charles-ray-eames (accessed 6 August 2015).

3 Carla Hartman and Lucia Atwood, telephone interview with the author, 15 April 2015.

4 Barbara Fahs Charles, telephone interview with the author, 23 June 2015.

5 Elizabeth Wilson, 'Bohemian Dress', in Valerie Steele, ed., *Encyclopedia of Clothing and Fashion, Volume 1: Academic Dress to Eyeglasses* (Farmington Hills, MI: Charles Scribner's Sons, 2005), p. 172.

6 Pat Kirkham, *Charles and Ray Eames: Designers of the Twentieth Century* (Cambridge, MA: MIT Press, 1995), p. 63.

7 Oral history interview with Ray Eames, 28 July – 20 August 1980, Archives of American Art Oral History Program, Smithsonian Institution, Washington DC, transcript available online at www.aaa.si.edu/collections/interviews/oral-history-interview-ray-eames-12821#transcript (accessed 6 August 2015).

8 Fahs Charles, telephone interview.

9 Ray attended the May Friend Bennett School in Millbrook, New York, between 1931 and 1933.

10 Hartman and Atwood, telephone interview.

11 Ray Eames to Charles Eames, 25 August 1955, II:6, Folder 8, The Papers of Charles and Ray Eames, Manuscript Division, Library of Congress, Washington DC (hereafter cited as Eames Papers).

12 Tina Beebe, quoted in Ruth La Ferla, 'Ray Eames: How She Dressed', *On the Runway* (blog), *New York Times*, 12 December 2011, http://runway.blogs.nytimes.com/2011/12/12/ray-eames-how-she-dressed/?_r=0 (accessed 6 August 2015).

13 Hartman and Atwood, telephone interview.

14 Daniel Delis Hill, *American Menswear: From the Civil War to the Twenty-First Century* (Lubbock, TX: Texas Tech University Press, 2011), p. 53.

15 Hartman and Atwood, telephone interview.

16 Margaret McAleer, Senior Archives Specialist, Manuscript Division, Library of Congress, Washington DC, telephone interview with the author, 10 June 2015.

17 Fahs Charles, telephone interview.

18 Ray Eames, quoted in Keith Colquhoun, 'Innovator in Earth Shoes', *Observer*, 2 November 1975, p. 16.

19 Martin H. Landey, of Martin Landey, Arlow Advertising Inc., to Ray Eames, 1 April 1975, II:75, Folder 'Kalsø Earth Shoes', Eames Papers.

20 The robes were originally designed for the Herman Miller Mixed Chorus, with the colours of the robes symbolizing the four primary voice parts, from soprano (yellow) to bass (purple). When Herman Miller disbanded the choir in 1960, the robes were given to Hope College in Holland, Michigan, where they became the performing apparel of the Chapel Choir. The robe design is still in use today.

21 II:173, New York World's Fair Uniforms Folder, Eames Papers.

22 Charles and Ray Eames, *S-73 (Sofa Compact)* [1954], *The Films of Charles and Ray Eames, Volume 6* (Chatsworth, CA: Image Entertainment, 2005), DVD.

23 Kirkham, *Charles and Ray Eames*, p. 74.

*Context as Destiny: The Eameses from Californian Dreams to the Californiafication of Everywhere*

1 Peter Smithson, 'Just a Few Chairs and a House: An Essay on the Eames-Aesthetic', *Architectural Design*, September 1966, pp. 443–5.

2 Alison and Peter Smithson, 'But Today We Collect Ads', *Ark*, no. 18, November 1956. This essay contains the first recorded use of the term 'Pop art'.

3 Alison and Peter Smithson, *Changing the Art of Inhabitation: Mies' Pieces, Eames' Dreams, the Smithsons* (London: Artemis, 1994), p. 81.

4 There are two versions of the film *Powers of Ten*. The first, made in 1968, was titled *Rough Sketch of a Proposed Film Dealing with the Powers of the Ten and the Relative Size of Things in the Universe*; the second, from 1977, was called *Powers of Ten: A Film Dealing with the Relative Size of Things in the Universe, and the Effect of Adding Another Zero*.

5 The scene on the Chicago lakeshore referred to here is from the second version of *Powers of Ten* (1977);

in the first version of the film (1968), the analogous scene takes place on a golf course in Florida.

6 According to Charles Eames, the 'entire structural steel was erected by 5 men in 16 hours'. Charles Eames, quoted in 'Life in a Chinese Kite: Standard Industrial Products Assembled in a Spacious Wonderland', *Architectural Forum*, September 1950, p. 96.

7 Chuck Ranberg and Anne Flett, 'Call Me Irresponsible', *Frasier*, season 1, episode 7, dir. James Burrows, aired 28 October 1993.

8 Smithson, 'Just a Few Chairs and a House', p. 445.

9 The *Whole Earth Catalog* was an American counterculture magazine and product catalogue published by Stewart Brand between 1968 and 1974.

10 Richard Barbrook and Andy Cameron, 'The Californian Ideology', *Science as Culture*, vol. 6, no. 26, 1996, pp. 44–72.

CELEBRATION AS A HUMAN NEED

*Introduction*

Epigraph: Corita Kent, in Kent and Jan Steward, *Learning by Heart: Teachings to Free the Creative Spirit* (New York: Bantam Books, 1992), p. 198.

1 Immaculate Heart College, *2nd Irregular Bulletin*, November 1956.

2 Corita Kent (1918–1986) was chair of the Immaculate Heart College art department from 1964 until 1968, when she left the college to pursue her own artistic career. Kent was an activist for civil rights and anti-war causes; her concern for social justice often shaped the assignments she set for her art classes. In 1965 Kent and her students created a 'Peace on Earth' exhibition as a Christmas display for the IBM showroom in New York. They were asked to modify the exhibition after it was deemed not festive enough and too direct a protest against the Vietnam War. Kent's own work was an outlet for her activism, and she was a celebrated graphic artist, working mainly in serigraphs (silk-screen prints).

3 *Everyday Art*, vol. 33, Winter 1954–5.

4 *Circus* consisted of photographs and soundtracks amassed by Charles over several years and then assembled into a slideshow for his first Charles Eliot Norton Lecture at Harvard University in 1970.

5 Charles Eames, lecture notes for Penrose Memorial Lecture, American Philosophical Society, Philadelphia, April 1974, II:218, The Papers of Charles and Ray Eames, Manuscript Division, Library of Congress, Washington DC.

*The Travelling Eameses*

1 *Two Baroque Churches in Germany*, 1955, film, 10:30 min.

*Celebrating Connections: From Aby Warburg's 'Iconology of the Interval' to the 'New Kinds of Models' of Charles and Ray Eames*

1 'Mnemosyne' refers to the Greek goddess of the same name, mother of the nine muses and the personification of memory in Greek mythology; 'atlas' refers to the German use of the word to mean 'album' or 'printed collection'. Warburg's *Mnemosyne Atlas* was published posthumously in book form as *Der Bilderatlas Mnemosyne*, ed. Martin Warnke and Claudia Brink (Berlin: Akademie Verlag, 2000).

2 The British art historian Kenneth Clark, who was a student of Warburg, described him as 'without doubt the most original thinker on art-history of our time … [He] entirely changed the course of art historical studies.' Kenneth Clark, *Another Part of the Wood: A Self-Portrait* (London: Murray, 1974), p. 189.

3 Charles described the importance of connections to design in the film *ECS* (1961).

4 Lawrence Alloway, 'Eames' World', *Architectural Association Journal*, vol. LXXII, no. 804, July–August 1956, p. 55.

5 Charles Eames, 'Grist for Atlanta paper version', I:217, Folder 15, The Papers of Charles and Ray Eames, Manuscript Division, Library of Congress, Washington DC (hereafter cited as the Eames Papers), quoted in Beatriz Colomina, 'Enclosed by Images: The Eameses' Multimedia Architecture', *Grey Room*, no. 2, Winter 2001, pp. 17, 29.

6 Charles Eames, quoted in Digby Diehl, 'Charles Eames: Q & A', *Los Angeles Times West Magazine*, 8 October 1972, p. 14.

7 E. P. Richardson, in A. H. Girard and W. D. Laurie Jr, eds, *For Modern Living* (exhib. cat.), Detroit Institute of Arts, September–November 1949, pp. 7, 81.

8 Peter Smithson, 'Just a Few Chairs and a House: An Essay on the Eames-Aesthetic', *Architectural Design*, September 1966, p. 443.

9 Rt Hon. Tony Benn, MP, 'A Tribute to Charles Eames', speech delivered at the American Embassy, London, 8 November 1978, II:62, Folder 'Tony Benn, 1977–8', Eames Papers.

10 Jehane Burns's notes for Charles Eames's second Charles Eliot Norton lecture, I:217, Folder 10, Eames Papers. The Eameses were greatly influenced by György Kepes's book *Language of Vision* (Chicago: Paul Theobald, 1944).

SAMPLE LESSONS

*Introduction*

Epigraph: Charles Eames, script for the film *A Communications Primer*, 1953.

1 Leaflet announcing *A Rough Sketch for a Sample Lesson for a Hypothetical Course*, 1953.

2 Owen Gingerich, 'A Conversation with Charles Eames', *American Scholar*, vol. 46, 1977, p. 331.

3 Charles and Ray Eames referred to the 'lecture' as *A Rough Sketch for a Sample Lesson for a Hypothetical Course*, while George Nelson called it *Art X*.

4 *A Rough Sketch* was presented twice, first at the University of Georgia in Athens and later at a series of six showings over three days at the University of California, Los Angeles, in May 1953.

5 The topic for Charles Eames's series of six Norton Lectures at Harvard University was announced as 'Problems Relating to Visual Communication and the Visual Environment'.

6 Charles's appointment as Regents' Professor at UCLA involved delivering a ten-week course.

7 In 1978 the theme of the annual International Design Conference in Aspen was 'Making Connections' (a title taken from the exhibition *Connections: The Work of Charles and Ray Eames*, held at UCLA in 1976–7). Charles delivered the title lecture at the conference.

8 Leaflet advertising the film *A Communications Primer*, 1953.

9 In order to compile the *India Report*, Charles and Ray Eames took a three-month research trip to India in 1957–8. The report was initiated by the Indian government and sponsored by the Ford Foundation.

*Page 230*

1 Claude Elwood Shannon (1916–2001) was an American mathematician, electronics engineer and cryptographer.

2 Norbert Wiener (1894–1964) was an American mathematician and philosopher. He was professor of mathematics at MIT and pioneered the development of cybernetics.

3 John von Neumann (1903–1957) was a Hungarian-born American mathematician and physicist, known for his work on game theory and in computer programming. Von Neumann was also a crucial figure in the development of the hydrogen bomb.

4 See Charles Eames to Ian McCallum, 3 September 1954; II:17, Folder 'McCallum, Ian, Architectural Review, Alcoa Do Nothing Machine, 1958–1959', The Papers of Charles and Ray Eames, Manuscript Division, Library of Congress, Washington DC.

*Page 232*

1 See lecture transcripts cited in 'Architecture 1 and 2, University of California, Berkeley', in Daniel Ostroff, ed., *An Eames Anthology* (New Haven and London: Yale University Press, 2015), pp. 120–27.

*Towards a Communication-Oriented Society: The Eameses' India Report*

1 Charles and Ray Eames, *The India Report*, April 1958, Part I (emphasis in original).

2 As the historian Gyan Prakash has noted, by the middle of the nineteenth century the East India Company had used the postal service, telegraph system and railways to forge a 'unified, secure, and productive colony'. Gyan Prakash, *Another Reason: Science and the Imagination of Modern India* (Princeton, NJ: Princeton University Press, 1999), p. 161.

3 'Behaviour patterns are pre-programmed, pre-set', and, 'It is in this climate that handicrafts flourish – changes take place by degrees – there are moments of violence but the security is in the status quo.' Charles and Ray Eames, *India Report*, Part I.

4 Members of the struggle for Indian independence, particularly Mahatma Gandhi, embraced this artisanal imagery in the form of the Swadeshi (which translates as 'self-reliance') and Khadi ('handspun cloth') movements. The village, with its social and economic structures, was a pre-colonial ready-made for Gandhi, the unit of 'true democracy in India'. On the 'cult of craft' and the independence struggle, see Saloni Mathur, *India by Design: Colonial History and Cultural Display* (Berkeley, CA: University of California Press, 2007), pp. 27–51. On Gandhi and the village, see Government of India, *Building from Below: Mahatma Gandhi and Acharya Vinoba Bhave on Village Self-Government* (New Delhi: Ministry of Community Development and Co-operation, Government of India, 1960), p. 16.

5 Charles and Ray Eames, *India Report*, Part I. As the historian Olivier Zunz has noted, altering behaviour patterns had been an objective of American philanthropic organizations since the early decades of the twentieth century. However, it reached new levels of funding and interest in the Ford Foundation's programmes of the 1950s. On the rise of behaviourism, see Olivier Zunz, *Why the American Century?* (Chicago: University of Chicago Press, 1998), pp. 57–61; on the Ford Foundation's application of social science, see Olivier Zunz, *Philanthropy in America: A History* (Princeton, NJ: Princeton University Press, 2012), pp. 184–5.

6 Charles and Ray Eames, *India Report*, Part II.

7 See Stuart W. Leslie and Robert Kargon, 'Exporting MIT: Science, Technology, and Nation-Building in India and Iran', *Osiris*, vol. 21, no. 1, 2006, pp. 110–30.

8 *The Government of India's Scientific Policy Resolution* (New Delhi: Government of India, 1958), pp. 1–2.

9 In an attempt to define the pedagogy of a school of art and design, the NID's administrators, Gautam and Gira Sarabhai, chose a quote from the Illinois Institute of Technology in Chicago: 'Design is that professional branch of art which combines the aesthetic sensitivity and free creativity of the artist with the scientific knowledge and intellectual discipline of the technologist for a socially useful purpose.' See *Report '63/69* (Ahmedabad: National Institute of Design, 1969), p. 1.

10 Prasanta C. Mahalanobis, *The Approach of Operational Research to Planning in India* (Bombay: Asia Publishing House, 1963 [1955]), p. 71.

11 '"Textiles and Ornamental Arts of India" on View at The Museum of Modern Art', press release, The Museum of Modern Art, New York, 13 April 1955, p. 3.

12 See Nick Cullather, *The Hungry World: America's Cold War Battle against Poverty in Asia* (Cambridge, MA: Harvard University Press, 2010), pp. 135–6.

13 The Non-Aligned Movement was established to resist collectively any foreign interference in the developing world (namely, by Western nations and the Soviet Union).

14 *Ford Foundation Annual Report* (New York: Ford Foundation, 1955), p. 94.

15 See Government of India, *Industrial Policy Resolution* (New Delhi: Government of India, 1956), Parts 5, 13, 15 and 20; and *Second Five Year Plan* (New Delhi: Government of India, 1956), Chapter 20.

16 Telefax from Douglas Ensminger, Ford Foundation Representative in India, to the Ford Foundation offices in New York, 4 December 1956, Ford Foundation Archives.

17 'Two New Films By Charles And Ray Eames', press release, The Museum of Modern Art, New York, 1 March 1956, p. 2.

18 The Eameses acknowledged both Shannon and Wiener at the end of *A Communications Primer*. Wiener popularized his theories of communications systems in *The Human Use of Human Beings: Cybernetics and Society* (Boston, MA: Houghton Mifflin, 1950). A schematic diagram of a general communications system from Shannon and Warren Weaver's *The Mathematical Theory of Communication* (Urbana: University of Illinois Press, 1949) was extremely important to the Eameses' description of communication in the film.

19 At the time of his collaboration with the Eameses, George Nelson (1908–1986) was a renowned industrial designer/architect and a former editor of the widely read journal *Architectural Forum*. In 1953 he would go on to found *Industrial Design* magazine.

20 Fred Turner, *The Democratic Surround: Multimedia and American Liberalism from World War II to the Psychedelic Sixties* (Chicago: University of Chicago Press, 2013), pp. 254–5.

21 Charles and Ray Eames, *India Report*, Part I.

22 *Ibid.*

23 *Ibid.*

24 *Ibid.*

25 *Ibid.*

26 Don Wallance, *Shaping America's Products* (New York: Reinhold, 1956), p. 177. Wallance, a furniture and industrial designer with a strong interest in the arts and crafts, was recommended by the Ford Foundation as an alternative to the Eameses should they be unable to travel to India. See Douglas Ensminger to Alfred C. Wolf, 6 February 1957, Ford Foundation Archives.

27 In contrast to interacting with the lota as a physical object lesson, Charles's photos of lotas created a series of visual object lessons – an indexical set of 'talking witnesses'.

28 Saloni Mathur, 'Charles and Ray Eames in India', *Art Journal*, vol. 70, no. 1, Spring 2011, p. 46.

29 Charles and Ray Eames, *India Report*, Part I.

30 Ravi Kalia, *Gandhinagar: Building National Identity in Postcolonial India* (Columbia: University of South Carolina Press, 2004), p. 64.

31 *Ibid.*, p. 58.

32 'Immense Task before India: Need for Creating Classless Society Pandit Nehru's Call for Co-operative Effort', *The Times of India*, 13 February 1949, p. 1.

33 Patel studied at the College of Art in Madras (1949–53) before taking up postgraduate studies in painting, sculpture and ceramics at the École des Beaux-Arts in Paris. Vyas, born and raised in Uganda, studied industrial design in the early 1950s at the Central School of Art and Design in London. At NID, Patel and Vyas eventually became, respectively, Design Director for Visual Communication and Design Director for Product Design.

34 Alexander Keefe, 'Subcontinental Synth: David Tudor and the First Moog in India', *East of Borneo*, 30 April 2013, www.eastofborneo.org/articles/subcontinental-synth-david-tudor-and-the-first-moog-in-india (accessed 10 June 2015).

35 In fact, following the publication of the *India Report*, the Ford Foundation and the Government of India hired Ernst Scheidegger, an adjunct professor of communications at HfG, and Vilhelm Wohlert, an architect and professor from the Royal Danish Academy of Fine Arts, to make a second report on how to enact the Eameses' vision. They recommended close cooperation between students and faculty in a workshop style of learning – similar to HfG's programme of training. This close relationship with HfG would ultimately backfire on the Sarabhais. See R. K. Banerjee, '40 Years of NID', unpublished manuscript, pp. 8–9.

36 In common with students at HfG, those enrolled at the NID, regardless of their field of interest, received instruction in cybernetics, social psychology, agronomics and ergonomics/human engineering. For a comparison of the schools' curriculums, see *Ulm 1: Quarterly Bulletin of the Hochschule für Gestaltung*, October 1958, p. 23, and *National Institute of Design: Documentation 1964–69* (Ahmedabad: National Institute of Design, 1969), pp. 13, 91.

37 'A Scheme for a Tangential Fan', devised in collaboration with Hans Gugelot and Ernst Reichl at HfG, and a costly proposal for the India Pavilion at Expo '70 in Osaka, Japan, were just two examples of projects that had little to do with issues facing India. See *National Institute of Design: Documentation 1964–69*, pp. 28, 60–61.

38 Report from J. S. Sandhu to Charles Eames, 16 September 1970, I:44, Folder 2, The Papers of Charles and Ray Eames, Manuscript Division, Library of Congress, Washington DC (hereafter cited as Eames Papers).

39 Sandhu wrote: 'Churning out Swiss or German graphics with esoteric typography is one thing – to be able to communicate these to the Indian masses is another.' *Ibid.*, p. 9.

40 Douglas Ensminger to Gautam Sarabhai, 8 November 1968, I:44, Folder 33, Eames Papers.

41 On the follow-up report, see note 35, above.

42 *Report '63/69* (Ahmedabad: National Institute of Design, 1969), p. 39.

43 Charles Eames to Sharada Prasad, 6 November 1972, I:44, Folder 4, Eames Papers.

44 A decorated war veteran and former chief of staff of the Indian Navy, Soman was selected on the basis of his supposedly 'excellent connections in Delhi'. The Sarabhais wanted Soman to act as a liaison between the institute and Delhi, 'while the internal work would be carried on by the Directing Board'. This did not happen. From the outset, Soman and Gautam failed to agree on the boundaries of their respective remits, and the two men butted heads over pedagogy and administrative duties. A consistent complaint about Soman from the NID's faculty related to his insistence that they participate in morning drill exercises. See Banerjee, '40 Years of NID', p. 43.

45 I:44, Folder 2, Eames Papers.

46 In June 1971 Ford Foundation representative Harry Wilhelm wrote rather tersely to Ray: 'Given our present circumstances, the Ford Foundation's support to the institute may be more moral than financial, but we will attempt to follow the precepts you suggest.' *Ibid.*

47 In a letter to the Eameses dated 10 January 1972, Gira Sarabhai wrote: 'The appointment of Admiral Soman as administrative head has been a disaster. He is remarkably stupid – pig-headed. If he continues to be here he will surely liquidate whatever little there is at NID.' I:45, Folder 2, Eames Papers.

48 Soman's tenure as the administrative director of the NID lasted from 1 October 1970 to 3 July 1972. For more on this subject, see *Parliamentary Debates, Rajya Sabha: Official Report*, vol. 81, nos 1–8, 1972, p. 77.

49 Romesh Thaper, *Report of the Review Committee on the National Institute of Design*, February 1974, p. 9.

Portions of this essay were presented at the Yale Modern South Asia Workshop in 2013. The author wishes to thank members of this workshop, Esther Choi and Catherine Ince for their invaluable feedback on initial drafts.

*Page 248*

1 Children from the Werkplaats Children's Community School in Bilthoven, the Netherlands, worked with Boeke to create the pictures. See Kees Boeke, *Cosmic View: The Universe in 40 Jumps* (New York: John Day Company, 1957), p. 4.

2 *Cosmic View (test)*, 1963, film, 3 min.

*Page 251*

1 Philip and Phylis Morrison, 'A Happy Octopus: Charles and Ray Learn Science and Teach it with Images', in Donald Albrecht *et al.*, *The Work of Charles and Ray Eames: A Legacy of Invention* (New York: Abrams, 1997), p. 108.

INFORMATION MACHINES

*Introduction*

1 Charles Eames, first draft of 'An Architectural Model is an Information Device', 1975, II:218, Folder 'Jehane Burns file; Charles Eames lectures', The Papers of Charles and Ray Eames, Manuscript Division, Library of Congress, Washington DC.

2 Rt Hon. Tony Benn, MP, 'A Tribute to Charles Eames', speech delivered at the American Embassy, London, 8 November 1978, II:62, Folder 'Tony Benn, 1977–8', The Papers of Charles and Ray Eames, Manuscript Division, Library of Congress, Washington DC.

*Communicating America: Moscow, 1959*

1 The United States Information Agency (1953–99) was a government body dedicated to supporting American interests abroad through cultural

exchanges and broadcasting. It closely followed the work of the Eameses, and often included Eames films in its libraries. The agency funded the international tour of *The World of Franklin and Jefferson* (1975–7).

2  George Nelson, quoted in Stanley Abercrombie, *George Nelson: The Design of Modern Design* (Cambridge, MA: MIT Press, 2000), p. 164.

3  Visual art also featured prominently. Visitors could see an exhibition of modern American sculpture and painting, as well as a version of the landmark photography exhibition *The Family of Man*. Curated by Edward Steichen, *The Family of Man* was first shown in 1955 at The Museum of Modern Art, New York. It consisted of 503 photographs of people from around the world, and was intended as an assertion of both global fellowship and photography as a universal language. The USIA funded a tour of the exhibition to thirty-seven foreign countries, where it served to promote associations between its egalitarian and democratic ideals and America's international reputation.

4  The Eameses were unaware that the Russian name for the flowers (*nezabutki*) also directly translates as 'forget me not'. This fortuitous coincidence ensured that the image carried the same association of friendship for Russian viewers as it did for Americans.

*Page 273*

1  In a letter to John E. Burchard, dean of the Massachusetts Institute of Technology, dated 13 July 1959, Charles wrote: 'Ray and I have just finished the charrette to end all. We have been doing a film presentation for the American National Exhibition at Moscow, and tonight we go there – over the Pole – with the prints under our arms.' II:16, Folder 'Massachusetts Institute of Technology, Cambridge, Mass., 1952–1959', The Papers of Charles and Ray Eames, Manuscript Division, Library of Congress, Washington DC.

*Squaring the Hypothetical Circle: Getting Around Mathematica*

Epigraph: Bertrand Russell, *Introduction to Mathematical Philosophy* (London: George Allen & Unwin, 1919), p. 3

1  Eric Schuldenfrei, *The Films of Charles and Ray Eames: A Universal Sense of Expectation* (London: Routledge, 2015), p. 105.

2  James R. Newman, *The World of Mathematics*, 4 vols (New York: Simon & Schuster, 1956), vol. 3, p. 1,485.

3  Other devices and exhibits include 'Mathematical Model Case', 'Möbius Band', 'Multiplication Cube', funhouse trick mirrors and two double-sided stanchions containing didactic panels.

Special thanks are owed to my curatorial colleague and mentor Marc Greuther, director of historical resources and chief curator at The Henry Ford, who is the reason why *Mathematica* calls the museum its new home; to the Eames family, Foundation and Office; and to my friend Steve Aldana, who was the catalyst for my first writings about the Eameses, and co-pilot on many architecture-fuelled adventures.

*Page 280*

1  *Architectural Record*, no. 7, July 1964, p. 2.

*Peaks of Perpetual Excitement: Exhibition-Making at the Eames Office*

1  Charles Eames, 'Language of Vision: The Nuts and Bolts', *Bulletin of the American Academy of Arts and Sciences*, vol. 28, no. 1, October 1974, p. 17. The circus was a recurring theme in the Eames Office. I first heard Charles talk about it in the autumn of 1967 as I was sorting through some photographs he had taken of the Ringling Bros. and Barnum & Bailey Circus in the late 1940s.

2  'Eames', interview with Charles Eames by S. M. Pruys, *Algemeen Handelsblad*, 14 June 1969, translation in I:263, Folder 3, The Papers of Charles and Ray Eames, Manuscript Division, Library of Congress, Washington DC (hereafter cited as Eames Papers).

3  The Museum of Science, Boston, since 1981 (originally at the Museum of Science and Industry, Chicago) and, since 2002, the New York Hall of Science (originally at the California Museum of Science and Industry,

Los Angeles). At the time of writing, the exhibition (combined elements from the New York World's Fair and the Pacific Science Center, Seattle) is due to open at a third venue, The Henry Ford in Dearborn, Michigan, within the next couple of years.

4  Charles Eames, quoted in 'How "A World of Numbers ... and Beyond" was Created', California Museum of Science and Industry, Los Angeles, press kit for *Mathematica*, opening 24 March 1961, collection of Robert Staples and Barbara Fahs Charles.

5  David Paul, 'Report of the Eames Photo Trip, April 20–30, 1973', memorandum to William R. Davis, 4 May 1973, collection of Robert Staples and Barbara Fahs Charles.

6  Recollection of the author, especially during work on *A Computer Perspective*.

7  Charles Eames, 'Language of Vision', p. 34 (emphasis in original).

8  Kevin Roche, 'A Conversation', *Perspecta*, vol. 19, 1982, p. 169.

9  Office of Charles and Ray Eames, 'Meeting with Malcolm Gordon', 26 May 1966, II:167, Folder 3, Eames Papers.

10  Kevin Roche, interview with the author, 19 March 2013.

11  Charles Eames, quoted in Paul Schrader, 'Poetry of Ideas: The Films of Charles Eames', *Film Quarterly*, Spring 1970, p. 12.

12  Schrader, 'Poetry of Ideas', p. 13.

13  Charles Eames, notes for a March 1970 presentation in Italy, II:167, Folder 5, Eames Papers.

14  Frank Taylor, Director of Museums, Smithsonian Institution, to John Szarkowski, Director, Department of Photography, The Museum of Modern Art, 16 June 1967, I:172, Folder 10, Eames Papers.

15  Charles Eames to Lloyd Herman, Administrative Officer, Smithsonian Institution, 30 October 1967, I:172, Folder 8, Eames Papers.

16  Charles Eames to Frank Taylor, Director of Museums, Smithsonian Institution, 22 December 1967, I:172, Folder 10, Eames Papers.

17  'Miss Barbara Charles of our office, who is coordinating all data on the 1,500 photographs used, is on recuperation leave.' Charles Eames to the BBC, 18 June 1968, in response to a rather sharp enquiry as to why its photographs had not been quickly returned, I:170, Folder 10, Eames Papers.

18  The Poor People's Campaign for economic justice was initiated by Martin Luther King Jr. Following his assassination in April 1968, it was continued by Ralph Abernathy and other civil rights leaders, who brought caravans of poor people from around the United States to Washington DC in mid-May that year. A total of 3,000 people were housed in Resurrection City. The documentary photographer Jill Freedman, who was living in the mud-soaked temporary community, shared her photographs with us; we shared with her the hot shower in our hotel room.

19  Wolf Von Eckardt, '"Photography in the City" Show Exciting', *Washington Post*, 30 June 1968, p. G8.

20  Charles Eames to Frank Taylor, 5 August 1968, I:172, Folder 10, Eames Papers.

21  McCandlish Phillips, 'Designers of Show on Indian Leaders Find Task Is an Exciting Chase', *New York Times*, 20 January 1965, p. 1.

22  Katherine Kuh, 'Nehru: A Visual Biography', *Saturday Review*, 20 February 1965, p. 42.

23  Ashoke Chatterjee, interview with Shilpa Das and Sanchari Mahapatra, 2011, quoted in Shilpa Das, ed., *50 Years of the National Institute of Design: 1961–2011* (Ahmedabad: National Institute of Design, 2013), p. 76. Chatterjee was a young communications officer at the International Development Bank when he volunteered to work on the installation of *Nehru* in Washington DC. There, he met the Eameses, beginning a decade of discussions on design. In 1975 Chatterjee was made executive director of NID.

24  Vikas Satwalekar, 'Heart of the Matter ...', *Indian Architect and Builder*, vol. 25, no. 1, September 2011, p. 55.

25  H. Y. Sharada Prasad, 'A Master Designer Who Cared: Tribute to Charles Eames', *Communicator*, July–October 1978, reprint, I:46, Folder 3, Eames Papers.

*The Artefacts of Innovation*

1  On 21 August 1978, just months before the 'Inventions' exhibition was due to open, Charles Eames died of a heart attack. A significant amount

of work had already been produced for the exhibition, but neither IBM nor the USIA would complete the project and it was never shown, suggesting it was the Eames Office that had been the driving force behind such initiatives.

2  Charles and Ray Eames, 'Inventions: The Artifacts of Innovation Notes', 1 August 1978, Los Angeles, I:155, Folder 6, The Papers of Charles and Ray Eames, Manuscript Division, Library of Congress, Washington DC (hereafter cited as Eames Papers).

3  Charles and Ray Eames, 'Inventions: The Artifacts of Innovation Notes', December 1977, Los Angeles, I:154, Folder 6, Eames Papers.

4  The exhibition was to travel to Ottawa, London, Paris, Rome, Berlin, Athens, Peking, Jakarta, New Delhi, Tokyo, Moscow, Cairo, Tehran, Tel Aviv, Lagos and Brasilia.

5  IBM and USIA, 'Inventions: The Artifacts of Innovation General Conditions of IBM/USIA Arrgreement', 1977, I:154, Folder 5, Eames Papers.

6  The Eameses' preliminary study of the history of the pacemaker is incorrect, as the first fully implantable pacemaker was implanted in 1958 at the Karolinska Institute in Sweden.

7  IBM and USIA, 'Inventions: The Artifacts of Innovation General Conditions of IBM/USIA Arrgreement'.

8  Charles and Ray Eames, 'Innovation and Invention Preface', December 1977, I:154, Folder 6, Eames Papers.

9  Eameses, 'Inventions: The Artifacts of Innovation Notes', December 1977.

10  Charles Eames, 'Notes to Gerard Piel from Charles Eames', February 1977, I:64, Folder 2, Eames Papers.

11  Charles Eames, 'Smithsonian Lecture Notes', 1977, Washington DC, I:217, Folder 24, Eames Papers.

12  Charles and Ray Eames, 'First Notes on a Fine Arts Center Associated with the Metropolitan Museum of Art', 1977, Los Angeles, I:218, Folder 7, Eames Papers.

13  *Ibid.*

14  Charles Eames, 'A Report to President Howard Johnson', 1969, Los Angeles, I:218, Folder 6, Eames Papers.

15  Charles Eames, 'MIT Lecture Notes', 1 July 1976, I:217, Folder 19, Eames Papers.

16  The conference's theme, 'Making Connections', related directly to the exhibition *Connections: The Work of Charles and Ray Eames*, held in Los Angeles in 1976: the organizer of the 28th IDCA, Ralph Caplan, had written an essay in the exhibition's catalogue titled 'Making Connections'. Charles Eames, 'International Design Conference Notes', 11 June 1978, I:217, Folder 27, Eames Papers.

17  Charles Eames, 'Norton Lecture Four Notes', Harvard Norton Lecture Series, I:217, Folder 10, Eames Papers.

18  Charles's notes continue: '(mathematician should no more think of delegating his film to "creative" film-makers than of delegating his journal article to a "creative" essay-writer)'. Eames, 'International Design Conference Notes'.

19  Charles and Ray Eames, dir., *Cable: The Immediate Future*, 1972, 10 min.

20  *Ibid.*

21  'What Is a House?', diagram by Charles and Ray Eames in *Arts & Architecture*, July 1944.

22  Eames, 'Smithsonian Lecture Notes'.

23  Charles and Ray Eames, 'Innovation and Invention Notes', December 1977, I:154, Folder 6, Eames Papers.

# Contributors

*Anthony Acciavatti* is on faculty at Columbia University in the City of New York, and is a PhD candidate in the history of science, Department of History at Princeton University. He is the author of *Ganges Water Machine: Designing New India's Ancient River* (2015).

*Barbara Fahs Charles* is a former staff member at the Eames Office (1967–1971) and founder of Staples & Charles Ltd, a design practice specializing in museums.

*Eames Demetrios* is the grandson of Charles and Ray Eames and Director of the Eames Office, which communicates, preserves and extends the work of Charles and Ray Eames.

*Kristen Gallerneaux* is Curator of Communication & Information Technology at the Henry Ford Museum, Michigan.

*Amy Gallick* is a preservation specialist in the Moving Image Section at the Library of Congress Packard Campus for Audio-Visual Conservation in Culpeper, Virginia.

*Catherine Ince* is curator of the exhibition *The World of Charles and Ray Eames* and editor of this publication. Ince is Curator at Barbican Art Gallery, where she specializes in architecture and design.

*Sam Jacob* is principal of Sam Jacob Studio for architecture and design; Professor of Architecture at UIC, Chicago; Director of Night School at the Architectural Association, London; and Visiting Professor at Yale School of Architecture.

*Lotte Johnson* is assistant curator of the exhibition *The World of Charles and Ray Eames* and assisted with this publication. Johnson is Assistant Curator at Barbican Art Gallery, where she specializes in twentieth-century and contemporary art.

*Professor Pat Kirkham* is Professor Emerita at Bard Graduate Center, New York, and has written widely on design, film and gender. Her publications include books on Charles and Ray Eames, Saul Bass, Eva Zeisel, women designers in the United States 1900–2000, diversity and the gendered object. She is currently working on a book on the Eameses and Hollywood.

*Alison Moloney* is Curator and Research Fellow, International Exhibitions Programme at the London College of Fashion.

*Luke Naessens* is Exhibitions Assistant at the Barbican Art Gallery; he assisted with the exhibition *The World of Charles and Ray Eames* and this publication.

*Dr Steve Parnell* is an architect, critic and lecturer, specializing in post-war architectural history, at the Department of Architecture, Planning & Landscape, Newcastle University.

*Elizabeth St George* is a research associate in the European Sculpture and Decorative Arts Department at the Metropolitan Museum of Art, New York. She is also a lecturer at Pratt Institute and a doctoral candidate at the Bard Graduate Center, New York.

*Dr Eric Schuldenfrei* is a co-founder of ESKYIU, an associate professor and the Associate Dean for Special Projects and Communications in the University of Hong Kong Faculty of Architecture.

# Index

*Italic* page numbers refer to illustrations.

Aalto, Alvar 143
Ahmedabad, India: Calico Museum of Textiles 245, 246; National Institute of Design (NID) 226, 242–3, 245–6, *245*, 294, *294*, 295; Sanskar Kendra (museum) 245, 294
Ain, Gregory *35*, 43
aircraft manufacture 22, *32*, 33, *33*, 34, *34*, *35*, 89
Albinson, Don *4*, 12, 18, 23, *49*, 113, 116, *141*
Alloway, Lawrence 124–5, 215
Aluminium Group (furniture collection) 138, 154, *154*, *164*, *271*
American Abstract Artists 18
Apple (corporation) 165, 167
Aquarium *see* National Aquarium project
*Architectural Association Journal* 124–5
*Architectural Design* (magazine) 100, *102*, *103*, 188–9, 207
*Architectural Forum* (magazine) *65*
'Architectural Model is an Information Device, An' (lecture) 266
*Architectural Review* (magazine) 100
Armstrong-Jones, Antony *283*
Arnold, Rebecca 149
Art X (educational application) 125, 233–40, *237–9*
*Arts & Architecture* (magazine) 14, *38*, 46, 62; Case Study House programme 62, 64, *64–5*, 73, 103; covers *19*, *22*, *40*, *45*, *46*, *163*; 'What is a House?' (article) *302*, 304
Ashby, Gordon *118*
Aspen, Colorado: International Design Conference 15, *225*, 226, 304
Atlanta, Georgia 266; SciTrek (museum) 277

Bailey, Stuart and Lucia 288
*Banana Leaf* (film) 12, *247*
Banham, Reyner 100, 103, *104–5*, 105
Banker, Suresh *294*
Bauer, Catherine 141
Bauer, Dale *118*
Bauhaus 18, *42*, 166
Beebe, Tina 150
Beer, Henry *298*
Benn, Anthony Wedgwood (Tony) *16*, 210, 216, 266
Berkeley, University of California 182, 215, 226, 232, 241
Bernstein, Elmer 113, 230, 288
Bertoia, Harry 18, 22, *35*, 42, 43
*Better Call Saul* (television series) 166
'Beware of Imitations' (advertising material) 162, *162–3*
Beyoncé 166
*Bhagavad Gita* 23, 226
Bill, Max 14
Bishop, Frances *141*
*Black Ships, The* (film) 303, *303*
*Blacktop* (film) 22, 200
Blitzer, Wolf 166
Boeke, Kees: *Cosmic View* 248
Borges, Jorge Luis 205
Boston: Museum of Science 277
Brawne, Michael 103
*Bread* (film) 200
British Museum, London *301*
Bronowski, Judith 248, *248*
Browne, Michael 207
Brühwiler, Paul *249*, *293*, *301*
Brutalism 100–103
Bungay, Richard *118*
Burns, Jehane 13, *300*

*Cable: The Immediate Future* (film) 304, *304*
Cage, John 246

California, and Eameses' design ethic 164–7
California Museum of Science and Industry, Los Angeles *276*, 277, *278*, *279*
Capacchione, Lucia *118*, *273*
Caplan, Ralph 13
card games 5, 20, 124, 126, *126–8*, 128, *189*, 215–16
Case Study House No. 8 *see* Eames House
Case Study House No. 9 64, *66*, *67*, 71, *71*, 76, *76–7*, 97
Casson, Sir Hugh 106
Castiglioni, Achille and Pier Giacomo 14
chairs: metal 23, *41*, *48*, 138, *141*; moulded-plywood 12, 21, *21*, 22, 23, *25*, *41*, 43, 46, *47–52*, 85; plastic/fibreglass *1*, *13*, *22*, 23, 43, 138, *138–47*, 146; wire 146, *188*; *see also* Aluminium Group; Lounge Chair and Ottoman; Tandem Seating
Chaise, La (chaise longue) 14, *141*
Chaparos, Nick *273*
Chaplin, Sir Charlie *120*, 121
Charles, Barbara Fahs 150, 151, *290*, *291*, *298*
Chicago: Merchandise Mart, *Good Design* exhibition (1950) 14, *14*, 23; Museum of Science and Industry 277; O'Hare Airport *155*
children's furniture *13*, *50*, 51
*Circus* (slideshow) *169–76*, 178, 215
clothes (of Eameses) 118, 148–51
CNN (news channel) 166
collecting and hoarding 103, 114–15, 117, 150, 167, 178, 210, 216
*Communications Primer, A* (film) 23, 125, 201, 215, 226, 230, *230–31*, 244
*Computer Perspective, A* (exhibition) *214*, 215, 266, 291, 298, *298–9*
Connor, Jay *141*
Corbusier, Le 18, 138; Sanskar Kendra 245, 294; Unité d'Habitation 95, 100
Cranbrook Academy of Art, Michigan 18, 23, 42, 113

Daigoro, Takayama 212, *212–13*
Dalwadi, P. M. *294*
*Day of the Dead* (film) 191, *191*, 206–7
De Pree, D. J. 15, 52
Deleuze, Gilles 215
Derrida, Jacques 215
*Design Q&A* (film) 256, *256*
Detroit Institute of Arts: *For Modern Living* (1949) *2*, 14, 23, 143, *143–5*, 216
Dinkeloo, John *see* KRJDA (architectural practice)
Dodd, Lamar 233, 234
*Domus* (magazine) 113, 150, 178
Donges, Richard (Dick) *118*, *248*
dress (of Eameses) 118, 148–51
Dreyfuss, Henry *119*, 121, 210
Dunne, Philip and Amanda 288
Dwan, Virginia 288

Eames House, Los Angeles (Case Study House No. 8): design and construction *3*, 20, 23, *42*, 44, 62, *63–75*, 64, *82–97*, 85–96, 276–7; hosting and entertaining 106–21, *106–7*, *110–12*, *117*, *119–21*; influence 14, 99–105, *101*; studio 184, *184–7*
Eames Office, Venice, California *4–5*, 12–13, *13*, 23, *33*, 41–2, 118, *182–3*
Eames Storage Unit (ESU) *13*, *137*
eBay (website) 167
education *see* pedagogy
Ensminger, Douglas 246
Entenza, John 22, 62, 64, 71, *71*, 103, 115, 304
entertaining and hosting, Eameses' 106–21, *106–7*, *110–12*, *117*, *119–21*
Eppinger, James 52
Evans, Edward S. 22, 28
Evans Products Company 22, 23, 28, 51
*Everyday Art Quarterly* *138*, 178

exhibitions (designed by Eameses) 266–305; *see also A Computer Perspective*; IBM Pavilion, New York World's Fair; *Jawaharlal Nehru: His Life and His India*; *Mathematica: A World of Numbers … and Beyond*; National Aquarium project; *Photography and the City*; *The World of Franklin and Jefferson*
*Exponents* (film) 304

Fellini, Federico 205
Festival of Britain (1951) 14
Feynman, Richard 196, 208
*Film Quarterly* 193–208
films 12, 23, 43–4, 115, 166, 184, 193–208, 210; *see also Banana Leaf*; *The Black Ships*; *Blacktop*; *Bread*; *Cable: A Communications Primer*; *Day of the Dead*; *Design Q&A*; *Exponents*; *House: After Five Years of Living*; *IBM at the Fair*; National Aquarium project; *Parade*; *Powers of Ten*; *S-73 (Sofa Compact)*; *Sumo Wrestler*; *SX-70*; *Toccata for Toy Trains*; *Tops*; *Traveling Boy*; *Two Baroque Churches in Germany*
Fleck, Glen *2*, 118, *118*, *177*, *288*, *292*, 293, 294, 298
*For Modern Living* (exhibition, 1949) *2*, 14, 23, 143, *143–5*, 216
Ford, Henry 21, 22, 278
Ford Foundation 242, 243–4, 246
Foucault, Michel 215
Fraser, Charles *4*
*Frasier* (television series) 166, *166*
Fuller, Buckminster 15, 122, 245, 268
Funke, Alex 251

Galentine, Wheaton 202
Gandhi, Indira *245*, 246, 294
*G.E.M.* (slideshow) 52, *53–60*, 215
Georgia, University of 125, 226, 233–40, 244
Germany: Eameses' travel in 210
Giacomo, Pier *see* Castiglioni, Achille
Girard, Alexander and Susan 14, 15, 43, 113, 125, 143, 178, 191, 210, 226, 234, 244, 266, 294, *294*
gliders 22, 34, *34*, 35
*Glimpses of the U.S.A.* (multi-screen presentation) 14, 16, 43, 113, 181, *197*, 210, 266, 268, 273, *273–5*
Godard, Jean-Luc 205, 206
*Good Design* (exhibition, 1950) 14, *14*, 23
Gordon, Malcolm S. 291, 296
Gould, Jerome 226
Graham, Martha 18
Gropius, Walter 18
Grotell, Maija 23

Hamilton, Richard 14
Hang-It-All (clothes rack) *306*
Harford, Betty *120*
Harris, Margaret 'Percy' 22, 210
Harvard University: Norton Lectures 12, 21, 42, 215, 216, 226
Hawks, Howard 205
Henderson, Nigel *100*, *147*, 188
Henry Ford Museum, Michigan 21, 277, 278
Herman Miller Furniture Company 13, 14, 15, 22, 23, 43, 52, 146; advertisements 162, *162–3*; showroom *137*, 138, *156–9*, 157
Heuvel, Dirk van den 103
Hofmann, Hans 18
Hostick, Robert *118*
*House: After Five Years of Living* (film) 62, 103
House of Cards (card deck) 5, 14, 20, 124, 126, *126–7*, *189*, 215–16, *299*
*House of Science* (multi-screen presentation) 196–7, 208, 266, *307*
Houseman, John 288
Hurst, Samuel and Melinda 288

IBM (corporation) 15, 16, 165, 230, 247, 280, 301, 303; Automatic Language Translation Machine *281*; Corporate Exhibit Center 291, 298, *298*, *300*; Optical Scanning and Information Retrieval System *284–5*; RAMAC computer 268, *271*; *see also A Computer Perspective*; *Mathematica: A World of Numbers … and Beyond*
*IBM at the Fair* 289
IBM Pavilion, New York World's Fair (1964–5) 151, 266, 277, *277*, *278*, 280, *280–85*; 'Information Machine' 16, 266, 287–9, *287*; Ovoid Theater *15*, 16, *281*, 282, *282*, *286*, 287; Sherlock Holmes puppet show 207, *282*; *see also Think*
Immaculate Heart College, Los Angeles *107*, 113, 178, *179*, 255
Independent Group 14, 100, 165
India: National Institute of Design (NID) 226, 242–3, 245–6, *245*, 294, *294*, 295
*India* (slideshow) 216, *217–24*
*India Report* (1958) 210, 226, 242–6, 294
Institute of Contemporary Arts, London: *Parallel of Life and Art* (1953) 98, 100, 103
'Inventions: The Artifacts of Innovation' (unfinished exhibition project) 303
*Iron Man 2* (film) 166
*Isaac Newton: Physics for a Moving Earth* (exhibition) *300*, 301

Jacobsen, Robert *141*
Jain, Minakshi *294*
Japan 121, 210, 212
*Jawaharlal Nehru: His Life and His India* (exhibition) 44, 210, *245*, 246, 291, 294–5, *294–5*
Jeakins, Dorothy 149

Kane, Nancy *2*, *118*, *273*
Keefe, Alexander 246
Kelley, Sister Helen 255
Kenmochi, Isamu 210
Kennedy, John F. 118
Kennedy, Robert 293
Kennedy, Sylvia *5*
Kent, Corita 178, *180–83*, 184
Kepes, György 216
Kerve, Padmaker *294*
Khrushchev, Nikita 268
Kirkham, Pat 149, 210
Kirwan, Michael 204
Knoll, Florence 42, 143
Knox, Alexander 210
*Konditorei* (slideshow) 210, *211*, 215
Krasner, Lee *306*
Kratka, Charles *141*
KRJDA (architectural practice) 42, 280, 291, 292, 296

*Lecture 1* (slideshow) 22
Lederborn, Christian and Henrietta *120*
Lee, Tsung-Dao 21
Lethaby, William 117
Levy, Don 202
Library of Congress 150, 303
*Life* (magazine) 84, 273
Lohse, Richard 14
Lounge Chair and Ottoman 22–3, 48, *48*, 138, 152, *152–3*, 166

McAleer, Margaret 151
McCoy, Esther 41–4, 117
McLaren, Norman 200, 202
*Mad Men* (television series) 166
Masey, Jack 113, 268, 273, *273*
Massachusetts Institute of Technology (MIT) 16; *MIT Report* 304
*Mastermind* (television series) 166, *167*
*Mathematica: A World of Numbers … and Beyond* (exhibition) 20, 44, 204, *247*, *267*, 276–8, *276–9*, 291, 295, *305*
Mathsson, Bruno 143
Matsumoto, Sosei *120*, 121
Matter, Herbert 22, 43, *46*
Meek, Parke *4*, *177*, 248, *248*, *273*

Metropolitan Museum of Art, New York 291, *301*, 303–4
Mexico 23, 191, 210
MGM Film Studios 12, 21, 22
Middleton, Robin 100
Mies van der Rohe, Ludwig 18, 100, 103, 138, 141
Miller, J. Irwin 154
MIT *see* Massachusetts Institute of Technology
Mitchell, Jill *185*
*Mnemosyne Atlas* (Warburg) 215–16, *216*
Modi, Rohit *294*
Moffat, Ivan 121
MoMA *see* Museum of Modern Art, New York
Moore, Charles 44
Morris, William 114, 117, 166
Morrison, Philip and Phylis 252
Moscow World's Fair (1959): American National Exhibition 16, 113, 181, *197*, 210, 266, 268, *268–75*
*Moveable Feasts and Changing Calendars* (exhibition) *300*
*Movie Sets* (slideshow) 12, 128, *129–36*
multi-screen presentations *see* slideshows
Museum of Modern Art, New York (MoMA) 16, 138; *The Family of Man* (1955) 293; 'International Competition for Low-Cost Furniture Design' (1948) 23, *140*, 141, *142*; *New Furniture Designed by Charles Eames* (1946) 52; 'Organic Design in Home Furnishings' competition (1940) 12, 18, *20*, 21, *21*, 42–3; *Textiles and Ornamental Arts of India* (1955) 243, 294; *see also Good Design* exhibition

Nakashima, George 246
Narashiman, N. V. L. *294*
National Aquarium project 42, 202, 204–5, *205*, 207, 291–3, *292*, 296, *296–7*; *see also Tanks*
Native American culture 115, 210
Nehru, Jawaharlal 243; *Jawaharlal Nehru: His Life and His India* (exhibition) 44, 210, *245*, 246, 291, 294–5, *294–5*
Nelson, George 15, 23, 43, 52, 113, 125, 226, 233–40, 244, 266, 268, 272–3, *273*
Neuhart, John *5*, 12, *118*, *273*
Neutra, Richard 24, 159
New Brutalism *see* Brutalism 100–103
New York Hall of Science 277
New York World's Fair (1964–5) 202, 280, 287; *see also* IBM Pavilion
Newman, James R. 277
Newton, Sir Isaac 277; *Isaac Newton: Physics for a Moving Earth* (exhibition) *300*, 301
NID *see* India, National Institute of Design
Nixon, Richard 268
Noguchi, Isamu *120*, 121
Nolan, Doris *48*, 210
Noyes, Eliot *2*, 21, 42, 46

Oppewall, Jeanine *300*
Orlan, Ted 248

Paatero, Antti 248
Pairs (card game) 128, *128*
Panchasara, Haribhai 294, *294*
Paolozzi, Sir Eduardo *100*, *147*, 188
*Parade* (film) 181, 190, 200
Paris: Grand Palais *301*; Musée des Arts Décoratifs, *What is Design?* (1969) *225*
Passalacqua, Sam *296*
Patel, Dashrath 245, 294, *294*
Patel, Ishu *294*
Paul, David 291
Pearce, Peter *5*, *118*, *273*
pedagogy 15–16, 23, 125, 180–83, 215, 226–46, 304
performance *114*, 115, *115*, 116

*Photography and the City: The Evolution of an Art and a Science* (exhibition) *265*, *290*, 291, *291*, *292–3*, 293–4
Pierson, Frederick and Polly 288–9
Plyformed Wood Company 26, 28
plywood, moulding techniques 12, 21, 22–3, 24, *25*, 36, *36*, *37*, 85
Ponti, Lisa *106*
Poole, Mairea *118*, *177*
*Powers of Ten* (film) *3*, 6, 20, 165–6, *165*, 202–4, 207, 226, 248, *248–53*, 251–2
Prasad, H. Y. Sharada 294, 295
Price, Vincent 115

*Railroad* (slideshow) 215, 232
Rainer, Yvonne 246
Rainey, Ford *120*, 121
Raugh, Michael *118*
Read, Sir Herbert 124
Redheffer, Raymond 291, 304
Reithard, Bill *118*
Resnais, Alain 206
Revell Toy House 138, 160, *160–61*
Richardson, E. P. 216
Ritter, Enrichetta 113
*Road Race* (slideshow) 215, 232
Robbe-Grillet, Alain 206
Roche, Kevin *see* KRJDA (architectural practice)
Rockefeller Foundation 230, 246
Rogers, Ernesto N. 14
Rohmer, Eric 206
Rosenthal, Tony and Halina 113
*Rough Sketch for a Sample Lesson for a Hypothetical Course, A* 12, 15, 16, 201, *227–9*, 229, 266
Ruskin, John 199
Russell, Bertrand, 3rd Earl 276
Russell, Sir Gordon 141

*S-73 (Sofa Compact)* (film) 151, *151*
Saarinen, Eero 12, 18, 21, 42, 64, 116, 143, 154, 280, *306*
Saarinen, Eliel 18, 42, 116
Saarinen, Loja 116
St George, Elizabeth 210
St Louis, Missouri 18
Sandhu, J. S. 246
Santa Fe, New Mexico: Museum of International Folk Art 191
Sarabhai, Gautam and Gira 245–6
Sasaki, Miyoko 212, *273*
Satwalekar, Vikas 295
Schrader, Paul 194–208
Scott, Wendell G. 26
sculptures: moulded-plywood 36, *36*, *37*
Sears, Roebuck & Co. (retailers) 151, 165, 167
*Seascape* (slideshow) 215, 232
Seattle: Pacific Science Center 277, 278
Seattle World's Fair (1962): *House of Science* exhibit 196–7, 208, 266, *307*
Shah, Haku *242*, *243*
Shannon, Claude 230, 244
Shawlee, Joan 288
Shiell, Irwin 289
Shulman, Julius *72–9*, *73*, *112*
slideshows and multi-screen presentations 12, 22, 115, 202, 215, 266–8; *see also* Art X; *Circus*; *G.E.M.*; *Glimpses of the U.S.A.*; *House of Science*; *India*; *Movie Sets*; *Railroad*; *Road Race*; *Seascape*; *Tanks*; *Think*; *Townscape*
*Small Hydromedusan: Polyorchis Haplus, A* (film) 292, 296
Smithson, Alison and Peter 62, 99–103, *100*, 115, 146, *147*, 165, 167, 198–9, 207, 216; 'And Now Dhamas Are Dying Out in Japan' (article) 188–9; *Changing the Art of Inhabitation* (book) 103; Hunstanton School *99*, 100, 103; *Parallel of Life and Art* (exhibition) *98*, 100, 103; Robin Hood Gardens, London 166; Upper Lawn Pavilion, Wiltshire *101*, 103
Smithsonian Institution, Washington DC 16, 291, 293, *295*, 303

Snow, C. P. 197, 208
*Sofa Compact* (film) 151, *151*
Soman, A. B. 246
*Space 1999* (television series) 166
*Spirit of St Louis, The* (film) 210
splints, moulded-plywood 12, 22, *26–7*, 28, *29*, *30–31*
Stackpole, Peter *61*, *80–84*, 84, *97*, *123*, *168*
Staples, Robert *5*, 12, *118*, 294, *294*, *298*
*Stars of Jazz* (television programme) 209
Staub, Christian *294*
Steichen, Edward 293
Steinberg, Saul *13*, 42, *139*, *143*, *168*, 190
stretchers 22, 26, *27*
*Sumo Wrestler* (film) 212
Sussman, Deborah *2*, 12, 15, 43, 113, 115, 118, *161*, *162*, *177*, 191, *267*, *282*, 294
Swenson, Richard *5*
*SX-70* (film) *307*
Sypher, Wylie 205, 206

Tandem Seating (public furniture range) 138, *155*
*Tanks* (slideshow) *6*, *257–64*, 296
Taylor, Crombie 289
Taylor, Frank 293
teaching *see* pedagogy
television 166, 209, 304
Thackrey, M. Y. *294*
Thaper, Romesh 246
*Think* (multi-screen presentation) *6*, 196, 199, *265*, 287–9, *288–9*
Tigrett Enterprises 122
*Time* (magazine) 22, 273
Time-Life Building, New York 277
*Toccata for Toy Trains* (film) *177*, 178, 200
Tokyo: National Museum of Modern Art 210
Tondreau, Bill 298
*Tops* (film) 200–201, *200–201*, 202, 209, *209*
*Townscape* (slideshow) 215, 232
Toy, The *13*, 122, *122–3*
toys *13*, 121–5, *122–3*; moulded-plywood 22–3, *50*; Revell Toy House 138, 160, *160–61*; tops *192*, 200–201, *200–201*, *209*; *see also* card games
*Traveling Boy* (film) 178, 190, *190*
travelling, Eameses' 191, 210
Tree, Iris *120*, 121
*Tron: Legacy* (film) 166
Tudor, David 246
Turner, Fred 244
*Two Baroque Churches in Germany* (film) 202, 206–7
*2001: A Space Odyssey* (film) 203

UCLA (University of California, Los Angeles) 141, 226
Udall, Stuart 291, 292
Ulm, Germany: Hochschule für Gestaltung 246
United States Information Agency (USIA) 268, 291, 303
Usher, Frederick *141*, 289

Venice, California 41; Eames Office *4–5*, 12–13, *13*, 23, *33*, 41–2, 118, *182–3*
Von Eckardt, Wolf 293
von Neumann, John 230
Vyas, H. Kumar 245, 294, *294*

Wachsmann, Konrad *114*, 115
Warburg, Aby 215–16
Washington, DC: Dulles Airport 155; Library of Congress 150, 303; National Aquarium (proposed) 42, 202, 204–5, *205*, 207, 255, 291–3, *292*, 296, *296–7*; Smithsonian Institution 16, 291, 293, *295*, 303
Watson, Thomas J. 15
Weiner, Michael 251
Wheeler, Monroe 243
Whitechapel Art Gallery, London: *This is Tomorrow* (1956) 100, *100*, *147*
Whitney, John *273*
*Whole Earth Catalog* 167, 255, *255*

Wiener, Norbert 230, 244
Wilder, Billy and Audrey 12, 113, 116, 118, *119*, 128, 210, 273, 289; proposed house for 78, *78–81*
Wills, John A. *22*, 146
Winter, John 85–96
Woermann, Catherine Dewey 18
*World of Franklin and Jefferson, The* (exhibition) 151, 266, 291, 301, *301*
World's Fairs *see* Moscow World's Fair; New York World's Fair; Seattle World's Fair
Wright, Frank Lloyd 18, 245
Wright, Orville and Wilbur 21
Wurster, William W. 232

Yamaguchi, Yoshiko (Shirley) *120*, 121
Yang, Chen Ning 21

Zenith Plastics 138, 146

# Backgrounds for archival texts

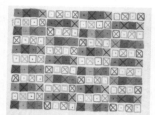
Ray Eames
Study for Crosspatch textile design, 1945

Student work completed in response to problem set by Charles Eames during his visiting professorship at the School of Architecture, University of California, Berkeley, 1953–4

California poppies in the Eames House meadow

Eggs with applied paper hearts in the Eames House

Poppies in the Eames House meadow

A table setting in the Eames House

Bow tie worn by Ray Eames

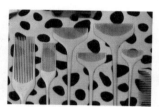
Combs arranged in the Eames House

Kites on the wall of 901

Graphics room at 901, 1988
Photograph by Shelley Mills

Charles Eames with toy train, c. 1957

Alcoa Solar Do-Nothing Machine, 1957

Fibreglass stacking chairs

Tools at 901

Eames Office staff members wearing toy masks, c. 1950

Still from *Goods* slideshow, 1971

Student work completed in response to problem set by Charles Eames during his visiting professorship at the School of Architecture, University of California, Berkeley, 1953–4

Frame from *G.E.M.* slideshow

Wall of circus posters
Photograph by Charles Eames

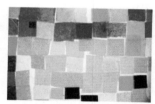
Gift wrapping, 1956

# Archival texts

Esther McCoy, 'An Affection for Objects', originally published in *Progressive Architecture*, no. 54, August 1973, pp. 64–7

John Winter, 'Eames House', originally published in *Great Buildings of the World: Modern Buildings* (London: Paul Hamlyn, 1969), pp. 110–21
Republished with permission of Martha Winter

Paul Schrader, 'Poetry of Ideas: The Films of Charles Eames', originally published in *Film Quarterly*, vol. 23, no. 3, Spring 1970, pp. 2–16
Republished with permission of University of California Press – Journals; permission conveyed through Copyright Clearance Center, Inc.

George Nelson, 'Art X: The Georgia Experiment', originally published in *Industrial Design*, no. 5, October 1954, pp. 44–51
Republished with permission of George Nelson Estate and F+W

## Additional image captions

### COVER

*Front, clockwise from top left*

Exterior of the Eames House

Ray Eames
Study for a room display for the exhibition
*For Modern Living*, 1949
The Work of Charles and Ray Eames,
Prints & Photographs Division, Library
of Congress, Washington DC

Wire Chairs with bird, 1953
Photograph by Charles Eames

Asterisk originally used in House
of Cards, picture and pattern decks

Final artwork from *Powers of Ten: A Film
Dealing with the Relative Size of Things
in the Universe and the Effect of Adding
Another Zero*, 1977

Ray Eames posing with cat photograph,
December 1970
Photograph by Charles Eames

*Back, clockwise from top left*

Photoshoot for an image used on the
Polyhedron showroom display for Eames
furniture, 25 May 1954

Alex Matter sitting on the moulded-
plywood elephant, 1945
Photograph by Herbert Matter

Charles and Ray Eames sitting on the
La Chaise prototype, 1948

Installation view of *Think*, IBM Pavilion,
New York World's Fair, 1964–5

LAR armchair with sketch by Saul
Steinberg, c. 1950–52
Collection Vitra Design Museum

Doris Nolan sitting on a tilt-back side
chair, c. 1946

### PAGES 1–6

*Page 1*

Charles and Ray Eames sitting on the
La Chaise prototype, 1948

Exterior of the Eames House

*Pages 2–3*

Ray Eames
Study for a room display for the exhibition
*For Modern Living*, 1949
The Work of Charles and Ray Eames,
Prints & Photographs Division, Library
of Congress, Washington DC

Eli Noyes, Ray Eames, Charles Eames,
Deborah Sussman, Glen Fleck and
Eliot Noyes posing against wall of 901,
September 1963

Eames House, 1949
Photograph by Julius Shulman

Final artwork from *Powers of Ten: A Film
Dealing with the Relative Size of Things
in the Universe and the Effect of Adding
Another Zero*, 1977

*Pages 4–5*

Eames Office staff photographed in
901 for *Vogue* magazine, 15 August 1959
From left: Don Albinson, Nancy Kane,
Charles Fraser, Parke Meek, Richard
Swenson, Robert Staples, Charles
Eames, Ray Eames, Peter Pearce, Sylvia
Kennedy, Dale Bauer and John Neuhart

Exterior of 901
Photograph by Eames Demetrios

Wax Crayons card from House of Cards,
picture deck, 1952

*Page 6*

Frame from *Tanks* slideshow

Final artwork from *Powers of Ten: A Film
Dealing with the Relative Size of Things
in the Universe and the Effect of Adding
Another Zero*, 1977

Installation view of *Think*, IBM Pavilion,
New York World's Fair, 1964–5

## Image credits

All images are courtesy and copyright
Eames Office LLC; additional copyright
holders and sources are listed below.
Every effort has been made to trace
additional copyright holders and to
obtain their permission for the use of
copyright material.

Courtesy The Work of Charles and Ray
Eames, Prints & Photographs Division,
Library of Congress, Washington DC
*2 (top left), 144–5, cover*: LC-DIG-
ppmsca-39682; *13 (centre)*: LC-DIG-
ds-07660; *15*: LC-DIG-ds-07494;
*34 (top)*: LC-DIG-ds-07483; *30–31*:
LC-DIG-ppmsca-39299; *47 (top)*:
LC-DIG-ppmsca-39680, LC-DIG-
ds-07500; *66–7*: LC-DIG-ppmsca-33528,
LC-DIG-ppmsca-05613, LC-
USZC4-6242, LC-DIG-ppmsca-33530;
*78, 79 (centre)*: LC-DIG-ppmsca-39685,
LC-DIG-ppmsca-39687, LC-DIG-
ppmsca-05750; *119 (top)*: LC-DIG-
ds-07697; *137 (bottom)*: LC-DIG-
ppmsca-39686u; *154 (bottom)*: LC-DIG-
ds-05399u; *156 (bottom)*: LC-DIG-
ppmsca-39687; *157 (top)*: LC-DIG-
ppmsca-39297; *162 (top, centre)*:
LC-DIG-ds-07658, LC-DIG-ds-07659;
*192*: LC-USZ62-135746; *212–13*: LC-DIG-
ds-07495, LC-DIG-ds-07496; *250–1*:
LC-DIG-ppmsca-39079, LC-DIG-
ppmsca-39085, LC-DIG-ppmsca-39083,
LC-DIG-ppmsca-39369, LC-DIG-
ppmsca-39082; *280*: LC-DIG-
ppmsca-39690; *282 (top)*: LC-DIG-
ds-07471; *286*: LC-DIG-ppmsca-39689

© J. Paul Getty Trust. Getty Research
Institute, Los Angeles (2004.R.10)
*2–3 (top right), 72–7, 112*

Courtesy The Papers of Charles and
Ray Eames, Manuscript Division, Library
of Congress, Washington DC
*16*: II:28, Folder 18; *104–5*: I:11, Folder 10;
*108–9*: II:227, Folder 3; *119 (bottom)*: II:6,
Folder 1; *128*: II:173, Folder 12; *146 (top)*:
II:141, Folder 7; *150, 152 (top)*: II:6, Folder 8;
*160*: II:189, Folder 9; *162 (bottom), 163
(left, bottom right)*: II:141, Folder 6; *179*:
II:11, Folder 12; *229*: II:OV 38; *232–41*: II:
215; *254, 255 (top)*: I:143; *320*: II:12, Folder 1

© The Museum of Modern Art, New York
*21 (bottom)*

From the collections of The Henry Ford
*22, 281 (bottom right), 285*

Photograph by Grant Young
*27 (top right)*

Image from the Eames Office project
'From the Collection of Ray Eames:
Furniture Designed by Charles and Ray
Eames', 1988. Photograph by Andrew
Neuhart
*27 (left)*

From *Arts & Architecture* magazine
© David Travers and Eames Office, LLC.
Reprinted with permission
*40, 45–6, 64, 65 (bottom)*

© 2015 The Museum of Modern Art/
Scala, Florence
*47, 140, 142*

Yale University Art Gallery
*49 (bottom)*

The LIFE Picture Collection/Getty
Images
*61 (top), 80–4, 97, 123, 168, 177*

*Architectural Forum* magazine
*65 (top)*

© Tate, London 2015
*98*

RIBA Library Photographs Collection
*99–100, 101 (top)*

Smithson Family Collection
*101 (bottom), 188–9*

Reprinted with permission of John Wiley
& Sons Ltd
*102–3, 188–9*

Courtesy Architectural Association
*124–5*

Courtesy Walker Art Center Archives,
Minneapolis, Minnesota, USA
*138*

Courtesy the Mayor Gallery. © Tate,
London 2015
*147 (bottom)*

Photograph by Tim McQuaide
*149*

www.iancookphotography.com
*151 (bottom)*

Photo by NBC/NBCU Photo Bank
via Getty Images
*166*

© BBC Photo Library
*167*

Reprinted with permission of Corita Art
Center
*180–3*

© The Warburg Institute
*216*

www.wholeearthcatalog.com
*255 (bottom)*

© Jack Masey
*269 (top)*

Courtesy Dan I. Slobin
*270 (top right)*

National Archives and Records
Administration
*270, 271 (bottom right)*

© Vitra Design Museum Archive
*271 (top)*

Photo credit: Elliott Erwitt, Magnum
Photos, New York, NY
*271 (bottom left)*

Courtesy Kevin Roche
*281 (top)*

Courtesy of International Business
Machines Corporation, © International
Machines Corporation
*281 (bottom right), 284 (top)*

The Washington Post via Getty Images
*290*

Courtesy Robert Staples and Barbara
Fahs Charles
*294 (centre)*

Courtesy Minakshi Jain
*294 (bottom)*

Smithsonian Institution Archives,
MAH-X3805-H
*295*

Collection Vitra Design Museum
© The Saul Steinberg Foundation/
Artists Rights Society (ARS), New York
*Cover, fourth row, second from left*

First published in the United Kingdom in 2015 by Thames & Hudson Ltd
in association with Barbican Art Gallery on the occasion of the exhibition
*The World of Charles and Ray Eames*, curated by Catherine Ince

21 October 2015 – 14 February 2016

First paperback edition published in 2018

Thames & Hudson Ltd
181A High Holborn, London WC1V 7QX

Barbican Art Gallery, Barbican Centre
Silk Street, London EC2Y 8DS
barbican.org.uk

Edited by Catherine Ince with Lotte Johnson
Designed by John Morgan studio

British Library Cataloguing-in-Publication Data
A catalogue record for this book is available from
the British Library

ISBN 978-0-500-29462-8

Printed and bound in Slovenia by DZS-Grafik d.o.o.

To find out about all our publications, please visit
www.thamesandhudson.com. There you can subscribe
to our e-newsletter, browse or download our current
catalogue, and buy any titles that are in print.

Exhibition Curator: Catherine Ince
Assistant Curator: Lotte Johnson
Exhibition Assistant: Luke Naessens
Curatorial Trainee: Mairia Evripidou

Exhibition Design: 6a architects

Exhibition Graphic Design: John Morgan studio